SECOND EDITION

Discovering Philosophy

Matthew Lipman
Montclair State College

Prentice-Hall, Inc., Englewood Cliffs, New Jersey 07632

Library of Congress Cataloging in Publication Data

LIPMAN, MATTHEW, comp.
Discovering philosophy.

1. Philosophy—Addresses, essays, lectures.
I. Title.
B21.L5 1977 100 76-55006
ISBN 0-13-216127-3

10 9 8 7 6 5 4 3 2 1

Prentice-Hall International, Inc., *London*
Prentice-Hall of Australia Pty. Limited, *Sydney*
Prentice-Hall of Canada, Ltd., *Toronto*
Prentice-Hall of India Private Limited, *New Delhi*
Prentice-Hall of Japan, Inc., *Tokyo*
Prentice-Hall of Southeast Asia Pte. Ltd., *Singapore*
Whitehall Books Limited, *Wellington, New Zealand*

Contents

V. The World At Large 365

by David G. Lewis

Portraits

I

POLITICAL REASONING

1

Introduction

The fundamental aim of political and social philosophy, it would seem, is the devising of a theory of justice that would appropriately prevail among all human beings.

But, it is generally argued, for there to be justice, a minimal condition is that power reside only in those who are legitimately entitled to exercise it. Who then are the legitimate custodians of power?

Thus it falls to political philosophy to consider the basis of sovereignty in any society, for sovereignty involves precisely the problem of the right to rule, and in whose name rules are to be made.

Ifwe ignore the risk of oversimplification, we may speak of three basic models of political organization:

1. One traditional model sees the State as that institution in society which monopolizes the use of force or violence. Yet the State, founded on force, is the sole source of law. Thus, according to this view, the group that makes up or controls the State, having the power to make whatever laws it chooses, is in a position to claim legitimacy for whatever use of power it wishes. All government, however disguised so as to appear altruistic or benevolent, is in essence self-serving: there is nothing to prevent those who control the State from using it for their own purposes, whatever those purposes are.

2. But a contrasting view is that the legal tradition in time begins to live a life of its own and comes to transcend all human institutions, including the State itself. Those who make the laws come and go, but the laws once made do not. They stay on, entrenching themselves deeper and deeper into the nature of human society. Thus, government under law comes to be regarded as a genuine approximation of ideal justice, replacing those forms of government that are based merely on force.

3. Still another view is that sovereignty resides only in the peoples of the world. Political power is therefore theirs alone to dispose of, just as they are also said to have a natural and ultimate right to the planet they inhabit and to all its goods. Although political power may be temporarily delegated, so as to be concentrated in relatively few hands, the ultimate objective is a world in which political powers, like everything else social

and public, must be distributed equitably in accordance with basic human rights, rather than vested in those who have amassed the force to seize and hold it. Thus, justice is seen from this third standpoint as the equitable distribution of political and social powers in a world so affluent as to be freed from vicious competitiveness, a distribution in accordance with the claims that all persons may make simply by virtue of their membership in mankind.

Now it has been observed that none of these three models is particularly concerned to cultivate the individual in all of his uniqueness or to give him room to develop the variety of his possibilities. Even though an equitable arrangement might be devised whereby the goods of the world were to be fairly distributed over the face of the earth and the claims of men upon one another were to be equitably met, the individual would still not be assured that society would suffer him to develop himself to the utmost, to be sovereign over his own life and utterances, free to think for himself, make his own decisions, amplify his own capacity for growth, or maximize his own creativity. It has therefore been maintained that political philosophy must come to terms with the problem of the claims of the person to a liberty that is not under the control of legitimized social power.

Political and social philosophy must also consider proposals for the bringing about of social changes, just as it must consider theoretical justifications of the maintenance of social stability. Nor are the values that men place upon stability and change to be neglected. For there are those who feel that to maintain existing or traditional social arrangements is to accede to and accept the stored-up wisdom of mankind, the accrued experience of the species as embodied in its prevailing customs and institutions. Others insist that the best framework for society is indeed tradition only if what is meant is the tradition of progress—of a society perpetually engaged in self-correction, constantly in search of its own improvement.

Still others insist, as has already been indicated, that neither stability nor progress are in themselves decisive, but that what is important is free individuality, which cannot be assured by compliance with the social order, but requires instead the compliance of that order for its own enhancement.

And, finally, there are those for whom government and social arrangements alike are never more than remedial and restitutive, a redressing of wrongs, a returning from imbalance to balance, a healing of wounds, with only minor and occasional forays to investigate new possibilities of political and social experience.

Political and social philosophy is thus a forum for the advancing and consideration of theories such as the foregoing—consideration being given to their language and logic as much as to their substance. It considers the claims of those who are articulate enough to make them and endeavors to surmise the possible claims of those who are mute. In so doing, it ranges over the vast terrain of power and law, of rights and responsibilities, of progress and tradition, of conflict and cooperation, of freedom and constraint. Though often explored, that terrain remains in many ways a wilderness and is frequently the scene of new revelations and enchanting discoveries regarding the possibilities of human beings in their perpetual search for satisfactory forms of social life.

In the selection from *The Republic*, the Socrates of Plato is portrayed as a participant in a brilliant debate with Thrasymachus. The latter, though perhaps arrogant and cynical, is a powerful and resourceful opponent. Socrates elicits from him the classic formulation of the tough-minded definition of justice, that it is whatever is in the interest of the stronger party, i.e., the rulers. But Socrates implies that just the opposite may be the case—that justice is whatever is in the interest of the governed. In his last and most audacious pronouncement, Thrasymachus insists that men are of such a nature that they prize only success and care little as to how such success was attained. If a person pretends to think well of justice, it is only to protect himself from other men by deluding them into respectability.

Hobbes and Marx, each in his own way, continue the emphasis of Thrasymachus on the need for a hard-headed theory of political arrangements. Hobbes postulates that, wherever government is lacking, men live in accordance with their instincts, which are inherently belligerent. Society is therefore founded upon the need for security in the face of this constant danger of anarchic violence and the misery that results from it. However, Marx argues that the "war of every man against every man" is not the result of human nature, but of the historical emergence of economic competition. Thus, while agreeing with Hobbes and Thrasymachus about the brutality of social existence under certain conditions, Marx contends that the movement of history is inevitably in the direction of the ideal social state hinted at by Socrates, in which power would be exercised only in the interests of those over whom it is exercised. In the final selection by Marx, the question of *fairness* is raised so insistently that subsequent writers seeking to define a just distribution of benefits and opportunities must either take Marx's formulation into account or risk creating the impression that they are failing to confront the issue.

Quinton's cautious analysis sets forth the claims and counterclaims associated with three of the major approaches to political obligation: intrinsic theories, extrinsic theories, and organic theories. He then shows contrasting ideological usages of such concepts of political ends as "liberty," "justice," and "democracy," and concludes that political dialogue is justified by the inconsistencies that, Quinton contends, are normally discovered in the customary formulations of those ends.

What is the conservative temperament? It is a propensity, Oakeshott tells us in this sympathetic profile of a political disposition, to enjoy and preserve present benefits. It is an outlook resigned to inevitable changes but suspicious of innovation. It is a readiness to respect formal procedures, even if this means tolerating what is abominable.

Liberty, as Lewis sees the notion in this defense of liberal values, is essential to our rationality and to our existence as persons. Liberty characterizes action in conformity with those rational requirements that a person sets for himself. Lewis traces several such imperatives, such as that a person act in a way he will not later regret and that persons accord one another mutual respect. From these self-imposed requirements of rationality, Lewis seeks to sketch the outlines of a free and just society, in which both competition and cooperation engage in constructive exercise.

Thus, if Oakeshott can be said to question whether rational enterprise is of any significant value whatsoever in the management of men's political destinies, Lewis makes the question of rationality central. But Lowenthal, avoiding the issues of personal character and human rationality altogether, concentrates on the conditions necessary for the achievement of a democratic socialism. While he sees that such a society must necessarily involve intelligent planning, he acknowledges that authoritarian regimes have likewise turned to planning in the twentieth century. He therefore holds to the achievement of the separation of productive labor from wage compensation, so that the distribution of the benefits of productivity can be handled more equitably in terms of individual deserts. At the same time, he insists upon the importance of democratic involvement in the transition to non-capitalist forms of social organization.

Central to political philosophy is the notion of justice, as Plato surmised when he made the analysis of that concept the backbone of *The Republic*. In recent years, the notion has been put forth that justice can be understood in terms of fairness. Rawls does not consider fairness and justice to be identical. But he contends that in a hypothetical "state of nature," where the parties are supposedly rational and mutually disinterested, the initial conditions are essentially fair. Under such conditions, Rawls suggests, persons would accept equality in the assignment of basic rights and duties, and would consider just those inequalities that would compensate the least advantaged members of society, rather than such inequalities as make for the "common good."

In an alternative approach, after distinguishing formal from material conceptions of justice, Feinberg proceeds to analyze a number of principles that can be considered relevant to a more precise understanding of the term. His analysis of *equality*, *need*, and *merit* as alternative (but not mutually exclusive) ways in which justice might be conceived is both careful and suggestive.

2

The Politics of Force

PLATO

(427–347 B.C.)

Plato's family was an aristocratic one, and while he was still young, it was thought that he might enter politics. But he became deeply attached to Socrates, whose conviction and resultant death shocked Plato profoundly. Leaving Athens, Plato travelled for some years. This was a formative period for his philosophy, and from it is believed to have come such dialogues as the Apology, Euthyphro, Crito, *and* Meno. *Arriving in Sicily, Plato was invited to the court of Dionysius I at Syracuse. But he displeased Dionysius and was expelled. Now about forty, Plato returned to Athens, where he founded a school known as the Academy, which was to include among its students the youthful Aristotle. The school flourished, and Plato found time to continue his writing. His earlier dialogues had seemed to emphasize the views of Socrates rather than his own, a characteristic that persisted through the* Symposium *and the earlier parts of the* Republic. *However, the tone gradually became more critical, as in the* Sophist, *and particularly in the* Parmenides. *After twenty years of directing the Academy, Plato again found himself in Sicily, this time as the tutor of Dionysius II. It appeared to be an excellent opportunity to train a philosopher-king, but court intrigues and a war terminated the studies, and Plato returned to the Academy. Five years later he again was persuaded to visit Dionysius II, but this time a quarrel ensued, and Plato was kept a virtual prisoner for a year. Once more he settled down in Athens, writing such late works as the* Timaeus *and the* Laws. *It is said that he remained hard at work on his writings up to the very end of his life, dying at the age of eighty.*

THE STRONG AND THE JUST

Listen then, Thrasymachus began. What I say is that "just" or "right" means nothing but what is to the interest of the stronger party. Well, where is your applause? You don't mean to give it me.

I will, as soon as I understand, I said. I don't see yet what you mean by right being the interest of the stronger party. For instance, Polydamas, the athlete, is stronger than we are, and it is to his interest to eat beef for the sake of his muscles; but surely you don't mean that the same diet would be good for weaker men and therefore be right for us?

You are trying to be funny, Socrates. It's a low trick to take my words in the sense you think will be most damaging.

No, no, I protested; but you must explain.

Don't you know, then, that a state may be ruled by a despot, or a democracy, or an aristocracy?

Of course.

And that the ruling element is always the strongest?

Yes.

Well then, in every case the laws are made by the ruling party in its own interest; a democracy makes democratic laws, a despot autocratic ones, and so on. By making these laws they define as "right" for their subjects whatever is for their own interest, and they call anyone who breaks them a "wrongdoer" and punish him accordingly. That is what I mean: in all states alike "right" has the same meaning, namely what is for the interest of the party established in power, and that is the strongest. So the sound conclusion is that what is "right" is the same everywhere: the interest of the stronger party.

Now I see what you mean, said I; whether it is true or not, I must try to make out. When you define right in terms of interest, you are yourself giving one of those answers you forbade to me; though, to be sure, you add "to the stronger party."

An insignificant addition, perhaps!

Its importance is not clear yet; what is clear is that we must find out whether your definition is true. I agree myself that right is in a sense a matter of interest; but when you add "to the stronger party," I don't know about that. I must consider.

Go ahead, then.

I will. Tell me this. No doubt you also think it is right to obey the men in power?

I do.

Are they infallible in every type of state, or can they sometimes make a mistake?

From The Republic of Plato *(I. 336 B–344E), translated by Francis M. Cornford (Oxford University Press, Inc., 1945, pp. 16–26). By permission of the Oxford University Press, Oxford.*

Of course they can make a mistake.

In framing laws, then, they may do their work well or badly?

No doubt.

Well, that is to say, when the laws they make are to their own interest; badly, when they are not?

Yes.

But the subjects are to obey any law they lay down, and they will then be doing right?

Of course.

If so, by your account, it will be right to do what is not to the interest of the stronger party, as well as what is so.

What's that you are saying?

Just what you said, I believe; but let us look again. Haven't you admitted that the rulers, when they enjoin certain acts on their subjects, sometimes mistake their own best interests, and at the same time that it is right for the subjects to obey, whatever they may enjoin?

Yes, I suppose so.

Well, that amounts to admitting that it is right to do what is not to the interest of the rulers or the stronger party. They may unwittingly enjoin what is to their own disadvantage; and you say it is right for the others to do as they are told. In that case, their duty must be the opposite of what you said, because the weaker will have been ordered to do what is against the interest of the stronger. You with your intelligence must see how that follows.

Yes, Socrates, said Polemarchus, that is undeniable.

No doubt, Cleitophon broke in, if you are to be a witness on Socrates' side.

No witness is needed, replied Polemarchus; Thrasymachus himself admits that rulers sometimes ordain acts that are to their own disadvantage, and that it is the subjects' duty to do them.

That is because Thrasymachus said it was right to do what you are told by the men in power.

Yes, but he also said that what is to the interest of the stronger party is right; and, after making both these assertions, he admitted that the stronger sometimes command the weaker subjects to act against their interests. From all which it follows that what is in the stronger's interest is no more right than what is not.

No, said Cleitophon; he meant whatever the stronger *believes* to be in his own interest. That is what the subject must do, and what Thrasymachus meant to define as right.

That was not what he said, rejoined Polemarchus.

No matter, Polemarchus, said I; if Thrasymachus says so now, let us take him in that sense. Now, Thrasymachus, tell me, was that what you intended to say—that right means what the stronger thinks is to his interest, whether it really is so or not?

Most certainly not, he replied. Do you suppose I should speak of a man as "stronger" or "superior" at the very moment when he is making a mistake?

I did think you said as much when you admitted that rulers are not always infallible.

That is because you are a quibbler, Socrates. Would you say a man deserves to be called a physician at the moment when he makes a mistake in treating his patient and just in respect of that mistake; or a mathematician, when he does a sum wrong and just in so far as he gets a wrong result? Of course we do commonly speak of a physician or a mathematician or a scholar having made a mistake; but really none of these, I should say, is ever mistaken, in so far as he is worthy of the name we give him. So strictly speaking—and you are all for being precise—no one who practises a craft makes mistakes. A man is mistaken when his knowledge fails him; and at that moment he is no craftsman. And what is true of craftsmanship or any sort of skill is true of the ruler: he is never mistaken so long as he is acting as a ruler; though anyone might speak of a ruler making a mistake, just as he might of a physician. You must understand that I was talking in that loose way when I answered your question just now; but the precise statement is this. The ruler, in so far as he is acting as a ruler, makes no mistakes and consequently enjoins what is best for himself; and that is what the subject is to do. So, as I said at first, "right" means doing what is to the interest of the stronger.

Very well, Thrasymachus, said I. So you think I am quibbling?

I am sure you are.

You believe my questions were maliciously designed to damage your position?

I know it. But you will gain nothing by that. You cannot outwit me by cunning, and you are not the man to crush me in the open.

Bless your soul, I answered, I should not think of trying. But, to prevent any more misunderstanding, when you speak of that ruler or stronger party whose interest the weaker ought to serve, please make it clear whether you are using the words in the ordinary way or in that strict sense you have just defined.

I mean a ruler in the strictest possible sense. Now quibble away and be as malicious as you can. I want no mercy. But you are no match for me.

Do you think me mad enough to beard a lion or try to outwit a Thrasymachus?

You did try just now, he retorted, but it wasn't a success.

Enough of this, said I. Now tell me about the physician in that strict sense you spoke of: is it his business to earn money or to treat his patients? Remember, I mean your physician who is worthy of the name.

To treat his patients.

And what of the ship's captain in the true sense? Is he a mere seaman or the commander of the crew?

The commander.

Yes, we shall not speak of him as a seaman just because he is on board a ship. That is not the point. He is called captain because of his skill and authority over the crew.

Quite true.

And each of these people has some special interest?

No doubt.

And the craft in question exists for the very purpose of discovering that interest and providing for it?

Yes.

Can it equally be said of any craft that it has an interest, other than its own greatest possible perfection?

What do you mean by that?

Here is an illustration. If you ask me whether it is sufficient for the human body just to be itself, with no need of help from without, I should say, Certainly not; it has weaknesses and defects, and its condition is not all that it might be. That is precisely why the art of medicine was invented: it was designed to help the body and provide for its interests. Would not that be true?

It would.

But now take the art of medicine itself. Has that any defects or weaknesses? Does any art stand in need of some further perfection, as the eye would be imperfect without the power of vision or the ear without hearing, so that in their case an art is required that will study their interests and provide for their carrying out those functions? Has the art itself any corresponding need of some further art to remedy its defects and look after its interests; and will that further art require yet another, and so on for ever? Or will every art look after its own interests? Or, finally, is it not true that no art needs to have its weaknesses remedied or its interests studied either by another art or by itself, because no art has in itself any weakness or fault, and the only interest it is required to serve is that of its subject-matter? In itself, an art is sound and flawless, so long as it is entirely true to its own nature as an art in the strictest sense—and it is the strict sense that I want you to keep in view. Is not that true?

So it appears.

Then, said I, the art of medicine does not study its own interest, but the needs of the body, just as a groom shows his skill by caring for horses, not for the art of grooming. And so every art seeks, not its own advantage—for it has no deficiencies—but the interest of the subject on which it is exercised.

It appears so.

But surely, Thrasymachus, every art has authority and superior power over its subject.

To this he agreed, though very reluctantly.

So far as arts are concerned, then, no art ever studies or enjoins the interest of the superior or stronger party, but always that of the weaker over which it has authority.

Thrasymachus assented to this at last, though he tried to put up a fight. I then went on:

So the physician, as such, studies only the patient's interest, not his own. For as we agreed, the business of the physician, in the strict sense, is not to make money for himself, but to exercise his power over the patient's body; and the ship's captain, again, considered strictly as no mere sailor, but in command of the crew, will study and enjoin the interest of his subordinates, not his own.

He agreed reluctantly.

And so with government of any kind: no ruler, in so far as he is acting as ruler, will study or enjoin what is for his own interest. All that he says and does will be said and done with a view to what is good and proper for the subject for whom he practises his art.

At this point, when everyone could see that Thrasymachus' definition of justice had been turned inside out, instead of making any reply, he said:

Socrates, have you a nurse?

Why do you ask such a question as that? I said. Wouldn't it be better to answer mine?

Because she lets you go about sniffling like a child whose nose wants wiping. She hasn't even taught you to know a shepherd when you see one, or his sheep either.

What makes you say that?

Why, you imagine that a herdsman studies the interests of his flocks or cattle, tending and fattening them up with some other end in view than his master's profit or his own; and so you don't see that, in politics, the genuine ruler regards his subjects exactly like sheep, and thinks of nothing else, night and day, but the good he can get out of them for himself. You are so far out in your notions of right and wrong, justice and injustice, as not to know that "right" actually means what is good for someone else, and to be "just" means serving the interest of the stronger who rules, at the cost of the subject who obeys; whereas injustice is just the reverse, asserting its authority over those innocents who are called just, so that they minister solely to their master's advantage and happiness, and not in the least degree to their own. Innocent as you are yourself, Socrates, you must see that a just man always has the worst of it. Take a private business: when a partnership is wound up, you will never find that the more honest of two partners comes off with the larger share; and in their relations to the state, when there are taxes to be paid, the honest man will pay more than the other on the same amount of property; or if there is money to be distributed, the dishonest will get it all. When either of them hold some public office, even if the just man loses in no other way, his private affairs at any rate will suffer from neglect, while his principles will not allow him to help himself from the public funds; not to mention the offence he will give to his friends and relations by refusing to sacrifice those principles to do them a good turn. Injustice has all the opposite advantages. I am speaking of the type I described just now, the man who can get the better of other people on a large scale: you must fix your eye on him, if you want to judge how much it is to one's own interest not to be just. You can see that best in the most consummate form of injustice, which rewards wrongdoing with supreme welfare and happiness and reduces its victims, if they won't retaliate in kind, to misery. That form is despotism, which uses force or fraud to plunder the goods of others, public or private, sacred or profane, and to do it in a wholesale way. If you are caught committing any one of these crimes on a small scale, you are punished and disgraced; they call it sacrilege, kidnapping, burglary, theft and brigandage. But if, besides taking their property, you turn all your countrymen into slaves, you will hear no more of those ugly names; your countrymen themselves will call you the happiest of men and bless your name, and so will everyone who hears of such a complete triumph of injustice; for when people denounce injustice, it is because they are afraid of suffering wrong, not of doing it. So true is it, Socrates, that injustice, on a grand enough scale, is superior to justice in strength and freedom and autocratic power; and "right" as I said at first, means simply what serves the interest of the stronger party; "wrong" means what is for the interest and profit of oneself.

THOMAS HOBBES

(1588–1679)

It is said that Hobbes was born prematurely because his mother was frightened by the Spanish Armada, and Hobbes himself remarks that these circumstances may have been the cause of his own timidity. But while he may have been anxious by temperament, Hobbes was a bold and incisive thinker, and a clear, vigorous writer.

In his earlier years, he worked as a private tutor successively to several patrons. On a number of occasions he toured the Continent, and became acquainted with Galileo, Descartes, and other leaders of the revolt against medieval scholasticism. He was fascinated by geometry, and by the possibilities of the newly developing physical science. Returning to England in 1637, where intensive constitutional struggles were taking place, he privately circulated a work offering a social contract theory of the state, and containing the view that sovereignty was derived from the people. Fearing that he would be punished for holding such views, Hobbes fled England, remaining in exile in Paris for eleven years. His De cive *was printed in 1647, and the* Leviathan *appeared in 1651, in which year he fled from France back to the England of Charles II. In his later years he busied himself with mathematics and physics, defended himself from charges of blasphemy, and at the age of eighty-four wrote a playful autobiography in Latin verse. Still later, in 1673–75, he produced translations of the* Iliad *and the* Odyssey, *and was still writing up to the year of his death.*

TERROR AND CIVILIZATION

Hereby it is manifest that, during the time men live without a common power to keep them all in awe, they are in that condition which is called war, and such a war as is of every man against every man. For war consists not in battle only, or the act of fighting, but in a tract of time wherein the will to contend by battle is sufficiently known; and therefore the notion of *time* is to be considered in the nature of war as it is in the nature of weather. For as the nature of foul weather lies not in a shower or two of rain but in an inclination thereto of many days together, so the nature of war consists not in actual fighting but in the known disposition thereto during all the time there is no assurance to the contrary. All other time is peace.

Whatsoever, therefore, is consequent to a time of war where every man is enemy to every man, the same is consequent to the time wherein men live without other security than what their own strength and their own invention shall furnish them withal. In such condition there is no place for industry, because the fruit thereof is uncertain: and consequently no culture of the earth; no navigation nor use of the commodities that may be imported by sea; no commodious building; no instruments of moving and removing such things as require much force; no knowledge of the face of the earth; no account of time; no arts; no letters; no society; and , which is worst of all, continual fear and danger of violent death; and the life of man solitary, poor, nasty, brutish, and short.

It may seem strange to some man that has not well weighed these things that nature should thus dissociate and render men apt to invade and destroy one another; and he may therefore, not trusting to this inference made from the passions, desire perhaps to have the same confirmed by experience. Let him therefore consider with himself—when taking a journey he arms himself and seeks to go well accompanied, when going to sleep he locks his doors, when even in his house he locks his chests, and this when he knows there be laws and public officers, armed, to revenge all injuries shall be done him—what opinion he has of his fellow subjects when he rides armed, of his fellow citizens when he locks his doors, and of his children and servants when he locks his chests. Does he not there as much accuse mankind by his actions as I do by my words? But neither of us accuse man's nature in it. The desires and other passions of man are in themselves no sin. No more are the actions that proceed from those passions till they know a law that forbids them, which, till laws be made, they cannot know, nor can any law be made till they have agreed upon the person that shall make it.

From Thomas Hobbes: Leviathan, *copyright © 1958 by The Liberal Arts Press, Inc., reprinted by permission of the Liberal Arts Press Division of the Bobbs-Merrill Company, Inc. Pp. 106–109, 170–173, 175–178.*

It may peradventure be thought there was never such a time nor condition of war as this, and I believe it was never generally so over all the world; but there are many places where they live so now. For the savage people in many places of America, except the government of small families, the concord whereof depends on natural lust, have no government at all and live at this day in that brutish manner as I said before. Howsoever, it may be perceived what manner of life there would be where there were no common power to fear by the manner of life which men that have formerly lived under a peaceful government use to degenerate into in a civil war.

But though there had never been any time wherein particular men were in a condition of war one against another, yet in all times kings and persons of sovereign authority, because of their independency, are in continual jealousies and in the state and posture of gladiators, having their weapons pointing and their eyes fixed on one another—that is, their forts, garrisons, and guns upon the frontiers of their kingdoms, and continual spies upon their neighbors—which is a posture of war. But because they uphold thereby the industry of their subjects, there does not follow from it that misery which accompanies the liberty of particular men.

To this war of every man against every man, this also is consequent: that nothing can be unjust. The notions of right and wrong, justice and injustice, have there no place. Where there is no common power, there is no law; where no law, no injustice. Force and fraud are in war the two cardinal virtues. Justice and injustice are none of the faculties neither of the body nor mind. If they were, they might be in a man that were alone in the world, as well as his senses and passions. They are qualities that relate to men in society, not in solitude. It is consequent also to the same condition that there be no propriety, no dominion, no *mine* and *thine* distinct; but only that to be every man's that he can get, and for so long as he can keep it. And thus much for the ill condition which man by mere nature is actually placed in, though with a possibility to come out of it consisting partly in the passions, partly in his reason.

The passions that incline men to peace are fear of death, desire of such things as are necessary to commodious living, and a hope by their industry to obtain them. And reason suggests convenient articles of peace, upon which men may be drawn to agreement. These articles are they which otherwise are called the Laws of Nature. . . .

The only way to erect such a common power as may be able to defend them from the invasion of foreigners and the injuries of one another, and thereby to secure them in such sort as that by their own industry and by the fruits of the earth they may nourish themselves and live contentedly, is to confer all their power and strength upon one man, or upon one assembly of men that may reduce all their wills, by plurality of voices, unto one will; which is as much as to say, to appoint one man or assembly of men to bear their person, and everyone to own and acknowledge himself to be author of whatsoever he that so bears their person shall act or cause to be acted in those things which concern the common peace and safety, and therein to submit their wills every one to his will, and their judgments to his judgment. This is more than consent or concord; it is a real unity of them all in one and the same person, made by covenant of every man with every man, in such manner as if every man should say to every man, *I authorize and give up my right of governing myself to this man, or to this assembly of men, on this condition, that you give up your right to him and authorize all his actions in like manner*. This done, the multitude so united in one person is called a commonwealth, in Latin civitas. This is the generation of that great leviathan (or rather, to speak more reverently, of that *mortal god*) to which we owe, under the *immortal God*, our peace and defense. For by this authority, given him by every particular man in the commonwealth, he has the use of so much power and strength conferred on him that, by terror thereof, he is enabled to form the wills of them all to peace at home and mutual aid against their enemies abroad. And in him consists the essence of the commonwealth, which, to define it, is *one person, of whose acts a great multitude, by mutual covenants one with another, have made themselves every one the author, to the end he may use the strength and means of them all as he shall think expedient for their peace and common defense*. And he that carries this person is called sovereign and said to have *sovereign power*; and everyone besides, his subject.

The attaining to this sovereign power is by two ways. One, by natural force, as when a man makes his children to submit themselves and their children to his government, as being able to destroy them if they refuse, or by war subdues his enemies to his will, giving them their lives on that condition. The other is when men agree among themselves to submit to some man or assembly of men voluntarily, on confidence to be protected by him against all others. This latter may be called a political commonwealth, or commonwealth by *institution*, and the former a commonwealth by *acquisition*. . . .

Liberty, or freedom, signifies properly the absence of opposition—by opposition I mean external impediments of motion—and may be applied no less to irrational and inanimate creatures than to rational. For whatsoever is so tied or environed as it cannot move but within a certain space, which space is determined by the opposition of some external body, we say it has not liberty to go farther. And so of all living creatures while they are imprisoned or restrained with walls or chains, and of the water while it is kept in by banks or vessels that otherwise would spread itself into a larger space, we use to say they are not at liberty to move in such manner as without those external impediments they would. But when the impediment of motion is in the constitution of the thing itself, we use not to say it wants the liberty but the power to move—as when a stone lies still or a man is fastened to his bed by sickness.

And according to this proper and generally received meaning of the word, a freeman *is he that in those things which by his strength and wit he is able to do is not hindered to do what he has a will to*. But when the words *free* and *liberty* are applied to anything but *bodies*, they are abused, for that which is not subject to motion is not subject to impediment; and therefore, when it is said, for example, the way is free, no liberty of the way is signified but of those that walk in it without stop. And when we say a gift is free, there is not meant any liberty of the gift but of the giver, that was not bound by any law or covenant to give it. So when we *speak freely*, it is not the liberty of voice or pronunciation but of the man, whom no law has obliged to speak otherwise than he did. Lastly, from the use of the word *free will*, no liberty can be inferred of the will, desire, or inclination but the liberty of the man, which consists in this: that he finds no stop in doing what he has the will, desire, or inclination to do.

Fear and liberty are consistent, as when a man throws his goods into the sea for *fear* the ship should sink, he does it nevertheless very willingly, and may refuse to do it if he will: it is therefore the action of one that was *free*; so a man sometimes pays his debt only for *fear* of imprisonment, which, because nobody hindered him from detaining, was the action of a man at *liberty*. And generally all actions which men do in commonwealths for *fear* of the law are actions which the doers had *liberty* to omit.

Liberty and *necessity* are consistent, as in the water that has not only *liberty* but a *necessity* of descending by the channel; so likewise in the actions which men voluntarily do, which, because they proceed from their will, proceed from *liberty*, and yet—because every act of man's will and every desire and inclination proceeds from some cause, and that from another cause, in a continual chain whose first link is in the hand of God, the first of all causes—proceed from *necessity*. . . .

To come now to the particulars of the true liberty of a subject—that is to say, what are the things which, though commanded by the sovereign, he may nevertheless without injustice refuse to do—we are to consider what rights we pass away when we make a commonwealth, or, which is all one, what liberty we deny ourselves by owning all the actions, without exception, of the man or assembly we make our sovereign. For in the act of our *submission* consists both our *obligation* and our *liberty*, which must therefore be inferred by arguments taken from thence, there being no obligation on any man which arises not from some act of his own, for all men equally are by nature free. And because such arguments must either be drawn from the express words, *I authorize all his actions*, or from the intention of him that submits himself to his power, which intention is to be understood by the end for which he so submits, the obligation and liberty of the subject is to be derived either from those words or others equivalent, or else from the end of the institution of sovereignty—namely, the peace of the subjects within themselves and their defense against a common enemy.

First, therefore, seeing sovereignty by institution is by covenant of every one to every one, and sovereignty by acquisition by covenants of the vanquished to the victor or child to the parent, it is manifest that every subject has liberty in all those things the right whereof cannot by covenant be transferred. I have shown before in the fourteenth chapter that covenants not to defend a man's own body are void. Therefore, if the sovereign command a man, though justly condemned, to kill, wound, or maim himself, or not to resist those that assault him, or to abstain from the use of food, air, medicine, or any other thing without which he cannot live, yet has that man the liberty to disobey.

If a man be interrogated by the sovereign or his authority concerning a crime done by himself, he is not bound, without assurance of pardon, to confess it; because no man, as I have shown in the same chapter, can be obliged by covenant to accuse himself.

Again, the consent of a subject to sovereign power is contained in these words: *I authorize, or take upon me, all his actions*; in which there is no restriction at all of his own former natural liberty, for by allowing him to *kill me* I am not bound to kill myself when he commands me. It is one thing to say: *kill me, or my fellow, if you please;* another thing to say, *I will kill myself, or my fellow*. It follows therefore, that—

No man is bound by by the words themselves either to kill himself or any other man, and consequently that the obligation a man may sometimes have, upon the command of the sovereign, to execute any dangerous or dishonorable office depends not on the words of our submission but on the intention, which is to be understood by the end thereof. When, therefore, our refusal to obey frustrates the end for which the sovereignty was ordained, then there is no liberty to refuse; otherwise there is.

Upon this ground, a man that is commanded as a soldier to fight against the enemy, though his sovereign have right enough to punish his refusal with death, may nevertheless in many cases refuse, without injustice—as when he substitutes a sufficient soldier in his place, for in this case he deserts not the service of the commonwealth. And there is allowance to be made for natural timorousness, not only to women, of whom no such dangerous duty is expected, but also to men of feminine courage. When armies fight, there is on one side or both a running away; yet when they do it not out of treachery but fear, they are not esteemed to do it unjustly but dishonorably. For the same reason, to avoid battle is not injustice but cowardice. But he that enrolls himself a soldier, or takes impressed money, takes away the excuse of a timorous nature, and is obliged not only to go to the battle but also not to run from it without his captain's leave. And when the defense of the commonwealth requires at once the help of all that are able to bear arms, everyone is obliged; because otherwise the institution of the commonwealth, which they have not the purpose or courage to preserve, was in vain.

To resist the sword of the commonwealth in defense of another man, guilty or innocent, no man has liberty; because such liberty takes away from the sovereign the means of protecting us, and is therefore destructive of the very essence of government. But in case a great many men together have already resisted the sovereign power unjustly, or committed some capital crime for which every one of them expects death, whether have they not the liberty then to join together and assist and defend one another? Certainly they have, for they but defend their lives, which the guilty man may as well do as the innocent. There was indeed injustice in the first breach of their duty; their bearing of arms subsequent to it, though it be to maintain what they have done, is no new unjust act. And if it be only to defend their persons, it is not unjust at all. But the offer of pardon takes from them to whom it is offered the plea of self-defense, and makes their perseverance in assisting or defending the rest unlawful.

KARL MARX

(1818–1883)

Karl Marx studied at the universities of Bonn and Berlin, where he came under the influence of Hegelian philosophy. After completing his Ph.D. at the University of Jena in 1842, he became a newspaper editor. Moving to Paris, he met Friedrich Engels, who became his lifelong friend and collaborator, and the two began writing works dealing with socialist theory. Marx's Manifesto of the Communist Party *(1848) is a powerful statement of his views, and has been of enormous historical importance. Settling permanently in London, Marx wrote his monumental* Das Kapital, *the first of whose three volumes appeared in 1867. He is often considered to have been the nineteenth-century individual whose views most powerfully influenced the society and culture of the succeeding century.*

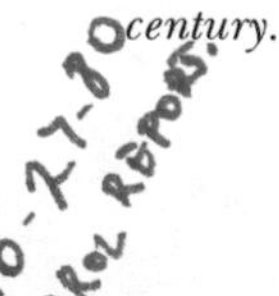

TRANSFORMING INJUSTICE INTO JUSTICE

1. BOURGEOIS AND PROLETARIANS

The history of all hitherto existing society is the history of class struggles.

Freeman and slave, patrician and plebeian, lord and serf, guild-master and journeyman, in a word, oppressor and oppressed, stood in constant opposition to one another, carried on an uninterrupted, now hidden, now open fight, a fight that each time ended, either in a re-volutionary re-constitution of society at large, or in the common ruin of the contending classes.

In the earlier epochs of history, we find almost everywhere a com-plicated arrangement of society into various orders, a manifold gradua-tion of social rank. In ancient Rome we have patricians, knights, plebeians, slaves; in the middle ages, feudal lords, vassals, guildmasters, journeymen, apprentices, serfs; in almost all of these classes, again, sub-ordinate gradations.

The modern bourgeois society that has sprouted from the ruins of feudal society, has not done away with class antagonisms. It has but es-tablished new classes, new conditions of oppression, new forms of strug-gle in place of the old ones.

Our epoch, the epoch of the bourgeoisie, possesses, however, this distinctive feature; it has simplified the class antagonisms. Society as a whole is more and more splitting up into two great hostile camps, into two great classes directly facing each other: Bourgeoisie and Proletariat.

From the serfs of the middle ages sprang the chartered burghers of the earliest towns. From these burgesses the first elements of the bourgeoisie were developed.

The discovery of America, the rounding of the Cape, opened up fresh ground for the rising bourgeoisie. The East-Indian and Chinese markets, the colonization of America, trade with the colonies, the in-crease in the means of exchange and in commodities generally, gave to commerce, to navigation, to industry, an impulse never before known, and thereby, to the revolutionary element in the tottering feudal society, a rapid development.

The feudal system of industry, under which industrial production was monopolized by close guilds, now no longer sufficed for the growing wants of the new markets. The manufacturing system took its place. The guild-masters were pushed on one side by the manufacturing middle-

From The Communist Manifesto *(1848), and from the* Critique of the Gotha Program *(1875).*

class; division of labor between the different corporate guilds vanished in the face of division of labor in each single workshop.

Meantime the markets kept ever growing, the demand, ever rising. Even manufacture no longer sufficed. Thereupon, steam and machinery revolutionized industrial production. The place of manufacture was taken by the giant, Modern Industry, the place of the industrial middle-class, by industrial millionaires, the leaders of whole industrial armies, the modern bourgeois.

Modern industry has established the world-market, for which the discovery of America paved the way. This market has given an immense development to commerce, to navigation, to communication by land. This development has, in its turn, reacted on the extension of industry; and in proportion as industry, commerce, navigation, railways extended, in the same proportion the bourgeoisie developed, increased its capital, and pushed into the background every class handed down from the Middle Ages.

We see, therefore, how the modern bourgeoisie is itself the product of a long course of development, of a series of revolutions in the modes of production and of exchange.

Each step in the development of the bourgeoisie was accompanied by a corresponding political advance of that class. An oppressed class under the sway of the feudal nobility, an armed and self-governing association in the mediaeval commune, here independent urban republic (as in Italy and Germany), there taxable "third estate" of the monarchy (as in France), afterwards, in the period of manufacture proper, serving either the semi-feudal or the absolute monarchy as a counterpoise against the nobility, and, in fact, corner stone of the great monarchies in general, the bourgeoisie has at last, since the establishment of Modern Industry and of the world-market, conquered for itself, in the modern representative State, exclusive political sway. The executive of the modern State is but a committee for managing the common affairs of the whole bourgeoisie.

The bourgeoisie, historically, has played a most revolutionary part.

The bourgeoisie, wherever it has got the upper hand, has put an end to all feudal, patriarchal, idyllic relations. It has pitilessly torn asunder the motley feudal ties that bound man to his "natural superiors," and has left remaining no other nexus between man and man than naked self-interest, than callous "cash payment." It has drowned the most heavenly ecstasies of religious fervor, of chivalrous enthusiasm, of philistine sentimentalism, in the icy water of egotistical calculation. It has resolved personal worth into exchange value, and in place of the numberless indefeasible chartered freedoms, has set up that single, unconscionable freedom—Free Trade. In one word, for exploitation, veiled by religious and political illusions, it has substituted naked, shameless, direct, brutal exploitation.

The bourgeoisie has stripped of its halo every occupation hitherto honored and looked up to with reverent awe. It has converted the physician, the lawyer, the priest, the poet, the man of science, into its paid wage-laborers.

The bourgeoisie has torn away from the family its sentimental veil, and has reduced the family relation to a mere money relation.

The bourgeoisie has disclosed how it came to pass that the brutal display of vigor in the Middle Ages, which Reactionists so much admire, found its fitting complement in the most slothful indolence. It has been the first to show what man's activity can bring about. It has accomplished wonders far surpassing Egyptian pyramids, Roman aqueducts, and Gothic cathedrals; it has conducted expeditions that put in the shade all former Exoduses of nations and crusades.

The bourgeoisie cannot exist without constantly revolutionizing the instruments of production, and thereby the relations of production, and with them the whole relations of society. Conservation of the old modes of production in unaltered form, was, on the contrary, the first condition of existence for all earlier industrial classes. Constant revolutionizing of production, uninterrupted disturbance of all social conditions, everlasting uncertainty and agitation distinguish the bourgeois epoch from all earlier ones. All fixed, fast-frozen relations, with their train of ancient and venerable prejudices and opinions, are swept away, all new-formed ones become antiquated before they can ossify. All that is solid melts into air, all that is holy is profaned, and man is at last compelled to face with sober senses, his real conditions of life, and his relations with his kind.

The need of a constantly expanding market for its products chases the bourgeoisie over the whole surface of the globe. It must nestle everywhere, settle everywhere, establish connections everywhere.

The bourgeoisie has through its exploitation of the world-market given a cosmopolitan character to production and consumption in every country. To the great chagrin of Reactionists, it has drawn from under the feet of industry the national ground on which it stood. All old-established national industries have been destroyed or are daily being destroyed. They are dislodged by new industries, whose introduction becomes a life and death question for all civilized nations, by industries that no longer work up indigenous raw material, but raw material drawn from the remotest zones; industries whose products are consumed, not only at home, but in every quarter of the globe. In place of the old wants, satisfied by the productions of the country, we find new wants, requiring for their satisfaction the products of distant lands and climes. In place of the old local and national seclusion and self-sufficiency, we have intercourse in every direction, universal inter-dependence of nations. And as in material, so also in intellectual production. The intellectual creations of individual nations become common property. National one-sidedness and narrow-mindedness become more and more impossible, and from the numerous national and local literatures there arises a world-literature.

The bourgeoisie, by the rapid improvement of all instruments of production, by the immensely facilitated means of communication, draws all, even the most barbarian, nations into civilization. The cheap prices of its commodities are the heavy artillery with which it batters down all Chinese walls, with which it forces the barbarians' intensely obstinate hatred of foreigners to capitulate. It compels all nations, on pain of extinction, to adopt the bourgeois mode of production; it compels them to introduce what it calls civilization into their midst, i.e., to become bourgeois themselves. In a word, it creates a world after its own image.

The bourgeoisie has subjected the country to the rule of the towns. It has created enormous cities, has greatly increased the urban population as compared with the rural, and has thus rescued a considerable part of the population from the idiocy of rural life. Just as it has made the country dependent on the towns, so it has made barbarian and semi-barbarian countries dependent on the civilized ones, nations of peasants on nations of bourgeois, the East on the West.

The bourgeoisie keeps more and more doing away with the scattered state of the population, of the means of production, and of property. It has agglomerated population, centralized means of production, and has concentrated property in a few hands. The necessary consequence of this was political centralization. Independent, or but loosely connected provinces, with separate interests, laws, governments and systems of taxation, became lumped together in one nation, with one government, one code of laws, one national class-interest, one frontier and one customs-tariff.

The bourgeoisie, during its rule of scarce one hundred years, has created more massive and more colossal productive forces than have all preceding generations together. Subjection of Nature's forces to man, machinery, application of chemistry to industry and agriculture, steam-navigation, railways, electric telegraphs, clearing of whole continents for cultivation, canalization of rivers, whole populations conjured out of the ground—what earlier century had even a presentiment that such productive forces slumbered in the lap of social labor?

We see then: the means of production and of exchange on whose foundation the bourgeoisie built itself up, were generated in feudal society. At a certain stage in the development of these means of production and of exchange, the conditions under which feudal society produced and exchanged, the feudal organization of agriculture and manufacturing industry, in one word, the feudal relations of property became no longer compatible with the already developed productive forces; they became so many fetters. They had to burst asunder; they were burst asunder.

Into their places stepped free competition, accompanied by a social and political constitution adapted to it, and by the economical and political sway of the bourgeois class.

A similar movement is going on before our own eyes. Modern bourgeois society with its relations of production, of exchange and of property, a society that has conjured up such gigantic means of production and of exchange, is like the sorcerer, who is no longer able to control the powers of the nether world whom he has called up by his spells. For many a decade past the history of industry and commerce is but the history of the revolt of modern productive forces against modern conditions of production, against the property relations that are the conditions for the existence of the bourgeoisie and of its rule. It is enough to mention the commercial crises that by their periodical return put on its trial, each time more threateningly, the existence of the entire bourgeois society. In these crises a great part not only of the existing products, but also of the previously created productive forces, are periodically destroyed. In these crises there breaks out an epidemic that, in all earlier epochs, would have seemed an absurdity—the epidemic of over-production. Society suddenly finds itself put back into a state of momentary barbarism; it appears as if a famine, a universal war of devastation had cut off the supply of every means of subsistence; industry and commerce seem to be destroyed; and why? Because there is too much civilization, too much means of subsistence, too much industry, too much commerce. The productive forces at the disposal of society no longer tend to further the development of the conditions of bourgeois property; on the contrary, they have become too powerful for these conditions, by which they are fettered, and so soon as they overcome these fetters, they bring disorder into the whole of bourgeois society, endanger the existence of bourgeois property. The conditions of bourgeois society are too narrow to comprise the wealth created by them. And how does the bourgeoisie get over these crises? On the one hand by enforced destruction of a mass of productive forces; on the other, by the conquest of new markets, and by the more thorough exploitation of the old ones. That is to say, by paving the way for more extensive and more destructive crises, and by diminishing the means whereby crises are prevented.

The weapons with which the bourgeoisie felled feudalism to the ground are now turned against the bourgeoisie itself. . . .

The essential condition for the existence, and for the sway of the bourgeois class, is the formation and augmentation of capital; the condition for capital is wage-labor. Wage-labor rests exclusively on competition between the laborers. The advance of industry, whose involuntary promoter is the bourgeoisie, replaces the isolation of the laborers, due to competition, by their revolutionary combination, due to association. The development of Modern Industry, therefore, cuts from under its feet the very foundation on which the bourgeoisie produces and appropriates products. What the bourgeoisie therefore produces, above all, are its own grave-diggers. Its fall and the victory of the proletariat are equally inevitable.

What is "a fair distribution"?

Do not the bourgeois assert that the present-day distribution is "fair"? And is it not, in fact, the only "fair" distribution on the basis of the present-day mode of production? Are economic relations regulated by legal conceptions or do not, on the contrary, legal relations arise from economic ones? Have not also the socialist sectarians the most varied notions about "fair" distribution?. . . .

What we have to deal with here is a communist society, not as it has *developed* on its own foundations, but, on the contrary, just as it *emerges* from capitalist society, which is thus in every respect, economically, morally, and intellectually, still stamped with the birthmarks of the old society from whose womb it emerges. Accordingly, the individual producer receives back from society—after the deductions have been made—exactly what he gives to it. What he has given to it is his individual quantum of labor. For example, the social working day consists of the sum of the individual hours of work; the individual labor time of the individual producer is the part of the social working day contributed by him, his share in it. He receives a certificate from society that he has furnished such and such an amount of labor (after deducting his labor for the common funds), and with this certificate he draws from the social stock of means of consumption as much as costs the same amount of labor. The same amount of labor which he has given to society in one form he receives back in another.

Here obviously the same principle prevails as that which regulates the exchange of commodities, as far as this is exchange of equal values. Content and form are changed because under the altered circumstances no one can give anything except his labor, and because, on the other hand, nothing can pass to the ownership of individuals except individual means of consumption. But, as far as the distribution of the latter among the individual producers is concerned, the same principle prevails as in the exchange of commodity equivalents: a given amount of labor in one form is exchanged for an equal amount of labor in another form.

Hence *equal right* here is still in principle—*bourgeois right*, although principle and practice are no longer at loggerheads, while the exchange of equivalents in commodity exchange exists only *on the average* and not in the individual case.

In spite of this advance this *equal right* is still constantly stigmatized by a bourgeois limitation. The right of the producers is *proportional* to the labor they supply; the equality consists in the fact that measurement is made with an *equal standard*, labor.

But one man is superior to another physically or mentally, and so supplies more labor in the same time, or can labor for a longer time; and labor, to serve as a measure, must be defined by its duration or intensity, otherwise it ceases to be a standard of measurement. This *equal* right is an unequal right for unequal labor. It recognizes no class differences because everyone is only a worker like everyone else, but it tacitly recognizes unequal individual endowment and thus productive capacity as natural privileges. *It is, therefore, a right of inequality, in its content, like every right*. Right by its very nature can consist only in the application of an equal standard; but unequal individuals (and they would not be different individuals if these were not unequal) are measurable only by an equal point of view, are taken from one *definite* side only, for instance, in the present case, are regarded *only as workers*, and nothing more is seen in them, everything else being ignored. Further, one worker is married, another not; one has more children than another, and so on and so forth. Thus, with an equal performance of labor, and hence an equal share in the social consumption fund, one will in fact receive more than another, one will be richer than another, and so on. To avoid all these defects, right instead of being equal would have to be unequal.

But these defects are inevitable in the first phase of communist society as it is when it has just emerged after prolonged birth pangs from capitalist society. Right can never be higher than the economic structure of society and the cultural development conditioned by it.

In a higher phase of communist society, after the enslaving subordination of the individual to the division of labor, and therewith also the antithesis between mental and physical labor, has vanished; after labor has become not only a means of life but life's prime want; after the productive forces have also increased with the all-round development of the individual, and all the springs of cooperative wealth flow more abundantly—only then can the narrow horizon of bourgeois right be crossed in its entirety and society inscribe on its banners: "From each according to his ability, to each according to his needs!"

3

Understanding Political Arrangements

ANTHONY QUINTON

(b. 1925)

Quinton became a university lecturer at Oxford in 1950, having previously received his education there. He has also taught in America–at Swarthmore College and at Stanford University. Quinton is well known for his contributions to philosophical periodicals and anthologies. He has also published The Nature of Things *(1973).*

GOVERNMENT AND OBLIGATION

1. POLITICAL OBLIGATION

The problem of political obligation—why should I, or anyone, obey the state—has always been the fundamental problem of political philosophy. The question it raises must be distinguished from two others with which it can easily be confused and it is also somewhat ambiguous itself. First, to ask why I *should* obey the state is not to ask why I *do*, though one answer to the latter question (viz. because I think I ought to) raises the former. People obey governments and abide by the law to a very great extent, no doubt, from force of habit and because it does not often occur to them to do anything else. When the possibility of disobedience does occur to them, in cases where there is an obvious clash between the demands of the state and private interests or moral conviction, they are restrained by fear of the probable consequences of disobedience. But people may also be prompted to obey the state by the conviction that they are morally obliged to do so. To inquire into the justification of this belief is to confront the problem of political obligation.

The other question with which that of the justification of obedience is often confused is that of how the state and its laws came into existence in the first place. The two issues look so very different at first glance that it may be hard to understand how they can ever have been run together. One explanation is that many obligations arise from something that has happened in the past: from a positive undertaking, for example, as in a marriage ceremony, or from the coming into existence of a particular state of affairs, as when a man recognizes his responsibility for injuries caused by his carelessness or for children brought into the world by his sexual activities.

A related point, emphasized by Hume, is that people generally regard prescription or customary acceptance as the solidest foundation of a right, though this may be less true now than it was in the eighteenth century. Another consideration is that when the state was created, if there ever was such a moment, the question of whether to obey was a live issue for everyone involved. More generally the confusion between the two questions is assisted by the habit of describing the problem of political obligation as concerned with the *origins* or *foundations* of the state, a mode of expression which can be interpreted historically or justificatorily. At any rate the two questions are entirely distinct. As Hume argued, even if the first states did originate in a contractual agreement between their members this has no bearing on our situation now: we do not inherit our ancestors' promissory obligations, and the states we live under originated for the most part in violent seizure of power.

With the question why I should obey the state extricated from others with which it may be confused, we can go on to consider what precisely it means. It has usually been taken to ask how it is that I am under a *moral obligation* to obey the state. But this is not the only meaning it can have, nor is it the most fruitful one. Morality, strictly so called, has no proprietary hold over the word 'ought'. We can also ask what makes it reasonable, sensible or prudent for me to obey the state. This goes to the opposite extreme from the narrowly moral interpretation of the question and might seem to invite only such obvious and unilluminating answers as that I am likely to be sent to prison if I do not obey. But between the two extremes there is a third possibility. We may ask: what makes it a generally good or desirable thing for me, or anyone, to obey the state? Here the rationality of political obedience is identified neither with its moral obligatoriness nor with its conduciveness to strictly personal interest and advantage. A great deal of what we ought to do is reasonable in this sense without being either morally obligatory or immediately advantageous.

There are three main kinds of solution to the problem of political obligation. First, there are what I shall call intrinsic theories, which derive the rationality or obligatoriness of obedience from the intrinsic character of the state. Secondly, at the other extreme, are extrinsic theories, which justify the state by reference, direct or indirect, to the purposes it serves, to the valuable consequences which flow from its possession of effective power. Finally, there are organic theories, which transform the problem by arguing that it implies a mistaken, 'abstract' conception of the relations between the state and the individual citizen.

The simplest of intrinsic theories is *traditionalism*, the view that the state ought to be obeyed because it always has been, Hume's prescription in its most elementary form. A historically important variant is the *divine right* theory which holds that we should obey the state because God has commanded us to do so. The theory of divine right can take a legitimist form, in which the criterion of divine authorization is something other than the possession of effective power, or it can be conformist, enjoining obedience to the powers that be whoever they are and however they acquired their position.

A more intellectually appetizing kind of intrinsic theory is the doctrine of *aristocracy*, which attributes intrinsic authority to the best people, picked out by their wisdom, ancient lineage, heroic qualities (as in fascism) or even wealth. In practice intrinsic theories soon lose their formal purity since any rational argument to justify obedience to traditional rulers, or to the best people, must rest on the pre-eminent capacity of the recommended rulers for realizing ends desired or valued by those called upon to obey them. This fate of intrinsic theories shows their affinity to deontological accounts of morally right action, which are liable to the same loss of identity. According to the deontologist such moral principles of right action as that one should keep promises or tell the truth are self-evident to the moral intelligence. They do not need justification in terms of the valuable results of general adherence to them and are only harmed and enfeebled if such justification is attempted. They do not need it since they retain their validity in cases where good results do not accrue: one should keep a promise even though no-one will be better off for one's doing so. If such principles are made dependent on the production of good consequences, it is argued, morality is degraded into calculating expediency. But few deontologists are brazen enough to insist that a trivial promise should be kept whatever happens, that one should leave someone drowning in a lonely spot to his fate in order to make a promised appearance at a tea-party. A rigidly deontological theory of political obligation, one that holds the principle that one should obey the state to be simply a self-evident truth, is conceivable. But this will not be very plausible unless 'state' is redefined in terms which guarantee that only rulers who rule well qualify for the description.

Extrinsic theories are the political correlates of teleological accounts of morally right action which define a right action as one from which it is reasonable to expect good consequences. In the doctrine of the *social contract*, the most famous of extrinsic theories, the connexion between obligation and good consequences is indirect. According to the contractarian I ought to obey the state because I have somehow promised or undertaken to do so. But the commitment from which my obligation arises is not conceived as arbitrary, purposeless and unconditional. It is entered into for the sake of some ultimate end (for example, security in Hobbes's version, the protection of natural rights in Locke's). Its binding force is conditional on the effectiveness of the state in realizing the end in question. For this reason a contract theory can never be absolutist. It cannot, in the manner of some intrinsic theories, assign unlimited authority to the state. Political obligation may always lapse and the state's authority be forfeited if the conditions of the contract are not satisfied.

Two main objections to the contract theory should be mentioned. First, since most people give no explicit undertaking to obey the state, there is a difficulty about identifying the thing they do which is to be interpreted as their making an implicit promise to obey. There is a dilemma here. If the supposedly contractual act is not voluntary, such as passively benefiting from the protection of the armed forces, it cannot be regarded as a promise. If it is voluntary, such as voting in an election, failure to perform it is not generally recognized as relieving a man from his obligations as a citizen. Secondly, there is Hume's favourite objection that the good ends for which the promise was made are sufficient to justify obedience to the state by themselves and without the intermediary of a highly speculative act of moral commitment. This leads to the conceptually more economical view of *utilitarianism*, that obedience to the state is justified on directly teleological grounds as a necessary condition of the general welfare, the advantage of society at large.

The *organic theory* of political obligation is implied by the doctrine of a general or real will advanced by Rousseau and Hegel. The theories considered so far, intrinsic and extrinsic, conceive the fundamental political situation as one in which some men, the citizens, are seen as quite distinct from and wholly subordinate to others, the state. This, the organic theorist maintains, is at any rate unnecessary and undesirable and perhaps, metaphysically considered, is an illusion. In any properly constituted political system, perhaps in any effectively functioning one, the state is or represents the better selves of the citizens, their real, general, impersonal, moral will as contrasted with their private, particular, irrationally self-regarding will. In a political system so conceived the citizens in obeying the state are following the promptings of their real or better natures, subjecting their irrational and self-interested passions to the control of their social and moral reason. Rousseau thought that an organic and genuinely obligatory political system was hard to attain, possible only in communities with small populations and directly democratic institutions. Hegel believed that it was approximated to in every effective state, to the extent at least that it was historically possible that it should be. Rousseau's hyperdemocratic ideal seems as impossible of achievement as Hegel's bland redescription of the facts of political life seems unrealistically complacent.

The analytic philosopher of politics does not give the general problem of political obligation so central a place in the subject as his traditional predecessors. It has the merit of raising conceptual questions about arguments designed to establish the rightness of action and of drawing attention to the difference between power, the ability to secure obedience, and authority, the right to expect it. But of more interest than the problem they have in common are the different values which theorists of political obligation, to the extent that their reasoning is teleological, see it as the state's justifying function to serve. The problem of political obligation represents the citizen as confronted by a single absolute choice between obedience and resistance, between conformity and treason. Even in the least democratic societies the scope of an individual's political action is seldom so brutally circumscribed. Whether or not he has the formal right to vote, to organize political associations and to convert others to his way of thinking, he will have many means at his disposal for bringing pressure to bear on the government, its acts, its composition, its institutional form. The values that are relevant to the ultimate choice between submission and rebellion are also relevant to a much more extensive range of political choices. It is more profitable to consider the ends of government on their own, detached from their traditional involvement with a single extreme issue of political action. . . .

2. THE ENDS OF GOVERNMENT

An ideology prescribes ends for government. It lays down certain ends as those to be pursued through political activity and through political institutions. The simplest kind of ideology describes an ideal society or utopia in which the ideologist's values are fully realized. Here the ideological aim is quite explicit. At the other extreme a theory of political obligation can serve an ideological purpose more indirectly. In it the preferred ends will appear as necessary conditions for justifying the state's authority.

There are objections to both procedures. Utopias, concentrating on the long-range goal of political endeavour, neglect the problems that arise about getting to the destination. Not all of these problems are practical. The realization of one part of the ideal may bring unexpected results in its train which obstruct the realization of the remainder. One ideological defect of theories of political obligation was pointed out at the end of the last section. The scope of an individual's political action is not confined to deciding whether or not to obey the state. He can usually bring some influence to bear on its selection of policies, its composition and its institutional form, even in societies that are not formally democratic. Another defect is that the essential conditions of political obligation, though they will be included in one's ideals, are not usually wholly coincident with them. Only if I take the wildly extreme position of refusing to admit an obligation to obey any government but a wholly ideal one will the conditions of political obligation and the principles of political action in general be identical.

The first task of the political philosopher in this field, and on one view his whole responsibility there, is to clarify the concepts of political ends. In the light of such a clarification he can critically examine the arguments that are used to support the choice of political ends. The conflicting conceptions that prevail of the political ends he is concerned with express ideological disagreements and this makes it hard to operate with strict neutrality and detachment. Opposing ideologists try to pre-empt words like *liberty, justice* and *democracy* for the type of political arrangement they favour. The political philosopher can keep himself from being embroiled only if he confines himself to articulating the way in which different ideological groups use the terms in which they proclaim their ideals.

A plain example of this kind of ideological competition over a concept is provided by liberty. The negative conception of liberty favoured by liberal individualists is repudiated by collectivists in the interests of positive liberty. Negative liberty is absence of interference by states, groups or individuals with the activities of individual men. For interference to be an infringement of liberty it must be directed against activities those interfered with actually want to carry out, it must be intended to have this effect and it must work through disincentives serious enough to be proper objects of fear. Positive liberty, being commonly defined as the ability to do what I *really* want to do, turns out to be very much like my ability to do what I ideally ought to want to do. The conflict is not resolved by simply giving different names to the two kinds of liberty and recognizing that one party favours the one and its proponents the other. For both parties agree that liberty ultimately consists in being able to do what you want to do. But they disagree as to what this is and about how we are to find out what it is.

There is a similar distinction between competing concepts of democracy. Here, however, it is the positive conception that is the more traditional: the view of Rousseau that a state is democratic to the extent that its acts express the common will of its citizens. The opposite view conceives democracy as a peaceful way of getting rid of governments with which the majority of the citizens are dissatisfied rather than as a means for the direct realization of their political aims. Both parties agree that democracy is in some sense government *by* the people. As for the rest of Lincoln's formula: all government claims to be *for* the people and all government is *of* the people—of whom else could it be? They disagree about how this agreed purpose is best brought about.

There is some slight analogy between these opposed views of liberty and democracy and two views about the nature of justice. The negative view would be that the state ought not to treat its citizens differently unless there is some relevant difference between them. Its positive opposite number is that the state should seek to eliminate or compensate for the natural inequalities of advantage that there are amongst them. It could be argued that there is no real difference here, since what one side sees as a natural inequality which the state ought to do something about the other side could recognize as a relevant difference justifying difference of treatment.

The most elementary form of justice is the impartial administration of the law. This can be represented as a kind of equality since it involves no account being taken in the judicial treatment of citizens of those differences between them that are not mentioned in the law itself. But laws that are justly administered can still be unjust in themselves if the differences of judicial treatment they prescribe are in some way unreasonable. While few would deny that equality is one principle, perhaps the fundamental principle, of justice, few would maintain that it is the whole of justice. The principle of equal treatment must be qualified by the recognition that people have different needs and, because of the services they have done, different deserts. Justice might seem to be the most comprehensive of political ends, with the possible exception of the common good, but on any definition it can come into collision with other widely shared values. Unequal distribution of income or property may be defended on the ground that it promotes general economic welfare. By according privileges to a naturally well-endowed minority it calls forth specially productive effort. Those who favour the maintenance of some productive inequalities—and there are, as the practice of professedly egalitarian societies suggests, few who would wish to exclude them altogether—are reluctant to say they approve a measure of injustice, But in this they are perhaps as unreasonable as those who find it hard to admit that the penal institutions of society are designed to reduce the liberty of evildoers.

Everyone agrees that it is an essential function of the state to preserve the security of its citizens. Hobbes held its preservation by a sovereign to be the sufficient condition of justified obedience to him, thus placing it above all other political values. Later political theorists have taken a less gloomy view of the costs of achieving it and have been prepared to accept some risk to security for the sake of other political ends. The general agreement there is about it accounts for the fact that it poses no serious conceptual problems.

One political value that has not yet been mentioned has had a very large influence on the course of political history but is seldom emphasized in works of political theory. This is prosperity. In so far as it does occur in theory it is as a slightly embarrassing aspect of the common good. No doubt its somewhat unspiritual character is responsible for this neglect. Until fairly recent times governments have taken no very direct part in its pursuit. They have confined themselves to legal regulation of the conditions of economic activity by controlling the currency, levying customs duties, limiting hours of work, granting monopolies and so forth. Only in the last century have they undertaken the direct management of productive enterprises and, as a result of more extensive economic knowledge, taken up the positive planning of the economy. The explicit ideological motive for much of this extension of the state's control of economic life has been socialistic, and has been based on considerations of justice rather than of prosperity. A major problem here is to determine how large a part of the common good material prosperity is. The ideology of laissez-faire maintains that the common good will be most fully realized in a society with a freely competitive economic system. But the economic theory on which this ideology is based includes the concept of social cost which applies to deprivations inflicted on the community by the competitive pursuit of wealth which the market mechanism does not correct.

The simplest way of recommending a political value is to assert that men have a self-evident natural right that it should be secured to them. The doctrine of axiomatic natural laws drew much of its appeal from its connexion with the idea that the principles of morality are divine commands. With the recession of that idea arguments of a teleological kind have come to be generally relied on. In some cases these arguments are utilitarian in the narrow, traditional sense. Such is the inference that liberty is good because the kind of restraint in whose absence it consists is unpleasant. On the other hand, in his famous defence of liberty John Stuart Mill, a professed utilitarian, recommended it as the indispensable condition for the discovery of new truths and the preservation of old ones, without stopping to consider the bearing of truth on utility in the sense of happiness.

Political theorists have very often fastened on one political end or other as supremely valuable and have argued that everything a reasonable man would consider good will be achieved by its pursuit. In doing so they have been led to extend the concept of their prime value so that it covers things far outside the original field of its application. Socialists have represented poverty as a kind of unfreedom while conservatives have objected to limitations of the privileges of wealth as cases of injustice. But there is no need to assume that all political ends are ultimately identical, that in pursuing any of them to the limit we must in the end realize all the others. It certainly seems that there are direct conflicts between them. Liberty and equality are often at odds with one another, as are liberty and security, or prosperity and justice. If the concepts of political ends are clearly articulated and understood, an effective kind of rational discussion about them is possible which has no real point if they are all so stretched that they run into one another.

4

The Politics of Stability and Change

MICHAEL OAKESHOTT

(b. 1901)

In his student years, Oakeshott attended St. George's School, as well as Gonville and Caius College, Cambridge. In 1925 he became a Fellow at Gonville and Caius. His earliest significant work was Experience and Its Modes *(1933). After serving in the British Army between 1940 and 1945, Oakeshott completed his study of Hobbes'* Leviathan, *which appeared in 1946. He taught at Nuffield College, Oxford, in 1949, and the following year was appointed University Professor of Political Science at the London School of Economics and Political Science, University of London—a post which he still holds. A collection of his essays, many of which appeared earlier in* Scrutiny, *were collected and published in 1962 under the title* Rationalism in Politics. *He became a Fellow of the British Academy in 1966.*

ON BEING CONSERVATIVE

The common belief that it is impossible (or, if not impossible, then so unpromising as to be not worth while attempting) to elicit explanatory general principles from what is recognized to be conservative conduct is not one that I share. It may be true that conservative conduct does not readily provoke articulation in the idiom of general ideas, and that consequently there has been a certain reluctance to undertake this kind of elucidation; but it is not to be presumed that conservative conduct is less eligible than any other for this sort of interpretation, for what it is worth. Nevertheless, this is not the enterprise I propose to engage in here. My theme is not a creed or a doctrine, but a disposition. To be conservative is to be disposed to think and behave in certain manners; it is to prefer certain kinds of conduct and certain conditions of human circumstances to others; it is to be disposed to make certain choices. And my design here is to construe this disposition as it appears in contemporary character, rather than to transpose it into the idiom of general principles.

The general characteristics of this disposition are not difficult to discern, although they have often been mistaken. They center upon a propensity to use and to enjoy what is available rather than to wish for or to look for something else; to delight in what is present rather than what was or what may be. Reflection may bring to light an appropriate gratefulness for what is available, and consequently the acknowledgment of a gift or an inheritance from the past; but there is no mere idolizing of what is past and gone. What is esteemed is the present; and it is esteemed not on account of its connections with a remote antiquity, nor because it is recognized to be more admirable than any possible alternative, but on account of its familiarity: not, *Verweile doch, du bist so schön,* but, *Stay with me because I am attached to you.*

If the present is arid, offering little or nothing to be used or enjoyed, then this inclination will be weak or absent; if the present is remarkably unsettled, it will display itself in a search for a firmer foothold and consequently in a recourse to and an exploration of the past; but it asserts itself characteristically when there is much to be enjoyed, and it will be strongest when this is combined with evident risk of loss. In short, it is a disposition appropriate to a man who is acutely aware of having something to lose which he has learned to care for; a man in some degree rich in opportunities for enjoyment, but not so rich that he can afford to be indifferent to loss. It will appear more naturally in the old than in the young, not because the old are more sensitive to loss but because

From Rationalism in Politics *by Michael Oakeshott,* *© 1962 in English by Michael Oakeshott, Basic Books Inc., Publishers, New York, and Methuen & Co., Ltd., London, pp. 168–173, 194–196.*

they are apt to be more fully aware of the resources of their world and therefore less likely to find them inadequate. In some people this disposition is weak merely because they are ignorant of what their world has to offer them: the present appears to them only as a residue of inopportunities.

To be conservative, then, is to prefer the familiar to the unknown, to prefer the tried to the untried, fact to mystery, the actual to the possible, the limited to the unbounded, the near to the distant, the sufficient to the superabundant, the convenient to the perfect, present laughter to utopian bliss. Familiar relationships and loyalties will be preferred to the allure of more profitable attachments; to acquire and to enlarge will be less important than to keep, to cultivate, and to enjoy; the grief of loss will be more acute than the excitement of novelty or promise. It is to be equal to one's own fortune, to live at the level of one's own means, to be content with the want of greater perfection which belongs alike to oneself and one's circumstances. With some people this is itself a choice; in others it is a disposition which appears, frequently or less frequently, in their preferences and aversions, and is not itself chosen or specifically cultivated.

Now, all this is represented in a certain attitude towards change and innovation; change denoting alterations we have to suffer and innovation those we design and execute.

Changes are circumstances to which we have to accommodate ourselves, and the disposition to be conservative is both the emblem of our difficulty in doing so and our resort in the attempts we make to do so. Changes are without effect only upon those who notice nothing, who are ignorant of what they possess, and apathetic to their circumstances; and they can be welcomed indiscriminately only by those who esteem nothing, whose attachments are fleeting, and who are strangers to love and affection. The conservative disposition provokes neither of these conditions: the inclination to enjoy what is present and available is the opposite of ignorance and apathy and it breeds attachment and affection. Consequently, it is averse from change, which appears always, in the first place, as deprivation. A storm which sweeps away a copse and transforms a favorite view, the death of friends, the sleep of friendship, the desuetude of customs of behavior, the retirement of a favorite clown, involuntary exile, reversals of fortune, the loss of abilities enjoyed and their replacement by others—these are changes, none perhaps without its compensations, which the man of conservative temperament unavoidably regrets. But he has difficulty in reconciling himself to them, not because what he has lost in them was intrinsically better than any alternative might have been or was incapable of improvement, nor because what takes its place is inherently incapable of being enjoyed, but because what he has lost was something he actually enjoyed and had learned how to enjoy and what takes its place is something to which he has acquired no attachment. Consequently, he will find small and slow changes more tolerable than large and sudden; and he will value highly every appearance of continuity. Some changes, indeed, will present no difficulty; but, again, this is not because they are manifest improvements but merely because they are easily assimilated: the changes of the seasons are mediated by their recurrence and the growing up of children by its continuousness. And, in general, he will accommodate himself more readily to changes which do not offend expectation than to the destruction of what seems to have no ground of dissolution within itself.

Moreover, to be conservative is not merely to be averse from change (which may be an idiosyncrasy); it is also a manner of accommodating ourselves to changes, an activity imposed upon all men. For, change is a threat to identity, and every change is an emblem of extinction. But a man's identity (or that of a community) is nothing more than an unbroken rehearsal of contingencies, each at the mercy of circumstance and each significant in proportion to its familiarity. It is not a fortress into which we may retire, and the only means we have of defending it (that is, ourselves) against the hostile forces of change is in the open field of our experience; by throwing our weight upon the foot which for the time being is most firmly placed, by cleaving to whatever familiarities are not immediately threatened and thus assimilating what is new without becoming unrecognizable to ourselves. The Masai, when they were moved from their old country to the present Masai reserve in Kenya, took with them the names of their hills and plains and rivers and gave them to the hills and plains and rivers of the new country. And it is by some such subterfuge of conservatism that every man or people compelled to suffer a notable change avoids the shame of extinction.

Changes, then, have to be suffered; and a man of conservative temperament (that is, one strongly disposed to preserve his identity) cannot be indifferent to them. In the main, he judges them by the disturbance they entail and, like everyone else, deploys his resources to meet them. The idea of innovation, on the other hand, is improvement. Nevertheless, a man of this temperament will not himself be an ardent innovator. In the first place, he is not inclined to think that nothing is happening unless great changes are afoot and therefore he is not worried by the absence of innovation: the use and enjoyment of things as they are occupies most of his attention. Further, he is aware that not all innovation is, in fact, improvement; and he will think that to innovate without improving is either designed or inadvertent folly. Moreover, even when an innovation commends itself as a convincing improvement, he will look twice at its claims before accepting them. From his point of view, because every improvement involves change, the disruption entailed has always to be set against the benefit anticipated. But when he has satisfied himself about this, there will be other considerations to be taken into the account. Innovating is always an equivocal enterprise, in which gain and loss (even excluding the loss of familiarity) are so closely interwoven that it is exceedingly difficult to forecast the final up-shot: there is no such thing as an unqualified improvement. For, innovating is an activity which generates not only the "improvement" sought, but a new and complex situation of which this is only one of the components. The total change is always more extensive than the change designed; and the whole of what is entailed can neither be foreseen nor circumscribed. Thus, whenever there is innovation there is the certainty that the change will be greater than was intended, that there will be loss as well as gain and that the loss and the gain will not be equally distributed among the people affected; there is the chance that the benefits derived will be greater than those which were designed; and there is the risk that they will be off-set by changes for the worse.

From all this the man of conservative temperament draws some appropriate conclusions. First, innovation entails certain loss and possible gain, therefore, the onus of proof, to show that the proposed change may be expected to be on the whole beneficial, rests with the would-be innovator. Secondly, he believes that the more closely an innovation resembles growth (that is, the more clearly it is intimated in and not merely imposed upon the situation) the less likely it is to result in a preponderance of loss. Thirdly, he thinks that an innovation which is a response to some specific defect, one designed to redress some specific disequilibrium, is more desirable than one which springs from a notion of a generally improved condition of human circumstances, and is far more desirable than one generated by a vision of perfection. Consequently, he prefers small and limited innovations to large and indefinite. Fourthly, he favours a slow rather than a rapid pace, and pauses to observe current consequences and make appropriate adjustments. And lastly, he believes the occasion to be important; and, other things being equal, he considers the most favourable occasion for innovation to be when the projected change is most likely to be limited to what is intended and least likely to be corrupted by undesired and unmanageable consequences.

The disposition to be conservative is, then, warm and positive in respect of enjoyment, and correspondingly cool and critical in respect of change and innovation: these two inclinations support and elucidate one another. The man of conservative termperament believes that a known good is not lightly to be surrendered for an unknown better. He is not in love with what is dangerous and difficult; he is unadventurous; he has no impulse to to sail uncharted seas; for him there is no magic in being lost, bewildered, or shipwrecked. If he is forced to navigate the unknown, he sees virtue in heaving the lead every inch of the way. What others plausibly identify as timidity, he recognizes in himself as rational prudence; what others interpret as inactivity, he recognizes as a disposition to enjoy rather than to exploit. He is cautious, and he is disposed to indicate his assent or dissent, not in absolute, but in graduated terms. He eyes the situation in terms of its propensity to disrupt the familiarity of the features of his world. . . . Of the many entailments of this view of things that might be pointed to, I will notice one, namely, that politics is an activity unsuited to the young, not on account of their vices but on account of what I at least consider to be their virtues.

Nobody pretends that it is easy to acquire or to sustain the mood of indifference which this manner of politics calls for. To rein-in one's own beliefs and desires, to acknowledge the current shape of things, to feel the balance of things in one's hand, to tolerate what is abominable, to distinguish between crime and sin, to respect formality even when it appears to be leading to error, these are difficult achievements; and they are achievements not to be looked for in the young.

Everybody's young days are a dream, a delightful insanity, a sweet solipsism. Nothing in them has a fixed shape, nothing a fixed price; everything is a possibility, and we live happily on credit. There are no obligations to be observed; there are no accounts to be kept. Nothing is specified in advance; everything is what can be made of it. The world is a mirror in which we seek the reflection of our own desires. The allure of violent emotions is irresistible. When we are young we are not disposed to make concessions to the world; we never feel the balance of a thing in our hands—unless it be a cricket bat. We are not apt to distinguish between our liking and our esteem; urgency is our criterion of importance; and we do not easily understand that what is humdrum need not be despicable. We are impatient of restraint; and we readily believe, like Shelley, that to have contracted a habit is to have failed. These, in my opinion, are among our virtues when we are young; but how remote they are from the disposition appropriate for participating in the style of government I have been describing. Since life is a dream, we argue (with plausible but erroneous logic) that politics must be an encounter of dreams, in which we hope to impose our own. Some unfortunate people, like Pitt (laughably called "the Younger"), are born old, and are eligible to engage in politics almost in their cradles; others, perhaps more fortunate, belie the saying that one is young only once, they never grow up. But these are exceptions. For most there is what Conrad called the "shadow line" which, when we pass it, discloses a solid world of things, each with its fixed shape, each with its own point of balance, each with its price; a world of fact, not poetic image, in which what we have spent on one thing we cannot spend on another; a world inhabited by others besides ourselves who cannot be reduced to mere reflections of our own emotions. And coming to be at home in this commonplace world qualifies us (as no knowledge of "political science" can ever qualify us), if we are so inclined and have nothing better to think about, to engage in what the man of conservative disposition understands to be political activity.

C.I. LEWIS

(1883-1964)

Clarence Irving Lewis was for many years among the most eminent of American philosophers. Born in Stoneham, Massachusetts, he attended Harvard University, receiving his A.B. there in 1906, and his Ph.D. in 1910. The following year he joined the faculty of philosophy at the University of California, remaining there for nine years. In 1920 he returned to Harvard, where he taught during the last thirty-three years of his career. He was made Edward Pierce Professor of Philosophy in 1930. Lewis delivered the Carus lectures in 1945, and the Woodbridge lectures in 1954. His best-known books are Mind and the World Order *(1929) and* An Analysis of Knowledge and Valuation *(1946). Following his retirement he published two additional works:* The Ground and Nature of the Right *(1955) and* Our Social Inheritance *(1957).*

THE MEANING OF LIBERTY

Man has long since subordinated to himself all other creatures inhabiting the earth which are big enough for him to see. And this control is rapidly being extended to the micro-organisms. He has already learned sufficiently well how to bend the processes of nature to his purposes so that human life need lack nothing essential—provided only we can learn to exercise a foresight extending beyond the single generation, and cease to squander natural resources which are limited and irreplaceable. Nothing external to man can now prevent him from going forward to realization of that destiny which his peculiar endowment makes possible. The remaining problem is man's control of himself, in his relations to other men. For, due to circumstances which men themselves have created, they can no longer live like predatory animals, or in groups which maintain themselves by aggression upon others. The issues of public morals now emerge as those which primarily affect the future of humanity. If, as has been assumed for two thousand years and more, men are rational, then this problem also will be resolved; but our assurance that civilization may not shortly end in suicide can only be as strong as that presumption. The crux of this problem concerns social institutions founded upon liberty; for civilization arises and progresses by the initiative of free men, freely cooperating in society.

From "The Meaning of Liberty," Revue Internationale de Philosophie, *Deuxième Année, 6, pp. 14–22.*

Liberty is the rational creature's ownership of himself. It consists in the exercise by the individual of his natural capacity for deliberate decision and self-determined action, subject only to restraints which find a sanction in that rationality which all men claim in common. As such, liberty is essential to personality. Man is born free in the sense that he discovers himself as an individual in discovering that this ability to act by deliberate decision belongs to his nature. He maintains his individuality only through the exercise of this capacity. He cannot renounce this privilege; and to deprive him of it is to deny him the right of existence as a person.

The concept of liberty cannot, however, be separated from its reference to rationality, as the capacity of the individual to understand the consequences of his own acts and hence to govern them by reference to what is good, and his acknowledgement of an imperative so to do. Deliberate decision would be unmeaning, apart from the distinction of desirable from undesirable; and the possibility of self-determined action would be pointless where there should be no recognition that what is desirable has an imperative significance for action. Self-conscious personality requires such understanding and acceptance of responsibility for what one does; and the presence of this capacity in another is a condition of our recognition of him as a fellow human.

The question of liberty can arise only amongst men and in their relations to other men. We may say of another animal that it is free, meaning only that it is able to behave according to the dictates of its own nature without other hindrances than those which are natural and usual to its environment; or that it is not free when circumstances which are artificial or abnormal prevent such behavior. But this vague conception of animal freedom is not that of liberty. Man also may find that the natural environment leaves open the way to his desire, or that the laws and circumstances of nature defeat his purposes; but he does not consider that his liberty is affected by such conditions unless they result from the deliberate acts of other men.

Liberty, then, is not to be identified with absence of impediments to what we wish, or human freedom with attainment of our purposes. Even if such purposes stand as comprehensive and perennial goals of human endeavor, it is at most the pursuit of these, and not their assurance, which could be accounted a liberty of the individual or regarded as a right.

Furthermore, the liberty of man distinguishes itself from the merely physical freedom of the animal to behave according to his compulsive drives by the human recognition of imperatives. Man's deliberation in action has reference to the government of his momentary impulses by consideration of their foreseeable consequences, and his acceptance of responsibility for these. Any restriction of action which is implicit in such rationality cannot be accounted a curtailment of the liberty of the individual since it springs from an imperative of his own nature.

The first such dictate is the imperative so to act that he will not later regret his decision and be sorry for what he has done or for what he might have done but failed to do. Without the possibility of such self-approval or self-condemnation, and the recognition of some kind of rightness or some wrongness in actions done or contemplated, there would be no self-consciousness of personality. If it should be asked what ground this imperative has, then there can be no other answer than this; that it belongs to human nature to be thus concerned for the future and not merely for the present, and to blame ourselves for weakness of will if we allow our actions to be governed by impulse or by present satisfaction or dissatisfaction, without respect to future consequences. To attribute the imperative so recognized to rationality, is not to postulate some inscrutable and separate faculty in man, but merely to name a pervasive and familiar feature of human living and doing by an appropriate and traditional name. To lack such concern for the future, or feel no imperative to govern one's conduct by reference to it, is to lack a prime requisite of human personality. If any being have no sense of these, then there can be no ground on which we could commend such critique of conduct to him; merely we should have to refuse him recognition as a fellow human, and be obliged to defend ourselves from unhappy consequences of his behavior as best we may, including the use of force if necessary.

This first imperative of reason may be regarded as prudential only and directed to the consequences of action for ourselves. But already the implication of respect for others is contained within it. Criticism of action by reference to self-interest alone, still bespeaks a rightness or a wrongness which is objective in the sense that if this action is to be regarded as rationally justified in one's own case, then it must have the same justification for every other rational being under like circumstances. Thus it is a basic condition of human association each recognize as right that only in his conduct toward his fellows which he is satisfied to recognize as similarly sanctioned in their conduct toward himself. We might, following Kant, call this second rule of reason the Categorical Imperative. It does not, however, have all the consequences which Kant thought to derive from it, and we shall speak of it instead as the Law of Justice.

It follows from this law that no man may, with right, seek to profit from association with others, and fail to condemn in himself those modes of action which, if adopted generally, would destroy the conditions of such profitable association, or dispel the possibility that others may similarly profit from associating themselves with him. And by this law of mutual respect, no rational being can claim as a liberty in his relation with others anything which he does not equally recognize as a liberty of others against himself. Thus all men must be equal before any law which can be rational and valid. Whoever would claim a right of action he does not accord to every other, either contravenes the basis of all rightness, or he refuses recognition of fellowship to those whom his action affects, and in so doing forfeits any claim to be treated as rational and a fellow being by them.

This basic principle of justice does not, however, dictate that it is an obligation of each to act with equal consideration for the *ends* of others as for one's own. If one should willingly accord to others the privilege of giving some priority to their private ends, in determining what they justifiably do, then a similar degree and manner of acting from self-interest may be justified in one's own case. Thus what the law of justice requires is mutual respect, not love: it does not command that the individual be equally concerned for others as for himself, but only that he respect the freedom of others in acting, it may be, pursuant to their own interest, as he wishes them to respect his similar freedom of action. It would indeed be a horrid world in which justice was not supplemented by human sympathy, and in which beings who, by being rational, are able to comprehend a suffering or enjoyment not their own, should fail to be moved to compassion as well as to just dealing with one another. Consonantly, although this law of mutual respect is a basic moral principle, it is to be doubted that it provides, as Kant thought, a sufficient ground for the whole of morals. Nevertheless, it does constitute a sufficient critique for those public and social institutions which affect the liberties of men; because, admitting the higher command that men love one another and the moral obligation to conserve the ends of others equally with one's own, still that higher law is not one the observance of which any man can demand of another toward himself, or would wish to see socially enforced—if social enforcement of it were conceivable.

It is a paradox affecting application of the conception that happiness for all constitutes an obligation for each, that happiness—at least for normal men—must include the privilege, in some measure, of achieving happiness for themselves and in ways of their own choosing. The fundamental liberty to be an individual includes this right to a measure of privacy; the right to be free, in what principally affects himself, of a solicitude on the part of others which goes beyond the mutual respect of equals. We do not choose that others generally should concern themselves for our happiness in the same way as for their own—unless they remember that happiness includes this privilege of privacy: we wish, rather, to reserve that kind of relationship for those toward whom we feel, and with whom we choose to establish, some closer bond. Paternalism toward the individual cannot be justified by the greatest happiness principle, or in fact by any other which is compatible with mutual respect. External interference with individuals, or with any freely cooperating group, is sanctioned only when their conduct injuriously affects others than themselves.

Thus, in the consideration of liberty, a line must be drawn between the moral dictate that the rational being is free to act in those ways only which he willingly recognizes as a like freedom of others against himself, and any higher or further moral precept such as the law of compassion. And the social enforcement of any dictate not derivative from this principle of justice, even though that dictate claim a moral ground, may still be an invasion of the private right of self-determination in action.

Furthermore, this consideration implies that no positive law of an organized society can rightfully be imposed upon the individual without his acceptance, and that the validity of government rests upon the consent of the governed. This is the case because the law of justice, while antecedent to or independent of any further fact, is a formal principle or rule of criticism only, and by itself alone does not determine any specific manner of action as a liberty reserved to the individual, nor any particular demand of an organized society, as a justified and enforceable restriction upon the action of individuals. The concrete content of morals requires for its determination some additional reference, beyond abstract principles of rationality, to the needs and purposes of men, which are not grounded in, but only criticized by, their reason. It is in point, for example, that the physically able and mentally astute might choose to see a broader field of unregulated initiative of action reserved to individuals generally; while those less capable, or those more moved by sympathy and less concerned for their merely private interests, might choose to see all men restricted more narrowly, for the sake of the general welfare. Whether a *laissez-faire* economy or state capitalism, or something in between, represents the ideal of social justice, is not determined by any *a priori* principle of justice: and individual adherence to one or another such ideal must depend upon the empirically determined consequences of that manner of organizing the social economy which is in question, and upon the relative value assigned to such consequences; for example, the relative value of the larger freedom of individual initiative and, possibly, the greater productivity under private enterprise, as against the greater security of individuals and, perhaps, the gain in distributing goods more nearly according to need, under socialism.

In fact, the antithesis of competition and cooperation serves to illustrate that general type of problem concerning social justice which has no solution on *a priori* principles alone; though in this connection we must remember that competition is by no means confined to the economic. A mode of action may be called competitive insofar as the success of one individual or one party militates against the equal success of others; and may be called cooperative insofar as the success of one party furthers the like success of others also. Without some kind or manner of the competition of individuals in society, there could be no liberty whatever, and men would reduce their social status to that of those insects for which the biological unit is the hive or colony, in which no individual can possess any rights because none has any genuinely independent existence. It is also doubtful whether, apart from all competition, progress would be possible. On the other hand, without some kind or manner of cooperation, implying restriction upon permissable individual initiative, there could be no civilization, and men would remain forever in a Hobbesian state of nature. It suggests itself that one empirical criterion with respect to such problems lies in the damage or the profit to society at large—as against the competing parties merely—of allowing a mode of competition or of forbidding that kind of individual initiative. The social damage of warfare, for example, is immense, and the social gains from it are altogether dubious; and the net social gain or loss from economic competition is now being weighed in the balance; while the competition of scientists and artists for professional rewards and standing may be altogether beneficent in its social consequences.

These considerations, however, lie to one side of our major question, which concerns the general problem of social authority and individual liberty under the principle that, *a priori*, every man is entitled a freedom of action which is restricted only by his willingness to accord that same liberty to others; and hence that no government is valid save by consent of the governed.

Historically, the cause of liberty has received a major support from social-contract theories, including the myth of an original state of nature. However sound the conclusions drawn from such conceptions, these premises are of course as far as possible from the truth—excepting only the fact that the manner and scope of social cooperation is likely to become more complex and extended with every major advance of civilization. So far as we know, normal human life has always been a group life, and liberty has never existed save under law. The binding character of the principle that the validity of any social authority rests upon the consent of those over whom it extends derives rather from the fact that self-conscious personality cannot exist without self-determination; and if there be no worth and dignity in persons, then there is no value in anything whatever, and the questions of right and wrong and justice are unmeaning. A society which should deny this ground of its authority in the individual wills of those who lie under this rule would deny the basis for the justification of anything and hence of itself.

What is principally needed here is an interpretation of this word "consent," which is in accord with basic social facts. And this, I would suggest, lies in the consideration already alluded to, that no man can rationally claim the advantages of cooperation while dissenting, by his action, from those restrictions by which alone this cooperation is possible and may attain those common ends for the sake of which it is undertaken. Men assent to the institutions of civilized society for physical security in place of "the warfare of each against all," but also from the more important interest they have in sharing the multifarious and impressive advantages of civilized life, which are impossible of achievement without the correspondingly complex modes of cooperative organization in an enduring and progressive social order.

Whoever reaps such advantages, tacitly consents to the institutions essential for their production and preservation. And it is further implied that if the individual hold a dissident opinion concerning particulars of the social organization, he will advance these opinions within the framework of the social order itself, and not by seeking its disruption, so long as he gives adherence to that general framework and desires to continue sharing benefits dependent on it.

But this of course will be true only when the social organization is one which reflects the general will of those included in it; and no regime is valid which comes into being or is imposed by violence or any form of *force majeure*—unless or until such a regime is confirmed by the freely expressed assent of those who are subject to it. And no rule remains valid beyond the moment in which such assent would be withdrawn if free-speaking were permitted. In practice, this can only mean that no government is valid save one by the freely elected representatives of the people, and of all of them, and one whose representative character is continuously maintained by frequent recourse to such free election.

Further, no government can validly restrict the right of any dissident individual to withdraw from its jurisdiction by emigration. Even an overwhelming majority, though they have every right to organize as they see fit, for pursuit of common ends, cannot justly impose its will on any individual who chooses to withhold his cooperation, abjure any benefits of it, and remove himself from the field affected by their cooperative activities.

Freedom of thought and speech, of peaceable assembly and unrestricted publication, are implicit in the right of all to alter the particulars of their social organization according to the common will; and of individuals to further that which they deem desirable, by persuasion of their fellows and appeal to their common rationality.

These and other concrete implications of the fundamental principle of justice stand clear in the history of our western civilization, and represent the crucial points of its application in practice. These traditionally defended liberties are assured by the basic law of justice itself, and independently of any empirical fact, save only such as universally obtain and may always be presumed.

RICHARD LOWENTHAL

(b. 1908)

After attending the universities of Berlin and Heidelberg, Richard Lowenthal was for some years a free-lance journalist and commentator in England. In 1959–60, he was a research associate at Harvard, and later was a visiting professor at Columbia. He has also been associated with the Center for Advanced Study in the Behavioral Sciences at Stanford. Since 1961, Lowenthal has been Professor of International Relations at the Free University in West Berlin. He is the author of Issues in the Future of Asia *(1969),* World Communism: The Disintegration of a Secular Faith, *and of numerous articles on Communism, East-West relations, and modern revolutionary movements.*

BEYOND CAPITALISM

1. IS CAPITALIST PLANNING POSSIBLE?

[There are four basic methods by which the state can stimulate economic activity within the framework of capitalism.] First, the state can raise mass consumption by increasing consumer power among the poorer strata of the population and can thus stimulate production. Second, it can encourage the production of investment goods in order to increase the general productivity of the economy and thus similarly start an increased flow of consumer goods. Third, it can direct investments toward purposes which are unproductive from the viewpoint of individual consumption and thus of social utility, for instance, armaments or ostentatious public buildings. Fourth, as long as it is not a world power, it can concentrate investment on pushing exports, thus making them equally independent of domestic consumption.

The first two types of stimulation clearly can be continued only on the basis of increasing welfare of the mass of the population within the planning state. The third type depends essentially on a continuation of arms production which is capable of devouring far greater investments than any other form of unproductive expenditure known to modern so-

This selection is a translation by Kurt Shell of portions of Jenseits des Kapitalismus *by Paul Sering (pseud.), published in 1948 by Verlag der Wiener Volksbuchhandlung, Vienna. The translated portions appeared in* Man in Contemporary Society *(New York: Columbia University, Press, 1951), Vol. 2, of which pp. 304–307, and 313–316 appear here.*

ciety. The fourth, based on export, can in the long run be planned only if the importing countries are made economically and finally politically dependent on the planning state. It demands economic and political expansion. The choice thus is only between two main directions of planning: welfare planning on one hand, imperialist planning on the other.

In England's wartime planning such a choice never arose. Planning came about under pressure of external necessity. There was a state of war and the subordination of all other needs to those of war production was required and recognized by all classes. But in 1933 Roosevelt and Hitler had the opportunity to decide freely the direction of their planning. And they chose different ways.

Roosevelt's New Deal administration consciously took the way of adding to the purchasing power of the working masses and of increasing general productive capacity; easing of credit for home building; reducing debts and interest charges for farmers; wage increases for labor directly through arbitration and indirectly through legal recognition of trade unions; attempts at lowering monopoly prices; productive emergency work paid at normal rates; and the gigantic project aiming at the improvement of the Tennessee Valley, a territory comprising several states, by means of dam construction, electrification, irrigation, and distribution of fertilizer at reduced cost.

Hitler's Third Reich equally consciously went the way of rearmament and planned imperialist expansion: super highways, increase of steel-producing capacity, arms production proper, *Ersatz* production, and simultaneous systematic integration of neighboring countries into the German planning system by means of trade treaties of a new type bringing the entire economy of these countries into dependence on German foreign trade planning long before their military occupation.

And here we come to a discovery decisive for the character of planned capitalism: Hitler's planning inevitably led to war and could be maintained only by means of totalitarian dictatorship—but under these conditions it functioned as expected. Roosevelt's planning led to increased welfare and to the President's reelection in four electoral campaigns in spite of the pressure exerted by the great majority of the capitalist press, but it failed to function beyond a certain point. This point can be exactly determined. Roosevelt succeeded in stimulating production from the side of purchasing power, but private investments never reached the scope desired and expected by the administration. Unemployment was reduced by millions, but full employment was never achieved.

The reason for this difference in development is easily seen: Hitler's planning was supported from the beginning by the decisive groups of big German capitalists. In minor questions they had to subordinate themselves, but generally they did not have to be forced to cooperate—the plan was their own plan. Roosevelt's plan, with its stress on mass consumer power, its support for trade unions, and its increase of wages at the expense of profits, from the beginning met the resistance of a large number of capitalists. Though many entrepreneurs had only to gain from economic stimulation, regardless by what method it was achieved, they nevertheless all feared to lose in the long run by Roosevelt's social policy. They felt that his plan did not eliminate their risks but rather increased them from the political side.

Indeed it is impossible for state planning to eliminate the risk for entrepreneurs in production for mass consumption to the same extent as in production of socially useless items for the account of the state. Consumer goods are produced in every modern society—in systems of free capitalism, planned capitalism, and socialism—for a market, which means that the consumers have a choice, within broad limits, on what consumer goods they wish to spend their income. In the case of arms and munitions, fortresses and super-highways, even in the case of production of exports to dependent countries, the state can guarantee in advance the absorption of the product. . . . In the production of consumer goods for the domestic market, particularly the domestic market of a free country, such state guarantees for the absorption of specific goods are impossible.

Even if the state were to buy the entire output of a particular item at profitable prices and then distribute it free or at reduced prices to the consumers—and something of this sort one could imagine in the case of housing, cheap motor cars, etc.—this would hurt rather than help capitalist production in its totality. The market for other goods serving the same needs, old apartment houses, for example, or bicycles, would be seriously shaken; the risk eliminated from one branch of production would be transferred—as in the case with successful monopolies—to other branches, and the total scope of capitalist production would be eliminated. For the extension of such methods to ever larger segments of consumer goods production can only end in the transformation of these branches of production into socialized public services.

But actually more is here at stake than the risk of the individual branch of production. Welfare planning is possible only through direct increase in the worker's share of the national income, which means an automatic lowering of the share derived from capital ownership whose source is capitalist profit. Here we meet the fundamental dilemma of all capitalist production: the dependence of every increase in production on growing consumption on the one hand and growing profit on the other. Elimination of this dilemma by planning can succeed only where an essential part of investment is consciously directed into channels independent of consumption by the working masses. Production of bombs has the advantage over the production of more useful items in that their sale is independent of the level of the wages paid out.

Roosevelt's planning, for the very reason that it aimed at a progressive raising of mass consumption, was incapable of assuring America's capitalists the same freedom from risks which Hitler assured Germany's capitalists. For this reason American capitalists hesitated to undertake new investments—and in a capitalist framework willingness to invest on the part of capitalists is essential for the functioning of the system. Roosevelt could have rendered it unessential only if he had been ready and sufficiently strong to take measures which, instead of merely aiming at encouragement of private investments, had led to their extensive replacement by public investments—socialist measures. Replacement of private profit by social need as the motive power for investment is more than planning within the framework of capitalist property—it requires the shattering of this framework.

While it is thus true that planning within the capitalist framework can be *attempted* by various forces and for diverse purposes, it can be *successfully* carried out in this framework in only one direction, that of imperialist planning. In the opposite direction, that of welfare planning, it must either break through the frame of the profit system or it must fail. . . .

VII. SOCIALIST PLANNING

The question arises whether under present technical and economic conditions, under conditions of hierarchic and bureaucratic production methods which create the need for planning, a third way actually exists: whether socialism, though not a scientific necessity in the sense of being inevitable, represents nevertheless a scientifically recognizable and politically realizable possibility in our time. . . .

Socialization of the means of production is not identical with their nationalization by law. What is important is the effective control of society over the utilization of the means of production, not their juridical ownership by the state. In a planned economy control over factories which legally still are the property of small owners can be effectively transferred into the hands of the state planning authority.

As long as monopoly ownership is not attacked, all state planning, whether democratic or dictatorial, remains dependent on the cooperation of the monopoly capitalists and therefore more or less subject to the pressure of their interests in contrast to the interests of society. Expropriation of other owners of capital, other owners of the means of production, is not equally a *prerequisite* for the socialist development. . . . The process of substituting salaried managers for private owners in the real direction of production begins under "free" capitalism and is hastened by every form of planned economy. The more effective the planning, the more private ownership of individual enterprises loses its concrete power and functional meaning, the readier is the owner himself to surrender his legal title along with the risk and to transform himself into a state functionary or the functionary of a public enterprise. Such a development is the natural social consequence, not the prerequisite, of socialist planning. Socialists are not interested in forcing . . . the "little man" to surrender rights to which he is still attached. The necessity for expropriation is strictly a question of economic power. Where large property ownership reveals itself as a concentration of power, where it becomes a center of resistance to the socialist planning goals, there this resistance can be broken only through expropriation. Where private ownership of individual enterprises lacks this characteristic of power, there the socialist state power is not interested in creating for itself artificial difficulties by expropriating persons whose productive activities it is incapable of replacing.

Equally, it is not decisive for the nature of planning whether expropriation of monopoly capitalists takes place with or without compensation. Ownership of a decisive share of a large bank's or a large industry's stock represents a power position. Ownership of government bonds or of bank deposits in the same amount which cannot be transformed into such stock represents no power position but merely a title to income. Practically, the necessity for compensation frequently arises from the impossibility to draw a legally effective distinction between large and small shareholders and from the desire to avoid harm to the small savers.

From the standpoint of the community's effective control over the means of production such compensation is indeed quite harmless. Its danger for the socialist development lies in its effect on income distribution. Large cash capital . . . represents a claim to unearned income. The socialist answer to this danger is the progressive capital levy which taxes away all property above the limit of middle-class well-being. Such a capital levy is an extraordinarily important weapon in the struggle for socialist justice and for equality of opportunity for individual development. It is not however a *precondition* of socialist planning; on the contrary, it is one of the measures which become possible only within the framework of socialist planning and bear witness to the socialist character of this planning.

The second demand, that the state must be democratic, flows from the concept of socialization, from the effective social control over the means of production, and from the bureaucratic tendency inherent in modern organization of production. Only when the bureaucratic hierarchy is subjected to effective democratic control can it be prevented from gradually closing itself off as a caste and from making public planning the instrument for the consolidation of a new class rule. Only when planning is truly and not merely fictionally carried on *by* the people can it in the long run remain planning *for* the people. But the people, society, the working classes, these are millions of people with diverse interests, knowledge, and capacities. Planning is technically a highly complicated process in which comparatively few specialized experts located at decisive points must continually make responsible decisions. The question arises in what sense planning *can* be democratic; in what sense planning by the people can be real.

First of all, the basic decisions of every economic plan are not of a technical but of a political nature. Experts can gauge a country's productive capacity at a particular time and from this calculate what living standard and thus what income level of the working masses is compatible with a given investment program and vice versa. But the decision as to which of the technically possible alternatives is *desirable*, how much should be currently consumed and how much provided for the improvement of the productive apparatus, for the creation of new industries or roads, does not depend on experts. If the alternatives are clearly presented, every citizen is capable of making a decision on these according to his understanding and interest. The people can plan in the sense that they can freely decide in what direction and at what speed they wish to develop their productive apparatus, for what long-term purposes they are willing to make short-term sacrifices or vice versa, when and for the sake of which groups the immediate improvement of the living standard must be given priority vis-à-vis long-term tasks.

The decision is in exactly the same degree a decision between different economic interests as any political decision in a capitalist democracy. It is a decision not only between present and future interests, but also between the interests of peasants and workers, of unskilled helpers and specialized bureaucrats, of welfare recipients in need of support and gainfully employed recipients of wages. It is a dangerous fallacy to assume that with the elimination of monopolistic exploitation all interest conflicts will be submerged in the fraternal unity of all the toilers. Planning, on the contrary, consists in the discovery of a concrete compromise between the continuously conflicting partial interests of various groups of working people. And if planning is to be democratic, it must allow as much play for the representation of these special interests as is in any way compatible with effective planning.

From this it follows that planning cannot be democratic unless freedom exists for organized representation and propagation of diverse viewpoints—thus freedom to form parties. The mere existence of economic group organizations, like trade unions, peasant leagues, etc., is not enough. The same persons often have diverse interests, as producers and consumers, as savers and wage earners, etc., and only the freedom for every individual to decide for himself which interest he gives priority to at any given moment can assure democratic decision-making. Where only economic organizations face each other, as in the "corporate state" conceived by many conservative opponents of democracy, there is no room for influencing public opinion and for the changing balance which the free voter establishes between partial interests. . . . It remains decisive for the democratic character of planning that interests be freely represented, not merely behind closed doors but in the struggle for public opinion, and that the compromise achieved in this struggle be not simply legislated by the leadership of the state.

The Ultimate Goal—Socialism. What do we mean by socialism? To this question the answer is the same today as a hundred years ago: abolition of classes and elimination of wage work. But today, when we live through the first phase of socialist planning, it becomes necessary to explain in somewhat more concrete terms the meaning of these words.

Abolition of classes cannot mean the end of functional division of labor. It must mean that the functional division of labor, and particularly the differences between performance and supervision, must not be profound; that children of diverse occupational backgrounds must have equal opportunities for development, must have an equal chance according to their ability to contribute to the common purposes of society. Beyond this, abolition of social classes must mean that income differences existing at the beginning of socialist planning will steadily diminish. The precondition is, first of all, increase in the productivity of labor, increase in disposable goods and disposable leisure. The classless society can be achieved only to the extent that—in Marx's words—"the springs of wealth flow faster." For the more goods that can be placed at the disposal of each member of society, the less importance attaches to additional income as an incentive to effort; the more must ideal and collective stimulants, the will to contribute to the whole, replace the material stimulus of income and the more easily can they do so.

This replacement, however, is the prerequisite for the real elimination of wage work. After the misery and hopelessness of the recent capitalist crisis the overwhelming majority of people are today satisfied if they are merely assured of a wage sufficient to meet their modest needs. They hardly feel the fundamental indignity implicit in the concept of a wage—namely, that man is worthy to receive the necessities of life from society only in the exact measure in which his contribution to production in the market is deemed worthy of compensation. All work for wages is "dehumanization" in that it transforms man from an end into a means of production—and this is at first just as true for wage work in a planned economy as for wage work under "free" capitalism. The special feature of socialist planning is that it strives to transcend this situation and indeed does lead beyond it.

It can do so in one way, and one way only. The larger a society's resources become, the larger is the share of life's necessities which can be assured to the working member of society independent of the "value" of his labor effort, not as compensation but as a right: "to each according to his needs." That which at present we call public services—the right to free education, to free medical care—is the beginning of this development, like many forms of social insurance. Tomorrow an advanced society can make housing a public service and establish the right to a home along with the other basic rights of a working man. And once this road has been taken, no limit exists to the severance of real income from compensation for labor performed except society's productivity.

5

The Politics of Justice

JOHN RAWLS

(b. 1921)

Rawls, born in Maryland, was educated at Princeton, where he also taught philosophy from 1950-52. Later he taught at Cornell, and subsequently at Harvard. He was a Fulbright scholar at Oxford for a year and has specialized, at Harvard, in moral and political philosophy.

ADVANTAGE TO THE DISADVANTAGED

My aim is to present a conception of justice which generalizes and carries to a higher level of abstraction the familiar theory of the social contract as found, say, in Locke, Rousseau, and Kant.[1] In order to do this we are not to think of the original contract as one to enter a particular society or to set up a particular form of government. Rather, the guiding idea is that the principles of justice for the basic structure of society are the object of the original agreement. They are the principles that free and rational persons concerned to further their own interests would accept in an initial position of equality as defining the fundamental terms of their association. These principles are to regulate all further agreements; they specify the kinds of social cooperation that can be entered into and the forms of government that can be established. This way of regarding the principles of justice I shall call justice as fairness.

Thus we are to imagine that those who engage in social cooperation choose together, in one joint act, the principles which are to assign basic rights and duties and to determine the division of social benefits. Men are to decide in advance how they are to regulate their claims against one another and what is to be the foundation charter of their society. Just as each person must decide by rational reflection what constitutes his good, that is, the system of ends which it is rational for him to pursue, so a group of persons must decide once and for all what is to count among them as just and unjust. The choice which rational men would make in this hypothetical situation of equal liberty, assuming for the present that this choice problem has a solution, determines the principles of justice.

In justice as fairness the original position of equality corresponds to the state of nature in the traditional theory of the social contract. This original position is not, of course, thought of as an actual historical state of affairs, much less as a primitive condition of culture. It is understood as a purely hypothetical situation characterized so as to lead to a certain

---

[1]As the text suggests, I shall regard Locke's *Second Treatise of Government*, Rousseau's *The Social Contract*, and Kant's ethical works beginning with *The Foundations of the Metaphysics of Morals* as definitive of the contract tradition. For all of its greatness, Hobbes's *Leviathan* raises special problems. A general historical survey is provided by J. W. Gough, *The Social Contract*, 2nd ed. (Oxford, The Clarendon Press, 1957), and Otto Gierke, *Natural Law and the Theory of Society*, trans. with an introduction by Ernest Barker (Cambridge, The University Press, 1934). A presentation of the contract view as primarily an ethical theory is to be found in G. R. Grice, *The Grounds of Moral Judgment* (Cambridge, The University Press, 1967). See also §19, note 30.

conception of justice.[2] Among the essential features of this situation is that no one knows his place in society, his class position or social status, nor does any one know his fortune in the distribution of natural assets and abilities, his intelligence, strength, and the like. I shall even assume that the parties do not know their conceptions of the good or their special psychological propensities. The principles of justice are chosen behind a veil of ignorance. This ensures that no one is advantaged or disadvantaged in the choice of principles by the outcome of natural chance or the contingency of social circumstances. Since all are similarly situated and no one is able to design principles to favor his particular condition, the principles of justice are the result of a fair agreement or bargain. For given the circumstances of the original position, the symmetry of everyone's relations to each other, this initial situation is fair between individuals as moral persons, that is, as rational beings with their own ends and capable, I shall assume, of a sense of justice. The original position is, one might say, the appropriate initial status quo, and thus the fundamental agreements reached in it are fair. This explains the propriety of the name "justice as fairness": it conveys the idea that the principles of justice are agreed to in an initial situation that is fair. The name does not mean that the concepts of justice and fairness are the same, any more than the phrase "poetry as metaphor" means that the concepts of poetry and metaphor are the same.

Justice as fairness begins, as I have said, with one of the most general of all choices which persons might make together, namely, with the choice of the first principles of a conception of justice which is to regulate all subsequent criticism and reform of institutions. Then, having chosen a conception of justice, we can suppose that they are to choose a constitution and a legislature to enact laws, and so on, all in accordance with the principles of justice initially agreed upon. Our social situation is just if it is such that by this sequence of hypothetical agreements we would have contracted into the general system of rules which defines it. Moreover, assuming that the original position does determine a set of principles (that is, that a particular conception of justice would be chosen), it will then be true that whenever social institutions satisfy these principles those engaged in them can say to one another that they are cooperating on terms to which they would agree if they were free and equal persons whose relations with respect to one another were fair. They could all view their arrangements as meeting the stipulations which they would acknowledge in an initial situation that embodies widely accepted and reasonable constraints on the choice of principles. The general recogni-

---

[2]Kant is clear that the original agreement is hypothetical. See *The Metaphysics of Morals,* pt. I *(Rechtslehre)*, especially §§ 47, 52; and pt. II of the essay "Concerning the Common Saying: This May Be True in Theory but It Does Not Apply in Practice," in *Kant's Political Writings,* ed. Hans Reiss and trans. by H. B. Nisbet (Cambridge, The University Press, 1970), pp. 73–87. See Georges Vlachos, *La Pensée politique de Kant* (Paris, Presses Universitaires de France, 1962), pp. 326-335; and J. G. Murphy, *Kant: The Philosophy of Right* (London, Macmillan, 1970), pp. 109–112, 133–136, for a further discussion.

tion of this fact would provide the basis for a public acceptance of the corresponding principles of justice. No society can, of course, be a scheme of cooperation which men enter voluntarily in a literal sense; each person finds himself placed at birth in some particular position in some particular society, and the nature of this position materially affects his life prospects. Yet a society satisfying the principles of justice as fairness comes as close as a society can to being a voluntary scheme, for it meets the principles which free and equal persons would assent to under circumstances that are fair. In this sense its members are autonomous and the obligations they recognize self-imposed.

One feature of justice as fairness is to think of the parties in the initial situation as rational and mutually disinterested. This does not mean that the parties are egoists, that is, individuals with only certain kinds of interests, say in wealth, prestige, and domination. But they are conceived as not taking an interest in one another's interests. They are to presume that even their spiritual aims may be opposed, in the way that the aims of those of different religions may be opposed. Moreover, the concept of rationality must be interpreted as far as possible in the narrow sense, standard in economic theory, of taking the most effective means to given ends. I shall modify this concept to some extent, but one must try to avoid introducing into it any controversial ethical elements. The initial situation must be characterized by stipulations that are widely accepted.

In working out the conception of justice as fairness one main task clearly is to determine which principles of justice would be chosen in the original position. To do this we must describe this situation in some detail and formulate with care the problem of choice which it presents. These matters I shall take up in the immediately succeeding chapters. It may be observed, however, that once the principles of justice are thought of as arising from an original agreement in a situation of equality, it is an open question whether the principle of utility would be acknowledged. Offhand it hardly seems likely that persons who view themselves as equals, entitled to press their claims upon one another, would agree to a principle which may require lesser life prospects for some simply for the sake of a greater sum of advantages enjoyed by others. Since each desires to protect his interests, his capacity to advance his conception of the good, no one has a reason to acquiesce in an enduring loss for himself in order to bring about a greater net balance of satisfaction. In the absence of strong and lasting benevolent impulses, a rational man would not accept a basic structure merely because it maximized the algebraic sum of advantages irrespective of its permanent effects on his own basic rights and interests. Thus it seems that the principle of utility is incompatible with the conception of social cooperation among equals for mutual advantage. It appears to be inconsistent with the idea of reciprocity implicit in the notion of a well-ordered society. Or, at any rate, so I shall argue.

I shall maintain instead that the persons in the initial situation would choose two rather different principles: the first requires equality in the assignment of basic rights and duties, while the second holds that social and economic inequalities, for example inequalities of wealth and authority, are just only if they result in compensating benefits for everyone, and in particular for the least advantaged members of society. These principles rule out justifying institutions on the grounds that the hardships of some are offset by a greater good in the aggregate. It may be expedient but it is not just that some should have less in order that others may prosper. But there is no injustice in the greater benefits earned by a few provided that the situation of persons not so fortunate is thereby improved. The intuitive idea is that since everyone's well-being depends upon a scheme of cooperation without which no one could have a satisfactory life, the division of advantages should be such as to draw forth the willing cooperation of everyone taking part in it, including those less well situated. Yet this can be expected only if reasonable terms are proposed. The two principles mentioned seem to be a fair agreement on the basis of which those better endowed, or more fortunate in their social position, neither of which we can be said to deserve, could expect the willing cooperation of others when some workable scheme is a necessary condition of the welfare of all.[3] Once we decide to look for a conception of justice that nullifies the accidents of natural endowment and the contingencies of social circumstances as counters in quest for political and economic advantage, we are led to these principles. They express the result of leaving aside those aspects of the social world that seem arbitrary from a moral point of view.

The problem of the choice of principles, however, is extremely difficult. I do not expect the answer I shall suggest to be convincing to everyone. It is, therefore, worth noting from the outset that justice as fairness, like other contract views, consists of two parts: (1) an interpretation of the initial situation and of the problem of choice posed there, and (2) a set of principles which, it is argued, would be agreed to. One may accept the first part of the theory (or some variant thereof), but not the other, and conversely. The concept of the initial contractual situation may seem reasonable although the particular principles proposed are rejected. To be sure, I want to maintain that the most appropriate conception of this situation does lead to principles of justice contrary to utilitarianism and perfectionism, and therefore that the contract doctrine provides an alternative to these views. Still, one may dispute this contention even though one grants that the contractarian method is a useful way of studying ethical theories and of setting forth their underlying assumptions.

Justice as fairness is an example of what I have called a contract theory. Now there may be an objection to the term "contract" and related expressions, but I think it will serve reasonably well. Many words have misleading connotations which at first are likely to confuse. The terms "utility" and "utilitarianism" are surely no exception. They too have unfortunate suggestions which hostile critics have been willing to exploit;

---

[3]For the formulation of this intuitive idea I am indebted to Allan Gibbard.

yet they are clear enough for those prepared to study utilitarian doctrine. The same should be true of the term "contract" applied to moral theories. As I have mentioned, to understand it one has to keep in mind that it implies a certain level of abstraction. In particular, the content of the relevant agreement is not to enter a given society or to adopt a given form of government, but to accept certain moral principles. Moreover, the undertakings referred to are purely hypothetical: a contract view holds that certain principles would be accepted in a well-defined initial situation.

The merit of the contract terminology is that it conveys the idea that principles of justice may be conceived as principles that would be chosen by rational persons, and that in this way conceptions of justice may be explained and justified. The theory of justice is a part, perhaps the most significant part, of the theory of rational choice. Furthermore, principles of justice deal with conflicting claims upon the advantages won by social cooperation; they apply to the relations among several persons or groups. The word "contract" suggests this plurality as well as the condition that the appropriate division of advantages must be in accordance with principles acceptable to all parties. The condition of publicity for principles of justice is also connoted by the contract phraseology. Thus, if these principles are the outcome of an agreement, citizens have a knowledge of the principles that others follow. It is characteristic of contract theories to stress the public nature of political principles. Finally there is the long tradition of the contract doctrine. Expressing the tie with this line of thought helps to define ideas and accords with natural piety. There are then several advantages in the use of the term "contract." With due precautions taken, it should not be misleading. . . .

Infringements of fair equality of opportunity are not justified by a greater sum of advantages enjoyed by others or by society as a whole. The claim (whether correct or not) must be that the opportunities of the least favored sectors of the community would be still more limited if these inequalities were removed. One is to hold that they are not unjust, since the conditions for achieving the full realization of the principles of justice do not exist.

Having noted these cases of priority, I now wish to give the final statement of the two principles of justice for institutions. For the sake of completeness, I shall give a full statement including earlier formulations.

First Principle

Each person is to have an equal right to the most extensive total system of equal basic liberties compatible with a similar system of liberty for all.

Second Principle

Social and economic inequalities are to be arranged so that they are both:

(a) to the greatest benefit of the least advantaged, consistent with the just savings principle, and

(b) attached to offices and positions open to all under conditions of fair equality of opportunity.

First Priority Rule (The Priority of Liberty)

The principles of justice are to be ranked in lexical order and therefore liberty can be restricted only for the sake of liberty. There are two cases:

(a) a less extensive liberty must strengthen the total system of liberty shared by all;

(b) a less than equal liberty must be acceptable to those with the lesser liberty.

Second Priority Rule (The Priority of Justice over Efficiency and Welfare)

The second principle of justice is lexically prior to the principle of efficiency and to that of maximizing the sum of advantages; and fair opportunity is prior to the difference principle. There are two cases:

(a) an inequality of opportunity must enhance the opportunities of those with the lesser opportunity;

(b) an excessive rate of saving must on balance mitigate the burden of those bearing this hardship.

General Conception

All social primary goods—liberty and opportunity, income and wealth, and the bases of self-respect—are to be distributed equally unless an unequal distribution of any or all of these goods is to the advantage of the least favored.

By way of comment, these principles and priority rules are no doubt incomplete. Other modifications will surely have to be made, but I shall not further complicate the statement of the principles. It suffices to observe that when we come to nonideal theory, we do not fall back straightway upon the general conception of justice. The lexical ordering of the two principles, and the valuations that this ordering implies, suggest priority rules which seem to be reasonable enough in many cases. By various examples I have tried to illustrate how these rules can be used and to indicate their plausibility. Thus the ranking of the principles of justice in ideal theory reflects back and guides the application of these principles to nonideal situations. It identifies which limitations need to be dealt with first. The drawback of the general conception of justice is that it lacks the definite structure of the two principles in serial order. In more extreme and tangled instances of nonideal theory there may be no alternative to it. At some point the priority of rules for nonideal cases will fail; and indeed, we may be able to find no satisfactory answer at all. But we must try to postpone the day of reckoning as long as possible, and try to arrange society so that it never comes.

JOEL FEINBERG

(b. 1926)

Feinberg was born in Detroit and educated at the University of Michigan. He has taught at Brown, Princeton, U.C.L.A., and, since 1967, at Rockefeller University. He has also been a Fellow at the Center for Studies in the Behavioral Sciences. A specialist in ethics, political and social philosophy, and the philosophy of law, his publications include Reason and Responsibility *(1965),* Moral Concepts *(1969), and* Doing and Deserving *(1970).*

SOCIAL JUSTICE

The problems of justice of most direct concern to social theory are those that necessarily involve comparisons of the claims of more than one person, and require that some sort of balance be struck between them. Occasions for these interpersonal comparisons do not by any means exhaust all the occasions of justice. In some contexts, an individual's rights or deserts alone determine what is due him, and once we have come to a judgment of his due, that judgment cannot be logically affected by subsequent knowledge of the condition of other parties. When our task is to do noncomparative justice (as we might call it) to each of a large number of individuals, we do not compare them with each other, but rather compare each in turn with an objective standard and judge each "on his own merits." Equality of treatment, therefore, is no part of the concept of noncomparative (individual) justice, even though it is a central element in comparative (social) justice. If we treat *everybody* unfairly by the relevant noncomparative standard, but equally and impartially so, we have done an injustice to each that is barely mitigated by the equal injustice done all the others.[1]

---

[1]Cf. the sports column of *Newsweek*, Sept. 14, 1970, p. 123, in which the toughness of the late professional football coach, Vincent Lombardi, is discussed: "Tackle Henry Jordan's oft-quoted remark indicated the fairness of the coach: 'He treated us all the same. Like dogs.' "

Our concern in this chapter will be with judgments of fairness that are essentially comparative. The main occasions for social or comparative justice are: the allocation of burdens and benefits, the legislation and administration of general rules, and the voluntary coming together in cooperative undertakings, or in games and other competitive activities. Comparative injustice under all these headings consists in the creation or modification of a *relation* between parties: unfair discrimination, arbitrary exclusion, favoritism, inappropriate partisanship or partiality, inconsistent rule-enforcement, "freeloading" in a cooperative undertaking, or putting one party at a relative disadvantage in a competition.

The basic principle of comparative justice is that like cases are to be treated alike and different cases to be treated differently. If Doe gets a large share and Roe a small share in a distribution, our sense of justice is not satisfied until we learn of some respect in which Doe and Roe differ that underlies and justifies this difference in treatment. If Doe and Roe are exactly alike in every respect, but one is given more than the other, the discrimination in their treatment is totally arbitrary, and *arbitrary discrimination* is the essence of comparative injustice. Indeed, many writers[2] hold that the principle of like treatment for like cases is more than simply one among many ethical principles vying for our allegiance, but is rather an instance of a more general principle that is constitutive of *rationality* itself. One would violate this more general principle by ascribing different geometrical properties to two identical isosceles triangles, or by holding that a given physical event was a lonely exception to Newton's Laws, as much as by denying equal protection of the law to those citizens who have black skins.

Any two persons or things will differ in *some* respects, and it is always possible to cite some difference between them in support (more precisely, in *justicization*)[3] of differences in the way they are treated. Clearly, then, comparative justice requires more than that difference in treatment be based on differences in characteristics. The underlying differences between individuals that justicize differences in their treatment must be *relevant* differences, and the underlying similarities that justicize similar treatment must be *relevant* similarities. Injustice is done when individuals who are alike in every relevant respect (not in absolutely every

---

[2]E.g., Isaiah Berlin, "Equality As An Ideal," *Proceedings of the Aristotelian Society,* LVI (1955–56); Chaim Perelman, *The Idea of Justice and the Problem of Argument* (New York: Humanities Press, Inc., 1963), pp. 1–60.

[3]I borrow this useful term from W. K. Frankena, "The Concept of Social Justice," in *Social Justice,* ed. R. B. Brandt (Englewood Cliffs, N.J.: Prentice-Hall, Inc., 1961), p. 5, and A. D. Woozley, "Injustice," *American Philosophical Quarterly,* IX (1972). To *justify* an act is to show that it is on balance and in the last analysis, all things considered, *right*. To *justicize* an act is to show only that it is *just*, and therefore tends to be right. Since (as we have seen) not all just acts are right, and not all right acts are just, the distinction between justicization and on-balance justification is useful.

respect) are treated differently, or when individuals who are different in some relevant respect are treated alike.

The principle of like treatment, then, is only a starting place in the analysis of comparative justice, and needs supplementation by criteria for determining the relevance of differences. For that reason, the like treatment principle is usually said to be merely a *formal principle of justice,* and the criteria of relevance for various contexts of justice with which it must be supplemented are called *material principles of justice.*[4] A formal principle of justice, in the words of a recent writer on the subject, "contains a completely unspecified variable whereas material principles con-constitute different ways of replacing the variable by a constant."[5] The principle that persons who are alike in the relevant respects must be treated alike, while persons who are unalike in the relevant respects must be treated unalike and in direct proportion to the differences between them is formal in the defined sense, since it fails completely to specify which respects are relevant. The principle that social wealth should be distributed to each in proportion to his contribution (or, alternately, his ability, need, rank, or virtue) is a material principle, since it at least goes a long way toward specifying which characteristics are relevant to the justice of distributions of social wealth.

The principle that like cases should be treated alike is put too hastily by some equalitarian writers in the form of a "presumption for equality." It is commonly said, for example, that although it is absurd to think that justice requires us to treat all men exactly alike, it does require that we give them equal treatment until we have good reason not to do so, that "the burden of proof is on the person who wants to treat people differently from one another. . . ."[6] But this presumptive principle is by no means identical in meaning or implications to the formal principle as we have formulated it. Our formal principle (which derives from Aristotle) would have us: (1) treat alike (equally) those who are the same (equal) in relevant respects, and (2) treat unalike (unequally) those who are unalike (unequal) in relevant respects, in direct proportion to the differences (inequalities) between them. The equalitarian presumptivist formulation completely ignores the second part of this principle in insisting that all and only departures from *equal* treatment need justification. Clearly, what needs justification according to the double formula above are: (1) departures from identical (equal) treatment when individuals seem to be

---

[4]The best explication I know of the distinction between formal and material principles of justice is that of Louis I. Katzner, "An Analysis of the Concept of Justice" (Ph.D. dissertation, University of Michigan, 1968). I am heavily indebted to that excellent work in the paragraphs that follow.

[5]Katzner, "An Analysis of the Concept of Justice," p. 2.

[6]Katzner, "An Analysis of the Concept of Justice," p. 37, paraphrasing S. Benn and R. S. Peters, *Social Principles and the Democratic State* (London: George Allen and Unwin Ltd., 1959), p. 111.

the same (equal) in relevant respects, *and* (2) departures from different (unequal) treatment when individuals seem to be different (unequal) in relevant respects. Where the "burden of proof" actually lies in a given case, then, depends upon what is given (believed or known) about the relevant traits of the individuals involved, and also upon the particular context of justice and its governing norms and maxims. The presumption in favor of equal treatment holds when the individuals involved are believed, assumed, or expected to be equal in the relevant respects, whereas the presumption in favor of *unequal* treatment holds when the individuals involved are expected to be different in the relevant respects.

Consider some examples. If two pupils both violate the same rule but one is given a more severe penalty, we would *presume* (knowing no more facts) that a comparative injustice had been committed by the teacher. Unless some relevant difference between the two offenders or their offenses could be brought to light by the teacher, we would treat the presumption as decisive. On the other hand, consider the example cited by Louis Katzner to show that sometimes the "burden of proof" is on those who advocate equality of treatment. A testator whose sole survivor is his son leaves one half of his estate to that son and, "equally," one half to another person of the son's age. The two inheritors are different in a respect we normally take to be relevant in such contexts, namely that one is a member of the testator's immediate family whereas the other is not. Because of this *given* relevant difference, the father has the burden of presenting a justification for *treating two people equally* that will override the presumption that they should be treated differently.

The equalitarian presumptivist principle, then, errs in overlooking cases in which our antecedent expectations about the existence of characteristics agreed to be relevant creates a presumption in favor of inequality. The disguised normative character of the principle ("disguised" when it is claimed to be the formal principle of comparative justice), and, more importantly, its ultimately arbitrary character, are shown by a consideration of how it would apply to cases where no expectation exists about the equal or unequal degree to which relevant characteristics are possessed by those subject to our treatment. The presumptive principle, in these cases, tells us to presume even in our ignorance that equal treatment is called for, that individuals about whom we know nothing should nevertheless be treated equally unless or until grounds for distinction between them can be found. In this instance, the presumptive principle clearly reveals itself as not "merely formal"; it purports to be a decisive guide to our conduct. Thus, a controversial (and indeed very doubtful!) normative principle is presented in the guise of a purely formal principle of reason supposedly definitive of the very nature of comparative justice. The moral of the story is this: Don't confuse an *exceptive principle* ("Treat all men alike *except* where there are relevant differences between them") with a *presumptive principle* ("Treat all men alike *until it can be shown* that there are relevant differences between them"). The exceptive principle is indeed formal, providing no guide to action or grounds for presuming either equality or inequality in the case in which we are ignorant of the characteristics of the men to be treated. The presumptive principle has us presume equal treatment even in this case, and that would be to make a presumption every bit as arbitrary as the presumption in favor of *unequal* treatment in the absence of knowledge of the relevant similarities and differences of the persons involved.

Stating the correct principles of *material justice* (criteria of relevance) is a task of a different order from that involved in formulating the principle of formal justice. Deciding which material principles to adopt requires us to enter the moral arena itself, where basic attitudes are in profound opposition, and social interests and political parties contend. The issues involved here, being substantive moral questions rather than questions of conceptual analysis with no direct normative implications, cannot be settled decisively by appeals to "the very definition of the concept of justice." We shall have to bring in normative principles from the outside so that justice can have substance and provide direction.

The choice of material principles is sometimes severely limited by the context itself, and is therefore not particularly difficult or controversial. We should not discriminate between persons who are alike in all relevant respects; but which respects are relevant depends upon the occasion for justice, on our purposes and objectives, and on the internal rules of the "game" we are playing. There is no one kind of characteristic that is relevant in all contexts, no single material principle that applies universally. In short, what we seek when we look for a material principle is what H. L. A. Hart has called "a shifting or varying criterion used in determining when, *for any given purpose*, cases are alike or different."[7] Hart went on to make the interesting suggestion that there is an analogy between relevance to a given purpose and other relational notions: "In this respect, justice is like the notions of what is genuine [real], or tall, or warm, which contain an implicit reference to a standard which varies with the classification of the thing to which they are applied."[8] Thus, the standard of tallness varies depending on whether we are speaking of children, men, women, buildings, or mountains. There is no vicious "relativism" in this variation, and no skeptical affront to reason. It is useful to have words whose criteria of application vary in understood ways with the context, and "relevant" (as it occurs in formulations of the formal principle of comparative justice) is such a word.

Having rejected a number of material principles that clearly fail to satisfy the "fair opportunity" requirement, we are still left with as many as five candidates for our acceptance. (It is in theory open to us to accept two or more of these five as valid principles, there being no a priori necessity that the list be reduced to one.) These are: (1) the principle of

---

[7]H. L. A. Hart, *The Concept of Law* (Oxford: The Clarendon Press, 1961), p. 156 (emphasis added).

[8]Hart, *The Concept of Law*, p. 156.

perfect equality; (2) the principle[s] of need; (3) the principles of merit and achievement; (4) the principle of contribution (or due return); (5) the principle of effort (or labor). I shall discuss each of these briefly.

(i) EQUALITY

The principle of perfect equality obviously has a place in any adequate social ethic. Every human being is equally a human being, and as we saw in Chapter 6, that minimal qualification entitles all human beings equally to certain absolute human rights: positive rights to non-economic "goods" that by their very natures cannot be in short supply, negative rights not to be treated in cruel or inhuman ways, and negative rights not to be exploited or degraded even in "humane" ways. It is quite another thing, however, to make the minimal qualification of humanity the ground for an absolutely equal distribution of a country's *material wealth* among its citizens. A strict equalitarian could argue that he is merely applying Aristotle's formula of proportionate equality (presumably accepted by all parties to the dispute) with a criterion of relevance borrowed from the human rights theorists. Thus, distributive justice is accomplished between *A* and *B* when the following ratio is satisfied:

$$\frac{A\text{'s share of } P}{B\text{'s share of P}} = \frac{A\text{'s possession of Q}}{B\text{'s possession of Q}}$$

Where *P* stands for economic goods, *Q* must stand simply for "humanity" or "a human nature," and since every human being possesses *that Q* equally, it follows that all should also share a society's economic wealth (the *P* in question) equally.

The trouble with this argument is that its major premise is no less disputable than its conclusion. The standard of relevance it borrows from other contexts where it seems very little short of self-evident, seems controversial, at best, when applied to purely economic contexts. It seems evident to most of us that merely being human entitles *everyone*—bad men as well as good, lazy as well as industrious, inept as well as skilled—to a fair trial if charged with a crime, to equal protection of the law, to equal consideration of his interests by makers of national policy, to be spared torture or other cruel and inhuman treatment, and to be permanently ineligible for the status of chattel slave. Adding a right to an equal share of the economic pie, however, is to add a benefit of a wholly different order, one whose presence on the list of goods for which mere humanity is the sole qualifying condition is not likely to win wide assent without further argument.

It is far more plausible to posit a human right to the satisfaction of (better: to an opportunity to satisfy) one's *basic* economic needs, that is, to enough food and medicine to remain healthy, to minimal clothing, housing, and so on. As Hume pointed out,[9] even these rights cannot exist under conditions of extreme scarcity. Where there is not enough to go around, it cannot be true that everyone has a right to an equal share[10]. But wherever there is moderate abundance or better—wherever a society produces more than enough to satisfy the *basic needs of everyone*—there it seems more plausible to say that mere possession of basic human needs qualifies a person for the opportunity to satisfy them. It would be a rare and calloused sense of justice that would not be offended by an affluent society, with a large annual agricultural surplus and a great abundance of manufactured goods, which permitted some of its citizens to die of starvation, exposure, or easily curable disease. It would certainly be *unfair* for a nation to produce more than it needs and not permit some of its citizens enough to satisfy their basic biological requirements. Strict equalitarianism, then, is a perfectly plausible material principle of distributive justice when confined to affluent societies and basic biological needs, but it loses plausibility when applied to division of the "surplus" left over after basic needs are met. To be sure, the greater the degree of affluence, the higher the level at which we might draw the line between "basic needs" and merely "wanted" benefits, and insofar as social institutions create "artificial needs," it is only fair that society provide all with the opportunity to satisfy them.[11] But once the line has been drawn between what is needed to live a minimally decent life by the realistic standards of a given time and place and what is only added "gravy," it is far from evident that justice still insists upon absolutely equal shares of the total. And it is evident that justice does *not* require strict equality wherever there is reason to think that unequal distribution causally determines greater production and is therefore in the interests of everyone, even those who receive the relatively smaller shares.

Still, there is no way to *refute* the strict equalitarian who requires exactly equal shares for everyone whenever that can be arranged without discouraging total productivity to the point where everyone loses. No one would insist upon equal distributions that would diminish the size of the total pie and thus leave smaller slices for *everyone*; that would be opposed to reason. John Rawls makes this condition part of his "rational principle" of justice: "Inequalities are arbitrary unless it is reasonable to expect that they will work out to everyone's advantage. . . ."[12] We are left then with a version of strict equalitarianism that is by no means evidently true and yet is impossible to refute. That is the theory that purports to

---

[9]David Hume, *Enquiry Concerning the Principles of Morals* Part III (LaSalle, Ill. The Open Court Publishing Company, 1947). Originally published in 1777.

[10]Except in the "manifesto sense" of "right" discussed on p. 67.

[11] This point is well made by Katzner, "An Analysis of the Concept of Justice," pp. 173–203.

[12]John Rawls, "Justice as Fairness," *The Philosophical Review*, LXVII (1958), 165.

apply not only to basic needs but to the total wealth of a society, and allows departures from strict equality when, *but only when*, they will work out to everyone's advantage. Although I am not persuaded by this theory, I think that any adequate material principle will have to attach great importance to keeping differences in wealth within reasonable limits, even after all basic needs have been met. One way of doing this would be to raise the standards for a "basic need" as total wealth goes up, so that differences between the richest and poorest citizens (even when there is no real "poverty") are kept within moderate limits.

(ii) NEED

The principle of need is subject to various interpretations, but in most of its forms it is not an independent principle at all, but only a way of mediating the application of the principle of equality. It can, therefore, be grouped with the principle of perfect equality as a member of the equalitarian family and contrasted with the principles of merit, achievement, contribution, and effort, which are all members of the nonequalitarian family. Consider some differences in "needs" as they bear on distributions. Doe is a bachelor with no dependents; Roe has a wife and six children. Roe must satisfy the needs of eight persons out of his paycheck, whereas Doe need satisfy the needs of only one. To give Roe and Doe equal pay would be to treat Doe's interests substantially *more* generously than those of anyone in the Roe family. Similarly, if a small private group is distributing food to its members (say a shipwrecked crew waiting rescue on a desert island), it would not be fair to give precisely the same quantity to a one hundred pounder as to a two hundred pounder, for that might be giving one person all he needs and the other only a fraction of what he needs—a difference in treatment not supported by any relevant difference between them. In short, to distribute goods in proportion to basic needs is not really to depart from a standard of equality, but rather to bring those with some greater initial burden or deficit up to the same level as their fellows.

The concept of a "need" is extremely elastic. In a general sense, to say that *S* needs *X* is to say simply that if he doesn't have *X* he will be harmed. A "basic need" would then be for an *X* in whose absence a person would be harmed in some crucial and fundamental way, such as suffering injury, malnutrition, illness, madness, or premature death. Thus we all have a basic need for foodstuffs of a certain quantity and variety, fuel to heat our dwellings, a roof over our heads, clothing to keep us warm, and so on. In a different but related sense of need, to say that *S* needs *X* is to say that without *X* he cannot achieve some specific purpose or perform some specific function. If they are to do their work, carpenters needs tools, merchants need capital and customers, authors need paper and publishers. Some helpful goods are not strictly needed in this sense: an author with pencil and paper does not really need a typewriter to write a book, but he may need it to write a book speedily, efficiently, and conveniently. We sometimes come to rely upon "merely helpful but unneeded goods" to such a degree that we develop a strong habitual dependence on them, in which case (as it is often said) we have a "psychological" as opposed to a material need for them. If we don't possess that for which we have a strong psychological need, we may be unable to be happy, in which case a merely psychological need for a functional instrument may become a genuine need in the first sense distinguished above, namely, something whose absence is harmful to us. (Cutting across the distinction between material and psychological needs is that between "natural" and "artificial" needs, the former being those that can be expected to develop in any normal person, the latter being those that are manufactured or contrived, and somehow implanted in, or imposed upon, a person.) The more abundant a society's material goods, the higher the level at which we are required (by the force of psychological needs) to fix the distinction between "necessities" and "luxuries"; what *everyone* in a given society regards as "necessary" tends to become an actual, basic need.

(iii) MERIT AND ACHIEVEMENT

The remaining three candidates for material principles of distributive justice belong to the nonequalitarian family. These three principles would each distribute goods in accordance, not with need, but with *desert*; since persons obviously differ in their deserts, economic goods would be distributed unequally. The three principles differ from one another in their conceptions of the relevant *bases of desert* for economic distributions. The first is the principle of *merit*. Unlike the other principles in the nonequalitarian family, this one focuses not on what a person has *done* to deserve his allotment, but rather on what kind of person he is—what characteristics he has.

Two different types of characteristic might be considered meritorious in the appropriate sense: skills and virtues. Native skills and inherited aptitudes will not be appropriate desert bases, since they are forms of merit ruled out by the fair opportunity requirement. No one deserves credit or blame for his genetic inheritance, since no one has the opportunity to select his own genes. Acquired skills may seem more plausible candidates at first, but upon scrutiny they are little better. First, all acquired skills depend to a large degree on native skills. Nobody is born knowing how to read, so reading is an acquired skill, but actual differences in reading skill are to a large degree accounted for by genetic differences that are beyond anyone's control. Some of the differences are no doubt caused by differences in motivation afforded different children, but again the early conditions contributing to a child's motivation are also largely beyond his control. We may still have some differences in acquired skills that are to be accounted for solely or primarily by differences in the degree of practice, drill, and perseverance expended by persons with roughly equal opportunities. In respect to these, we can propitiate the requirement of fair opportunity, but only by nullifying the significance of acquired skill as such, for now skill is a relevant basis of desert only to the extent that it is a product of one's own effort. Hence, *effort* becomes the true basis of desert (as claimed by our fifth principle, discussed below), and not simply skill as such.

Those who would propose rewarding personal *virtues* with a larger than average share of the economic pie, and punishing defects of character with a smaller than average share, advocate assigning to the economic system a task normally done (if it is done at all) by noneconomic institutions. What they propose, in effect, is that we use retributive criteria of distributive justice. Our criminal law, for a variety of goods reasons, does not purport to punish people for what they are, but only for what they do. A man can be as arrogant, rude, selfish, cruel, insensitive, irresponsible, cowardly, lazy, or disloyal as he wishes; unless he *does* something prohibited by the criminal law, he will not be made to suffer legal punishment. At least one of the legal system's reasons for refusing to penalize character flaws as such would also explain why such defects should not be listed as relevant differences in a material principle of distributive justice. The apparatus for detecting such flaws (a "moral police"?) would be enormously cumbersome and impractical, and its methods so uncertain and fallible that none of us could feel safe in entrusting the determination of our material allotments to it. We could, of course, give roughly equal shares to all except those few who have *outstanding* virtues—gentleness, kindness, courage, diligence, reliability, warmth, charm, considerateness, generosity. Perhaps these are traits that deserve to be rewarded, but it is doubtful that larger economic allotments are the appropriate vehicles of rewarding. As Benn and Peters remind us, "there are some sorts of 'worth' for which rewards in terms of income seem inappropriate. Great courage in battle is recognized by medals, not by increased pay."[13] Indeed, there is something repugnant, as Socrates and the Stoics insisted, in paying a man to be virtuous. Moreover, the rewards would offer a pecuniary motive for certain forms of excellence that require motives of a different kind, and would thus tend to be self-defeating.

The most plausible nonequalitarian theories are those that locate relevance not in meritorious traits and excellences of any kind, but rather in prior doings: not in what one is, but in what one has done. Actions, too, are sometimes called "meritorious," so there is no impropriety in denominating the remaining families of principles in our survey as "meritarian." One type of action-oriented meritarian might cite *achievement* as a relevant desert basis for pecuniary rewards, so that departures from equality in income are to be justicized only by distinguished achievements in science, art, philosophy, music, athletics, and other basic

---

[13]Benn and Peters, *Social Principles and the Democratic State*, p. 139.

areas of human activity. The attractions and disadvantages of this theory are similar to those of theories which I rejected above that base rewards on skills and virtues. Not all persons have a fair opportunity to achieve great things, and economic rewards seem inappropriate as vehicles for expressing recognition and admiration of noneconomic achievements. . . .

If we assume that the criterion of a just outcome for distributions of economic goods *can* be defined independently of the rules of any given procedure for distributing those goods, and can be used therefore as a test of the fairness of alternative procedures, then we must take the context of economic distribution to exemplify what Rawls calls "imperfect procedural justice." When we choose from the point of view of fairness among various capitalist, socialist, and mixed schemes for organizing an economy, we cannot hope to find a system that is certain to generate a just outcome in every instance, giving every citizen exactly his due as determined by an independent material criterion of distributive justice. Even assuming agreement on the criterion of a just distributive outcome, our choice is more like that between rival procedures for conducting a criminal trial, e.g., between the adversary system used in English-speaking countries and the inquisitorial system used elsewhere in Europe. For criminal trials we have an agreed upon conception of just outcomes: we want guilty men convicted and innocent men acquitted. What we must decide is, which alternative system of criminal procedure, subject to certain obvious restrictions set by other values, is likely to achieve these objectives in the higher percentage of cases? Similarly, in the choice among economic systems on the assumption of independent standards for just outcomes, we must decide which of the alternative systems of procedures will come closest to satisfying those standards, subject to the restrictions of such other values as efficiency and liberty.

On the other hand, we might prefer to take the problem of economic distribution to be a question of what Rawls calls "pure procedural justice," at least for that part of the problem that concerns the economic "surplus" that is left after basic needs have been satisfied equally for everyone. Our choice will hinge in large part on whether we take the economic arena to be basically cooperative or competitive, whether we think of our economic interrelations as a race for surplus riches with economic income as prizes for the swiftest, or "winnings" for the luckiest, or as some other kind of rule-governed "game" we all play or contest we all enter. In the end, our criteria of economic justice will reflect the way we *conceive* the economic sphere of life. Beyond the level of basic needs (interpreted in a realistic and generous way), even the model of the roulette wheel with its simple rules of pure procedural justice provides a possible, if unappealing, model. Given the universal satisfaction of basic human needs, those procedures for producing and distributing goods are best that best promote the common good, and there may be no clear and convincing criterion for the just distribution of "surplus goods" other than the fair operation of those procedures, whichever they may be.

6

Epilogue

PLATO, HOBBES, AND MARX

HOBBES. I've been rereading the *Republic*.

PLATO. Ah!

HOBBES. It struck me once again how much I was indebted to you. Even if I didn't always agree with the answers you proposed, you raised the right questions, and they're still relevant.

PLATO. The questions I raised were those that urgently needed to be raised. You'll recall that the public attitude towards philosophy at the time I wrote was quite negative. Even the young people would often shrug—as many appear to do today—meaning, "Why bother?" I think it forced me to be more dramatic than I might otherwise have been.

HOBBES. My own period had a weakness for rhetoric, so I cultivated a lean, dry style. It seldom inspired, but it often convinced.

PLATO. Very true. As for me, I was less concerned to convince than to inspire, for I wanted to expose not only ideas to men's minds, but the clash of ideas as well. I loved the excitement of intellectual battles, not the smug satisfaction of doctrinal victories. But these peculiar tendencies of mine would not have prevailed had the terrible pressure of events not injected into my life so keen a sense of mission and of urgency. Why, barely half a century before all had been radiant—golden poetry, golden drama, golden temples. When I came upon that scene, only the afterglow was there; men seemed forgetful of their past achievements . . . having long since forgotten how to achieve.

HOBBES. Looking back, the Age of Pericles must have seemed far more vivid to you than the Renaissance was to us. Yours was a tremendous cultural explosion occurring in a highly concentrated portion of time and space; ours was more diffuse.

PLATO. It was as you say, but of course we didn't realize it then. Apart from a few historians, there weren't many among us who had more than the faintest sense of history. Then, too, so many things were mingled in my mind—the fate of Athens, the fate of Greece, the fate of man, and the overwhelming symbolic fate of Socrates. Poor Athens, where men of genius once jostled and elbowed each other in the streets, where the bright Mediterranean sun shone down on a community itself illuminated by robust intelligence and knowing grace, had come to exhibit in my own time only squabbling and struggling, the echoes and shadows of which stretched far on ahead of us into the night. I looked back at the fifth century the way a sailor watches the shoreline of his homeland becoming ever more distant, ever more unrecoverable. Suddenly I realized how enormous was my responsibility. For it seemed as if man's response to the first great opportunity to become fully civilized—or should I say fully human?—although brilliant and thrilling at first, was now being leached and drained away into impotence. If there were not to be a relapse into barbarism, someone had to establish the intellectual foundations of a civilization. Foundational questions had to be asked, if there were to be a civilization rather than nothing. After all, we had doubted . . . Ah, Marx! Over here!

HOBBES. Dreadful fellow, really. Awfully clever, I'll admit, but quite dreadful.

PLATO. If you'd overlook your differences with him on the issue of private property, you might admit how much the two of you have in common.

MARX. The philosophers.

HOBBES. That we are—you too: theorists all.

PLATO. Oh, I'd hardly call my *Republic* a theory. I think of it rather as myth within myth, vision opening into vision, ideas which unfold and fold again, come to light and disappear into shadow. But the *Leviathan* is rock upon solid rock, and juts up out of the seventeenth century as the Acropolis juts up out of Athens. You're modern, even scientific. Indeed, I've been rereading the *Leviathan* for all the reasons I've told you, and for others of my own.

MARX. Did you enjoy seeing how he used your social contract theory in the *Leviathan?*

HOBBES. I was so much concerned to refute Aristotle's contention that society is a natural institution that I didn't think it necessary to observe that he was in turn reacting against your social contract theory, Plato.

PLATO. It was no more my "theory" than it was "mine", for I didn't originate it. But you were both welcome to it, and you both articulated it and elaborated upon it. Don't you see, Marx, how similar your depiction of ruthless, universal competition under capitalism is to Hobbes's notion of the "state of nature," with its "war of every man against every man"?

MARX. Perhaps. But he sees no way out except through legality, terror, and a State bloated beyond imagination, while I see beyond the State to the ultimate liberation of mankind from every spectre of deprivation and injustice.

HOBBES. But, like you, I tried to show that sovereignty—the right to rule—derives from the powers of the people themselves rather than from God. Human society is the result of the fact that, rather than fight incessantly among themselves, men prefer to institute a state that will enforce peace among them.

PLATO. And yet, this contention which both of you seem to insist on—that, physically and intellectually, men are pretty much alike—really! Aren't you exaggerating their similarities? I myself am convinced that the talent for ruling is spread unequally among men, so that some are more fit than others to be educated as future rulers.

HOBBES. I didn't deny that there were such differences. I merely maintained that they were politically insignificant. In politics, the important distinction is not that between clever rulers and stupid ones, but that between rulers, whether clever or stupid, whose edicts are backed up by force, as opposed to rulers, whatever their intelligence, who cannot enforce their edicts. You think the key to politics lies in intelligence; I happen to think it lies in force. In a well-run country, the laws, whether enlightened or not, are systematically and uniformly enforced, while in a poorly run country they are not.

PLATO. I never maintained that intelligent leadership could be effective without force. What I tried to show was that force is necessary to run a country, but that intelligence is indispensable to run it well.

HOBBES. You're forgetting human nature. Men's basic instincts are selfish and aggressive. Each wants to grab all he can for himself, and hold on to it as long as he can. So men come to fight among themselves, and they're deterred from fighting only by force or the threat of force. The more force you use on men, the more peaceable they become, and if you want them to be absolutely peaceful, then you must be prepared to create an absolute force over them.

MARX. I've seen all sorts of poverty, but there's nothing quite like the poverty of philosophy. No extravagant talk about a world where abundance is justly distributed so as to meet all men's legitimate needs; no wasteful discussion of the ways of minimizing the invidious distinctions among men, so as eventually to eliminate the need for repression; no concern to maximize human creativity and independence. No, in their straitened circumstances, philosophers seem able to touch upon only such minimal matters as force and constraint, law and order. What intellectual bankruptcy!

PLATO. Perhaps. But I think you'll find, if you reread the *Republic*, that I'm concerned in it to show the State as not so much repressive as remedial, healing and restitutive, and as acting in the interests of the ruled rather than in the interests of the rulers. But it really doesn't matter. As far as the twentieth century is concerned, the *Leviathan* and the *Manifesto* seem considerably more influential than the *Republic*.

HOBBES. It hardly surprises me that this should be so. After all, the problems of the twentieth century resemble in many ways those of the seventeenth. We were trying to come to grips with the disorder that existed within each nation. The twentieth century is grappling with political disorder on an international scale. But I think the solution I offered in the one instance would apply equally well in the other.

MARX. I didn't merely offer a solution. I predicted the outcome. My followers thought it would happen overnight; my critics said it couldn't happen ever. Both were wrong. It will come, but accompanied by a suffering even more intense and incalculable than I had imagined.

PLATO. You may not be wrong. In any event, I'm grateful that both of you and so many others have joined in the dialogue. For a time it seemed to me that I might be talking just to myself. But Aristotle gave me hope that the dialogue would continue, and I see that it has.

II

THE MORAL LIFE

7

Introduction

Perhaps one of the least questioned notions of modern ethical and political philosophies is that the two disciplines are continuous and homogeneous. Underlying this belief is the apprehension that if the two fields were separated, political philosophy would be deprived of all ethical content and would be discovered to be shamefully amoral. It has therefore been argued that the same criteria are applicable to both politics and ethics. Such an assumption, however, may well be questioned. For it could be argued that *all* rule-governed or policy-governed behavior is political, and that such considerations as the categorical imperative of Kant and the greatest happiness principle of Bentham and Mill are essentially political, having to do much more with justice than with morality. On this view, ethics would deal only with choice-governed behavior to which rules functioned in a tentative and auxiliary fashion, whereas political philosophy would concern itself solely with rule-governed conduct—i.e., with the devising of rules to which public choices could rationally conform.

From this standpoint, therefore, the distinction between the political and the ethical depends simply on whether the focus is on the making of policies or on the making of individual choices. The social legitimation of betting, gambling, prostitution, abortion, suicide, and so on, are questions of public policy, and such legitimation will very likely express a consensus of the public's views as to what is to the interest of the majority, and as to what it might be if everyone were to act in such and such a way. The conduct of persons in society will thereupon be policy-governed or rule-governed. But the individual who is contemplating whether or not to gamble or to commit suicide or to live with another person of the opposite sex without benefit of marriage is in an ethical situation in which moral rules, however rationally derived, are not binding policies but suggestive hypotheses for guidance in the making of a choice. For insofar as we accept our likeness with other human beings, we may be content to abide by the policies that govern the society in which we live, whether or not such policies have the force of legality. But insofar as we construe our situations as unique and therefore incommensurable with the situations of others, social rules and public policies will play only an auxiliary role in the way in which we come to our ethical decision.

It is for reasons such as these that *justice* has come to be seen as the dominant ideal of political philosophy, which deals with policy-governed or rule-governed conduct, while ethics, which is concerned with the theory of choice-governed conduct, takes as its guide the ideal of *freedom*.

Ethics, then, is the philosophy of personal conduct. On this point—and only on this point—there is some semblance of agreement. With every step we take beyond it, we plunge into a wilderness.

How are we to live? How are we to act? What are we to do? It is when we ask ourselves questions such as these that we begin to find ourselves drawn into a bewildering jungle of conflicting values.

But travellers have emerged, after years of anguished wandering about, and have sought to draw for us, as best they could, maps of the moral landscape. Crude maps, it is true, and possibly of dubious reliability, since they seem so much at odds with one another as to even the most salient and pronounced features of the terrain. But they are our only guides and models. Here, in brief, are a few of them:

1. *Morality as conscientious, industrious service*. In a factory, as is well-known, the ordinary workman is little troubled by the question of what he is to do. His job has precise specifications. Management has indicated to him in no uncertain terms just what he must do and how he must do it. Should he fail to perform as he is expected to, he may find himself no longer employed in that factory. And it is similarly, according to this first conception, that morality should be construed. A Management (which one cannot doubt exists) expects us to conduct ourselves in the world in accordance with a system of living which that governing body has designed. The system can be neither criticized nor challenged. It is enough that one has one's duties and that one carries them out as conscientiously, efficiently, and industriously as possible. The moral person is a humble laborer in the service of a wisely providential system. One expects no reward for such labor, for to be permitted to serve so benevolent a Management is itself the greatest blessing one can hope to enjoy.

2. *Morality as descriptive science*. Men's diverse behaviors are carefully observed and noted. Certain uniformities are discovered; for instance, it is found that human behavior exhibits a conspicuous tendency to proceed in the direction of, say, happiness. It is therefore assumed that happiness is the natural (and indeed, universally acknowledged) goal of human life. The only issues with which morality must deal, therefore, are questions of the means of obtaining that goal. The right way to live is the best or most expeditious way of achieving this highest prize that life has to offer. Reason, which we all possess, can therefore select for us the proper life-direction, and to the extent to which we arrange our lives reasonably, to this extent are we virtuous.

In this respect, consider Aristotle's functional and naturalistic approach to ethics: an axe is a thing that chops, so a good axe is one that chops well; an eye is a thing that sees, so good eyes are things that see well. Once we know the function of a thing, goodness is simply a matter of the degree of excellence in the performance of the function. Thus, man's function being to live in accordance with reason, the good man is one who performs such a function excellently. And since whatever performs its unique function well is in a state of well-being, the virtuous man's life is characterized by human well-being, or happiness.

3. *Morality as formal science*. Another map describes the wilderness as no wilderness at all, but as a rationally organized commonwealth. We all know that we must be consistent, for a world in which we all thought it our duty to be inconsistent would be so chaotic and absurd as to be unbearable. But if we are consistent, we cannot logically exempt ourselves from what we would deny the rest of mankind. Consequently it follows that our reason can construct rules of conduct applicable to everyone, and that we need ask only whether or not a rule is universalizable in order to know whether or not it is applicable.

Thus, Kant finds Aristotle's approach unacceptable because it defines human virtue in terms of its success in producing the goal of happiness, rather than in terms of perfect obedience to an overriding moral principle. Kant in fact denies that the consequences of an action can indicate the moral worth of that action. He claims instead that the act, to be right, must be in conformity with moral law, while the person who commits the act, to be considered virtuous, must be motivated solely by respect for such law. The virtuous person is therefore one who, purely for the sake of the law, does what the law requires. And what the law requires is that he do what all persons would want to do in such a situation.

4. *Morality as politics*. This map was produced by explorers who obviously followed trails traced by those who had devised the two maps last cited, for it contains features common to both. Morality is portrayed as a descriptive science, yet its demonstrations rest rather lightly on factual evidence, and the appeal is rather to consensus and the common good. The ideal of the moral life turns out to be identical with the ideal of the political life of the society, namely, "the greatest happiness of the greatest number." Happiness is defined as pleasure, and the pleasures that experienced men pursue are taken to be the most desirable goods of life.

One version of this approach is known as Utilitarianism. In its more extreme forms, with its stress upon pleasure as the goal of human action and its insistence upon dealing with particular situations in ways that need not be universalized, Utilitarianism appears to be the very opposite of Kantianism. But in the more moderate formulations of Utilitarianism and Kantianism, there would seem to be considerable convergence of their respective points of view.

As a Utilitarian, Mill finds Kant's formulation of ethics unacceptable, because it exaggerates the importance of personal motives, and rejects the role of consequences in determining the moral worth of an act.

To Mill, actions that generate more happiness among more people are better actions than those that are less productive of happiness of the same quality. Moreover, Mill fears that universal moral principles, such as Kant's, may turn out to be a disguised form of social tyranny, since they make no allowance for personal liberty, privacy, individuality, or creativity. Mill proposes that society acknowledge as beyond its jurisdiction all those actions that a person enjoys with respect only to himself, or which, if such actions affect other mature individuals, do so with the understanding and consent of those persons. Mill therefore rejects the notion that society should be permitted to dictate to a "rational and undeceived" adult the style of life he ought to lead, with the claim that it is for "his own good." Mill insists that, insofar as a person is sovereign over his own life, he must be free to do as he pleases with that life.

5. *Morality as art*. Every personal situation, according to this view, is utterly unique. Yet the moral situation is binding and authoritative: it demands that one do what is appropriate to it. One may have done other things in other situations, but here and now, at this time, in this place, one must recognize the moral compulsion of the situation as coercive, and must do what the situation requires. In this sense, a person's unique response to a moral situation is a recognition that the stage has been set, that he has been challenged to act, and that he must respond in an individualized and creative fashion, much as an artist, in the artistic situation, must wrestle with his media, and with his traditions, and with his emotions, in order to wring from them a work of art. To choose the right act requires imagination, inventiveness, and audacity.

6. *Morality as craft*. When morality is seen as industry, then moral acts appear to be mass-manufactured, identical with one another, as interchangeable as products falling off an assembly line. When morality is seen as art, moral acts have the same uniqueness as works of art are presumed to have. But these are two extremes, and in between there is a third alternative, which conceives of the moral agent as analogous to the craftsman. Like a craftsman, he is respectful of his roots and traditions, careful of his tools and materials, and respectful of time-honored methods of behaving. But the great works of pottery and furniture, of tapestry and decoration, demonstrate that fine craftsmen have always been prepared to innovate and initiate, although with modesty and caution. So, too, with the moral agent as craftsman: he well understands custom and established usage, and he pays his respects to them without grumbling. But while his departure from routine may not have the excitement and freshness of those to be found in art, they nevertheless bear the stamp of a responsible craftsman.

Obviously these charts are no more than glimpses of a very strange territory. In certain respects they are quite clearly at odds with one another.

Take the matter of rules. Some conceptions of ethics conceive its purpose to be the devising of codes of moral rules by which men can live. Others agree that rules are necessary, but argue that such rules may be obtained from some supernatural source, or directly from nature itself. Still others contend that, while men must live by moral rules, it is not the business of philosophical ethics to provide such rules. Instead, it is argued, ethics should provide no more than the underlying principle of all such rules, much as a constitution is the principle underlying the civil laws of a nation.

But there are those to whom any moral rule is anathema. They stress the importance of wholesome emotions like love and compassion, or they stress the importance of moral sensitivity and moral insight. Yet others maintain that emotions are quite unreliable and untrustworthy unless such feelings can be critically examined and understood. They therefore maintain that the emphasis should not be put upon the devising of rules of morality, but should be placed instead upon the rules of logical reasoning by means of which emotions, facts, values, and other components of moral situations must be examined.

But this last formulation pits intelligence against desires, and desires themselves are thought of by some as wholly irrational. One further conception of ethics therefore sees desires as themselves containing in each case a germ of judiciousness or intelligence, and it is precisely this cognitive germ that must be cultivated and developed, until our desires at last manifest themselves as intelligent, and we come to desire only what experience, reflection, and inquiry have certified to be desirable.

The more recent selections begin with Hare's detailed overview of the nature and scope of ethical philosophy. Hare meticulously sorts out the major differences among ethical theorists, so as to clarify the basic distinctions between ethics and morals, between objectivism and subjectivism, between prescriptivism and descriptivism, and among such traditional approaches as naturalism, intuitionism, and emotivism. Any setting forth of the classification of ethical arguments is liable to involve a degree of dreariness, but the patient reader will discover that the Hare essay can be very useful in the attempt to understand contemporary philosophical discourse about the moral life.

The essays by Schneewind and Hampshire may be seen to complement one another rather than delineate contrasting points of view. The model of ethics elaborated by Schneewind resembles the more general model of scientific understanding: moral principles are likened to formulations of particular scientific laws, while large-scale religious or cultural outlooks, or world-views within which a morality is embedded, are likened to more general scientific theories. Moral systems are decidedly fallible, Schneewind acknowledges, but nevertheless have the merit of being widely accepted, and as a consequence are able to give "shape and coherence and predictability to large segments of life." To Hampshire, each society has primary moral customs and prohibitions that are part and parcel of its world-view, and that are not adequately evaluated when isolated and dealt with in purely utilitarian terms. He contends that utilitarian optimism about rationality and progress can succeed all too well in draining custom and tradition of much of their significance, with the result that the instinctual and emotional barriers to anti-social behavior upon which civilizations are constructed may very well be eroded and disintegrated. Hampshire consequently rejects the utilitarian faith that human nature will be transformed through moral reasoning.

The problematic character of the family as an institution is pointed up by both the Wasserstrom and the Margolis selections. Wasserstrom's careful examination of the question of adultery raises such questions as whether sexual relationships are an indispensable part of marriage, whether sexual exclusiveness is an indispensable aspect of sexual intimacy, and whether the preservation of marriage must necessarily be presumed. The Wasserstrom article, in raising these and many additional questions regarding adultery, offers no answers to the questions it propounds. The Margolis essay, on the other hand, sets forth a specific proposal for a distinction between the institution of marriage and the institution of the family, so as to guarantee to marriage the rights of privacy and freedom, while guaranteeing to the family those benefits of justice that accrue to whatever is in the public domain. It is therefore possible to view the Margolis article as one of a variety of options open to society with respect to the stresses that have long been characteristic of marriage as an institution, but that are apparently becoming increasingly critical and intense.

The question of what each of us ought to do is approached in quite different terms by the existentialist Sartre and by the analytical philosopher Urmson. Sartre insists that each person is responsible for everyone, and uses the notion of exemplary behavior to show that no matter what it is we do, people will imitate us, and then seek to justify their behavior by citing what we had done as their excuse for doing likewise. Responsibility is therefore inescapable, and we must accept the burden of being models for everyone, hence responsible for everyone. Whether Sartre's approach is as applicable to the more mundane contexts of everyday life as it is to situations of dramatic moral crisis is a matter of debate. Urmson approaches the matter in an opposite fashion, first acknowledging that there are basic moral duties that everyone might be expected to perform, then arguing that in emergencies, one may very well do that which is far beyond one's duty to do. Thus, under certain specifiable conditions, actions become possible that do not fit the normally accepted compartmentalization of behavior as comprised of what we ought to do, what we ought not to do, and what is not our duty either to do or not do. Urmson concludes that while we can rightfully expect persons to do whatever is their basic duty as a minimum, we cannot demand ideal conduct from them, admirable as it is that some of them should be saintly or heroic.

Dewey's essay is characteristically forceful and incisive. He indicts the view that customs and traditions cannot be reconstructed as itself one of the chief sources of the preservation of unwholesome or unsuccessful cultural patterns. And he rejects the notion that such institutions as war and economic competition are the reflection of an underlying and very rigid instinctual complex known as "human nature." Here his views on human freedom and the plasticity of human impulse contrast sharply with the pessimism of Hobbes and Oakeshott. Dewey's belief that men can become more rational as individuals and can devise more rational institutions under which to live, if only they would thoroughly reconstruct their educational processes, extend democracy to all forms of social power, and use science as their model for the solution of social problems, is as unappealing to sceptics as it is to authoritarians and irrationalists. As a pragmatist, however, Dewey would be satisfied if the value of his proposals would be determined by no other criteria than the success of their application.

8

The Character of Morality

ARISTOTLE

(384 B.C.–322 B.C)

Aristotle was born in Stagira, in Thrace; his father was physician to the king of Macedonia. At the age of seventeen he came to Athens, and remained at Plato's Academy for almost twenty years. (Plato was forty-three years his senior.) After leaving the Academy, Aristotle traveled for some years, then became tutor to Alexander, son of the king of Macedonia. But the association lasted only two or three years, and in 335 B.C., Aristotle returned to Athens, where he set up the Lyceum. Here he wrote treatises on many scientific subjects, as well as on most areas of philosophy. He directed the Lyceum for twelve years, but left Athens when the death of Alexander unleashed a considerable tide of anti-Macedonian sentiment, which caused the Athenians to withdraw the honors they had extended him, and perhaps even to have threatened his life. This was in 323 B.C., and Aristotle died the following year. He and Plato continue to be the most influential thinkers in Western civilization, and they must be considered among the most profound.

OUTLINE OF A SCIENCE OF ETHICS

1. EVERY art and every kind of inquiry, and likewise every act and purpose, seems to aim at some good: and so it has been well said that the Good is that at which everything aims.

But a difference is observable among these aims or ends. What is aimed at is sometimes the exercise of a faculty, sometimes a certain result beyond that exercise. And where there is an end beyond the act, there the result is better than the exercise of the faculty.

Now since there are many kinds of actions and many arts and sciences, it follows that there are many ends also; *e.g.*, health is the end of medicine, ships of shipbuilding, victory of the art of war, and wealth of economy.

But when several of these are subordinated to some one art or science,—as the making of bridles and other trappings to the art of horsemanship, and this in turn, along with all else that the soldier does, to the art of war, and so on,—then the end of the master-art is always more desired than the ends of the subordinate arts, since these are pursued for its sake. And this is equally true whether the end in view be the mere exercise of a faculty or something beyond that, as in the above instances.

2. If then in what we do there be some end which we wish for on its own account, choosing all the others as means to this, but not every end without exception as a means to something else (for so we should go on *ad infinitum*, and desire would be left void and objectless),—this evidently will be the good or the best of all things.

And surely from a practical point of view it much concerns us to know this Good; for then, like archers shooting at a definite mark, we shall be more likely to attain what we want.

If this be so, we must try to indicate roughly what it is, and first of all to which of the arts and sciences it belongs.

It would seem to belong to the supreme art or science, that one which most of all deserves the name of master-art or master-science.

Now Politics[1] seems to answer to this description. For it prescribes which of the sciences a state needs, and which each man shall study, and up to what point; and to it we see subordinated even the highest arts, such as economy, rhetoric, and the art of war.

Since then it makes use of the other practical sciences, and since it further ordains what men are to do and from what to refrain, its end must include the ends of the others, and must be the proper good of man.

For though this good is the same for the individual and the state, yet the good of the state seems a grander and more perfect thing both to

From Nichomachean Ethics, *Book One.*

attain and to secure; and glad as one would be to do this service for a single individual, to do it for a people and for a number of states is nobler and more divine.

This then is the aim of the present inquiry, which is a sort of political inquiry.[2]

3. We must be content if we can attain to so much precision in our statement as the subject before us admits of; for the same degree of accuracy is no more to be expected in all kinds of reasoning than in all kinds of manufacture.

Now what is noble and just (with which Politics deals) is so various and so uncertain, that some think these are merely conventional and not natural distinctions.

There is a similar uncertainty also about what is good, because good things often do people harm: men have before now been ruined by wealth, and have lost their lives through courage.

Our subject, then, and our data being of this nature, we must be content if we can indicate the truth roughly and in outline, and if, in dealing with matters that are not amenable to immutable laws, *and* reasoning from premises that are but probable, we can arrive at probable conclusions.[3]

The reader, on his part, should take each of my statements in the same spirit; for it is the mark of an educated man to require, in each kind of inquiry, just so much exactness as the subject admits of: it is equally absurd to accept probable reasoning from a mathematician, and to demand scientific proof from an orator.

But each man can form a judgment about what he knows, and is called "a good judge" of that—of any special matter when he has received a special education therein, "a good judge" (without any qualifying epithet) when he has received a universal education. And hence a young man is not qualified to be a student of Politics; for he lacks experience of the affairs of life, which form the data and the subject-matter of Politics.

Further, since he is apt to be swayed by his feelings, he will derive no benefit from a study whose aim is not speculative but practical.

But in this respect young in character counts the same as young in years; for the young man's disqualification is not a matter of time, but is due to the fact that feeling rules his life and directs all his desires. Men of this character turn the knowledge they get to no account in practice, as we see with those we call incontinent; but those who direct their desires and actions by reason will gain much profit from the knowledge of these matters.

[1, 2] To Aristotle "Politics" is a much wider term than to us; it covers the whole field of human life, since man is essentially social in nature. It therefore encompasses what we would think of as the social sciences as well as social philosophy.

[3] The expression τὰ ως επὶ τὸ πολύ covers both (1) what is generally though not universally true, and (2) what is probable though not certain.

So much then by way of preface as to the student, and the spirit in which he must accept what we say, and the object which we propose to ourselves.

4. Since—to resume—all knowledge and all purpose aims at some good, what is this which we say is the aim of Politics; or, in other words, what is the highest of all realizable goods?

As to its name, I suppose nearly all men are agreed; for the masses and the men of culture alike declare that it is happiness, and hold that to "live well" or to "do well" is the same as to be "happy."

But they differ as to what this happiness is, and the masses do not give the same account of it as the philosophers.

The former take it to be something palpable and plain, as pleasure or wealth or fame; one man holds it to be this, and another that, and often the same man is of different minds at different times,—after sickness it is health, and in poverty it is wealth; while when they are impressed with the consciousness of their ignorance, they admire most those who say grand things that are above their comprehension.

Some philosophers, on the other hand, have thought that, beside these several good things, there is an "absolute" Good which is the cause of their goodness.

As it would hardly be worth while to review all the opinions that have been held, we will confine ourselves to those which are most popular, or which seem to have some foundation in reason.

But we must not omit to notice the distinction that is drawn between the method of proceeding from your starting-points or principles, and the method of working up to them. Plato used with fitness to raise this question, and to ask whether the right way is from or to your starting-points, as in the race-course you may run from the judges to the boundary, or *vice versâ*.

Well, we must start from what is known.

But "what is known" may mean two things: "what is known to us," which is one thing, or "what is known" simply, which is another.

I think it is safe to say that *we* must start from what is known to *us*.

And on this account nothing but a good moral training can qualify a man to study what is noble and just—in a word, to study questions of Politics. For the undemonstrated fact is here the starting-point, and if this undemonstrated fact be sufficiently evident to a man, he will not require a "reason why." Now the man who has had a good moral training either has already arrived at starting-points or principles of action, or will easily accept them when pointed out. But he who neither has them nor will accept them may hear what Hesiod says[4]—

"The best is he who of himself doth know;
Good too is he who listens to the wise;

[4]"Works and Days," 291-295.

> But he who neither knows himself nor heeds
> The words of others, is a useless man."

• • •

7. Leaving these matters, then, let us return once more to the question, what this good can be of which we are in search.

It seems to be different in different kinds of action and in different arts—one thing in medicine and another in war, and so on. What then is the good in each of these cases? Surely that for the sake of which all else is done. And that in medicine is health, in war is victory, in building is a house—a different thing in each different case, but always, in whatever we do and in whatever we choose, the end. For it is always for the sake of the end that all else is done.

If then there be one end of all that man does, this end will be the realizable good—or these ends, if there be more than one.

Our argument has thus come round by a different path to the same point as before. This point we must try to explain more clearly.

We see that there are many ends. But some of these are chosen only as means, as wealth, flutes, and the whole class of instruments. And so it is plain that not all ends are final.

But the best of all things must, we conceive, be something final.

If then there be only one final end, this will be what we are seeking—or if there be more than one, then the most final of them.

Now that which is pursued as an end in itself is more final than that which is pursued as means to something else, and that which is never chosen as means than that which is chosen both as an end in itself and as means, and that is strictly final which is always chosen as an end in itself and never as means.

Happiness seems more than anything else to answer to this description: for we always choose it for itself, and never for the sake of something else; while honor and pleasure and reason, and all virtue or excellence, we choose partly indeed for themselves (for, apart from any result, we should choose each of them), but partly also for the sake of happiness, supposing that they will help to make us happy. But no one chooses happiness for the sake of these things, or as a means to anything else at all.

We seem to be led to the same conclusion when we start from the notion of self-sufficiency.

The final good is thought to be self-sufficing [or all-sufficing]. In applying this term we do not regard a man as an individual leading a solitary life, but we also take account of parents, children, wife, and, in short, friends and fellow-citizens generally, since man is naturally a social being. Some limit must indeed be set to this; for if you go on to parents and descendants and friends of friends, you will never come to a stop. But this we will consider further on: for the present we will take self-sufficing to mean what by itself makes life desirable and in want of nothing. Now happiness is believed to answer to this description.

And further, happiness is believed to be the most desirable thing in the world, and that not merely as one among other goods things: if it were merely one among other good things [so that other things could be added to it], it is plain that the addition of the least of other goods must make it more desirable; for the addition becomes a surplus of good, and of two goods the greater is always more desirable.

Thus it seems that happiness is something final and self-sufficing, and is the end of all that man does.

But perhaps the reader thinks that though no one will dispute the statement that happiness is the best thing in the world, yet a still more precise definition of it is needed.

This will best be gained, I think, by asking, What is the function of man? For as the goodness and the excellence of a piper or a sculptor, or the practiser of any art, and generally of those who have any function or business to do, lies in that function, so man's good would seem to lie in his function, if he has one.

But can we suppose that, while a carpenter and a cobbler has a function and a business of his own, man has no business and no function assigned him by nature? Nay, surely as his several members, eye and hand and foot, plainly have each his own function, so we must suppose that man also has some function over and above all these.

What then is it?

Life evidently he has in common even with the plants, but we want that which is peculiar to him. We must exclude, therefore, the life of mere nutrition and growth.

Next to this comes the life of sense; but this too he plainly shares with horses and cattle and all kinds of animals.

There remains then the life whereby he acts—the life of his rational nature,[5] with its two sides or divisions, one rational as obeying reason, the other rational as having and exercising reason.

But as this expression is ambiguous,[6] we must be understood to mean thereby the life that consists in the exercise of the faculties; for this seems to be more properly entitled to the name.

The function of man, then, is exercise of his vital faculties [or soul] on one side in obedience to reason, and on the other side with reason.

But what is called the function of a man of any profession and the function of a man who is good in that profession are generically the same, *e.g.*, of a harper and of a good harper; and this holds in all cases

---

[5]*πρακτική τις του λόγον εχοντος*. Aristotle frequently uses the terms *πρᾶξις*, *πρακτ́ς*, *πρακτικός* in this wide sense, covering all that man does, *i.e.* all that part of man's life that is within the control of his will, or that is consciously directed to an end, including therefore speculation as well as action.

[6]For it might mean either the mere possession of the vital faculties, or their exercise.

without exception, only that in the case of the latter his superior excellence at his work is added; for we say a harper's function is to play the harp, and a good harper's to play the harp well.

Man's function then being, as we say, a kind of life—that is to say, exercise of his faculties and action of various kinds with reason—the good man's function is to do this well and beautifully.

But the function of anything is done well when it is done in accordance with the proper excellence of that thing.

Putting all this together, then, we find that the good of man is exercise of his faculties in accordance with excellence or virtue, or, if there be more than one, in accordance with the best and most complete virtue.

But to this we must add that the external circumstances of his life must also be perfect and complete: if one swallow or one fine day does not make a spring, neither does one day or any small space of time make a blessed or happy man.

This, then, may be taken as a rough outline of the good; for this, I think, is the proper method,—first to sketch the outline, and then to fill in the details. But it would seem that, the outline once fairly drawn, any one can carry on the work and fit in the several items which time reveals to us or helps us to find. And this indeed is the way in which the arts and sciences have grown; for it requires no extraordinary genius to fill up the gaps.

IMMANUEL KANT

(1724–1804)

The worldwide influence of Kant's work contrasts sharply with the seclusion of his life, spent in and near Königsberg, the Prussian city where he was born. He obtained his doctorate in 1755, and gave lectures as a Privatdozent *for the next fifteen years. Twice he failed to obtain a professorship at Köningsberg, although he refused appointments elsewhere. However in 1770 he received the chair of metaphysics and logic. His major work, the* Critique of Pure Reason, *was published in 1781, and was followed by the* Metaphysic of Morals *(1785), the* Critique of Practical Reason *(1788), and the* Critique of Judgment *(1790). Kant's philosophic achievements quickly became famous throughout Germany. In 1792, when the first part of his book* Religion within the Boundaries of Reason Alone *was published, the repressive Prussian regime turned its attention to him as the most important representative of free inquiry. Although publication of the remainder of the work was forbidden, Kant published it in 1794. In 1797 he ceased his public lectures, and while he continued to write, his powers diminished markedly in the years before his death.*

THE MORAL PERSON AND THE MORAL LAW

Nothing can possibly be conceived in the world, or even out of it, which can be called good without qualification, except a good will. Intelligence, wit, judgment, and the other *talents* of the mind, however they may be named, or courage, resolution, perseverance, as qualities of temperament, are undoubtedly good and desirable in many respects. But these gifts of nature may also become extremely bad and mischievous if the will which is to make use of these gifts, and which therefore constitutes what is called *character*, is not good. It is the same with the *gifts of fortune*. Power, riches, honor, even health, and the general well-being and contentment with one's condition which is called *happiness*, all inspire pride and often presumption if there is not a good will to correct the influence of these on the mind, and with this to rectify also the whole principle of acting and adapt it to its end. The sight of a being, not adorned with a single feature of a pure and good will, enjoying unbroken prosperity can never give pleasure to an impartial rational spectator. Thus a good will appears to constitute the indispensable condition for being even worthy of happiness.

Indeed, quite a few qualities are of service to this good will itself and may facilitate its action, yet have no intrinsic, unconditional value, but are always presupposing a good will; this qualifies the esteem that we justly have for these qualities and does not permit us to regard them as absolutely good. Moderation in the affections and passions, self-control and calm deliberation are not only good in many respects, but even seem to constitute part of the intrinsic worth of a person, but they are far from deserving to be called good without qualification, although they have been so unconditionally praised by the ancients. For without the principles of a good will, these qualities may become extremely bad. The coolness of a villain not only makes him far more dangerous, but also immediately makes him more abominable in our eyes than he would have been without it.

A good will is good not because of what it performs or effects, nor by its aptness for attaining some proposed end, but simply by virtue of the volition; that is, it is good in itself and when considered by itself is to be esteemed much higher than all that it can bring about in pursuing any inclination, nay even in pursuing the sum total of all inclinations. It might happen that, owing to special misfortune, or to the niggardly provision of a step-motherly nature, this will should wholly lack power to accomplish its purpose. If with its greatest efforts this will should yet achieve nothing and there should remain only good will (to be sure, not a

From *Foundations of the Metaphysics of Morals.*

mere wish but the summoning of all means in our power), then, like a jewel, good will would still shine by its own light as a thing having its whole value in itself. Its usefulness or fruitlessness can neither add to nor detract anything from this value. It would be, as it were, only the setting to enable us to handle it the more conveniently in common commerce and to attract to it the attention of those who are not yet experts, but not to recommend it to true experts or to determine its value.

However, there is something so strange in this idea of the absolute value of the mere will in which no account is taken of its utility, that notwithstanding the thorough assent of even common reason, a suspicion lingers that this idea may perhaps really be the product of mere high-flown fancy, and that we may have misunderstood the purpose of nature in assigning reason as the governor of the will. Therefore, we will examine this idea from this point of view:

We assume, as a fundamental principle, that no organ [designed] for any purpose will be found in the physical constitution of an organized being, except one which is also the fittest and best adapted for that purpose. Now if the proper object of nature for a being with reason and a will was its *preservation*, its *welfare*, in a word its happiness, then nature would have hit upon a very bad arrangement when it selected the reason of the creature to carry out this function. For all the actions which the creature has to perform with a view to this purpose, and the whole rule of its conduct would be far more surely prescribed by [its own] instinct, and that end [happiness] would have been attained by instinct far more certainly then it ever can be by reason. Should reason have been attributed to this favored creature over and above [such instinct], reason would only have served this creature for contemplating the happy constitution of its nature, for admiring it, and congratulating itself thereon, and for feeling thankful for it to the beneficent cause. But [certainly nature would not have arranged it so that] such a creature should subject its desires to that weak and deceptive guidance, and meddle with nature's intent. In a word, nature would have taken care that reason should not turn into *practical* exercise, nor have the presumption, with its feeble insight, to figure out for itself a plan of happiness and the means for attaining it. In fact, we find that the more a cultivated reason applies itself with deliberate purpose to enjoying life and happiness, so much more does the man lack true satisfaction. From this circumstance there arises in many men, if they are candid enough to confess it, a certain degree of *misology*; that is, hatred of reason, especially in the case of those who are most experienced in the use of reason. For, after calculating all the advantages they derive, not only from the invention of all the arts of common luxury, but even from the sciences (which then seem to them only a luxury of the intellect after all) they find that they have actually only brought more trouble upon themselves, rather than gained in happiness. They end by envying, rather than despising, the common run of men who keep closer to the guidance of mere instinct and who do not allow their reason to have much influence on their conduct. We must admit this much, that the judgment of those, who would diminish very much the lofty eulogies on the advantages which reason gives us in regard to the happiness and satisfaction of life, or would even deny these advantages altogether, is by no means morose or ungrateful for the goodness with which the world is governed. At the root of these judgments lies the idea that the existence of world order has a different and far nobler end for which, rather than for happiness, reason is properly intended. Therefore this end must be regarded as the supreme condition to which the private ends of man must yield for the most part.

Thus reason is not competent enough to guide the will with certainty in regard to its objects and the satisfaction of all our wants which it even multiplies to some extent; this purpose is one to which an implanted instinct would have led with much greater certainty. Nevertheless, reason is imparted to us as a practical faculty; that is, as one which is to have influence on the *will*. Therefore, if we admit that nature generally in the distribution of natural propensities has adapted the means to the end, nature's true intention must be to produce a *will*, which is not merely good as a *means* to something else but *good in itself*. Reason is absolutely necessary for this sort of will. Then this will, though indeed not the sole and complete good, must be the supreme good and the condition of every other good, even of the desire for happiness. Under these circumstances, there is nothing inconsistent with the wisdom of nature in the fact that the cultivation of the reason which is requisite for the first and unconditional purpose, does in many ways interfere, at least in this life, with the attainment of the second purpose: happiness, which is always relative. Nay, it may even reduce happiness to nothing without nature failing thereby in her purpose. For reason recognizes the establishment of a good will as its highest practical destination, and is capable of only satisfying its own proper kind in attaining this purpose: the attainment of an end determined only by reason, even when such an attainment may involve many a disappointment over otherwise desirable purposes.

Therefore we must develop the notion of a will which deserves to be highly esteemed for itself and is good without a specific objective, a notion which is implied by sound natural common sense. This notion needs to be clarified rather than expounded. In evaluating our actions this notion always takes first place and constitutes the condition of all the rest. In order to do this we will take the notion of duty which includes that of a good will, although implying certain subjective restrictions and hindrances. However, these hindrances, far from concealing it or rendering it unrecognizable, rather emphasize a good will by contrast and make it shine forth so much the brighter.

I omit here all actions which are already recognized as inconsistent with duty, although they may be useful for this or that purpose. The question whether these actions are done *from duty* cannot arise at all since they conflict with it. I also leave aside those actions which really conform to duty but to which men have *no* direct *inclination*, performing them because they are impelled to do so by some other inclination. For in this case we can readily distinguish whether the action which agrees with duty is done *out of duty* or from a selfish point of view. It is much harder to make this distinction when the action accords with duty and when besides the subject has a *direct* inclination toward it. For example, it is indeed a matter of duty that a dealer should not overcharge an inexperienced purchaser, and wherever there is much commerce the prudent tradesman does not overcharge, but keeps a fixed price for everyone, so that a child buys of him as well as any other. Men are thus *honestly* served; but this is not enough to make us believe that the tradesman has so acted from duty and from principles of honesty; his own advantage required it. It is out of the question in this case to suppose that he might have besides a direct inclination in favor of the buyers, so that out of love, as it were, he should give no advantage to one over another. Hence the action was done neither out of duty nor because of inclination but merely with a selfiish view. On the other hand, it is a duty to maintain one's life; in addition everyone also has a direct inclination to do so. But on this account the often anxious care which most men take of their lives has no intrinsic worth and their maxim has no moral import. No doubt they preserve their life *as duty requires*, but not *because duty requires*. The case is different, when adversity and hopeless sorrow have completely taken away the relish for life; if the unfortunate one, strong in mind, indignant at his fate rather than despondent or dejected, longs for death and yet preserves his life without loving it. [If he does this] not from inclination or fear but from duty, then his maxim has a moral worth.

To be beneficent when we can is a duty; besides this, there are many minds so sympathetically constituted that without any other motive of vanity or self-interest, they find a pleasure in spreading joy [about them] and can take delight in the satisfaction of others so far as it is their own work. But I maintain that in such a case, however proper, however amiable an action of this kind may be, it nevertheless has no true moral worth, but is on a level with other inclinations; e.g. the inclination to honor which, if it is happily directed to that which is actually of public utility and accordant with duty and consequently honorable, deserves praise and encouragement but not respect. For the maxim lacks the moral ingredient that such actions be done *out of duty*, not from inclination. Put the case [another way and suppose] that the mind of that philanthropist were clouded by sorrow of his own, extinguishing all sympathy with the lot of others, and that while he still has the power to benefit others in distress he is not touched by their trouble because he is absorbed with his own; suppose that he now tears himself out of this deadening insensibility, and performs the action without any inclination for it, but simply from duty; only then has his action genuine moral worth. Furthermore, if nature has put little sympathy into the heart of this or that man, if a supposedly upright man is by temperament cold and indifferent to the sufferings of others, perhaps because in respect of his own sufferings he is provided with the special gift of patience and fortitude so that he supposes or even requires that others should have the same; such a man would certainly not be the meanest product of nature. But if nature had not specially shaped him to be a philanthropist, would he not find cause in himself for attributing to himself a value far higher than the value of a good-natured temperament could be? Unquestionably. It is just in this that there is brought out the moral worth of the character which is incomparably the highest of all; namely, that he is beneficent, not from inclination, but from duty.

To secure one's own happiness is a duty, at least indirectly; for discontent with one's condition under pressure of many anxieties and amidst unsatisfied wants might easily become a great *temptation to transgression from duty*. But here again, without reference to duty, all men already have the strongest and most intense inclination to happiness, because it is just in this idea that all inclinations are combined in one total. But the precept for happiness is often of such a sort that it greatly interferes with some inclinations. Yet a man cannot form any definite and certain conception of the sum of satisfying all of these inclinations, which is called happiness. It is not then to be wondered at that a single inclination, definite both as to what it promises and as to the time within which it can be gratified, is often able to overcome such a fluctuating idea [as the precept for happiness.] For instance, a gouty patient can choose to enjoy what he likes and to suffer what he may, since according to his calculation, at least on this occasion he has not sacrificed the enjoyment of the present moment for a possibly mistaken expectation of happiness supposedly found in health. But, if the general desire for happiness does not influence his will, and even supposing that in his particular case health was not a necessary element in his calculation, there yet remains a law even in this case, as in all other cases; that is, he should promote his happiness not from inclination but from duty. Only in following duty would his conduct acquire true moral worth.

Undoubtedly, it is in this manner that we are to understand those passages of the Scripture in which we are commanded to love our neighbor, even our enemy. For love, as an affection, cannot be commanded, but beneficence for duty's sake can be, even though we are not impelled to such kindness by any inclination, and may even be repelled by a natural and unconquerable aversion. This is *practical* love and not *psychological*. It is a love originating in the will and not in the inclination of sentiment, in principles of action, not of sentimental sympathy.

The second proposition is: That an action done from duty derives its moral worth, *not from the purpose* which is to be attained by it, but from the maxim by which it is determined. Therefore the action does not depend on the realization of its objective, but merely on the *principle* of volition by which the action has taken place, without regard to any object of desire. It is clear from what precedes that the purposes which we may have in view for our actions, or their effects as regarded as ends and impulsions of the will, cannot give to actions any unconditional or moral worth. Then in what can their worth consist if it does not consist in the will as it is related to its expected effect? It cannot consist in anything but the *principle of the will*, with no regard to the ends which can be attained by the action. For the will stands between its *a priori* principle which is formal, and its *a posteriori* impulse which is material, as between two roads. As it must be determined by something, it follows that the will must be determined by the formal principle of volition, as when an action is done from duty, in which case every material impulse has been withdrawn from it.

The third proposition, which is a consequence of the preceding two, I would express thus: *Duty is the necessity of an action, resulting from respect for the law.* I may have an *inclination* for an object as the effect of my proposed action, but I cannot have *respect* for an object just for this reason: that it is merely an effect and not an action of will. Similarly, I cannot have respect for an inclination, whether my own or another's; I can at most, if it is my own, approve it; if it is another's I can sometimes even cherish it; that is, look on it as favorable to my own interest. Only the law itself which is connected with my will by no means as an effect but as a principle which does not serve my inclination but outweighs it, or at least in case of choice excludes my inclination from its calculation; only such a law can be an object of respect and hence a command. Now an action done from duty must wholly exclude the influence of inclination, and with it every object of the will, so that nothing remains which can determine the will objectively except the *law*, and [determine the will] subjectively except *pure respect* for this practical law, and hence [pure respect] for the maxim[1] to follow this law even to the thwarting of all my inclinations.

Thus the moral worth of an action does not consist of the effect expected from it, nor from any principle of action which needs to borrow its motive from this expected effect. For, all these effects, agreeableness of one's condition and even the promotion of the happiness of others, all this could have also been brought about by other causes so that for this there would have been no need of the will of a rational being. However, in this will alone can the supreme and unconditional good be found. Therefore the pre-eminent good which we call moral can consist in nothing other than *the concept of law* in itself, *which is certainly only possible in a rational being*, in so far as this conception, and not the expected effect, determines the will. This is a good which is already present in the person acting according to it, and we do not have to wait for good to appear in the result.[2]

---

[1]A maxim is the subjective principle of volition. The objective principle, that is, what would also serve all rational beings subjectively as a practical principle if reason had full power over desire; this objective principle is the practical *law*.

[2]Here it might be objected that I take refuge in an obscure feeling behind the word *respect* instead of giving a distinct solution of the question by a concept of reason. But, although respect is a feeling, it is not a feeling *received* through outside influence, but is self-generated by a rational concept, and therefore is specifically distinct from all feelings of the former kind, which may be related either to inclination or fear. What I recognize immediately as a law, I recognize with respect. This merely signifies the consciousness that my

But what sort of law can it be the conception of which must determine the will, even without our paying any attention to the effect expected from it, in order that this will may be called good absolutely and without qualification? As I have stripped the will of every impulse which could arise for it from obedience to any law, there remains nothing but the general conformity of the will's actions to law in general. Only this conformity to law is to serve the will as a principle; that is, I am never to act in any way other than *so I could want my maxim also to become a general law*. It is the simple conformity to law in general, without assuming any particular law applicable to certain actions, that serves the will as its principle, and must so serve it, if duty is not to be a vain delusion and a chimerical notion. The common reason of men in their practical judgments agrees perfectly with this and always has in view the principle suggested here. For example, let the question be: When in distress may I make a promise with the intention of not keeping it? I readily distinguish here between the two meanings which the question may have: Whether it is prudent, or whether it is in accordance with duty, to make a false promise. The former undoubtedly may often be the case. I [may] see clearly that it is not enough to extricate myself from a present difficulty by means of this subterfuge, but that it must be carefully considered whether there may not result from such a lie a much greater inconvenience than that from which I am now freeing myself. But, since in spite of all my supposed *cunning* the consequences cannot be foreseen easily; the loss of credit may be much more injurious to me than any mischief which I seek to avoid at present. That being the case, one might consider whether it would not be more *prudent* to act according to a general maxim, and make it a habit to give no promise except with the intention of keeping it. But, it is soon clear that such a maxim is still only based on the fear of consequences. It is a wholly different thing to be truthful from a sense of duty, than to be so from apprehension of injurious consequences. In the first case, the very conceiving of the action already implies a law for me; in the second case, I must first look about elsewhere to see what results may be associated with it which would affect me. For it is beyond all doubt wicked to deviate from the principle of duty; but to be

---

will is *subordinate* to a law, without the intervention of other influences on my sense. The immediate determination of the will by the law and the consciousness of this may be called *respect*, so that this may then be regarded as an effect of the law on the subject and not as the *cause* of it. In a word, respect is the conceiving of a value which reduces my self-love. Accordingly, respect is considered neither an object of inclination nor of fear, though it has something analogous to both. The *object* of respect is the *law* only, a law that we impose on *ourselves* and yet recognize as necessary in itself. We are subjected to it as a law without consulting self-love; but as imposed by us on ourselves, it is a result of our will. In the former aspect it has analogy to fear, in the latter to inclination. Respect for a person is properly only respect for the law (of honesty, etc.) of which he gives us an example. Since we also look on the improvement of our talents as a duty we consider that we see in a person of talents the *example of a law*, as it were, to become like him in this by effort and this constitutes our respect. All so-called moral *interest* consists simply in *respect* for the law.

unfaithful to my maxim of prudence may often be very advantageous to me, although it is certainly wiser to abide by it. However, the shortest way, and an unerring one, to discover the answer to this question of whether a lying promise is consistent with duty, is to ask myself, "Would I be content if this maxim of extricating myself from difficulty by a false promise held good as a general law for others as well as for myself?" Would I care to say to myself, "Everyone may make a deceitful promise when he finds himself in a difficulty from which he cannot extricate himself otherwise"? Then I would presently become aware that while I can decide in favor of the lie, I can by no means decide that lying should be a general law. For under such a law there would be no promises at all, since I would state my intentions in vain in regard to my future actions to those who would not believe my allegation, or, if they did so too hastily, they would pay me back in my own coin. Hence, as soon as such a maxim was made a universal law, it would necessarily destroy itself.

Therefore I do not need any sharp acumen to discern what I have to do in order that my will may be morally good. [As I am] inexperienced in the course of the world and incapable of being prepared for all its contingencies, I can only ask myself: "Can you will that your maxim should also be a general law?" If not, then my maxim must be rejected, not because of any disadvantage in it for myself or even for others, but because my maxim cannot fit as a principle into a possible universal legislation, and reason demands immediate respect from me for such legislation. Indeed, I do not *discern* as yet on what this respect is based; into this question the philosopher may inquire. But at least I understand this much: that this respect is an evaluation of the worth that far outweighs all that is recommended by inclination. The necessity of acting from *pure* respect for the practical law [of right action;] is what constitutes duty, to which every other motive must yield, because it is the condition of a will being good *in itself*, and the value of such a will exceeds everything.

Thus we have arrived at the principle of moral knowledge of common human reason. Although common men no doubt do not conceive this principle in such an abstract and universal form, yet they really always have it before their eyes and use it as the standard for their decision. It would be easy to show here how, with this compass in hand, men are well able to distinguish, in every case that occurs, what is good, bad, conformable to duty or inconsistent with it. Without teaching them anything at all new, we are only, like Socrates, directing their attention to the principle they employ themselves and [showing] that we therefore do not need science and philosophy to know what we should do to be honest and good and even wise and virtuous.

JOHN STUART MILL

(1806–1873)

Mill's early education was an intensive one, for he was a remarkably precocious child; he read Xenophon and Herodotus by his eighth year, and Plato by the time he was ten. His father, who was his only teacher, taught him to think for himself, but unfortunately neglected to allow for the natural development of other aspects of his son's personality. It was only with an inner struggle that, in his twenties, the younger Mill was able to break away from this pattern of overeducation, and to engage in a more tolerant quest for personal happiness. He had already begun, well before he was twenty, to contribute to political and economic newspapers and journals, and he continued to do so for many years. In 1843, Mill published his Logic, *an effort to formulate the methods of scientific investigation, and in 1848 his* Political Economy *appeared. Mill had long been associated with the India House in its government of the Indian colonies. When his wife died, he retired from official duties, and published some of his most trenchant and characteristic works,* On Liberty *(1859),* Representative Government *(1860), and* Utilitarianism *(1861). He was elected to Parliament in 1865 and spoke out often in the cause of freedom and reform. Throughout his life, he remained faithful to his father's precept—to investigate for himself whenever possible, rather than accept the authority of others.*

THE PRACTICE OF FREEDOM

The object of this Essay is to assert one very simple principle, as entitled to govern absolutely the dealings of society with the individual in the way of compulsion and control, whether the means used be physical force in the form of legal penalties, or the moral coercion of public opinion. That principle is, that the sole end for which mankind are warranted, individually or collectively, in interfering with the liberty of action of any of their number, is self-protection. That the only purpose for which power can be rightfully exercised over any member of a civilized community, against his will, is to prevent harm to others. His own good, either physical or moral, is not a sufficient warrant. He cannot rightfully be compelled to do or forbear because it will better for him to do so, because it will make him happier, because, in the opinions of others, to do so would be wise, or even right.

These are good reasons for remonstrating with him, or reasoning with him, or persuading him, or entreating him, but not for compelling him, or visiting him with any evil, in case he do otherwise. To justify that, the conduct from which it is desired to deter him must be calculated to produce evil to some one else. The only part of the conduct of any one, for which he is amenable to society, is that which concerns others. In the part which merely concerns himself, his independence is, of right, absolute. Over himself, over his own body and mind, the individual is sovereign.

It is, perhaps, hardly necessary to say that this doctrine is meant to apply only to human beings in the maturity of their faculties. We are not speaking of children, or of young persons below the age which the law may fix as that of manhood or womanhood. Those who are still in a state to require being taken care of by others, must be protected against their own actions as well as against external injury. For the same reason, we may leave out of consideration those backward states of society in which the race itself may be considered as in its nonage. The early difficulties in the way of spontaneous progress are so great, that there is seldom any choice of means for overcoming them; and a ruler full of the spirit of improvement is warranted in the use of any expedients that will attain an end, perhaps otherwise unattainable. Despotism is a legitimate mode of government in dealing with barbarians, provided the end be their improvement, and the means justified by actually effecting that end. Liberty, as a principle, has no application to any state of things anterior to the time when mankind have become capable of being improved by free and equal discussion. Until then, there is nothing for them but implicit obedience to an Akbar or a Charlemagne, if they are so fortunate as to

From On Liberty.

find one. But as soon as mankind have attained the capacity of being guided to their own improvement by conviction or persuasion (a period long since reached in all nations with whom we need here concern ourselves), compulsion, either in the direct form or in that of pains and penalties for non-compliance, is no longer admissible as a means to their own good, and justifiable only for the security of others.

It is proper to state that I forego any advantage which could be derived to my argument from the idea of abstract right, as a thing independent of utility. I regard utility as the ultimate appeal on all ethical questions; but it must be utility in the largest sense, grounded on the permanent interests of man as a progressive being. Those interests, I contend, authorize the subjection of individual spontaneity to external control, only in respect to those actions of each, which concern the interest of other people. If any one does an act hurtful to others, there is a *prima facie* case for punishing him, by law, or, where legal penalties are not safely applicable, by general disapprobation. There are also many positive acts for the benefit of others, which he may rightfully be compelled to perform; such as, to give evidence in a court of justice; to bear his fair share in the common defence, or in any other joint work necessary to the interest of the society of which he enjoys the protection; and to perform certain acts of individual beneficence, such as saving a fellow creature's life, or interposing to protect the defenceless against ill-usage, things which whenever it is obviously a man's duty to do, he may rightfully be made responsible to society for not doing. A person may cause evil to others not only by his actions but by his inaction, and in either case he is justly accountable to them for the injury. The latter case, it is true, requires a much more cautious exercise of compulsion than the former. To make any one answerable for doing evil to others, is the rule; to make him answerable for not preventing evil, is, comparatively speaking, the exception. Yet there are many cases clear enough and grave enough to justify that exception. In all things which regard the external relations of the individual, he is *de jure* amenable to those whose interests are concerned, and if need be, to society as their protector. There are often good reasons for not holding him to the responsibility; but these reasons must arise from the special expediencies of the case: either because it is a kind of case in which he is on the whole likely to act better, when left to his own discretion, than when controlled in any way in which society have it in their power to control him; or because the attempt to exercise control would produce other evils, greater than those which it would prevent. When such reasons as these preclude the enforcement of responsibility, the conscience of the agent himself should step into the vacant judgment-seat, and protect those interests of others which have no external protection; judging himself all the more rigidly, because the case does not admit of his being made accountable to the judgment of his fellow creatures.

But there is a sphere of action in which society, as distinguished from the individual, has, if any, only an indirect interest; comprehending all that portion of a person's life and conduct which affects only himself, or, if it also affects others, only with their free, voluntary, and undeceived consent and participation. When I say only himself, I mean directly, and in the first instance: for whatever affects himself, may affect others *through* himself; and the objection which may be grounded on this contingency, will receive consideration in the sequel. This, then, is the appropriate region of human liberty. It comprises, first, the inward domain of consciousness; demanding liberty of conscience, in the most comprehensive sense; liberty of thought and feeling; absolute freedom of opinion and sentiment on all subjects, practical or speculative, scientific, moral, or theological. The liberty of expressing and publishing opinions may seem to fall under a different principle, since it belongs to that part of the conduct of an individual which concerns other people; but, being almost of as much importance as the liberty of thought itself, and resting in great part on the same reasons, is practically inseparable from it. Secondly, the principle requires liberty of tastes and pursuits; of framing the plan of our life to suit our own character; of doing as we like, subject to such consequences as may follow; without impediment from our fellow-creatures, so long as what we do does not harm them, even though they should think our conduct foolish, perverse, or wrong. Thirdly, from this liberty of each individual, follows the liberty, within the same limits, of combination among individuals; freedom to unite, for any purpose not involving harm to others: the persons combining being supposed to be of full age, and not forced or deceived.

No society in which these liberties are not, on the whole, respected, is free, whatever may be its form of government; and none is completely free in which they do not exist absolute and unqualified. The only freedom which deserves the name, is that of pursuing our own good in our own way, so long as we do not attempt to deprive others of theirs, or impede their efforts to obtain it. Each is the proper guardian of his own health, whether bodily, or mental and spiritual. Mankind are greater gainers by suffering each other to live as seems good to themselves, than by compelling each to live as seems good to the rest. . . .

9

Shapes of Moral Theory

R. M. HARE

(b. 1919)

Educated at Balliol College, Oxford, Hare became White's Professor of Moral Philosophy at Corpus Christi College, Oxford, in 1966, a position he still occupies. His publications include The Language of Morals *(1952),* Freedom and Reason *(1963),* Practical Inferences *(1971),* Essays on Philosophical Method *(1971),* Essays on the Moral Concepts *(1972), and* Application of Moral Philosophy *(1972).*

ETHICS AND MORALS

I. INTRODUCTORY

Out of the many sorts of inquiry for which the term "ethics" has at one time or another been used, three groups of questions may be selected as the most important to distinguish from one another: (1) *Moral questions*: for example, "Ought I to do that?"; "Is polygamy wrong?": "Is Jones a good man?". In this sense "ethical" and "moral" mean much the same. (2) *Questions of fact about people's moral opinions:* for example, "What did Mohammed (*or* what does the British Middle Class, or what do I myself) in fact think (or say) about the rightness or wrongness of polygamy?" (3) *Questions about the meanings of moral words (for example, "ought", "right", "good", "duty"); or about the nature of the concepts or the "things" to which these words "refer"*: for example, "When Mohammed said that polygamy is not wrong, what was he saying?" These three sorts of questions being quite distinct, the use of the word "ethics" to embrace attempts to answer all three is confusing, and is avoided by the more careful modern writers. No generally accepted terminology for making the necessary distinctions has yet emerged; but in this article we shall distinguish between (1) morals, (2) descriptive ethics and (3) ethics, corresponding to the three sorts of questions listed above. The case for confining the word "ethics" (used without qualification) to the third sort of question is that ethics has usually been held to be a part of philosophy, and the third group of questions, which are analytical or logical inquiries, or, as older writers might say, metaphysical ones, is much more akin than the first two groups to other inquiries generally included in philosophy. Thus ethics (in the narrow sense) stands to morals in much the same relation as does the philosophy of science to science. The student of ethics will nevertheless have to get used to a variety of terminologies; he will find plain "ethics" used for what we have just called "morals" ("normative ethics" is another term used for this); and he will find, for what we have just called "ethics", the more guarded terms "the logic of ethics", "metaethics", "theoretical ethics", "philosophical ethics" and so on. Works called "ethics" usually contain questions and answers of all three kinds, and the student of ethics must be prepared to find in them ambiguous remarks in which it is not clear *what* sort of question the writer is trying to answer. It is, for example, only too easy to confuse a moral statement with a descriptive ethical one, especially when one is

From The Concise Encyclopedia of Western Philosophy & Philosophers, *edited by J. O. Urmson (New York: Hawthorne Books, Inc., 1960), pp. 130–138.*

talking about one's own moral views; but it is nevertheless vital to distinguish the moral judgment "It would be wrong to do that" from the descriptive ethical statement "I, as a matter of psychological fact, think that it would be wrong to do that." The first task, therefore, for anybody who takes up the subject, is to learn to distinguish these three types of questions from one another; and for this purpose the following rules may be found helpful. A writer is making a *moral* statement if he is thereby *committing* himself to a moral view or standpoint; if not (that is, if he is merely writing in a detached way about moral views which are or may be held by himself or other people), it is either a *descriptive ethical* or an *ethical* statement; and this is normally indicated by the form of the statement, the moral words being "insulated" by occurring inside a "that" -clause or quotation-marks. Which of the two it is can be decided in the following way: if the truth of the statement depends on what moral opinions are *actually held* by people, it is a *descriptive ethical* statement; but if its truth depends only on what is *meant* by certain words, or on *what people would be saying if* they voiced certain moral opinions, it is an *ethical* statement. Thus, for example, ethics in the narrow sense is concerned directly neither with whether polygamy *is* wrong (a moral question) nor with whether anybody in fact thinks it is wrong (a descriptive ethical question)—though ethics may have a bearing on these two questions, as mathematics has on physics; it is concerned with the question "Precisely what is one saying if one says that polygamy is wrong"?

II. RELATIONS BETWEEN THESE INQUIRIES

Throughout the history of the subject, the chief incentive to the undertaking of all three sorts of inquiry has been the hope of establishing conclusions of the first kind (that is, moral conclusions) by means of a philosophical inquiry. It is from this motive that inquiries of the second and especially the third kinds have mostly been undertaken. Clearly the study of the meaning of the moral words is closely related to the study of what makes arguments containing them cogent or otherwise. One of the best ways of obtaining a clear view of the subject is to consider the mutual relations between these three kinds of inquiry, and the bearing that they can have on one another.

(1) *Descriptive ethics and morals*. Some writers have proceeded directly from descriptive ethical premises to moral (normative ethical) conclusions. For example, the Greek hedonist Eudoxus argued that since everyone thought pleasure to be the good, it must *be* the good. In a similar way some modern writers have held that the task of the moral philosopher—the utmost he can do by way of establishing moral conclusions—is to examine carefully the opinions that are accepted by his society or by himself and reduce them to some sort of system. This is to take received opinions as data, and to regard as established a moral

system that can be shown to be consistent with them. This type of argumentation will not, however, appear convincing to anyone who considers the fact that a person (for example, in the ancient world) might have said "Everyone thinks that it is legitimate to keep slaves, but may it not be wrong?" Universal assent to a moral principle does not prove the principle; otherwise the moral reformer, who propounds for the first time a new moral principle, could be put out of court all too easily. Still less does it follow, from the fact that some limited set of people hold some moral opinion, that that opinion is right.

(2) *Descriptive ethics and ethics proper*. The commonest way, however, in which it has been sought to bring descriptive ethics to bear on moral questions is not directly but indirectly. It has been thought that a descriptive ethical inquiry might lead to conclusions about the *meanings* of moral terms (conclusions, that is to say, in ethics proper); and that in turn these might be used to prove moral conclusions. Those who have argued in this way have been attracted by a seductive analogy between moral terms and other predicates and adjectives. For example, it might be held possible to prove in the following way, to anyone who disputed it, that post-boxes in England are red: we should first establish by observation that everybody says that things are red when they have a certain recognizable quality, and that they are not red when they do not have this quality; we should conclude from this, that "red" *means* "having this quality". This is the first step. We should then ask our disputant to observe that post-boxes in England have this same quality; and since we have already established that "having this quality" is just what "red" *means*, he can no longer deny that the post-boxes are red. It might be thought possible to use the same arguments in ethics to prove, for example, that certain kinds of action are right. But unfortunately the analogy breaks down at both steps—at the step from descriptive ethics to ethics proper, and at the step from ethics to morals. That conclusions about what people *mean by* "right", for example, cannot be proved by finding out what they *call* right, is evident from the case of the moral reformer just mentioned. If he said that slavery was not right, when slavery was one of the things universally agreed to be right, he would, if the proposed argument were valid, be like a man who said that postboxes were not red when everybody agreed that they were red; we should be able to accuse such a man of misusing the word "red"—for "red" *means* the colour which post-boxes are, so how can he deny that they are red? But the moral reformer can deny that slavery is right while still using the word "right" in the same sense as that in which his contemporaries, who think that slavery is right, are using it. This example shows that there is an important difference between moral words and words like "red"—a difference which invalidates the superficially plausible argument from descriptive-ethical premisses to conclusions about the meanings of moral words.

(3) *Ethics and morals*. But the second step in the proposed argument is also invalid, for a very similar reason. We cannot, even if we can establish the meaning of the moral words, pass from this to conclusions of

substance about moral questions. This may be shown by the following example: suppose that there are two people who know everything about a certain action (including its circumstances and consequences), and still dispute, as they may, about whether it was wrong. Since they are in dispute, they must be using the word "wrong" with the same meaning; for if this were not so, there would be no real dispute, only a verbal confusion. But since they can continue to dispute, even though they are in agreement about the meaning of the word, it follows that knowledge of the meaning of the word cannot by itself, or even in conjunction with what they both know about the action, determine whether the action is wrong. Some *other* difference must remain between them (a moral difference) which is neither a difference about what the action is (for this they know in the fullest detail) nor about the meaning of "wrong" (for about this they are agreed). The plausible argument which we have just rejected is a particular application of a type of argument often used in philosophy, and known as "the argument from the paradigm case". Without discussing here whether the argument is cogent in other fields, we can see that it is not in ethics. The assumption that this argument has unrestricted force is linked with the assumption that to discover the use of a word is always to discover to what things it is correctly applied. This is not true of words like "is" and "not"; and it seems not to be true of moral words either. This assumption (to take another example) leaves us with no way of distinguishing between the uses of the two sets of words "Shut the door" and "You are going to shut the door"; for all the words in both sets, in so far as they "apply" to anything, apply to the *same* things.

III. NATURALISM

The arguments so far considered and rejected all exhibit a common feature. In them, moral conclusions are allegedly derived from premises which are not themselves moral judgments: in the one case the premise was a statement of sociological fact about what people think on a moral question; in the other it was a statement of linguistic fact about how (with what meaning) people use a certain word, together with another premise giving the description of an action whose wrongness is in dispute. This feature is common to a great many arguments which have been used by ethical thinkers; and it has been frequently stated that any argument which derives moral conclusions from non-moral premises must be invalid. A famous statement to this effect was made by Hume in *Treatise of Human Nature* (1739–40), III, I, i. Hume based his rejection of such arguments on the general logical principle that a valid argument cannot proceed from premises to some "new affirmation" not contained, at any rate implicitly, in the premises. The correctness of Hume's view ("no *ought* from an *is*") depends, therefore, on the assumption that moral judgments contain an element in their meaning (the essentially moral element) which is not equivalent, even implicitly, to anything in the conjunction of the premises. It is this assumption which is challenged by those ethical theories known as naturalist. The term "naturalist" has been used in a variety of ways, but will be used here as follows: an ethical theory is naturalistic if, and only if, it holds that moral judgments are equivalent in meaning to statements of non-moral fact.

It must be noted that, on this definition, a statement of moral opinion (that is to say a statement in the first of the three classes listed at the beginning of this article) cannot be called naturalistic; for naturalism is a view about the meanings of moral terms, and nobody is committed to any form of it who confines himself to merely *using* moral terms without taking up a view about their meaning, definition or analysis. In general, no view can be naturalistic unless, in the statement of the view, the moral words occur inside quotation marks or a "that"-clause or are *mentioned* (not used) in some other way, and remarks are made about their meaning or their equivalence to other expressions. That is to say, only statements in ethics proper, as contrasted with descriptive ethics and with morals, can be naturalistic. Thus the view that the right action (the action which ought to be done) in a given situation, is that which would produce the greatest balance of pleasure over pain, is not naturalistic, since it does not seek to *define* "right", but only to say what actions *are* right. To be a naturalist, a utilitarian of this sort would have to hold, in addition, that his view was true in virtue of the meaning of "right"—that is to say, that "right" *meant* "producing the greatest balance of pleasure over pain". If he refrains from trying to prove his theory in this way, "refutations of naturalism" pass over his head.

It must also be noticed that, on this definition of naturalism, to call a definition of a moral word "naturalistic" does not imply that the properties in terms of which it is being defined are empirical, that is, perceived by the five senses. As Moore, who coined the expression "the naturalistic fallacy", observed, the same "fallacy", as he thought it was, is committed if the properties are "properties of supersensible reality", given only that they are not moral properties. Thus a philosopher who *defines* "right" as meaning "in accordance with the will of God" is, in this sense, a naturalist, unless the word "God" itself is held to be implicitly a moral term. The most important argument by which Moore sought to "refute naturalism" may be restated as follows, using the example just quoted: if "right" meant the same as "in accordance with the will of God", then, "whatever is in accordance with the will of God is right" would mean the same as "whatever is in accordance with the will of God is in accordance with the will of God"; but according to our actual use of the words it seems to mean more than this mere tautology. (Note that, as before, there is nothing in this argument which forces anybody to abandon the *moral* view that whatever is in accordance with the will of God and only what is in accordance with it is right. It is only the attempt to make this view true by definition which is naturalistic). It has been held, though not by Moore, that what is wrong with naturalistic definitions is that they leave out the commendatory or prescriptive element in the meaning of words such as "right" and "good" (*see below*).

IV. INTUITIONISM

The work of Moore convinced most philosophers that naturalistic definitions of moral terms had to be ruled out. But Moore and his immediate followers showed a great reluctance to abandon what had been the traditional view of the way in which words have meaning. It was taken for granted that the way to explain the meaning of an adjective, for example, was to identify the property which it "stands for" or "is the name of"; all adjectives have the same logical function, that of "standing for" a property, and the differences between them are not differences in logical character, but simply differences between theproperties for which they "stand". When, therefore, it became accepted that moral adjectives did not stand for "natural" (that is, non-moral) properties, it was concluded that they must stand for peculiar moral properties, thought to be discerned by "intuition".

There are two main forms of ethical intuitionism. According to the first, we are supposed to intuit the rightness, goodness, etc. of concrete individual acts, people, etc.; general moral principles are arrived at by a process of induction, that is, by generalisation from a large number of these instances. According to the second, what we intuit are the general principles themselves (for example, "promise-breaking is wrong"); by applying these, we ascertain the moral properties of individual acts and people. The second view has the merit of emphasizing a very important fact about the logical character of moral words, namely that the moral adjectives, etc. differ from most other adjectives in the following way: we call a thing "red", for example, because of its redness and nothing else; it could be similar in every other way and yet not be red. But when we call a person "good" or an act "right", we call them good or right *because* they have certain other characteristics—for example, an act is called wrong because it is an act of promise-breaking, or good because it is the act of helping a blind man across a road. The intuitionists sometimes express this feature of moral adjectives by saying that they are the "names" of "consequential" or "supervenient" properties. Even if we reject the idea that all adjectives have meaning by being the names of properties, this remains an important discovery. It has sometimes been thought that Hume's "no *ought* from an *is*" was a denial that we can, for example, call an act good *because* it is an act of a certain kind. This is a misunderstanding; what Hume was denying was that it *logically followed*, from an act's being of a certain kind, that it is good. The difference is crucial, but obscure. It has been one of the main problems of recent ethics to give a satisfactory account of the connexion between, for example, goodness and what were called "good-making characteristics". The intuitionists reject the naturalist explanation of this connexion as due to an equivalence in meaning between moral words and words describing the characteristics of things in virtue of which we apply moral words to them. But they give no adequate positive account of the connexion, contenting themselves, for the most part, with saying that it is a "synthetic necessary" connexion discerned by "intuition". The explanatory force of this account is impaired by the failure to say clearly what "intuition " is or what is meant by "synthetic necessary connexion".

But the chief argument brought against ethical intuitionism of all sorts is the following, which is to be compared with that in section II (3). Intuition is supposed to be a way of knowing, or determining definitively and objectively, the truth or falsity of a given moral judgment. But suppose that two people differ on a moral question, and that both, as may well happen, claim to intuit the correctness of their own views. There is then no way left of settling the question, since each can accuse the other of being defective in intuition, and there is nothing about the intuitions themselves to settle which it is. It is often objected further, that what "moral intuitions" people have will depend on their various moral upbringings and other contingent causes. In fact, the intuitionists, who often claim to be "objectivists", belie this claim by appealing to a faculty of intuition which is unavoidably subjective. This illustrates the extreme difficulty, to be referred to below, of stating any clear distinction between "objective" and "subjective" in this field. Intuitionism enjoyed a wide popularity in the early years of this century; but it has now been abandoned even by some of its prominent supporters. Writers on ethics have tended, either to revert to some form of naturalism, open or disguised, or to pass on to one of the kinds of view, to be described below, which recognise that "good", "right", etc. have, logically, a quite different role from that of other adjectives, and that it may be misleading to call them "the names of properties".

V. RELATIVISM AND SUBJECTIVISM

Great confusion has been caused in ethics by lumping together, under the title "subjectivism", theories which are quite different from one another. Before considering subjectivism proper, we must first distinguish from it the *moral* view which is best called *relativism*. A typical relativist holds that we ought to do that, and that only, which we *think* we ought to do; on this theory, the mere having of a certain moral opinion by a man or a society makes that moral opinion correct for that man or society. Since this is a *moral* doctrine and not an *ethical* one (that is, since it says what we ought to do, not what "ought" means) it is not naturalistic (see above), but it is open to the objection that it makes it impossible to say that another man's moral judgment is wrong—indeed, it has the paradoxical consequence that two people who differ about a moral question must both be right. This seems to be at variance with the common use of the moral words; we have here an illustration of a way in which ethics (the study of the uses of the moral words) can have a negative bearing on a moral question—it enables us to *rule out* a moral view as involving logical paradox, but not to *prove* one. It may also be objected to relativism that it does not do what a moral principle is expected to do, viz. guide us in making our decisions on particular moral questions. For if I am wondering what to do, it is no use being told that I ought to do what I think I ought to do; for the trouble is that I do not know what to think. Relativism is mentioned, not for its own value, but because confusion of other views with it has bedevilled nearly all discussion of the views which we are about to consider. These are by contrast all ethical views (that is, views about the meanings of the moral words). They do not commit the holder of them to the acceptance or rejction of any substantive moral opinions.

The first is a form of naturalism, which is not now often avowedly held, but dates from a time when it was thought that a moral sentence must have meaning in the same way as other indicative sentences, viz. by being used to state that a certain object possesses a certain property (see above section IV). It being unplausible, for many reasons (some of which have been given in section III) to hold that the properties in question are "objective" properties of objects, it was suggested that they are "subjective" properties—that is, properties of being related in certain ways to states of mind of the maker of the statement in question. Thus "He is a good man" was held to mean "He, as a matter of psychological fact, arouses in me a certain mental state (for example, a feeling of approval)". This theory makes a moral judgment equivalent to a descriptive ethical statement (see above, section I). If it is taken literally, it is open to the objection that it makes moral disagreement impossible. For if two people say, one that a man is a good man, and the other that he is not, they are, on this view, not disagreeing with each other; for one of them means that he (the speaker) is in a certain mental state, and the other means that *he* (the second speaker) is not in that state; and between these statements there is no contradiction.

Because of this objection, the view has been generally abandoned in favour of others which hold that in a moral judgment we are not giving information about our mental state, but engaging in a use of language different from the giving of information. This development has been part of the recent realisation by philosophers that it is a mistake to regard all kinds of sentences as having the same logical character and role. For at least two reasons it is best to confine the name "subjectivism" to the view just considered, and not to extend it to those described below. First of all, the terms "objective" and "subjective" have a tolerably clear meaning, and draw a graspable distinction, when they are used to mark the difference between statements of "objective" fact about objects, and statements of "subjective" fact about the speaker (though even here there might be confusion; for in a sense it is an objective fact that the mind of the speaker is in a certain state). But the distinction gets lost when moral judgments are held not to be statements of fact, in the narrow sense, at all. This may be seen by comparing the case of imperatives (though it is not suggested that moral judgments resemble these in all respects). An imperative expresses neither an objective statement nor a subjective statement, since it does not express a statement at all; nor does it express a "subjective command"; for it is hard to understand what this would be. So, if it be asked "Is the command 'Shut the door' *about* the door or *about* the mind of the speaker?", the answer, in so far as the question is meaningful, must be "About the door". And in the same way the moral judgment "He is a good man" may be held to be, in the strongest possible sense, "about" the man in question, and not about the mind of the speaker, even by someone who holds that it is not (in the narrow sense) *a statement of fact* about the man. Thus criticisms of the theories to be described in the next section, on the ground that they turn moral judgments into remarks about the mind of the speaker, are misdirected, and should be reserved for subjectivism as described in the present section. The same applies to the criticism that these theories "make what is right depend on what the speaker thinks is right".

Secondly, the division between those views which hold that moral judgments are used to give some sort of information, and those which hold that they have a quite different function, is the most fundamental in ethics, and should not be concealed by using a term which straddles it. Views of the first sort (for example all the ethical views so far considered) are called "descriptivist"; views of other kinds, including those considered in the rest of this article, are called "non-descriptivist".

VI. EMOTIVISM

Though emotivism was, historically, the first kind of non-descriptivism to be canvassed, it is a mistake to think of it as the only kind, or even as commanding general support among non-descriptivists at the present time. It is common even now for non-descriptivists of all kinds to be misleadingly called "emotivists", even though their theories do not depend on any reference to the emotions. Emotivism proper embraces a variety of views, which may be held concurrently. According to the best-known, moral judgments have it as their function to "express" or "evince" the moral emotions (for example, approval) of the speaker. According to another version, their use is to arouse or evoke similar emotions in the person to whom they are addressed, and so stimulate him to actions of the kind approved. A. J. Ayer when he wrote *Language, Truth and Logic* (1936), which contains the most famous exposition of emotivism, attributed both these functions to moral judgments; but he has since abandoned emotivism, though remaining a non-descriptivist. C. L. Stevenson put forward a kindred view, with the difference that, instead of the word "emotion", he most commonly used the word "attitude". An attitude was usually thought of by him as a disposition to be in certain mental states or to do certain kinds of actions. Stevenson's "attitudes" are much closer to the "moral principles" of the older philosophers (especially Aristotle) than is usually noticed by those who use the misleading "objectivist-subjectivist" classification. Stevenson made the important qualification to his view that, besides their "emotive meaning" moral judgments may also have a "descriptive meaning". In one of his several "patterns of analysis" the meaning of a moral judgment is analysed into two components: (1) a non-moral assertion about, for example, an act (explicable naturalistically in terms of empirical properties of the act); and (2) a specifically moral component (the emotive meaning) whose presence prevents a naturalistic account being given of the meaning of the whole judgment. This specifically moral element in the meaning is the function which these judgments have of *expressing* attitudes and *persuading* or *influencing* people to adopt them, towards the act described. Stevenson's views did not, of course, find favour with descriptivists, and even non-descriptivists who have written after him, while recognizing the seminal importance of his work, have for the most part rejected the implied irrationalism of the view that the only specifically moral element in the meaning of moral terms is their emotive force. This, it has been felt, makes moral judgments too like rhetoric or propaganda, and does insufficient justice to the possibility of reasoned argument about moral questions. If moral argument is possible, there must be *some* logical relations between a moral judgment and other moral judgments, even if Hume was right to hold that a moral judgement is not derivable from statements of non-moral fact. Stevenson has some important things to say about moral arguments, but his account of them has been generally held to be inadequate.

VII. OUTSTANDING PROBLEMS

Most of the main problems which occupy ethical thinkers at the present time arise from the complexity of the meaning of moral terms, which combines two very different elements.

(1) *The evaluative or prescriptive meaning* (these more non-committal terms are now often preferred to Stevenson's "emotive meaning"). It is not necessary, and probably false, to attribute to moral judgments, as such, any impulsive or causative force or power to *make* or *induce us to* do what they enjoin; but even descriptivists sometimes admit that moral judgments have the function of *guiding* conduct. It is indeed fairly evident that in many typical cases we ask, for example, "What ought I to do?" because we have to decide what to do, and think that the answer to the "ought" question has a bearing on our decision greater and more intimate than that possessed by answers to questions of non-moral fact. To take another example, it is fairly evident that there is an intimate connexion between thinking A better than B, and preferring A to B, and between the latter and being disposed to choose A rather than B. This inti-

mate connexion is emphasized in the old tag (whose substance goes back to Socrates): "Whatever is sought, is sought under the appearance of its being good". It would follow from this that to call a thing good is thereby to offer guidance about choices, and the same might be said of the other moral terms. Descriptivists, however, refuse to admit that this feature is part of the *meaning* of moral terms.

Their principal opponents, who may be called "prescriptivists", hold that it *is* part of the meaning. Moral judgments, on this view, share with imperatives the characteristic that to utter one is to commit oneself, directly or indirectly, to some sort of precept or prescription about actual or conceivable decisions or choices. In typical cases, disagreement with a moral judgment is displayed by failure to act on it—as when someone has told me that the right thing to do is such and such, and I immediately do the opposite. Such a view does not, like the emotive theory, make moral argument impossible: for according to some prescriptivists logical relations may hold between prescriptions as well as between ordinary statements.

Prescriptivists have to face, like Socrates, the difficulty that in cases of so-called "weakness of will" we may choose to do something which we think bad or wrong. The most promising line for prescriptivists to take in answer to this objection is to point out that in such cases either the chooser is *unable* to resist the temptation (as is indicated by the expression "*weakness* of will"; cf. also St. Paul , Romans 7, 23); or else he thinks the thing bad or wrong only in some weaker, conventional sense, having the descriptive meaning of "bad" or "wrong" but lacking their prescriptive force.

(2) *The descriptive meaning*. The second main feature of moral judgments is that which distinguishes them from imperatives: whenever we make a moral judgment about, for example, an act, we must make it because of *something about* the act, and it always makes sense to ask what this something is (though it may be hard to put a reply into words). This (although it has been denied by some recent thinkers) follows from the "consequential" character of moral "properties" (see above, section IV). To every particular moral judgment then, there corresponds a universal judgment to the effect that a certain feature of the thing judged is, so far as it goes, a reason for making a certain moral judgment about it. For instance, if I say that a particular act is good because it is the act of helping a blind man across a road, I seem to be adhering thereby to the universal judgment that it is good to help blind people across roads (and not merely this particular blind man across this particular road). Those who accept this argument may be called "universalists"; and their opponents, who do not, may be called "particularists". A universalist is not committed to the view that, if it is a good act to help a blind man across a road on this occasion, it would be a good act on all occasions (for example, it would not be a good act if the blind man was known to be hopelessly lost and his destination lay on this side of the road); he is committed only to the view that it would be a good act in the absence of something to make

a difference between the two acts—something more than the mere numerical difference between the acts.

The universalist thesis is closely connected with the thesis that moral judgments, besides their function as prescriptions, have also a descriptive meaning (see above, section VI). On this view, in calling an act, for example, good, we are commending it (the prescriptive element in the meaning), but commending it because of something about it. These two elements are well summarized by the *Oxford English Dictionary's* first definition of "good": "The most general adjective of commendation, implying the existence in a high, or at least satisfactory, degree of characteristic qualities which are either admirable in themselves or useful for some purpose". The word "characteristic" is important; it draws attention to the fact that the word which follows "good" makes a difference to the qualities which a thing has to have in order to be called good (for example, a good strawberry does not have to have the same qualities as a good man). In the case of some words (for example, "knife"), if we know what they mean, we know some of the conditions that have to be fulfilled before we can call a thing of that kind good. Some philosophers (for example Plato and Aristotle) have held that the same is true of all words—that, for example, if we could determine "the nature of man" we should therefore be able to say what makes a man a good man. But this type of argument may be based on a false analogy between words like "man" and words like "knife".

A more promising way of bringing the universalist thesis to bear on moral arguments (and thus to some extent satisfying those who insist that ethical studies should be relevant to moral questions) is that exemplified by the "Golden Rule" and worked out in some detail (though obscurely) by Kant and his followers. In certain cases it may be a powerful argument, if a man is contemplating some act, to ask what it is about the act which makes him call it right, and whether, if some other act possessed the same features, but his own role in it were different, he would judge it in the same way. This type of argument occurs in two famous passages of Scripture (2 Samuel 12, 7 and Matthew 18, 32). It has been held that a judgment is not a *moral* judgement unless the speaker is prepared to "universalize his maxim". But this raises the vexed question of the criteria for calling judgments "moral judgments" a question which is beyond the scope of this article.

This question, and the whole problem of the relation between the prescriptive and the descriptive elements in the meaning of moral judgments, continues to tax ethical thinkers. It has been impossible in this article to do more than sketch the principal issues and give some account of their origin.

J. B. SCHNEEWIND

(b. 1930)

Having studied at Cornell and Princeton, Schneewind has taught philosophy at Chicago, Princeton, Yale, and Pittsburgh. He is now provost and vice-president of Hunter College. He has been a Mellon fellow and a Guggenheim fellow, and has concentrated upon ethics and Victorian studies.

CONVENTION AND CONVICTION

The model of knowledge which I shall use for discussing morality is the scientific model. It is almost inevitable that a cognitivist view of morality should stress the resemblances between science and ethics; yet to do so is not necessarily to escape from a demand for classical first principles. The ideal of reasoning, and the correlated ideal of knowledge, behind the belief in classical first principles, is a geometric and deductive ideal, and frequently leads to intuitionistic positions. But it can also lead to certain varieties of 'scientific' morality. Thus, Herbert Spencer's moral theory is essentially a deductive system based on a single classical first principle. What is supposed to be distinctively 'scientific' about it is that the principle is allegedly derived wholly from the discoveries of the positive sciences. J. S. Mill's version of utilitarianism is less wholeheartedly scientific than Spencer's view: Mill does not think that the single basic principle of morality can be scientifically proven. But every moral problem and every other rule of morality can, under the supervision of the utilitarian principle, be given purely scientific treatment (or will be susceptible of it, when the social sciences have matured). Still, one need not fall back on classical first principles when one attempts to show that morality can be understood along the lines of a science. There is at least one other way in which science can serve as a model, a way pointed out in certain of its aspects by John Dewey. It may be argued that what is scientific about morality is neither some basic principle or

From "Moral Knowledge and Moral Principles," *in* Knowledge and Necessity, *Royal Institute of Philosophy Lectures, Vol. 3, 1968-69 (London: Macmillan and Co., Ltd., 1970), pp. 255-262.*

principles on which it rests, nor its reliance on special sciences for most of the premises on which moral reasoning proceeds, but the general structure of its contents and its methods. Moral beliefs show the same kind of susceptibility to systematisation, criticism, revision, and re-systematisation that factual beliefs show. There are analogues to theory and data among our moral beliefs, and these can be understood as related in ways like those in which theory and data are related in the sciences. If we can show that this way of understanding morality is feasible, we shall have undercut the argument claiming that the model which commits us to classical first principles is the only possible one.

Principles of morality function in some ways like the formulations of laws which scientists propose. There are, at any given time, a number of specific judgments, rules and ideals, the correctness of which we have no hesitation in affirming. Formulations of moral principles serve to systematise and generalise these beliefs, and in doing so they articulate what may be called the spirit of our morality. They pick out the aspects of our less general beliefs which are not tied to specific circumstances and which would remain constant in a variety of situations. This enables them to express the point or rationale of specific moral convictions. And this in turn enables us to carry out a critical and explicit projection of our moral beliefs to new kinds of problems and new combinations of circumstances. The formulation of a principle to cover classes of cases where we know the rights and wrongs, and the application of the principle thus formed to the solution of difficulties which arise where we have no firm convictions, are analogous, in a rough but fairly clear way, to the formulation of a law to cover a set of well-established data and its use to predict results of new combinations of causal factors.

We must avoid taking too simple a view of this procedure, either in science or in morality. Recent work in the philosophy of science shows that it is misleading to think of each formulation of a scientific law as operating in isolation from every other formulation. Laws are expressed in the context of general theories, and they, as well as many of the concepts involved in assembling the data of the science, must be understood within that context. Similar points hold of morality. I do not mean to suggest that philosophical theories of ethics occupy the position of general theories in the sciences. What occupies the analogous position is rather the general world outlook—typically a religious outlook, or a non-religious world-view still conscious of its non-religiousness—in which a morality is embedded. A large part of the terms and beliefs of these general metaphysical views of life and the world are inseparably intertwined with what we tend to think of as distinctively moral beliefs. The very concepts by which we pick out subjects for moral predication may be rooted in religious or metaphysical propositions, and these in turn may be unintelligible without their evaluative and moral implications. Thus it will take a whole set of moral principles, understood against a metaphysical background, to articulate our moral beliefs adequately and to provide an intelligible and applicable projection of them to new problems. These complex interconnections give rise in morality to a phenomenon comparable to the use in scientific practice of 'theory-laden' observation terms. Many terms employed in the description of particular things and events carry strong theoretical implications, so that in using them we are committed to accepting certain scientific laws. Similarly, many of the terms used for describing our commonest actions and social relations have moral implications built into them. Those who use them are by that fact committed to at least the prima facie acceptance of certain moral directives: to say, e.g., that I am 'married to' so-and-so is to imply my acceptance of a directive against having sexual relations with anyone else. The moral implications of terms like this have been called 'practice-defining rules', and contrasted with 'summary rules'. It is not necessary that a comparison of moral principles with scientific laws should force us to accept the view that all moral principles are of the latter type. But it must equally be borne in mind that the vocabulary embodying practice-defining rules is itself open to alteration and in this respect like the theory-laden terms used in scientific observation.

If the relations between fact and theory in science are complex, so is the way in which the acceptability of a theory depends on the data it organises and the predictions it warrants. Laws that unify a large body of well-established facts and empirical generalisations, that enable us to make successful predictions over a wide range, and that suggest numerous points for further fruitful experiment and theory-construction, are not easily abandoned. A well-founded theory cannot be overthrown by the negative results of a single 'crucial experiment'. Logically speaking, it is always possible to defend a formulation of a law from a counter-instance by explaining the instance in terms of an *ad hoc* hypothesis, or by treating it as due to faulty instruments, bad observation, freakish accident, etc. In terms of the economy and strategy of research this is not always a bad move to make. It is only when the amount of evidence that must be avoided instead of absorbed grows fairly large, when the original theory becomes cumbrous and difficult to use because of the qualifications and adjustments needed to make it fit the evidence, that serious exploration of alternative theories takes place; and the existence of some viable alternative theory is needed before an accepted view will be abandoned. A new theory, if it is of the most attractive kind, will explain the evidence which told in favour of the older view—perhaps recasting it in a new terminology—and it will explain as well what was anomalous or required special hypotheses from the older standpoint. It will enable new areas of investigation to be developed and new types of prediction to be successfully made. It will, in short, perform the same functions as the replaced theory, but better.

If the study of the history of science is still at a comparatively early stage of development, the study of the history of moral systems has hardly even begun. At this point it can only be proposing a hypothesis to say that the pattern of thought revealed in studies of 'scientific revolutions' may be useful as a guide in investigating the development of norms and values. Still, even a rudimentary knowledge of history may allow us to see how this pattern could be relevant. Moral systems are used, not to predict, but to direct and evaluate conduct. They can fail to operate in any number of ways, as scientific theories can fail. Yet accepted systems have a definite value in virtue of the fact that they are widely accepted: they give shape and coherence and predictability to large segments of life, and they are therefore not lightly to be abandoned. Hence no single failure is likely to suffice to overthrow an accepted morality. As in the case of reasonably good theories, it is likely to take an accumulation of difficulties before serious investigation of alternatives occurs. These difficulties may arise from a number of causes. There can, for instance, be failure of relevance to prevalent problems. A morality developed within one type of social or economic situation may be carried over while technological or financial changes occur which effectively alter the nature of the society in which people accept it; and in the new situation the old directives may simply fail to cover recurring problems generally felt to be important. In such circumstances a morality also may fail by giving guidance which is not specific enough, or which it is not feasible to expect people to follow. R. H. Tawney's well-known discussion of the failure of the medieval church to provide an adequate set of precepts for action in a developing capitalist economy gives illustrations of these points. Either the types of monetary transaction vital to a capitalist economy were not covered by any of the standard directives or else they were covered by directives involved in concepts like that of usury and just price which it was no longer feasible to apply. People simply could not live in accordance with the dictates implied by those terms, and were forced to find new ways of organising their actions. Another kind of difficulty with a moral code arises when a change of circumstances transforms a once coherent set of practical demands into directives that repeatedly require incompatible or self-defeating actions. This is the sort of situation involved in what R. K. Merton calls 'anomie', where (roughly) socially acceptable goals can only be reached by breaking socially acceptable rules; and there are other types as well. Still another kind of difficulty with a moral system arises when the religious or metaphysical outlook with which it is involved ceases to be widely accepted: its categories may then cease to seem relevant to the daily problems people face, and therefore its judgments may be increasingly wide of the mark.

Complaints of these kinds about an accepted morality have often been answered by its defenders with the claim that the fault lies not in the moral code but in the social system which is changing in immoral directions, or in the weakness of men, which makes them less willing than usual to expend the effort needed to live up to moral demands, or in the faithlessness of men, which leads them to abandon the revealed truth, or in any of an innumerable variety of factors which allow one to admit the failure of the system to give useful guidance but to cling to the system nonetheless. As in similar cases where counter-evidence to a well-based scientific law is presented, this procedure has a definite justification. But in morality, as in science, it is not always used. There are times when abandoning a moral principle seems more reasonable than continuing to claim that it is true despite the numerous exceptions and qualifications it requires. And the abandonment of one principle is likely to involve repercussions in other parts of the system: the controversy over the morality of birth-control may be mentioned in illustration, touching as it does on the nature of the family, the function of sexual relations and the permissibility of pleasure, the place of women, the authority of various institutions, etc. In this connection it would be interesting to investigate the part played, in basic moral change, by the availability of some alternative system of morality, which would incorporate what is still held to be true in the old view while advancing to new insights on the points of difficulty in that view.

These brief comments may indicate some of the ways in which the structure of morality is like the structure of science, and may point towards an interpretation of moral principles and moral knowledge which does not force us to a belief in what I have called classical first principles. It may help to clarify the hypothesis being suggested if I add one or two further remarks.

The claim that morality is 'cognitive' and that we now have some moral knowledge is not the claim that all our moral convictions as they now stand are true or justifiable. We do not think any such implication to be involved in the claim that we have knowledge of geology or physics or mathematics. We are aware that many of the particular opinions and theories we now hold in these disciplines will eventually be discarded as mistaken, but we have no hesitation in claiming knowledge within these fields nonetheless. The situation is the same as regards morality. I have suggested that moral principles can be supported by showing that they provide adequate articulation of less general moral beliefs which are at a given time held without doubt. I do not mean to imply, however, that the beliefs to which we are at this moment committed are beyond criticism—far from it. Our morality has been derived from many sources and shaped by many influences. It is moreover deeply involved with our factual and religious or metaphysical beliefs. There is no guarantee that it is free from inconsistency, error, or superstition, either on the purely moral plane or in its non-moral involvements. Though it is bound to be our main starting-point in thinking about practical matters, we must assume that progress and improvement in moral knowledge are possible. This is no more, and no less, than we must assume in every area of thought where truth is an aim. Most moral philosophers, however, have thought of moral progress chiefly as the progressive improvement of the human race—as a slow growth in the degree to which men live up to the demands of morality. Few have considered the possibility that moral progress may consist primarily in the growth of moral knowledge. One reason for this may have been their acceptance of the presuppositions that lead to a demand for classical first principles. For on that view, if we do not now know at least the first principles of morality, we cannot really know anything of morality (though of course our opinions may be true). But if we already know the first principles of morality then whatever progress is to be made in our knowledge of the subject (discounting that which will result solely from the improvement of scientific knowledge) must be comparatively minor. The view being put forward here in opposition to this places no such block in the way of contemplating the improvement of even our most general or most cherished principles.

Does this view leave open the possibility that moral knowledge might be, or become, esoteric, the possession of a small group of experts? This did happen to scientific knowledge, yet we do not wish to grant that it could occur with respect to morality. Nor, indeed, are we required to grant it. Any claim to know something must be open to assessment by the relevant group of those qualified to judge. In the case of morality this group consists of those who are able and willing to live their lives—to the usual extent—under the guidance of moral directives understood as such, and not taken simply as customs or taboos or religious commands or positive laws. It is a necessary, if not a sufficient, condition of the justifiability of any claim to knowledge that those who are competent to judge should come to agree with the claim when they investigate it in the proper manner. Moral claims are no exception, and the disagreement of informed and thoughtful moral agents with our own moral assertions gives us a reason for being less confident of them. Still, disagreement, even when the reasons for it are given, is not refutation, and one defence of controversial opinions which must be admitted does leave an opening for the charge of esotericism. It must, I think, be granted that some people really are more insightful and sensitive, morally speaking, than others, and that these people may possibly be ahead of the majority in their grasp of the morality of a particular kind of action. But the distinction between insight and delusion—between wisdom and charlatanry—is no less real than that between science and quackery, and it involves the same basic point: eventually the community of competent judges will come to accept the one and reject the other, if it looks into the matter with sufficient care.

Our moral principles, then, must articulate our unshakable convictions and provide us with adequate guidance for future decisions. In addition they must be capable of calling forth agreement in a potentially unlimited community of moral agents. How can we be sure enough of any principles, under such stringent conditions, to claim that we know they are correct? Well, of course, our scientific theories and hypotheses must survive similar tests, and we manage to make this claim about some of them. And after all the quest for moral knowledge did not begin yesterday. The moral principles most of us accept have had to survive a fair amount of testing and sifting in the course of time. There is therefore a fair amount of evidence to show that they can give acceptable guidance and can form the nucleus of a moral community. To say that we *know* some of them to be correct is to express our reasoned confidence that they, or something very close to them, will, of those available for consideration, come out best in relation to all the evidence, future as well as past. It is also to express our decision, at least for the present, to hold to these principles despite any objections to or difficulties with them. This decision need be no more irrational than similar decisions made by scientists. The principles that we decide, in this fashion, to maintain are the ones we consider basic. The theory of classical first principles involves mistaking this kind of decision for a discovery that certain principles are basic because of their own inherent nature.

STUART HAMPSHIRE

(b. 1914)

Stuart Hampshire is Warden of Wadham College, Oxford, and is one of the better-known British philosophers associated with the analytical movement. He was born in Lincolnshire, England, and upon completing his graduate work in philosophy, became a Fellow of All Souls College and of New College, Oxford. Between 1960 and 1963, he served as Grote Professor of Mind and Logic at University College, London. His works include Spinoza *(1951),* Thought and Action *(1959), and* Freedom of the Individual *(1965).*

MORALITY AND PESSIMISM

III

A way of life is a complicated thing, marked out by many details of style and of manner, and also by particular activities and interests, which a group of people of similar dispositions in a similar social situation may share; consequently the group may become an imitable human type who transmits many of its habits and ideals to its descendants, provided that social change is not too rapid.

In rational reflection one may justify an intuitively accepted and unconditional prohibition as a common, expected feature of a recognizable way of life that on other grounds one values and find admirable, or as a necessary preliminary condition of this way of life. There are rather precise grounds in experience and in history for the reasonable man to expect that certain virtues, which he admires and values, can only be attained at the cost of certain others, and that the virtues typical of several different ways of life cannot be freely combined, as he might wish. Therefore a reasonable and reflective person will review the separate moral injunctions, which intuitively present themselves as having force and authority, as making a skeleton of an attainable, respect-worthy, and preferred way of life. He will reject those that seem likely in practice to

From Morality and Pessimism *by Stuart Hampshire (©Cambridge University Press 1972), pp. 28–33.*

conflict with others that seem more closely part of, or conditions of, the way of life that he values and admires, or that seem irrelevant to this way of life.

One must not exaggerate the degree of connectedness that can be claimed for the set of injunctions that constitute the skeleton of a man's morality. For example, it is a loose, empirical connection that reasonably associates certain sexual customs with the observation of certain family duties, and certain loyalties to the state or country with the recognition of certain duties in respect of property, and in time of war.

The phrase "way of life" is vague and is chosen for its vagueness. The unity of a single way of life, and the compatibility in practice of different habits and dispositions, are learned from observation, direct experience, and from psychology and history. We know that human nature naturally varies, and is deliberately variable, only within limits, and that not all theoretically compatible achievements and enjoyments are compatible in normal circumstances. A reasonable man may envisage a way of life, which excludes various kinds of conduct as impossible, without excluding a great variety of morally tolerable ways of life within this minimum framework. The moral prohibitions constitute a kind of grammar of conduct, showing the elements out of which any fully respectworthy conduct, as one conceives it, must be built.

The plurality of absolute prohibitions, and the looseness of their association with any one way of life that stresses a certain set of virtues, is to be contrasted with the unity and simplicity of utilitarian ethics. One might interpret the contrast in this way: to the utilitarian it is certain that all reasonable purposes are parts of a single purpose in a creature known to be governed by the pleasure principle or by a variant of it. The antiutilitarian replies: nothing is certain in the theory of morality, but, at a pretheoretical level, some human virtues fit together as virtues to form a way of life aspired to, and some monstrous and brutal acts are certainly vicious in the sense that they undermine and corrupt this way of life; and we can explain why they are, and what makes them so, provided that we do not insist upon either precision or certainty or simplicity in the explanation.

The absolute moral prohibitions, which I am defending, are not to be identified with Kant's categorical moral injunctions; for they are not to be picked out by the logical feature of being universal in form. Nor are they prescriptions that must be affirmed, and that cannot be questioned or denied, just because they are principles of rationality and because any contrary principles would involve a form of contradiction. They are indeed judgments of unconditional necessity, in the sense that they imply that what must be done is not necessary because it is a means to some independently valued end, but because the action is a necessary part of a way of life and ideal of conduct. The necessity resides in the nature of the action itself, as specified in the fully explicit moral judgment. The principal and proximate grounds for claiming that the action must, or must not, be performed are to be found in the characterization of the action offered within the prescription; and if the argument is pressed further, first a virtue or vice and then a whole way of life will have to be described.

But still a number of distinctions are needed to avoid misunderstandings. First, he who says, for example, "You must not give a judgment about this until you have heard the evidence," or, "I must stand by my friend in this crisis," claiming an absolute, and unconditional, necessity to act just so on this occasion, is not claiming an overriding necessity to act in this way in all circumstances. He has so far not generalized at all, as he would have generalized if he were to add "always" or "in all circumstances." The immediate grounds for the necessity of the action or abstention are indicated in the judgment itself. These particular actions, which are cases of the general type "respecting evidence" and "standing by friends," are said to be necessary on this occasion in virtue of having just this character, and in virtue of their being this type of action. In other painful circumstances, and on other occasions, other unconditional necessities, with other grounds, might be judged to have overriding claims.

In a situation of conflict, the necessities may be felt to be stringent, and even generally inescapable, and the agent's further reflection may confirm his first feeling of their stringency. Yet in the circumstances of conflict he has to make a choice, and to bring himself to do one of the normally forbidden things in order to avoid doing the other. He may finally recognize one overriding necessity, even though he would not be ready to generalize it to other circumstances. The necessity that is associated with such types of action—e.g., not to betray one's friends—is absolute and unconditional, in the sense that it is not relative to, or conditional upon, some desirable external end; but it is liable occasionally to conflict with other necessities.

A second distinction must be drawn. From the fact that a man thinks that there is nothing other than X that he can do in a particular situation, it does not follow that it is intuitively obvious to him that he must do X. Certainly he may have reached the conclusion immediately and without reflection; but he might also have reached the very same conclusion after weighing a number of arguments for and against. A person's belief that so-and-so must be done, and that he must not act in any other way, may be the outcome of the calculation of the consequences of not doing the necessary thing, always provided that he sees the avoidance of bringing about these consequences as something that is imposed on him as a necessity in virtue of the character of the action. The reason for the necessity of the action sometimes is to be found in its later consequences rather than in the nature and quality of the action evident at the time of action. In every case there will be a description of the action that shows the immediate ground for the necessity, usually by indicating the virtue or vice involved.

Different men, and different social groups, recognize rather different moral necessities in the same essential areas of moral concern. This is no more surprising, or philosophically disquieting, than the fact that different men, and different social groups, will order the primary virtues of men, and the features of an admirable way of life, differently. That the poverty-stricken and the destitute must be helped, just because they suffer, and that a great wrong does not demand a great punishment as retribution, are typical modern opinions about what must be done. Reasoning is associated with these opinions, as it is also with the different orderings of essential virtues; there are no conclusive proofs, or infallible intuitions, which put a stop to the adducing of new considerations. One does not expect that everyone should recognize the same moral necessities; but rather that everyone should recognize some moral necessities, and similar and overlapping ones, in the same, or almost the same, areas of moral concern.

A man's morality, and the morality of a social group, can properly be seen as falling into two parts: first, a picture of the activities necessary to an ideal way of life which is aspired to, and, second, the unavoidable duties and necessities without which even the elements of human worth, and of a respectworthy way of life, are lacking. The two parts are not rationally unconnected. To take the obvious classical examples: a betrayal of friends in a moment of danger, and for the sake of one's own safety, is excluded from the calculation of possibilities; one may lose perhaps everything else, but this cannot be done; the stain would be too great. And one may take public examples: an outrage of cruelty perpetrated upon undefended civilians in war would constitute a stain that would not be erased and would not be balanced against political success.

IV

How would a philosophical friend of the utilitarians respond to these suggestions? Among other objections he would certainly say that I was turning the clock back, suggesting a return to the moral philosophies of the past: absolute prohibitions, elementary decencies, the recognition of a plurality of prohibitions which do not all serve a single purpose—and with nothing more definite behind them than a form of life aspired to. This is the outline of an Aristotelian ethics; ancient doctrine. Modern utilitarians thought that men have the possibility of indefinite improvement in their moral thinking, and that they were confined and confused by their innate endowments of moral repugnances and emotional admirations. There was a sense of the open future in all their writing.

But hope of continuing improvement, if it survives at all, is now largely without evidence. Lowering the barriers of prohibition and making rational calculation of consequences the sole foundation of public policies have so far favored, and are still favoring, a new callousness in policy, a dullness of sensibility, and sometimes moral despair, at least in respect of public affairs. When the generally respected barriers of impermissible conduct are once crossed, and when no different unconditional barriers, within the same areas of conduct, are put in their place, then the special, apparently superstitious, value attached to the preservation of human life will be questioned. This particular value will no longer be distinguished by an exceptionally solemn prohibition; rather it will be assessed on a common scale alongside other desirable things. Yet it is not clear that the taking of lives can be marked and evaluated on a common scale on which increases of pleasure and diminutions of suffering are also measured. This is the suggested discontinuity which a utilitarian must deny.

Moral prohibitions in general, and particularly those that govern the taking of life, the celebration of the dead, and that govern sexual relations and family relations, are artifices that give human lives some distinctive, peculiar, even arbitrary human shape and pattern. They make human the natural phases of experience and lend them a distinguishing sense and direction, one among many possible ones. It is normal for men to expect these artificialities, without which their lives would seem to them inhuman. Largely for this reason a purely naturalistic and utilitarian interpretation of duties and obligations, permissions and prohibitions, in these areas, and particularly in the taking of human life, leaves uneasiness. The idea of morality is connected with the idea that taking human life is a terrible act, one which has to be regulated by some set of overriding constraints that constitute a morality; and the connection of ideas alleged here is not a vague one.

If there were a people who did not recoil from killing, and, what is a distinguishable matter, who seemed to attach no exceptional value to human life, they would be accounted a community of the subhuman; or, more probably, we would doubt whether their words and practices had been rightly interpreted and whether their way of life had been understood.

Yet the taking of life does not have any exceptional importance in utilitarian ethics, that is, in an ethics that is founded exclusively on the actual, ascertained desires and sentiments of men (unlike J. S. Mill's); the taking of life is morally significant in so far as it brings other losses with it. For a strict utilitarian (which J. S. Mill was not) the horror of killing is only the horror of causing other losses, principally of possible happiness; in cases where there are evidently no such losses, the horror of killing becomes superstition. And such a conclusion of naturalism, pressed to its limits, does produce a certain vertigo after reflection. It seems that the mainspring of morality has been taken away.

This vertigo is not principally the result of looking across a century of cool political massacres, undertaken with rational aims; it is also a sentiment with a philosophical thought behind it. A consistent naturalism displaces the prereflective moral emphasis upon respect for life, and for the preservation of life, on to an exclusive concern for one or other of the expected future products of being alive—happiness, pleasure, the satisfaction of desires. Respect for human life, independent of the use made of it, may seem to utilitarians a survival of a sacramental consciousness, or at least a survival of a doctrine of the soul's destiny, or of the unique relation between God and man. It had been natural to speak of the moral prohibitions against the taking of life as being respect for the sacredness of an individual life; and this phrase has no proper place, it is very reasonably assumed, in the thought of anyone who has rejected belief in supernatural sanctions.

But the situation may be more complicated. The sacredness of life, so called, and the absolute prohibitions against the taking of life, except under strictly defined conditions, may be admitted to be human inventions. Once the human origin of the prohibitions has been recognized, the prohibition against the taking of life, and respect for human life as such, may still be reaffirmed as absolute. They are reaffirmed as complementary to a set of customs, habits, and observances, which are understood by reference to their function, and which are sustained, partly because of, partly in spite of, this understanding: I mean sexual customs; family observances; ceremonial treatment of the dead; gentle treatment of those who are diseased and useless, and of the old and senile; customs of war and treatment of convicted criminals; political and legal safeguards for the rights of individuals; and some customary rituals of respect and gentleness in personal dealings.

This complex of habits, and the rituals associated with them, are carried over into a secular morality which makes no existential claims that a naturalist would dispute, and which still rejects the utilitarian morality associated with naturalism. The error of the optimistic utilitarian is that he carries the deritualization of transactions between men to a point at which men not only can, but ought to, use and exploit each other as they use and exploit any other natural objects, as far as this is compatible with general happiness. And at this point, when the mere existence of an individual person by itself has no value, apart from the by-products and uses of the individual in producing and enjoying desirable states of mind, there is no theoretical barrier against social surgery of all kinds. Not only is there no such barrier in theory, but, more important, the nonexistence of the barriers is explicitly recognized.

The draining of moral significance from ceremonies, rituals, manners, and observances that imaginatively express moral attitudes and prohibitions leaves morality incorporated only in a set of propositions and computations: thin and uninteresting propositions, when so isolated from their base in the observances, and manners, which govern ordinary relations with people, and which always manifest implicit moral attitudes and opinions. The computational morality, on which optimists rely, dismisses the nonpropositional and unprogrammed elements in morality altogether, falsely confident that these elements can all be ticketed and brought into the computations.

One may object that I now seem to be arguing for the truth of a doctrine by pointing to the evil consequences of its being disbelieved. This is not my meaning. I have been assuming that prohibitions against killing are primary moral prohibitions; secondly, that the customs and rituals that govern, in different societies, relations between the sexes, marriage, property rights, family relationships, and the celebration of the dead are primary moral customs; they always disclose the peculiar kind of respect for human life, and occasions for disrespect, that a particular people or society recognizes, and therefore their more fundamental moral beliefs and attitudes.

Ordinarily a cosmology, or metaphysics, is associated with morality, and, for Europeans, it has usually been a supernatural cosmology. When the supernatural cosmology is generally rejected, or no longer is taken seriously, the idea that human life has a unique value has to be recognized as a human invention. But it is not an invention from nothing at all. The rituals and manners that govern behavior and respect for persons already express a complex set of moral beliefs and attitudes, and embody a particular way of life. Affirmations of particular rights, duties, and obligations, the propositions of a morality, are a development and a correction of this inexplicit morality of ritual and manners.

Each society, each generation within it, and, in the last resort, each reflective individual, accepts and amends an established morality expressed in rituals and manners, and in explicit prohibitions; and an individual will do this in determining what kind of person he aspires to be and what are the necessary features of a desirable and admirable way of life as he conceives it. If these prohibitions, whatever they are, were no longer observed, and the particular way of life that depends on them was lost, and not just amended or replaced, no particular reason would be left to protect human life more than any other natural phenomenon.

The different manners of different societies provide, as an element in good manners, for the recognition of differences; so among the more serious moral constraints—serious in the sense that they regulate killing and sexuality and family relationships, and so the conditions of survival of the species—may be the requirement to respect moral differences, at least in certain cases. Provided that there are absolute prohibitions in the same domains with the same function, and provided that their congruence with a desired way of life is grasped, we may without irrationality accept the differences; and there may sometimes be a duty to avoid conflict or to look for compromise in cases of conflict.

Consider the intermediate case between manners in the restricted sense and absolute moral principles: a code of honor of a traditional kind. The different prohibitions of different codes are still recognized as codes of honor; and dishonor incurred in the breach of different disciplines is in each case recognizably dishonor, in virtue of the type of ideal behavior, and the way of life, that has been betrayed. Prohibitions in other moralities, very different from the moralities of honor, may be similarly diverse in content.

The question cannot be evaded: what is the rational basis for acting as if human life has a peculiar value, quite beyond the value of any other natural things, when one can understand so clearly how different people, for quite different reasons, have come to believe that it has a particular value and to affirm this in their different moralities? Is one not rationally compelled to follow the utilitarians in denying the autonomy of ethics, and the absoluteness of moral prohibitions, if one once comes to understand the social, psychological, and other functions which the prohibitions serve? If one reflectively adopts and reaffirms one or other of these moralities, together with its prohibitions, then it may seem that one must be accepting the morality for the sake of its uses and function, rather than for the reasoning associated with it; and this concedes the utilitarian's case.

The conclusion is not necessary. A morality, with its ordering of virtues and its prohibitions, provides a particular ideal of humanity in an ideal way of life; and this moral ideal explains where and why killing is allowed and also for what purposes a man might reasonably give his life; and in this sense it sets its own peculiar value on human life. One cannot doubt that there are causes, largely unknown, that would explain why one particular ideal has a hold upon men at a particular time and place, apart from the reasoning that they would use to defend it. And it seems certain that the repugnances and horror surrounding some moral prohibitions are sentiments that have both a biological and a social function.

But the attitude of a reflective man to these repugnances and prohibitions does not for this reason have to be a utilitarian one. One may on reflection respect and reaffirm the prohibitions, and the way of life that they protect, for reasons unconnected with their known or presumed functions—just as one may respect and adopt a code of manners, or a legal system, for reasons that are unconnected with the known functions of such codes and systems in general; and for reasons unconnected also with the known causes that brought these particular codes and systems into existence.

The reasons that lead a reflective man to prefer one code of manners, and one legal system, to another must be moral reasons; that is, he must find his reasons in some order of priority of interests and activities in the kind of life that he praises and admires and that he aspires to have, and in the kind of person that he wants to become. Reasons for the most general moral choices, which may sometimes be choices among competing moralities, must be found in philosophical reasoning, if they are found at all: that is, in considerations about the relation of men to the natural, or to the supernatural, order.

V

I will mention one inclining philosophical reason, which has in the past been prominent in moral theories, particularly in those of Aristotle and of Spinoza, and which influences me. One may on reflection find a particular set of prohibitions and injunctions, and a particular way of life protected by them, acceptable and respectworthy partly because this specifically conceived way of life, with its accompanying prohibitions, has in history appeared natural, and on the whole still feels natural, both to oneself and to others. If there are no countervailing reasons for rejecting this way of life, or for rejecting some distinguishing features of it, its felt and proven naturalness is one reason among others for accepting it.

This reason is likely to influence particularly those who, unlike utilitarians, cannot for other reasons believe that specific states of mind of human beings are the only elements of value in the universe: who, on the contrary, believe that the natural order as a whole is the fitting object of that kind of unconditional interest and respect that is called moral; that the peculiar value to be attached to human life, and the prohibitions against the taking of life, are not dependent on regarding and treating human beings as radically different from other species in some respects that cannot be specified in plain, empirical statements; that the exceptional value attached both to individual lives, and to the survival of the species as a whole, resides in the power of the human mind to begin to understand, and to enjoy, the natural order as a whole, and to reflect upon this understanding and enjoyment; and that, apart from this exceptional power, the uncompensated destruction of any species is always a loss to be avoided.

George Eliot and George Henry Lewes accepted a variant of Spinozistic naturalism close to the doctrine that I have been suggesting. But they still believed in the probability of future moral improvements, once superstitions had gone. Their ethics was still imbued with an optimism that was certainly not shared by Spinoza, and with a sense of an open and unconfined future for the species.

Spinoza's own naturalism was quite free from optimism about the historical future. He does not suggest that advanced, highly educated societies will for the first time be governed largely by the dictates of reason, and that human nature will radically change, and that the conflict between reason and the incapacitating emotions will be largely resolved. Rather he suggests an opposing view of history and of the future: that moral progress, in the proper sense of the increasing dominance of gentleness and of reason, is not to be expected except within very narrow limits. He thought he knew that as psycho-physical organisms people are so constructed that there must always in most men be recurrences of unreason alongside reason, and that in this respect social and historical change would be superficial in their consequences.

This pessimism, or at least lack of optimism, is compatible with a secular doctrine, akin to that of natural law, that represents many of the seemingly natural prohibitions of noncomputational morality as more likely to be endorsed than to be superseded by reflection. A moralist of this persuasion does not foresee a future in which rational computation will by itself replace the various imaginations, unconscious memories and habits, rituals and manners, which have lent substance and content to men's moral ideas, and which have partly formed their various ways of life.

Some of these ways of life, and certainly their complexity and variety, may be respected as an aspect of natural variety; and, like other natural phenomena, they may over the years be studied and explained, at least to some degree explained. From this point of view, that of natural knowledge, the species, if it survives, may perhaps make interesting advances. But this was not the utilitarians' hope; they looked for an historical transformation of human nature through new moral reasoning, and this has not occurred and is now not to be reasonably expected.

10

Marital Morality

RICHARD WASSERSTROM

(b. 1936)

Richard Wasserstrom, Professor of Philosophy and Law at the University of California at Los Angeles, is the author of The Judicial Decision *(1961). He has written many papers on the philosophy of law, and has edited* War and Morality *(1970),* Morality and the Law *(1971), and* Today's Moral Problems *(1975).*

IS ADULTERY IMMORAL?

Many discussions of the enforcement of morality by the law take as illustrative of the problem under consideration the regulation of various types of sexual behavior by the criminal law. It was, for example, the Wolfenden Report's recommendations concerning homosexuality and prostitution that led Lord Devlin to compose his now famous lecture, "The Enforcement of Morals." And that lecture in turn provoked important philosophical responses from H. L. A. Hart, Ronald Dworkin, and others.

Much, if not all, of the recent philosophical literature on the enforcement of morals appears to take for granted the immorality of the sexual behavior in question. The focus of discussion, at least, is whether such things as homosexuality, prostitution, and adultery ought to be made illegal even if they are immoral, and not whether they are immoral.

I propose in this paper to think about the latter, more neglected topic, that of sexual morality, and to do so in the following fashion. I shall consider just one kind of behavior that is often taken to be a case of sexual immorality—adultery. I am interested in pursuing at least two questions. First, I want to explore the question of in what respects adulterous behavior falls within the domain of morality at all: For this surely is one of the puzzles one encounters when considering the topic of sexual morality. It is often hard to see on what grounds much of the behavior is deemed to be either moral or immoral, for example, private homosexual behavior between consenting adults. I have purposely selected adultery because it seems a more plausible candidate for moral assessment than many other kinds of sexual behavior.

The second question I want to examine is that of what is to be said about adultery, without being especially concerned to stay within the area of morality. I shall endeavor, in other words, to identify and to assess a number of the major arguments that might be advanced against adultery. I believe that they are the chief arguments that would be given in support of the view that adultery is immoral, but I think they are worth considering even if some of them turn out to be nonmoral arguments and considerations.

A number of the issues involved seem to me to be complicated and difficult. In a number of places I have at best indicated where further philosophical exploration is required without having successfully conducted the exploration myself. The paper may very well be more useful as an illustration of how one might begin to think about the subject of sexual morality than as an elucidation of important truths about the topic.

Before I turn to the arguments themselves there are two preliminary points that require some clarification. Throughout the paper I shall refer to the immorality of such things as breaking a promise, deceiving someone, etc. In a very rough way, I mean by this that there is something morally wrong that is done in doing the action in question. I mean that the action is, in a strong sense, of "*prima facie*" *prima facie* wrong or unjustified. I do not mean that it may never be right or justifiable to do the action; just that the fact that it is an action of this description always does count against the rightness of the action. I leave entirely open the question of what it is that makes actions of this kind immoral in this sense of "immoral."

The second preliminary point concerns what is meant or implied by the concept of adultery. I mean by "adultery" any case of extramarital sex, and I want to explore the arguments for and against extramarital sex, undertaken in a variety of morally relevant situations. Someone might claim that the concept of adultery is conceptually connected with the concept of immorality, and that to characterize behavior as adulterous is already to characterize it as immoral or unjustified in the sense described above. There may be something to this. Hence the importance of making it clear that I want to talk about extramarital sexual relations. If they are always immoral, this is something that must be shown by argument. If the concept of adultery does in some sense entail or imply immorality, I want to ask whether that connection is a rationally based one. If not all cases of extramarital sex are immoral (again, in the sense described above), then the concept of adultery should either be weakened accordingly or restricted to those classes of extramarital sex for which the predication of immorality is warranted.

One argument for the immorality of adultery might go something like this: what makes adultery immoral is that it involves the breaking of a promise, and what makes adultery seriously wrong is that it involves the breaking of an important promise. For, so the argument might continue, one of the things the two parties promise each other when they get married is that they will abstain from sexual relationships with third persons. Because of this promise both spouses quite reasonably entertain the expectation that the other will behave in conformity with it. Hence, when one of the parties has sexual intercourse with a third person he or she breaks that promise about sexual relationships which was made when the marriage was entered into, and defeats the reasonable expectations of exclusivity entertained by the spouse.

In many cases the immorality involved in breaching the promise relating to extramarital sex may be a good deal more serious than that involved in the breach of other promises. This is so because adherence to this promise may be of much greater importance to the parties than is adherence to many of the other promises given or received by them in their lifetime. The breaking of this promise may be much more hurtful and painful than is typically the case.

Why is this so? To begin with, it may have been difficult for the non-adulterous spouse to have kept the promise. Hence that spouse may feel the unfairness of having restrained himself or herself in the absence of reciprocal restraint having been exercised by the adulterous spouse. In addition, the spouse may perceive the breaking of the promise as an indication of a kind of indifference on the part of the adulterous spouse. If you really cared about me and my feelings—the spouse might say—you would not have done this to me. And third, and related to the above, the spouse may see the act of sexual intercourse with another as a sign of affection for the other person and as an additional rejection of the non-adulterous spouse as the one who is loved by the adulterous spouse. It is not just that the adulterous spouse does not take the feelings of the spouse sufficiently into account, the adulterous spouse also indicates through the act of adultery affection for someone other than the spouse. I will return to these points later. For the present, it is sufficient to note that a set of arguments can be developed in support of the proposition that certain kinds of adultery are wrong just because they involve the breach of a serious promise which, among other things, leads to the intentional infliction of substantial pain by one spouse upon the other.

Another argument for the immorality of adultery focuses not on the existence of a promise of sexual exclusivity but on the connection between adultery and deception. According to this argument, adultery involves deception. And because deception is wrong, so is adultery.

Although it is certainly not obviously so, I shall simply assume in this paper that deception is always immoral. Thus the crucial issue for my purposes is the asserted connection between extramarital sex and deception. Is it plausible to maintain, as this argument does, that adultery always does involve deception and is on that basis to be condemned?

The most obvious person on whom deceptions might be practiced is the nonparticipating spouse; and the most obvious thing about which the nonparticipating spouse can be deceived is the existence of the adulterous act. One clear case of deception is that of lying. Instead of saying that the afternoon was spent in bed with A, the adulterous spouse asserts that it was spent in the library with B, or on the golf course with C.

There can also be deception even when no lies are told. Suppose, for instance, that a person has sexual intercourse with someone other than his or her spouse and just does not tell the spouse about it. Is that deception? It may not be a case of lying if, for example, the spouse is never asked by the other about the situation. Still, we might say, it is surely deceptive because of the promises that were exchanged at marriage. As we saw earlier, these promises provide a foundation for the reasonable belief that neither spouse will engage in sexual relationships with any other persons. Hence the failure to bring the fact of extramarital sex to the attention of the other spouse deceives that spouse about the present state of the marital relationship.

Adultery, in other words, can involve both active and passive deception. An adulterous spouse may just keep silent or, as is often the fact, the spouse may engage in an increasingly complex way of life devoted to the concealment of the facts from the nonparticipating spouse. Lies, half-truths, clandestine meetings, and the like may become a central feature of the adulterous spouse's existence. These are things that can and do happen, and when they do they make the case against adultery an easy one. Still, neither active nor passive deception is inevitably a feature of an extramarital relationship.

It is possible, though, that a more subtle but pervasive kind of deceptiveness is a feature of adultery. It comes about because of the connection in our culture between sexual intimacy and certain feelings of love and affection. The point can be made indirectly at first by seeing that one way in which we can, in our culture, mark off our close friends from our mere acquaintances is through the kinds of intimacies that we are prepared to share with them. I may, for instance, be willing to reveal my very private thoughts and emotions to my closest friends or to my wife, but to no one else. My sharing of these intimate facts about myself is from one perspective a way of making a gift to those who mean the most to me. Revealing these things and sharing them with those who mean the most to me is one means by which I create, maintain, and confirm those interpersonal relationships that are of most importance to me.

Now in our culture, it might be claimed, sexual intimacy is one of the chief currencies through which gifts of this sort are exchanged. One way to tell someone—particularly someone of the opposite sex—that you have feelings of affection and love for them is by allowing to them or sharing with them sexual behaviors that one doesn't share with the rest of the world. This way of measuring affection was certainly very much a part of the culture in which I matured. It worked something like this. If you were a girl, you showed how much you liked someone by the degree of sexual intimacy you would allow. If you liked a boy only a little, you never did more than kiss—and even the kiss was not very passionate. If you liked the boy a lot and if your feeling was reciprocated, necking, and possibly petting, was permissible. If the attachment was still stronger and you thought it might even become a permanent relationship, the sexual activity was correspondingly more intense and more intimate, although whether it would ever lead to sexual intercourse depended on whether the parties (and particularly the girl) accepted fully the prohibition on non-marital sex. The situation for the boy was related, but not exactly the same. The assumption was that males did not naturally link sex with affection in the way in which females did. However, since women did, males had to take this into account. That is to say, because a woman would permit sexual intimacies only if she had feelings of affection for the male and only if those feelings were reciprocated, the male had to have and express those feelings, too, before sexual intimacies of any sort would occur.

The result was that the importance of a correlation between sexual intimacy and feelings of love and affection was taught by the culture and assimilated by those growing up in the culture. The scale of possible positive feelings toward persons of the other sex ran from casual liking at the one end to the love that was deemed essential to and characteristic of marriage at the other. The scale of possible sexual behavior ran from brief, passionless kissing or hand-holding at the one end to sexual intercourse at the other. And the correlation between the two scales was quite precise. As a result, any act of sexual intimacy carried substantial meaning with it, and no act of sexual intimacy was simply a pleasurable set of bodily sensations. Many such acts were, of course, more pleasurable to the participants because they were a way of saying what the participants' feelings were. And sometimes they were less pleasurable for the same reason. The point is, however, that in any event sexual activity was much more than mere bodily enjoyment. It was not like eating a good meal, listening to good music, lying in the sun, or getting a pleasant back rub. It was behavior that meant a great deal concerning one's feelings for persons of the opposite sex in whom one was most interested and with whom one was most involved. It was among the most authoritative ways in which one could communicate to another the nature and degree of one's affection.

If this sketch is even roughly right, then several things become somewhat clearer. To begin with, a possible rationale for many of the rules of conventional sexual morality can be developed. If, for example, sexual intercourse is associated with the kind of affection and commitment to another that is regarded as characteristic of the marriage relationship, then it is natural that sexual intercourse should be thought properly to take place between persons who are married to each other. And if it is thought that this kind of affection and commitment is only to be found within the marriage relationship, then it is not surprising that sexual intercourse should only be thought to be proper within marriage.

Related to what has just been said is the idea that sexual intercourse ought to be restricted to those who are married to each other as a means by which to confirm the very special feelings that the spouses have for each other. Because the culture teaches that sexual intercourse means that the strongest of all feelings for each other are shared by the lovers, it is natural that persons who are married to each other should be able to say this to each other in this way. Revealing and confirming verbally that these feelings are present is one thing that helps to sustain the relationship; engaging in sexual intercourse is another.

In addition, this account would help to provide a framework within which to make sense of the notion that some sex is better than other sex. As I indicated earlier, the fact that sexual intimacy can be meaningful in the sense described tends to make it also the case that sexual intercourse can sometimes be more enjoyable than at other times. On this view, sexual intercourse will typically be more enjoyable where the strong feelings of affection are present than it will be where it is merely "mechanical."

This is so in part because people enjoy being loved, especially by those whom they love. Just as we like to hear words of affection, so we like to receive affectionate behavior. And the meaning enhances the independently pleasureable behavior.

More to the point, moreover, an additional rationale for the prohibition on extramarital sex can now be developed. For given this way of viewing the sexual world, extramarital sex will almost always involve deception of a deeper sort. If the adulterous spouse does not in fact have the appropriate feelings of affection for the extramarital partner, then the adulterous spouse is deceiving that person about the presence of such feelings. If, on the other hand, the adulterous spouse does have the corresponding feelings for the extramarital partner but not toward the nonparticipating spouse, the adulterous spouse is very probably deceiving the nonparticipating spouse about the presence of such feelings toward that spouse. Indeed, it might be argued, whenever there is no longer love between the two persons who are married to each other, there is deception just because being married implies both to the participants and to the world that such a bond exists. Deception is inevitable, the argument might conclude, because the feelings of affection that ought to accompany any act of sexual intercourse can only be held toward one other person at any given time in one's life. And if this is so, then the adulterous spouse always deceives either the partner in adultery or the nonparticipating spouse about the existence of such feelings. Thus extramarital sex involves deception of this sort and is for this reason immoral even if no deception vis-à-vis the occurrence of the act of adultery takes place.

What might be said in response to the foregoing arguments? The first thing that might be said is that the account of the connection between sexual intimacy and feelings of affection is inaccurate. Not inaccurate in the sense that no one thinks of things that way, but in the sense that there is substantially more divergence of opinion than that account suggests. For example, the view I have delineated may describe reasonably accurately the concepts of the sexual world in which I grew up, but it does not capture the sexual *weltanschauung* of today's youth at all. Thus, whether or not adultery implies deception in respect to feelings depends very much on the persons who are involved and the way they look at the "meaning" of sexual intimacy.

Second, the argument leaves to be answered the question of whether it is desirable for sexual intimacy to carry the sorts of messages described above. For those persons for whom sex does have these implications, there are special feelings and sensibilities that must be taken into account. But it is another question entirely whether any valuable end—moral or otherwise—is served by investing sexual behavior with such significance. That is something that must be shown and not just assumed. It might, for instance, be the case that substantially more good than harm would come from a kind of demystification of sexual behavior: one that would encourage the enjoyment of sex more for its own sake and one that would reject the centrality both of the association of sex with love and of love with only one other person.

I regard these as two of the more difficult, unresolved issues that our culture faces today in respect to thinking sensibly about the attitudes toward sex and love that we should try to develop in ourselves and in our children. Much of the contemporary literature that advocates sexual liberation of one sort or another embraces one or the other of two different views about the relationship between sex and love.

One view holds that sex should be separated from love and affection. To be sure sex is probably better when the partners genuinely like and enjoy each other. But sex is basically an intensive, exciting sensuous activity that can be enjoyed in a variety of suitable settings with a variety of suitable partners. The situation in respect to sexual pleasure is no different from that of the person who knows and appreciates fine food and who can have a very satisfying meal in any number of good restaurants with any number of congenial companions. One question that must be settled here is whether sex can be so demystified; another, more important question is whether it would be desirable to do so. What would we gain and what might we lose if we all lived in a world in which an act of sexual intercourse was no more or less significant or enjoyable than having a delicious meal in a nice setting with a good friend? The answer to this question lies beyond the scope of this paper.

The second view seeks to drive the wedge in a different place. It is not the link between sex and love that needs to be broken; rather, on this view, it is the connection between love and exclusivity that ought to be severed. For a number of the reasons already given, it is desirable, so this argument goes, that sexual intimacy continue to be reserved to and shared with only those for whom one has very great affection. The mistake lies in thinking that any "normal" adult will only have those feelings toward one other adult during his or her lifetime—or even at any time in his or her life. It is the concept of adult love, not ideas about sex, that, on this view, needs demystification. What are thought to be both unrealistic and unfortunate are the notions of exclusivity and possessiveness that attach to the dominant conception of love between adults in our and other cultures. Parents of four, five, six, or even ten children can certainly claim and sometimes claim correctly that they love all of their children, that they love them all equally, and that it is simply untrue to their feelings to insist that the numbers involved diminish either the quantity or the quality of their love. If this is an idea that is readily understandable in the case of parents and children, there is no necessary reason why it is an impossible or undesirable ideal in the case of adults. To be sure, there is probably a limit to the number of intimate, "primary" relationships that any person can maintain at any given time without the quality of the relationship being affected. But one adult ought surely be able to love two, three, or even six other adults at any one time without that love being different in kind or degree from that of the traditional, monogomous, lifetime marriage. And as between the individuals in these relationships, whether within a marriage or without, sexual intimacy is fitting and good.

The issues raised by a position such as this one are surely worth exploring in detail and with care. Is there something to be called "sexual love" which is different from parental love or the nonsexual love of close friends? Is there something about love in general that links it naturally and appropriately with feelings of exclusivity and possession? Or is there something about sexual love, whatever that may be, that makes these feelings especially fitting here? Once again the issues are conceptual, empirical, and normative all at once: What is love? How could it be different? Would it be a good thing or a bad thing if it were different?

Suppose, though, that having delineated these problems we were now to pass them by. Suppose, moreover, we were to be persuaded of the possibility and the desirability of weakening substantially either the links between sex and love or the links between sexual love and exclusivity. Would it not then be the case that adultery could be free from all of the morally objectionable features described so far? To be more specific, let us imagine that a husband and wife have what is today sometimes characterized as an "open marriage." Suppose, that is, that they have agreed in advance that extramarital sex is—under certain circumstances—acceptable behavior for each to engage in. Suppose, that as a result there is no impulse to deceive each other about the occurrence or nature of any such relationships, and that no deception in fact occurs. Suppose, too, that there is no deception in respect to the feelings involved between the adulterous spouse and the extramarital partner. And suppose, finally, that one or the other or both of these spouses then has sexual intercourse in circumstances consistent with these understandings. Under this description, so the agreement might conclude, adultery is simply not immoral. At a minimum, adultery cannot very plausibly be condemned either on the ground that it involves deception or on the ground that it requires the breaking of a promise.

At least two responses are worth considering. One calls attention to the connection between marriage and adultery; the other looks to more instrumental arguments for the immorality of adultery. Both issues deserve further exploration.

One way to deal with the case of the "open marriage" is to question whether the two persons involved are still properly to be described as being married to each other. Part of the meaning of what it is for two persons to be married to each other, so this argument would go, is to have committed oneself to have sexual relationships only with one's spouse. Of course, it would be added, we know that that commitment is not always honored. We know that persons who are married to each other often do commit adultery. But there is a difference between being willing to make a commitment to marital fidelity, even though one may fail to honor that commitment, and not making the commitment at all. Whatever the relationship may be between the two individuals in the case described above, the absence of any commitment to sexual exclusivity requires the conclusion that their relationship is not a marital one. For a commitment to sexual exclusivity is a necessary although not a sufficient condition for the existence of a marriage.

Although there may be something to this suggestion, as it is stated it is too strong to be acceptable. To begin with, I think it is very doubtful that there are many, if any, *necessary* conditions for marriage; but even if there are, a commitment to sexual exclusivity is not such a condition.

To see that this is so, consider what might be taken to be some of the essential characteristics of a marriage. We might be tempted to propose that the concept of marriage requires the following: a formal ceremony of some sort in which mutual obligations are undertaken between two persons of the opposite sex; the capacity on the part of the persons involved to have sexual intercourse with each other; the willingness to have sexual intercourse only with each other; and feelings of love and affection between the two persons. The problem is that we can imagine relationships that are clearly marital and yet lack one or more of these features. For example, in our own society, it is possible for two persons to be married without going through a formal ceremony, as in the common-law marriages recognized in some jurisdictions. It is also possible for two persons to get married even though one or both lacks the capacity to engage in sexual intercourse. Thus, two very elderly persons who have neither the desire nor the ability to have intercourse can, nonetheless, get married, as can persons whose sexual organs have been injured so that intercourse is not possible. And we certainly know of marriages in which love was not present at the time of the marriage, as, for instance, in marriages of state and marriages of convenience.

Counterexamples not satisfying the condition relating to the abstention from extramarital sex are even more easily produced. We certainly know of societies and cultures in which polygamy and polyandry are practiced, and we have no difficulty in recognizing these relationships as cases of marriages. It might be objected, though, that these are not counterexamples because they are plural marriages rather than marriages in which sex is permitted with someone other than with one of the persons to whom one is married. But we also know of societies in which it is permissible for married persons to have sexual relationships with persons to whom they were not married, for example, temple prostitutes, concubines, and homosexual lovers. And even if we knew of no such societies, the conceptual claim would still, I submit, not be well taken. For suppose all of the other indicia of marriage were present: suppose the two persons were of the opposite sex. Suppose they had the capacity and desire to have intercourse with each other, suppose they participated in a formal ceremony in which they understood themselves voluntarily to be entering into a relationship with each other in which substantial mutual commitments were assumed. If all these conditions were satisfied, we would not be in any doubt about whether or not the two persons were married even though they had not taken on a commitment of sexual exclusivity and even though they had expressly agreed that extramarital sexual intercourse was a permissible behavior for each to engage in.

A commitment to sexual exclusivity is neither a necessary nor a sufficient condition for the existence of a marriage. It does, nonetheless, have this much to do with the nature of marriage: like the other indicia enumerated above, its presence tends to establish the existence of a marriage. Thus, in the absence of a formal ceremony of any sort, an explicit commitment to sexual exclusivity would count in favor of regarding the two persons as married. The conceptual role of the commitment to sexual exclusivity can, perhaps, be brought out through the following example. Suppose we found a tribe which had a practice in which all the other indicia of marriage were present but in which the two parties were *prohibited* ever from having sexual intercourse with each other. Moreover, suppose that sexual intercourse with others was clearly permitted. In such a case we would, I think, reject the idea that the two were married to each other and we would describe their relationship in other terms, for example, as some kind of formalized, special friendship relation—a kind of heterosexual "blood-brother" bond.

Compare that case with the following. Suppose again that the tribe had a practice in which all of the other indicia of marriage were present, but instead of a prohibition on sexual intercourse between the persons in the relationship there was no rule at all. Sexual intercourse was permissible with the person with whom one had this ceremonial relationship, but it was no more or less permissible than with a number of other persons to whom one was not so related (for instance, all consenting adults of the opposite sex). Although we might be in doubt as to whether we ought to describe the persons as married to each other, we would probably conclude that they were married and that they simply were members of a tribe whose views about sex were quite different from our own.

What all of this shows is that *a prohibition* on sexual intercourse between the two persons involved in a relationship is conceptually incompatible with the claim that the two of them are married. The *permissibility* of intramarital sex is a necessary part of the idea of marriage. But no such incompatibility follows simply from the added permissibility of extramarital sex.

These arguments do not, of course, exhaust the arguments for the prohibition on extramarital sexual relations. The remaining argument that I wish to consider—as I indicated earlier—is a more instrumental one. It seeks to justify the prohibition by virtue of the role that it plays in the development and maintenance of nuclear families. The argument, or set of arguments, might, I believe, go something like this.

Consider first a farfetched nonsexual example. Suppose a society were organized so that after some suitable age—say, 18, 19, or 20—persons were forbidden to eat anything but bread and water with anyone but their spouse. Persons might still choose in such a society not to get married. Good food just might not be very important to them because they have underdeveloped taste buds. Or good food might be bad for them because there is something wrong with their digestive system. Or good food might be important to them, but they might decide that the enjoyment of good food would get in the way of the attainment of other things that were more important. But most persons would, I think, be led to favor marriage in part because they preferred a richer, more varied, diet to one of bread and water. And they might remain married because the family was the only legitimate setting within which good food was obtainable. If it is important to have society organized so that persons will both get married and stay married, such an arrangement would be well suited to the preservation of the family, and the prohibitions relating to food consumption could be understood as fulfilling that function.

It is obvious that one of the more powerful human desires is the desire for sexual gratification. The desire is a natural one, like hunger and thirst, in the sense that it need not be learned in order to be present within us and operative upon us. But there is in addition much that we do learn about what the act of sexual intercourse is like. Once we experience sexual intercourse ourselves—and in particular once we experience orgasm—we discover that it is among the most intensive, short-term pleasures of the body.

Because this is so, it is easy to see how the prohibition upon extramarital sex helps to hold marriage together. At least during that period of life when the enjoyment of sexual intercourse is one of the desirable bodily pleasures, persons will wish to enjoy those pleasures. If one consequence of being married is that one is prohibited from having sexual intercourse with anyone but one's spouse, then the spouses in a marriage are in a position to provide an important source of pleasure for each other that is unavailable to them elsewhere in the society.

The point emerges still more clearly if this rule of sexual morality is seen as of a piece with the other rules of sexual morality. When this prohibition is coupled, for example, with the prohibition on nonmarital sexual intercourse, we are presented with the inducement both to get married and to stay married. For if sexual intercourse is only legitimate within marriage, then persons seeking that gratification which is a feature of sexual intercourse are furnished explicit social directions for its attainment; namely marriage.

Nor, to continue the argument, is it necessary to focus exclusively on the bodily enjoyment that is involved. Orgasm may be a significant part of what there is to sexual intercourse, but it is not the whole of it. We need only recall the earlier discussion of the meaning that sexual intimacy has in our own culture to begin to see some of the more intricate ways in which sexual exclusivity may be connected with the establishment and maintenance of marriage as the primary heterosexual, love relationship. Adultery is wrong, in other words, because a prohibition on extramarital sex is a way to help maintain the institutions of marriage and the nuclear family.

Now I am frankly not sure what we are to say about an argument such as this one. What I am convinced of is that, like the arguments discussed earlier, this one also reveals something of the difficulty and complexity of the issues that are involved. So, what I want now to do—in the brief and final portion of this paper—is to try to delineate with reasonable precision what I take several of the fundamental, unresolved issues to be.

The first is whether this last argument is an argument for the *immorality* of extramarital sexual intercourse. What does seem clear is that there are differences between this argument and the ones considered earlier. The earlier arguments condemned adulterous behavior because it was behavior that involved breaking of a promise, taking unfair advantage, or deceiving another. To the degree to which the prohibition on extramarital sex can be supported by arguments which invoke considerations such as these, there is little question but that violations of the prohibition are properly regarded as immoral. And such a claim could be defended on one or both of two distinct grounds. The first is that things like promise-breaking and deception are just wrong. The second is that adultery involving promise-breaking or deception is wrong because it involves the straightforward infliction of harm on another human being—typically the nonadulterous spouse—who has a strong claim not to have that harm so inflicted.

The argument that connects the prohibition on extramarital sex with the maintenance and preservation of the institution of marriage is an argument for the instrumental value of the prohibition. To some degree this counts, I think, against regarding all violations of the prohibition as obvious cases of immorality. This is so partly because hypothetical imperatives are less clearly within the domain of morality than are categorical ones, and even more because instrumental prohibitions are within the domain of morality only if the end they serve or the way they serve it is itself within the domain of morality.

What this should help us see, I think, is the fact that the argument that connects the prohibition on adultery with the preservation of marriage is at best seriously incomplete. Before we ought to be convinced by it, we ought to have reasons for believing that marriage is a morally desirable and just social institution. And this is not quite as easy or obvious a task as it may seem to be. For the concept of marriage is, as we have seen, both a loosely structured and a complicated one. There may be all sorts of intimate, interpersonal relationships which will resemble but not be identical with the typical marriage relationship presupposed by the traditional sexual morality. There may be a number of distinguishable sexual and loving arrangements which can all legitimately claim to be called *marriages*. The prohibitions of the traditional sexual morality may be effective ways to maintain some marriages and ineffective ways to promote and preserve others. The prohibitions of the traditional sexual morality may make good psychological sense if certain psychological theories are true, and they may be purveyors of immense psychological mischief if other psychological theories are true. The prohibitions of the traditional sexual morality may seem obviously correct if sexual intimacy carries the meaning that the dominant culture has often ascribed to it, and they may seem equally bizarre when sex is viewed through the perspective of the counter-culture. Irrespective of whether instrumental arguments of this sort are properly deemed moral arguments, they ought not to fully convince anyone until questions like these are answered.

CLORINDA MARGOLIS

(b. 1930)

Clorinda Margolis is Associate Director of Preventive Services, Jefferson Community Health Center, and a member of the faculty, Department of Psychiatry and Human Behavior, Thomas Jefferson University. She has written extensively on social issues, including drugs, sexual roles, race relations, and euthanasia.

JOSEPH MARGOLIS

(b. 1924)

Joseph Margolis is Professor of Philosophy, Temple University, and Editor, Philosophical Monographs. *He is the author of numerous books including, most recently,* Negativities, The Limits of Life, *and* Art and Philosophy.

THE SEPARATION OF MARRIAGE AND FAMILY

The family and the marriage institution are obviously so central to the history of every society that it is hopeless to suppose that one could specify, quite objectively, the proper form of either or both. Proposals can be no more than reasonable adjustments of existing practices; that is, debate tends to be dialectical, focused on those possibilities of change that actual arrangements, which are themselves no more than the latest phase of accumulating changes, may support. Furthermore, marriage and the family are the natural magnets for every important

"The Separation of Marriage and the Family" was first commissioned to appear in Feminism and Philosophy, *edited by Mary Vetterling-Braggin, Frederick Elliston, and Jane English (Totowa, N. J.: Littlefield Adams, 1977). It appears here by arrangement with the authors and the editors.*

quarrel about the race—property and inheritance, personal relations, the care and education of the young, the initiation and monitoring of sex, the limits of personal freedom, the authority of the state and church, the distribution of public status. At one extreme, it is claimed that marriage is a sacrament or has a fixed and ordained function. At the other, only the historical contingencies are noted by which the nuclear family and its norms are seen to be the gradual result of a certain narrowing and a certain alteration of family relations since at least the Middle Ages.

The peculiarity of marriage is the intensity with which its norms are disputed, at the same time that its functional possibilities remain quite unclear. It appears at one and the same time to be a purely personal relationship, a sacrament or at least a serious institution guarded by moral or religious authorities, and a mere legal contract. It is in fact easy to see how it may be viewed exclusively along any one of these dimensions.

An interesting experiment suggests itself, therefore. Why not consider the separation of the interests of marriage and the family within the developing forms of contemporary Western life? One might almost say that that would not even be an experiment, would perhaps be no more than an elaboration of an actual tendency. For example, contemporary ease of divorce and insistence on the privacy of sexual and other personal relationships tend, in the context of the nuclear family, to drive the interests of marriage and family apart. Marriage increasingly tends to focus on the satisfaction of certain private interests; family, on at least certain public concerns regarding the well-being of dependents, the control of property and the like. Why not, therefore, consider what would be involved in construing marriage as essentially concerned with such private interests; and families, as essentially concerned with such public interests?

This need not be construed as an attack on existing institutions. It would offer us only a picture of certain rational options available to those who are already drifting in the direction of separating the two institutions. For instance, there is evidence of an increasing interest on the part of unmarried women to have and raise children. Wherever an older and a viable practice exists in which the interests of the family and the marriage couple converge harmoniously, there is no need to recommend—or even to explore, at least for the same reasons—the prospects of radically transforming our understanding of the marriage relationship. But in a society committed to tolerating plural conceptions of marriage, defending sexual and personal privacy as a matter of personal liberty, liberalizing both on legal and informal grounds the acceptability of separation and divorce, acknowledging the legitimacy of the view that the personal compatibility of mates is the primary or even exclusive justificatory basis for marriage, there is bound to be a realistic need to consider even radical possibilities.

No doubt the medieval marriage involved the institution of a personal relationship, but there is little reason to think it was ever construed romantically (certainly not in the technical sense); in fact it was effectively incompatible with romantic love. It surely never set a premium on a sustained and exclusive personal and distinctly sexualized love. The development of that conception resulted somehow from the gradual secularization, then sexualization, of romance and its identification with the utterly different notion of the functional harmony and mutual respect of marriage mates. The Vatican Council's pronouncement, reported in Pope Paul's *Humanae Vitae*, that "Marriage and conjugal love are by their nature ordained toward the begetting and educating of children," holds so closely to the earlier conception of marriage that it must seem, to orthodox Roman Catholics, like a contradiction in terms, to hear that Dutch priests have actually attempted to extend and to defend offering the marriage sacrament to homosexual couples. (The same issue of course appears outside Roman Catholic circles.) And yet, in our own day, the matter is blandly regarded by many as debatable, even within the Catholic tradition.

Again, *Humanae Vitae* declares explicitly that "directly willed and procured abortions, even if for therapeutic reasons, are to be absolutely excluded as licit means of regulating births"; also, that "direct sterilization, whether perpetual or temporary, whether of the man or of the woman" is to be outlawed. Obviously, this doctrine is rejected by many of the Christian faith, disputed even among Catholics, and notably inoperative in Western civil law. What is important about the pronouncement, however, quite apart from its substance, is that it presupposes a normative conceptual unity linking the function of individual persons, the function of the marriage relationship, and the function of the family initiated by marriage. To concede that such a unity may not obtain is, in our own time, hardly subversive: it is the standard claim of a very large number of persons and is as much institutionalized as the doctrine of *Humanae Vitae* itself. Furthermore, even where such a unity is admitted, as in other parts of the Christian community, the conception of the functions involved differs drastically from the view advanced by the Pope—so drastically, for instance, that divorce, abortion, sterilization, the legitimacy of homosexual marriage, contraception to avoid children, and the like are either flatly regarded as legitimate or, at the very least, debatable.

Consider then the extreme possibility. *If* marriage were a purely personal matter, the effective union of two (or even several) persons (of either sex), then the permanence of the relationship would depend entirely on the feelings and volitions of the parties affected. On that assumption, there would be absolutely no point in linking property rights, inheritance, social position, the "begetting and educating of children," even the monitoring of sex or obligations of child support or the support of spouses, with the institution of marriage. Two types of marriage would fit this extreme condition: first of all, an *informal* marriage, a personal agreement to cohabit, not legally binding but socially—possibly even religously or sacramentally—recognized; secondly, a term marriage, a legal agreement to cohabit for a determinate period, for purposes of a private nature, renewable by mutual consent.

Here, what strikes one at once is that, however reasonable it may be to protect the legal rights of children or other wards, legal constraints on marriage (not arising from the initiative of contracting parties) have very little to do with the kind of personal affection, cooperation, sexual interest that presumably would sustain either the informal or the (probably short-term) contractual marriage. In fact, families themselves might well be formed in quite different ways from those acknowledged at present. There is of course every evidence that so-called primitive societies draw rather sharp distinctions between the rights of families and the rights of marriage mates. It's quite conceivable, in our own society, that agreements obtain in which, though a party of either sex be a donor toward the begetting of children, families may be legally recognized (apart from divorce and death) in which only one parent, not necessarily the natural parent, and children begotten or adopted form the functioning family. The concept of a family is quite different from the concept of a marriage; even the so-called nuclear family is by no means the limiting form of viable families. Hence, the legal considerations involved in protecting a family, for instance limitations on the use of property in the interests of family or family members, may be sharply distinguished from the personal or contingent legal considerations involved in a marriage.

In this sense, a *family* is a social unit of *legal parents* and *offspring* or *wards*, whether natural or adopted; and a *marriage* is a social unit of *adults* or competent parties agreeing informally or by contract to cohabit, whatever arrangements of personal privacy they may agree to. It may be argued that the younger natural offspring of elderly parents have become the legal parents of their own natural parents (or, adoptively, of other wards of any age); and in general, the legal protection and control of families and their members will be seen to be a logically distinct matter from that of imposing legal constraints upon marriage.

One obvious place where the confusion of marriage and family interests has regularly obtained is where the income tax laws apply. If for example persons not legally married were permitted to file joint income tax returns or if the tax did not favor those legally married over those not married, there would be no gratuitous disadvantage to those who chose to live together in an informal marriage or who, though contractually married, intended to have no children. It is reasonably clear that the motivation for favoring married couples over the unmarried has to do with an anticipated link with the raising of families. But if the management of property and the assignment of children and wards were linked solely to families and not to marriages, there would be no need to consider marriage in the distribution of taxes; also, the widespread use of contraception and sterilization suggests that that linkage is becoming increasingly irregular. And even now, the assignment of children to parents must be determined, sometimes, where no actual marriage obtains; in particular, the very concept of illegitimacy depends on conflating the interests of marriage and family. Were there legal specifications for the individuation of families—*which did not depend on (or solely on) consent*—the category of illegitimacy could be quite simply eliminated. Obviously, the welfare laws of the United States, which bind unwed fathers to support their natural offspring, already is committed to the principle; nevertheless, the social and legal stigma of illegitimacy remains. Again, if the tax advantages of a given family were independently defensible, they could be sustained without any reference to marriage at all.

Clearly, the distinction of marriage and family requires a third form of contract, yielding what might be called a *contractual family (not* a marriage); that is, several parties might voluntarily contract to form a family. They might do this in either of two ways: first of all, by begetting children—whether they are married or not—which children they legally signify they intend to take responsibility for as wards; secondly, by adopting children—whether they are married or not. Conditions of eligibility may very reasonably be imposed, since the public community has an understandable interest in the care of children and wards and the control and management of property. Marriage as such, however, would not be a relevant consideration, since *its* function, *ex hypothesi*, is a matter exclusively of private concern; though the character and responsibility of individuals who happen to be or not to be married would, fairly, be considered relevant. The members of a family sharing responsibility on some admissible basis need not of course cohabit as a marriage unit; clearly, therefore, their legal responsibilities would be unaffected by the transience and the vagaries of the marriage relationship itself. It is even conceivable that, in the absence of a family contract or where such a contract is disallowed, children begotten by a given couple, whether married or not, would be assigned involuntarily to some legally recognized family; also, contractually initiated families might well have jurisdiction only in specified contexts. Again, a family might conceivably be contractually initiated by one party of either sex, where another might serve merely as a natural donor, as is very nearly already the case in the practice of artificial insemination, where the donor need be neither a member of the resulting family nor a party to any marriage; and of course the contracting parent(s)—one, two (of either sex), or more than two—may merely adopt children or wards, without entering into a marriage at all. The separation of marriage and family, therefore, suggests the viability both of homosexual marriages and of families composed of parents of one sex, as well as marriages and families composed of more than two adults or two parents.

These variations suggest the relative inflexibility of our current marriage customs. In fact, the history of family organization shows that the human race has always experimented boldly and with a great deal of variety in distinguishing marriage and family structures. In primitive matrilineal societies for instance, it is quite characteristic that the care and responsibility for children and the inheritance of property is sharply distinguished from the limited interests of those recognized as mated. Even in the most conservative setting of American life, the admission of day-care centers, boarding schools, the public educational system, compulsory health standards, the rights of children and the like argue that the effective jurisdiction of the nuclear family is largely a myth. And in other societies, for instance with a strong communal if not collective organization, the authority of parents is bound to be severely circumscribed by the prerogatives of the community itself. But why this should affect the purely private relations between or among parties to a marriage is not in the least clear—unless, that is, the very notion of private relations (part of the heritage of the liberal tradition of personal rights and liberties) is itself rejected. So it is entirely fair to say that the concept of the informal and term marriage are intelligible only within the conceptual tradition of personal liberties. In that sense, of course, they represent a partisan proposal. (Doubtless, however, analogues of these alternatives could be formulated for non-western traditions.)

Marriage, then, need not entail families and families need not entail marriages. Since birth control is legally permitted, both in and out of marriage, it cannot consistently be maintained that marriages must be legally controlled in order to further a biological objective, the reproduction of the race. In any event, the fantastic increase in the population of the world in our own century has made the restriction of births biologically more important than their encouragement. Also, artificial insemination would be a more reliable means of insuring the birth rate (if that were actually our prime concern); and marriage interests, on the evidence, might even interfere to some extent with the biological issue. Furthermore, since the legal protection of personal privacy is one of the strongest themes of the liberal tradition, it must appear increasingly arbitrary to interfere with the discreet expression of sexual preferences on the part of consenting adults or otherwise competent parties. Hence, if the legal control of property were generally distinguished from matters affecting marriage, and if the property rights of families and members of families and the rights of children (for example, regarding constraints on child abuse) and wards were legally specified, there would seem to be no reason at all why either informal or term marriages tailored to the idiosyncratic interests of participating parties should not be tolerated within the existing legal system.

The radical implications are obvious. For instance, there would no longer be a basis for the legal status of adultery, except perhaps contingently as grounds for the breach of a *particular* contract. Adultery would be irrelevant to a marriage by informal consent, might well be precluded or ignored by some term contract, and would in any case never as such provide grounds for a criminal action or for a civil action involving the custody of children or wards or the acquisition of property. So-called "open marriages" would not be a contradiction in terms; and of course homosexual and group marriages would no longer be anomalous. Considerations of child support, child custody, alimony, and the like would be radically altered, since they would not rest, wherever still relevant, exclusively on grounds of family responsibility. The result would be to disentangle the resolution of questions of divorce, property settlement, custody of children, and the like from just those complications that result from confusing family and marriage considerations. Conditions of divorce for instance might well be specified in a term contract or be legally construed as a matter of formal notice of some appropriate sort, without involving the law in any questions of intent, personal cruelty, or the like that might legitimately fall within the boundaries of personal privacy. Legal divorce proceedings, including settlement, therefore, could be entirely obviated. Neither children nor property would ever, logically or legally, involve the marriage relationship as such. The implied economies are actually startling—particularly for such a small conceptual adjustment (that is in any case already to some extent upon us).

The personal and moral or religious dimensions of marriage would, accordingly, be affected also. For one thing, in spite of *Humanae Vitae*, there is no consensus about the natural function of marriage or the family; it is not even clear that it makes sense to speak of the natural function of such a complex pair of institutions. Appeal to "the objective moral order established by God," however convincing to the faithful, is already implicitly more than questioned by a great many people. Still, there is no reason to think that those who participate (or would participate) in marriage (even informal and term marriage) are (or would be) disinclined to sanctify or dignify that relationship. The "natural" function interested parties tend to prefer is, clearly, harmonious cohabitation for whatever private purposes they may voluntarily subscribe to. In what conceivable sense, given the history of the institution to our own day, could this be said to be an illegitimate function? But if that function be conceded, it would be palpably unreasonable to disallow divorce, separation, annulment. In fact, in the liberal tradition, it is thought to be an improper use of the law to enforce directly, merely as such, any given moral or religious practice. On the other hand, the noticeable fragility of the marriage relationship—which, after all, is not the result of the innovations we are considering, but rather of the rigidity, confusion, inflexibility, insensitivity of existing customs to historical change itself—

requires, if marriage is to survive at all, a liberalized sense of the dignity or sanctity of that relationship.

One may, therefore, view divorce and separation not so much as a sign of the failure of marriage or a sign of a threat to the life of the institution, as a natural adjunct of the relationship. *If* marriage were viewed as a wholly personal and private relationship, there would be no plausible basis for denying that short-term contracts, termination or nonrenewal of a contract, divorce or separation for cause would be legitimate sources of relief against dissatisfaction or else of continuing liberty following satisfaction within contractual terms specified. If we could liberalize the conditions of marriage, so that those who wished to participate could experiment with whatever private arrangements they could jointly support in terms of personal taste and of whatever traditions of dignity and sanctity they could subscribe to, divorce, separation, annulment would come to be construed as the appropriate forms of terminating, rationally, an entirely private relationship—without affecting in the least the entirely distinct structure of whatever families the participating parties belong to and without implying anything at all of a pejorative nature about the marriage dissolved or terminated. What this means is that marriage cannot, on the hypothesis given, fail to become a relatively transient institution—at least for many—a source of continuing personal freedom and renewal for competent parties, weaving in and out of contact with more permanent and more fundamental family relations.

The issue is not whether it is realistic to invent new forms of marriage along the lines suggested or even to separate the concepts of marriage and family in the precise way indicated; it is rather to recognize that the impermanence, dissatisfaction, collision of values that characterize so much of contemporary marriage are effectively yielding such a separation—without, however, protecting either institution from the dislocations due to the other and without providing for the rational resolution of problems affecting either institution. For example, there is good reason to think that the incidence of juvenile delinquency and juvenile crime is in large measure due to the inertia, incompetence, inefficiency of isolated nuclear families regarding the rearing and control of their members. The transience of marriage obviously contributes to the instability of nuclear families. But it is, rather, the utter inadequacy of the nuclear family to come to grips with the broader problems of any community, that is both masked and confirmed against change by our insistence on subordinating the very existence of families to the condition of marriage. *If* marriages are as unstable as they appear to be and *if* families are as important as they are thought to be to the stable life of a community—for instance to the effectiveness of its moral values, to the rational management of its resources—then it cannot but be entirely irrational to conflate the two institutions or, worse, to make the institution of the family wholly or largely dependent on that of the more transient marriage.

There may well be, therefore, an actual need to experiment with separating the institutions in a more formal way—not just to speculate about the implications of such a change.

11

Conditions of Liberation

JEAN-PAUL SARTRE

(b. 1905)

A philosopher whose works have exercised considerable influence upon contemporary culture, Sartre is generally considered to be the most articulate exponent of the philosophy of existentialism. He was educated at the Lycée Henri IV and at the Ecole Normale Supérieure in Paris. Later he became a teacher at the Lycée du Havre, and from 1935 to 1942 taught philosophy at the Lycée Condorcet. With the outbreak of World War II he served in the French Army, and was a prisoner of war from 1940 to 1941. For the next three years he was active in the underground resistance movement. One of the founders of the journal Les Temps Modernes, *he still serves as one of its directors. In 1964 he was offered the Nobel Prize for Literature, but refused to accept it. Among his philosophical works are* Being and Nothingness *(1943, translated 1956);* Existentialism *(1946, translated 1947); and* Critique of Dialectical Reason *(1960). He has also written prolifically in fields other than philosophy. His most well-known novel is* Nausea *(1944), and he has written several plays, among which are* The Flies *(1942),* No Exit *(1944), and* The Prisoners of Altona *(1959), in addition to a considerable body of literary criticism.*

EACH ACT DEFINES MANKIND

What is meant by the term *existentialism?*. . .

Actually, it is the least scandalous, the most austere of doctrines. It is intended strictly for specialists and philosophers. Yet it can be defined easily. What complicates matters is that there are two kinds of existentialist; first, those who are Christian, among whom I would include Jaspers and Gabriel Marcel, both Catholic; and on the other hand the atheistic existentialists, among whom I class Heidegger, and then the French existentialists and myself. What they have in common is that they think that existence precedes essence, or, if you prefer, that subjectivity must be the starting point.

Just what does that mean? Let us consider some object that is manufactured, for example, a book or a paper-cutter: here is an object which has been made by an artisan whose inspiration came from a concept. He referred to the concept of what a paper-cutter is and likewise to a known method of production, which is part of the concept, something which is, by and large, a routine. Thus, the paper-cutter is at once an object produced in a certain way and, on the other hand, one having a specific use; and one can not postulate a man who produces a paper-cutter but does not know what it is used for. Therefore, let us say that, for the paper-cutter, essence—that is, the ensemble of both the production routines and the properties which enable it to be both produced and defined—precedes existence. Thus, the presence of the paper-cutter or book in front of me is determined. Therefore, we have here a technical view of the world whereby it can be said that production precedes existence.

When we conceive God as the Creator, He is generally thought of as a superior sort of artisan. Whatever doctrine we may be considering, whether one like that of Descartes or that of Leibnitz, we always grant that will more or less follows understanding or, at the very least, accompanies it, and that when God creates He knows exactly what He is creating. Thus, the concept of man in the mind of God is comparable to the concept of paper-cutter in the mind of the manufacturer, and, following certain techniques and a conception, God produces man, just as the artisan, following a definition and a technique, makes a paper-cutter. Thus, the individual man is the realisation of a certain concept in the divine intelligence.

In the eighteenth century, the atheism of the *philosophes* discarded the idea of God, but not so much for the notion that essence precedes existence. To a certain extent, this idea is found everywhere; we find it in Diderot, in Voltaire, and even in Kant. Man has a human nature; this human nature, which is the concept of the human, is found in all men,

From Existentialism, *Philosophical Library, New York (1945, trans. from the French in 1947 by Bernard Frechtman), pp. 14, 15–28, 34–39, 45–46, 49–51.*

which means that each man is a particular example of a universal concept, man. In Kant, the result of this universality is that the wild-man, the natural man, as well as the bourgeois, are circumscribed by the same definition and have the same basic qualities. Thus, here too the essence of man precedes the historical existence that we find in nature.

Atheistic existentialism, which I represent, is more coherent. It states that if God does not exist, there is at least one being in whom existence precedes essence, a being who exists before he can be defined by any concept, and that this being is man, or, as Heidegger says, human reality. What is meant here by saying that existence precedes essence? It means that, first of all, man exists, turns up, appears on the scene, and, only afterwards, defines himself. If man, as the existentialist conceives him, is indefinable, it is because at first he is nothing. Only afterward will he be something, and he himself will have made what he will be. Thus, there is no human nature, since there is no God to conceive it. Not only is man what he conceives himself to be, but he is also only what he wills himself to be after his thrust toward existence.

Man is nothing else but what he makes of himself. Such is the first principle of existentialism. It is also what is called subjectivity, the name we are labeled with when charges are brought against us. But what do we mean by this, if not that man has a greater dignity than a stone or table? For we mean that man first exists, that is, that man first of all is the being who hurls himself toward a future and who is conscious of imagining himself as being in the future. Man is at the start a plan which is aware of itself, rather than a patch of moss, a piece of garbage, or a cauliflower; nothing exists prior to this plan; there is nothing in heaven; man will be what he will have planned to be. Not what he will want to be. Because by the word "will" we generally mean a conscious decision, which is subsequent to what we have already made of ourselves. I may want to belong to a political party, write a book, get married; but all that is only a manifestation of an earlier, more spontaneous choice that is called "will." But if existence really does precede essence, man is responsible for what he is. Thus, existentialism's first move is to make every man aware of what he is and to make the full responsibility of his existence rest on him. And when we say that a man is responsible for himself, we do not only mean that he is responsible for his own individuality, but that he is responsible for all men.

The word subjectivism has two meanings, and our opponents play on the two. Subjectivism means, on the one hand, that an individual chooses and makes himself; and, on the other, that it is impossible for man to transcend human subjectivity. The second of these is the essential meaning of existentialism. When we say that man chooses his own self, we mean that every one of us does likewise; but we also mean by that that in making this choice he also chooses all men. In fact, in creating the man that we want to be, there is not a single one of our acts which does not at the same time create an image of man as we think he ought to be. To choose to be this or that is to affirm at the same time the value of what we choose, because we can never choose evil. We always choose the good, and nothing can be good for us without being good for all.

If, on the other hand, existence precedes essence, and if we grant that we exist and fashion our image at one and the same time, the image is valid for everybody and for our whole age. Thus, our responsibility is much greater than we might have supposed, because it involves all mankind. If I am a workingman and choose to join a Christian trade-union rather than be a communist, and if by being a member I want to show that the best thing for man is resignation, that the kingdom of man is not of this world, I am not only involving my own case—I want to be resigned for everyone. As as result, my action has involved all humanity. To take a more individual matter, if I want to marry, to have children; even if this marriage depends solely on my own circumstances or passion or wish, I am involving all humanity in monogamy and not merely myself. Therefore, I am responsible for myself and for everyone else. I am creating a certain image of man of my own choosing. In choosing myself, I choose man.

This helps us understand what the actual content is of such rather grandiloquent words as anguish, forlornness, despair. As you will see, it's all quite simple.

First, what is meant by anguish? The existentialists say at once that man is anguish. What that means is this: the man who involves himself and who realizes that he is not only the person he chooses to be, but also a law-maker who is, at the same time, choosing all mankind as well as himself, can not help escape the feeling of his total and deep responsibility. Of course, there are many people who are not anxious; but we claim that they are hiding their anxiety, that they are fleeing from it. Certainly, many people believe that when they do something, they themselves are the only ones involved, and when someone says to them, "What if everyone acted that way?" they shrug their shoulders and answer, "Everyone doesn't act that way." But really, one should always ask himself, "What would happen if everybody looked at things that way?" There is no escaping this disturbing thought except by a kind of double-dealing. A man who lies and makes excuses for himself by saying "not everybody does that," is someone with an uneasy conscience, because the act of lying implies that a universal value is conferred upon the lie.

Anguish is evident even when it conceals itself. This is the anguish that Kierkegaard called the anguish of Abraham. You know the story: an angel has ordered Abraham to sacrifice his son; if it really were an angel who has come and said, "You are Abraham, you shall sacrifice your son," everything would be all right. But everyone might first wonder, "Is it really an angel, and am I really Abraham? What proof do I have?"

There was a madwoman who had hallucinations; someone used to speak to her on the telephone and give her orders. Her doctor asked her, "Who is it who talks to you?" She answered, "He says it's God." What proof did she really have that it was God? If an angel comes to me, what proof is there that it's an angel? And if I hear voices, what proof is there that they come from heaven and not from hell, or from the subconscious, or a pathological condition? What proves that they are addressed to me? What proof is there that I have been appointed to impose my choice and my conception of man on humanity? I'll never find any proof or sign to convince me of that. If a voice addresses me, it is always for me to decide that this is the angel's voice; if I consider that such an act is a good one, it is I who will choose to say that it is good rather than bad.

Now, I'm not being singled out as an Abraham, and yet at every moment I'm obliged to perform exemplary acts. For every man, everything happens as if all mankind had its eyes fixed on him and were guiding itself by what he does. And every man ought to say to himself, "Am I really the kind of man who has the right to act in such a way that humanity might guide itself by my actions?" And if he does not say that to himself, he is masking his anguish.

There is no question here of the kind of anguish which would lead to quietism, to inaction. It is a matter of a simple sort of anguish that anybody who has had responsibilities is familiar with. For example, when a military officer takes the responsibility for an attack and sends a certain number of men to death, he chooses to do so, and in the main he alone makes the choice. Doubtless, orders come from above, but they are too broad; he interprets them, and on this interpretation depend the lives of ten or fourteen or twenty men. In making a decision he can not help having a certain anguish. All leaders know this anguish. That doesn't keep them from acting; on the contrary, it is the very condition of their action. For it implies that they envisage a number of possibilities, and when they choose one, they realize that it has value only because it is chosen. We shall see that this kind of anguish, which is the kind that existentialism describes, is explained, in addition, by a direct responsibility to the other men whom it involves. It is not a curtain separating us from action, but is part of action itself.

When we speak of forlornness, a term Heidegger was fond of, we mean only that God does not exist and that we have to face all the consequences of this. The existentialist is strongly opposed to a certain kind of secular ethics which would like to abolish God with the least possible expense. About 1880, some French teachers tried to set up a secular ethics which went something like this: God is a useless and costly hypothesis; we are discarding it; but, meanwhile, in order for there to be an ethics, a society, a civilization, it is essential that certain values be taken seriously and they they be considered as having an *a priori* existence. It must be obligatory, *a priori*, to be honest, not to lie, not to beat your wife, to have children, etc., etc. So we're going to try a little device which will make it possible to show that values exist all the same, inscribed in a heaven of ideas, though otherwise God does not exist. In other words—and this, I believe, is the tendency of everything called reformism in France—nothing will be changed if God does not exist. We shall find ourselves with the same norms of honesty, progress, and humanism, and we shall have made of God an outdated hypothesis which will peacefully die off by itself.

The existentialist, on the contrary, thinks it very distressing that God does not exist, because all possibility of finding values in a heaven of ideas disappears along with Him; there can no longer be an *a priori* Good, since there is no infinite and perfect consciousness to think it. Nowhere is it written that the Good exists, that we must be honest, that we must not lie; because the fact is we are on a plane where there are only men. Dostoievsky said, "If God didn't exist, everything would be possible." That is the very starting point of existentialism. Indeed, everything is permissible if God does not exist, and as a result man is forlorn, because neither within him nor without does he find anything to cling to. He can't start making excuses for himself.

If existence really does precede essence, there is no explaining things away by reference to a fixed and given human nature. In other words, there is no determinism, man is free, man is freedom. On the other hand, if God does not exist, we find no values or commands to turn to which legitimize our conduct. So, in the bright realm of values, we have no excuse behind us, nor justification before us. We are alone, with no excuses.

That is the idea I shall try to convey when I say that man is condemned to be free. Condemned, because he did not create himself, yet, in other respects is free; because, once thrown into the world, he is responsible for everything he does. The existentialist does not believe in the power of passion. He will never agree that a sweeping passion is a ravaging torrent which fatally leads a man to certain acts and is therefore an excuse. He thinks that man is responsible for his passion.

The existentialist does not think that man is going to help himself by finding in the world some omen by which to orient himself. Because he thinks that man will interpret the omen to suit himself. Therefore, he thinks that man, with no support and no aid, is condemned every moment to invent man. Ponge, in a very fine article, has said, "Man is the future of man." That's exactly it. But if it is taken to mean that this future is recorded in heaven, that God sees it, then it is false, because it would really no longer be a future. If it is taken to mean that, whatever a man may be, there is a future to be forged, a virgin future before him, then this remark is sound. But then we are forlorn. . . .

As for despair, the term has a very simple meaning. It means that we shall confine ourselves to reckoning only with what depends upon our will, or on the ensemble of probabilities which make our action possible. When we want something, we always have to reckon with probabilities. I may be counting on the arrival of a friend. The friend is coming by rail or street-car; this supposes that the train will arrive on schedule, or that the street-car will not jump the track. I am left in the realm of possibility; but possibilities are to be reckoned with only to the point where my action comports with the ensemble of these possibilities, and no further. The moment the possibilities I am considering are not rigorously involved by my action, I ought to disengage myself from them, because no God, no scheme, can adapt the world and its possibilities to my will. When Descartes said, "Conquer yourself rather than the world," he meant essentially the same thing.

The Marxists to whom I have spoken reply, "You can rely on the support of others in your action, which obviously has certain limits because you're not going to live forever. That means: rely on both what others are doing elsewhere to help you, in China, in Russia, and what they will do later on, after your death, to carry on the action and lead it to its fulfillment, which will be the revolution. You even *have* to rely upon that, otherwise you're immoral." I reply at once that I will always rely on fellow-fighters insofar as these comrades are involved with me in a common struggle, in the unity of a party or a group in which I can more or less make my weight felt; that is, one whose ranks I am in as a fighter and whose movements I am aware of at every moment. In such a situation, relying on the unity and will of the party is exactly like counting on the fact that the train will arrive on time or that the car won't jump the track. But, given that man is free and that there is no human nature for me to depend on, I can not count on men whom I do not know by relying on human goodness or man's concern for the good of society. I don't know what will become of the Russian revolution; I may make an example of it to the extent that at the present time it is apparent that the proletariat plays a part in Russia that it plays in no other nation. But I can't swear that this will inevitably lead to a triumph of the proletariat. I've got to limit myself to what I see.

Given that men are free and that tomorrow they will freely decide what man will be, I cannot be sure that, after my death, fellow-fighters will carry on my work to bring it to its maximum perfection. Tomorrow, after my death, some men may decide to set up Fascism, and the others may be cowardly and muddled enough to let them do it. Fascism will then be the human reality, so much the worse for us.

Actually, things will be as man will have decided they are to be. Does that mean that I should abandon myself to quietism? No. First, I should involve myself; then, act on the old saw, "Nothing ventured, nothing gained." Nor does it mean that I shouldn't belong to a party, but rather that I shall have no illusions and shall do what I can. For example, suppose I ask myself, "Will socialization, as such, ever come about?" I know nothing about it. All I know is that I'm going to do everything in my power to bring it about. Beyond that, I can't count on anything. Quietism is the attitude of people who say, "Let others do what I can't do." The doctrine I am presenting is the very opposite of quietism, since it declares, "There is no reality except in action." Moreover, it goes further, since it adds, "Man is nothing else than his plan; he exists only to the extent that he fulfills himself; he is therefore nothing else than the ensemble of his acts, nothing else than his life."

According to this, we can understand why our doctrine horrifies certain people. Because often the only way they can bear their wretchedness is to think, "Circumstances have been against me. What I've been and done doesn't show my true worth. To be sure, I've had no great love, no great friendship, but that's because I haven't met a man or woman who was worthy. The books I've written haven't been very good because I haven't had the proper leisure. I haven't had children to devote myself to because I didn't find a man with whom I could have spent my life. So there remains within me, unused and quite viable, a host of propensities, inclinations, possibilities, that one wouldn't guess from the mere series of things I've done."

Now, for the existentialist there is really no love other than one which manifests itself in a person's being in love. There is no genius other than one which is expressed in works of art; the genius of Proust is the sum of Proust's works; the genius of Racine is his series of tragedies. Outside of that, there is nothing. Why say that Racine could have written another tragedy, when he didn't write it? A man is involved in life, leaves his impress on it, and outside of that there is nothing. To be sure, this may seem a harsh thought to someone whose life hasn't been a success. But, on the other hand, it prompts people to understand that reality alone is what counts, that dreams, expectations, and hopes warrant no more than to define a man as a disappointed dream, as miscarried hopes, as vain expectations. In other words, to define him negatively and not positively. However, when we say, "You are nothing else than your life," that does not imply that the artist will be judged solely on the basis of his works of art; a thousand other things will contribute toward summing him up. What we mean is that a man is nothing else than a series of undertakings, that he is the sum, the organization, the ensemble of the relationships which make up these undertakings. . . .

Besides, if it is impossible to find in every man some universal essence which would be human nature, yet there does exist a universal human condition. It's not by chance that today's thinkers speak more readily of man's condition than of his nature. By condition they mean, more or less definitely, the *a priori* limits which outline man's fundamental situation in the universe. Historical situations vary; a man may be born a slave in a pagan society or a feudal lord or a proletarian. What does not vary is the necessity for him to exist in the world, to be at work there, to be there in the midst of other people, and to be mortal there. The limits are neither subjective or objective, or, rather, they have an objective and a subjective side. Objective because they are to be found everywhere and are recognizable everywhere; subjective because they are *lived* and are nothing if man does not live them, that is, freely determine his existence with reference to them. And though the configurations may differ, at least none of them are completely strange to me, because they all appear as attempts either to pass beyond these limits or recede from them or deny them or adapt to them. Consequently, every configuration, however individual it may be, has a universal value.

Every configuration, even the Chinese, the Indian, or the Negro, can be understood by a Westerner. "Can be understood" means that by virtue of a situation that he can imagine, a European of 1945 can, in like manner, push himself to his limits and reconstitute within himself the configuration of the Chinese, the Indian, or the African. Every configuration has universality in the sense that every configuration can be understood by every man. This does not at all mean that this configuration defines man forever, but that it can be met with again. Thre is always a way to understand the idiot, the child, the savage, the foreigner, provided one has the necessary information. . . .

Moral choice is to be compared to the making of a work of art. And before going any further, let it be said at once that we are not dealing here with an aesthetic ethics, because our opponents are so dishonest that they even accuse us of that. The example I've chosen is a comparison only.

Having said that, may I ask whether anyone has ever accused an artist who had painted a picture of not having drawn his inspiration from rules set up *a priori*? Has anyone ever asked, "What painting ought he to make?" It is clearly understood that there is no definite painting to be made, that the artist is engaged in the making of his painting, and that the painting to be made is precisely the painting he will have made. It is clearly understood that there are no *a priori* aesthetic values, but that there are values which appear subsequently in the coherence of the painting, in the correspondence between what the artist intended and the result. Nobody can tell what the painting of tomorrow will be like. Painting can be judged only after it has once been made. What connection does that have with ethics? We are in the same creative situation. We never say that a work of art is arbitrary. When we speak of a canvas of Picasso, we never say that it is arbitrary; we understand quite well that he was making himself what he is at the very time he was painting, that the ensemble of his work is embodied in his life.

The same holds on the ethical plane. What art and ethics have in common is that we have creation and invention in both cases. We can not decide *a priori* what there is to be done. . . . Man makes himself. He isn't ready made at the start. In choosing his ethics, he makes himself, and force of circumstances is such that he can not abstain from choosing one. We define man only in relationship to involvement. It is therefore absurd to charge us with arbitrariness of choice.

J. O. URMSON

(b. 1915)

J. O. Urmson is Fellow of Corpus Christi College, University of Oxford, and formerly Professor of Philosophy in the University of St. Andrews, and Visiting Associate Professor at Princeton University. His publications include The Concise Encyclopedia of Western Philosophy and Philosophers *(which he edited), and* Philosophical Analysis *(1956)*

SAINTS AND HEROES

Moral philosophers tend to discriminate, explicitly or implicitly, three types of action from the point of view of moral worth. First, they recognize actions that are a duty, or obligatory, or that we ought to perform, treating these terms as approximately synonymous; second, they recognize actions that are right in so far as they are permissible from a moral standpoint and not ruled out by moral considerations, but that are not morally required of us, like the lead of this or that card at bridge; third, they recognize actions that are wrong, that we ought not to do. Some moral philosophers, indeed, could hardly discriminate even these three types of action consistently with the rest of their philosophy; Moore, for example, could hardly recognize a class of morally indifferent actions, permissible but not enjoined, since it is to be presumed that good or ill of some sort will result from the most trivial of our actions. But most moral philosophers recognize these three types of action and attempt to provide a moral theory that will make intelligible such a threefold classification.

To my mind this threefold classification, or any classification that is merely a variation on or elaboration of it, is totally inadequate to the facts of morality; any moral theory that leaves room only for such a classification will in consequence also be inadequate. My main task in this paper will be to show the inadequacy of such a classification by drawing attention to two of the types of action that most conspicuously lie outside such a classification; I shall go on to hazard some views on what sort of theory will most easily cope with the facts to which I draw attention, but the facts are here the primary interest.

From Essays in Moral Philosophy, *ed. A. I. Melden (Seattle: University of Washington Press, 1958), pp. 198-216.*

We sometimes call a person a saint, or an action saintly, using the word "saintly" in a purely moral sense with no religious implications; also we sometimes call a person a hero or an action heroic. It is too clear to need argument that the words "saint" and "hero" are at least normally used in such a way as to be favorably evaluative; it would be impossible to claim that this evaluation is always moral, for clearly we sometimes call a person a saint when evaluating him religiously rather than morally and may call a person the hero of a game or athletic contest in which no moral qualities were displayed, but I shall take it that no formal argument is necessary to show that at least sometimes we use both words for moral evaluation.

If "hero" and "saint" can be words of moral evaluation, we may proceed to the attempt to make explicit the criteria that we implicitly employ for their use in moral contexts. It appears that we so use them in more than one type of situation, and that there is a close parallel between the ways in which the two terms "hero" and "saint" are used; we shall here notice three types of situation in which they are used which seem to be sufficiently different to merit distinction. As the first two types of situation to be noticed are ones that can be readily subsumed under the threefold classification mentioned above, it will be sufficient here to note them and pass on to the third type of situation, which, since it cannot be subsumed under that classification, is for the purposes of this paper the most interesting.

A person may be called a saint (1) if he does his duty regularly in contexts in which inclination, desire, or self-interest would lead most people not to do it, and does so as a result of exercising abnormal self-control; parallel to this a person may be called a hero (1) if he does his duty in contexts in which terror, fear, or a drive to self-preservation would lead most men not to do it, and does so by exercising abnormal self-control. Similarly for actions: an action may be called saintly (1) if it is a case of duty done by virtue of self-control in a context in which most men would be led astray by inclination or self-interest, and an action may be called heroic (1) if it is a case of duty done by virtue of self-control in a context in which most men would be led astray by fear or a drive for self-preservation. The only difference between the saintly and the heroic in this sort of situation is that the one involves resistance to desire and self-interest; the other, resistance to fear and self-preservation. This is quite a clear difference, though there may be marginal cases, or cases in which motives were mixed, in which it would be equally appropriate to call an action indifferently saintly or heroic. It is easy to give examples of both the heroic and the saintly as distinguished above: the unmarried daughter does the saintly deed of staying at home to tend her ailing and widowed father; the terrified doctor heroically stays by his patients in a plague-ridden city.

A person may be called a saint (2) if he does his duty in contexts in which inclination or self-interest would lead most men not to do it, not, as in the previous paragraph, by abnormal self-control, but without effort; parallel to this a person may be called a hero (2) if he does his duty in contexts in which fear would lead most men not to do it, and does so without effort. The corresponding accounts of a saintly (2) or heroic (2) action can easily be derived. Here we have the conspicuously virtuous deed, in the Aristotelian sense, as opposed to the conspicuously self-controlled, encratic deed of the previous paragraph. People thus purged of temptation or disciplined against fear may be rare, but Aristotle thought there could be such; there is a tendency today to think of such people as merely lucky or unimaginative, but Aristotle thought more highly of them than of people who need to exercise self-control.

It is clear that, in the two types of situation so far considered, we are dealing with actions that fall under the concept of duty. Roughly, we are calling a person saintly or heroic because he does his duty in such difficult contexts that most men would fail in them. Since for the purposes of this paper I am merely conceding that we do use the term "saintly" and "heroic" in these ways, it is unnecessary here to spend time arguing that we do so use them or in illustrating such uses. So used, the threefold classification of actions whose adequacy I wish to deny can clearly embrace them. I shall therefore pass immediately to a third use of the terms "heroic" and "saintly" which I am not merely willing to concede but obliged to establish.

I contend, then, that we may also call a person a saint (3) if he does actions that are far beyond the limits of his duty, whether by control of contrary inclination and interest or without effort; parallel to this we may call a person a hero (3) if he does actions that are far beyond the bounds of his duty, whether by control of natural fear or without effort. Such actions are saintly (3) or heroic (3). Here, as it seems to me, we have the hero or saint, heroic or saintly deed, par excellence; until now we have been considering but minor saints and heroes. We have considered the, certainly, heroic action of the doctor who does his duty by sticking to his patients in a plague-stricken city; we have now to consider the case of the doctor who, no differently situated from countless other doctors in other places, volunteers to join the depleted medical forces in that city. Previously we were considering the soldier who heroically does his duty in the face of such dangers as would cause most to shirk—the sort of man who is rightly awarded the Military Medal in the British Army; we have now to consider the case of the soldier who does more than his superior officers would ever ask him to do—the man to whom, often posthumously, the Victoria Cross is awarded. Similarly, we have to turn from saintly self-discipline in the way of duty to the dedicated, self-effacing life in the service of others which is not even contemplated by the majority of upright, kind, and honest men, let alone expected of them. . . .

But morality, I take it, is something that should serve human needs, not something that incidentally sweeps man up with itself, and to show that a morality was ideal would be to show that it best served man—man as he is and as he can be expected to become, not man as he would be if he were perfectly rational or an incorporeal angel. Just as it would be fatuous to build our machines so that they would give the best results according to an abstract conception of mechanical principles, and is much more desirable to design them to withstand to some extent our ham-fistedness, ignorance, and carelessness, so our morality must be one that will work. In the only sense of "ideal" that is of importance in action, it is part of the ideal that a moral code should actually help to contribute to human well-being, and a moral code that would work only for angels (for whom it would in any case be unnecessary) would be a far from ideal moral code for human beings. There is, indeed, a place for ideals that are practically unworkable in human affairs, as there is a place for the blueprint of a machine that will never go into production; but it is not the place of such ideals to serve as a basic code of duties.

If, then, we are aiming at a moral code that will best serve human needs, a code that is ideal in the sense that a world in which such a code is acknowledged will be a better place than a world in which some other sort of moral code is acknowledged, it seems that there are ample grounds why our code should distinguish between basic rules, summarily set forth in simple rules and binding on all, and the higher flights of morality of which saintliness and heroism are outstanding examples. These grounds I shall enumerate at once.

1. It is important to give a special status of urgency, and to exert exceptional pressure, in those matters in which compliance with the demands of morality by all is indispensable. An army without men of heroic valor would be impoverished, but without general attention to the duties laid down in military law it would become a mere rabble. Similarly, while life in a world without its saints and heroes would be impoverished, it would only be poor and not necessarily brutish or short as when basic duties are neglected.

2. If we are to exact basic duties like debts, and censure failure, such duties must be, in ordinary circumstances, within the capacity of the ordinary man. It would be silly for us to say to ourselves, our children and our fellow men, "This and that you and everyone else must do," if the acts in question are such that manifestly but few could bring themselves to do them, though we may ourselves resolve to try to be of that few. To take a parallel from positive law, the prohibition laws asked too much of the American people and were consequently broken systematically; and as people got used to breaking the law a general lowering of respect for the law naturally followed; it no longer seemed that a law was something that everybody could be expected to obey. Similarly in Britain the gambling laws, some of which are utterly unpractical, have fallen into contempt as a body. So, if we were to represent the heroic act of sacrificing one's life for one's comrades as a basic duty, the effect would be to lower the degree of urgency and stringency that the notion of duty does in fact possess. The basic moral code must not be in part too far beyond the capacity of the ordinary men on ordinary occasions, or a general breakdown of compliance with the moral code would be an inevitable

consequence; duty would seem to be something high and unattainable, and not for "the likes of us." Admirers of the Sermon on the Mount do not in practice, and could not, treat failure to turn the other cheek and to give one's cloak also as being on all fours with breaches of the Ten Commandments, however earnestly they themselves try to live a Christian life.

3. A moral code, if it is to be a code, must be formulable, and if it is to be a code to be observed it must be formulable in rules of manageable complexity. The ordinary man has to apply and interpret this code without recourse to a Supreme Court or House of Lords. But one can have such rules only in cases in which a type of action that is reasonably easy to recognize is almost invariably desirable or undesirable, as killing is almost invariably undesirable and promise-keeping almost invariably desirable. Where no definite rule of manageable complexity can be justified, we cannot work on that moral plane on which types of action can be enjoined or condemned as duty or crime. It has no doubt often been the case that a person who has gone off to distant parts to nurse lepers has thereby done a deed of great moral worth. But such an action is not merely too far beyond average human capacity to be regarded as a duty, as was insisted in (2) above; it would be quite ridiculous for everyone, however circumstanced, to be expected to go off and nurse lepers. But it would be absurd to try to formulate complicated rules to determine in just what circumstances such an action is a duty. This same point can readily be applied to such less spectacular matters as excusing legitimate debts or nursing sick neighbors.

4. It is part of the notion of a duty that we have a right to demand compliance from others even where we are interested parties. I may demand that you keep your promises to me, tell me the truth, and do me no violence, and I may reproach you if you transgress. But however admirable the tending of strangers in sickness may be it is not a basic duty, and we are not entitled to reproach those to whom we are strangers if they do not tend us in sickness; nor can I tell you, if you fail to give me a cigarette when I have run out, that you have failed in your duty to me, however much you may subsequently reproach yourself for your meanness if you do so fail. A line must be drawn between what we can expect and demand from others and what we can merely hope for and receive with gratitude when we get it; duty falls on one side of this line, and other acts with moral value on the other, and rightly so.

5. In the case of basic moral duties we act to some extent under constraint. We have no choice but to apply pressure on each other to conform in these fundamental matters; here moral principles are like public laws rather than like private ideals. But free choice of the better course of action is always preferable to action under pressure, even when the pressure is but moral. When possible, therefore, it is better that pressure should not be applied and that there should be encouragement and commendation for performance rather than outright demands and censure in the event of nonperformance. There are no doubt degrees in this matter. Some pressure may reasonably be brought to persuade a person

to go some way beyond basic duty in the direction of kindliness and forbearance, to be not merely a just man but also not too hard a man. But, while there is nothing whatever objectionable in the idea of someone's being pressed to carry out such a basic duty as promise-keeping, there is something horrifying in the thought of pressure being brought on him to perform an act of heroism. Though the man might feel himself morally called upon to do the deed, it would be a moral outrage to apply pressure on him to do such a deed as sacrificing his life for others.

These five points make it clear why I do not think that the distinction of basic duty from other acts of moral worth, which I claim to detect in ordinary moral thought, is a sign of the inferiority of our everyday moral thinking to that of the general run of moral theorists. It in no way involves anyone in acquiescing in a second best. No doubt from the agent's point of view it is imperative that he should endeavor to live up to the highest ideals of behavior that he can think of, and if an action falls within the ideal it is for him irrelevant whether or not it is a duty or some more supererogatory act. But it simply does not follow that the distinction is in every way unimportant, for it is important that we should not demand ideal conduct from others in the way in which we must demand basic morality from them, or blame them equally for failures in all fields. It is not cynicism to make the minimum positive demands upon one's fellow men; but to characterize an act as a duty is so to demand it.

Thus we may regard the imperatives of duty as prohibiting behavior that is intolerable if men are to live together in society and demanding the minimum of cooperation toward the same end; that is why we have to treat compliance as compulsory and dereliction as liable to public censure. We do not need to ask with Bentham whether pushpin is as good as poetry, with Mill whether it is better to be Socrates dissatisfied or a fool satisfied, or with Moore whether a beautiful world with no one to see it would have intrinsic worth; what is and what is not tolerable in society depends on no such nice discrimination. Utilitarians, when attempting to justify the main rules of duty in terms of a *summum bonum*, have surely invoked many different types of utilitarian justification, ranging from the avoidance of the intolerable to the fulfillment of the last detail of a most rarefied ideal.

Thus I wish to suggest that utilitarianism can best accommodate the facts to which I have drawn attention; but I have not wished to support any particular view about the supreme good or the importance of pleasure. By utilitarianism I mean only a theory that moral justification of actions must be in terms of results. We can be content to say that duty is mainly concerned with the avoidance of intolerable results, while other forms of moral behavior have more positive aims.

To summarize, I have suggested that the trichotomy of duties, indifferent actions, and wrongdoing is inadequate. There are many kinds of action that involve going beyond duty proper, saintly and heroic actions being conspicuous examples of such kinds and action. It has been my main concern to note this point and to ask moral philosophers to theorize in a way that does not tacitly deny it, as most traditional theories have. But I have also been so rash as to suggest that we may look upon our duties as basic requirements to be universally demanded as providing the only tolerable basis of social life. The higher flights of morality can then be regarded as more positive contributions that go beyond what is universally to be exacted; but while not exacted publicly they are clearly equally pressing *in foro interno* on those who are not content merely to avoid the intolerable. Whether this should be called a version of utilitarianism, as I suggest, is a matter of small moment.

JOHN DEWEY

(1859–1952)

A native of Vermont, Dewey graduated from the University of Vermont in 1879. After three years of teaching high school, he entered Johns Hopkins University, where he was particularly influenced by the courses he took under Charles Peirce—the philosopher who originally developed the theory of pragmatism—and the Hegelian George S. Morris. Dewey's doctoral thesis dealt with the psychology of Kant. Upon receiving his Ph.D. in 1884, he joined the faculty of philosophy at the University of Michigan, and taught there almost continuously until 1894. In that year he became head of the Department of Philosophy and Psychology at the University of Chicago, where he established his historic Laboratory School, out of whose innovative procedures he developed many of his pioneering educational theories. In 1904 he became a professor at Columbia University, first at Teachers College, then in the department of philosophy. He retired in 1930. Dewey was active in social reform movements, and was instrumental in founding the American Association of University Professors. He studied educational systems in China, Japan, Turkey, and Russia, and received honorary doctorates from Vermont, Johns Hopkins, Peking National University, and the University of Paris. In 1929 he delivered the Gifford lectures. Dewey was a prolific writer, and the following titles represent only a small portion of his work: Human Nature and Conduct *(1922),* Experience and Nature *(1925),* Philosophy and Civilization *(1931),* Art as Experience *(1934),* A Common Faith *(1934),* Logic: The Theory of Inquiry *(1938), and* Theory of Valuation *(1939).*

HUMAN NATURE, PRIVATE PROPERTY, AND WAR

I have come to the conclusion that those who give different answers to the question I have asked in the title of this article are talking about different things. This statement in itself, however, is too easy a way out of the problem to be satisfactory. For there is a real problem, and so far as the question is a practical one instead of an academic one, I think the proper answer is that human nature *does* change.

By the practical side of the question, I mean the question whether or not important, almost fundamental, changes in the ways of human belief and action have taken place and are capable of still taking place. But to put this question in its proper perspective, we have first to recognize the sense in which human nature does not change. I do not think it can be shown that the innate needs of men have changed since man became man or that there is any evidence that they will change as long as man is on the earth.

By "needs" I mean the inherent demands that men make because of their constitution. Needs for food and drink and for moving about, for example, are so much a part of our being that we cannot imagine any condition under which they would cease to be. There are other things not so directly physical that seem to me equally engrained in human nature. I would mention as examples the need for some kind of companionship; the need for exhibiting energy, for bringing one's powers to bear upon surrounding conditions; the need for both co-operation with and emulation of one's fellows for mutual aid and combat alike; the need for some sort of aesthetic expression and satisfaction; the need to lead and to follow; etc.

Whether my particular examples are well chosen or not does not matter so much as does recognition of the fact that there are some tendencies so integral a part of human nature that the latter would not be human nature if they changed. These tendencies used to be called instincts. Psychologists are now more chary of using that word than they used to be. But the word by which the tendencies are called does not matter much in comparison to the fact that human nature has its own constitution.

Where we are likely to go wrong after the fact is recognized that there is something unchangeable in the structure of human nature is the inference we draw from it. We suppose that the manifestation of these needs is also unalterable. We suppose that the manifestations we have got used to are as natural and as unalterable as are the needs from which they spring.

From The Rotarian *(February, 1938). The original title of the article, to which Dewey refers, was "Does Human Nature Change?"*

The need for food is so imperative that we call the persons insane who persistently refuse to take nourishment. But what kinds of food are wanted and used is a matter of acquired habit influenced by both physical environment and social custom. To civilized people today, eating human flesh is an entirely unnatural thing. Yet there have been peoples to whom it seemed natural because it was socially authorized and even highly esteemed. There are well-accredited stories of persons, needing support from others, who have refused palatable and nourishing foods because they were not accustomed to them; the alien foods were so "unnatural" they preferred to starve rather than eat them.

Aristotle spoke for an entire social order as well as for himself when he said that slavery existed by nature. He would have regarded efforts to abolish slavery from society as an idle and utopian effort to change human nature where it was unchangeable. For according to him it was not simply the desire to be a master that was engrained in human nature. There were persons who were born with such an inherently slavish nature that it did violence to human nature to set them free.

The assertion that human nature cannot be changed is heard when social changes are urged as reforms and improvements of existing conditions. It is always heard when the proposed changes in institutions or conditions stand in sharp opposition to what exists. If the conservative were wiser, he would rest his objections in most cases, not upon the unchangeability of human nature, but upon the inertia of custom; upon the resistance that acquired habits offer to change after they are once acquired. It is hard to teach an old dog new tricks and it is harder yet to teach society to adopt customs which are contrary to those which have long prevailed. Conservatism of this type would be intelligent and it would compel those wanting change not only to moderate their pace, but also to ask how the changes they desire could be introduced with a minimum of shock and dislocation.

Nevertheless, there are few social changes that can be opposed on the ground that they are contrary to human nature itself. A proposal to have a society get along without food and drink is one of the few that are of this kind. Proposals to form communities in which there is no cohabitation have been made and the communities have endured for a time. But they are so nearly contrary to human nature that they have not endured long. These cases are almost the only ones in which social change can be opposed simply on the ground that human nature cannot be changed.

Take the institution of war, one of the oldest, most socially reputable of all human institutions. Efforts for stable peace are often opposed on the ground that man is by nature a fighting animal and that this phase of his nature is unalterable. The failure of peace movements in the past can be cited in support of this view. In fact, however, war is as much a social pattern as is the domestic slavery which the ancients thought to be an immutable fact.

I have already said that, in my opinion, combativeness is a constituent part of human nature. But I have also said that the manifestations of these native elements are subject to change because they are affected by custom and tradition. War does not exist because man has combative instincts, but because social conditions and forces have led, almost forced, these "instincts" into this channel.

There are a large number of other channels in which the need for combat has been satisfied, and there are other channels not yet discovered or explored into which it could be led with equal satisfaction. There is war against disease, against poverty, against insecurity, against injustice, in which multitudes of persons have found full opportunity for the exercise of their combative tendencies.

The time may be far off when men will cease to fulfill their need for combat by destroying each other and when they will manifest it in common and combined efforts against the forces that are enemies of all men equally. But the difficulties in the way are found in the persistence of certain acquired social customs and not in the unchangeability of the demand for combat.

Pugnacity and fear are native elements of human nature. But so are pity and sympathy. We send nurses and physicians to the battlefield and provide hospital facilities as "naturally" as we change bayonets and discharge machine guns. In early times there was a close connection between pugnacity and fighting, for the latter was done largely with the fists. Pugnacity plays a small part in generating wars today. Citizens of one country do not hate those of another nation by instinct. When they attack or are attacked, they do not use their fists in close combat, but throw shells from a great distance at persons whom they have never seen. In modern wars, anger and hatred come after the war has started; they are effects of war, not the cause of it.

It is a tough job sustaining a modern war; all the emotional reactions have to be excited. Propaganda and atrocity stories are enlisted. Aside from such extreme measures there has to be definite organization, as we saw in the World War, to keep up the morale of even noncombatants. And morale is largely a matter of keeping emotions at a certain pitch; and unfortunately fear, hatred, suspicion, are among the emotions most easily aroused.

I shall not attempt to dogmatize about the causes of modern wars. But I do not think that anyone will deny that they are social rather than psychological, though psychological appeal is highly important in working up a people to the point where they want to fight and in keeping them at it. I do not think, moreover, that anyone will deny that economic conditions are powerful among the social causes of war. The main point, however, is that whatever the sociological causes, they are affairs of tradition, custom, and institutional organization, and these factors belong among the changeable manifestations of human nature, not among the unchangeable elements.

I have used the case of war as a typical instance of what is changeable and what is unchangeable in human nature, in their relation to schemes of social change. I have selected the case because it is an extremely difficult one in which to effect durable changes, not because it is an easy one. The point is that the obstacles in the way are put there by social forces which do change from time to time, not by fixed elements of human nature. This fact is also illustrated in the failures of pacifists to achieve their ends by appeal simply to sympathy and pity. For while, as I have said, the kindly emotions are also a fixed constituent of human nature, the channel they take is dependent upon social conditions.

There is always a great outburst of these kindly emotions in time of war. Fellow feeling and the desire to help those in need are intense during war, as they are at every period of great disaster that comes home to observation or imagination. But they are canalized in their expression; they are confined to those upon our side. They occur simultaneously with manifestation of rage and fear against the other side, if not always in the same person, at least in the community generally. Hence the ultimate failure of pacifist appeals to the kindly elements of native human nature when they are separated from intelligent consideration of the social and economic forces at work.

William James made a great contribution in the title of one of his essays, *The Moral Equivalents of War*. The very title conveys the point I am making. Certain basic needs and emotions are permanent. But they are capable of finding expression in ways that are radically different from the ways in which they now currently operate.

An even more burning issue emerges when there is proposed any fundamental change in economic institutions and relations. Proposals for such sweeping change are among the commonplaces of our time. On the other hand, the proposals are met by the statement that the changes are impossible because they involve an impossible change in human nature. To this statement, advocates of the desired changes are only too likely to reply that the present system or some phase of it is contrary to human nature. The argument *pro* and *con* then gets put on the wrong ground.

As a matter of fact, economic institutions and relations are among the manifestations of human nature that are most susceptible of change. History is living evidence of the scope of these changes. Aristotle, for example, held that paying interest is unnatural, and the Middle Ages re-echoed the doctrine. All interest was usury, and it was only after economic conditions had so changed that payment of interest was a customary and in that sense a "natural" thing, that usury got its present meaning.

There have been times and places in which land was held in common and in which private ownership of land would have been regarded as the most monstrous of unnatural things. There have been other times and places when all wealth was possessed by an overlord and his subjects held wealth, if any, subject to his pleasure. The entire system of credit so fundamental in contemporary financial and industrial life is a modern invention. The invention of the joint stock company with limited liability of individuals has brought about a great change from earlier facts and conceptions of property. I think the need of owning something is one of the native elements of human nature. But it takes either ignorance or a very lively fancy to suppose that the system of ownership that exists in the United States in 1938, with all its complex relations and its interweaving with legal and political supports, is a necessary and unchangeable product of an inherent tendency to appropriate and possess.

Law is one of the most conservative of human institutions; yet through the cumulative effect of legislation and judicial decisions it changes, sometimes at a slow rate, sometimes rapidly. The changes in human relations that are brought about by changes in industrial and legal institutions then react to modify the ways in which human nature manifests itself, and this brings about still further changes in institutions, and so on indefinitely.

It is for these reasons that I say that those who hold that proposals for social change, even of rather a profound character, are impossible and utopian because of the fixity of human nature, confuse the resistance to change that comes from acquired habits with that which comes from original human nature. The savage, living in a primitive society, comes nearer to being a purely "natural" human being than does civilized man. Civilization itself is the product of altered human nature. But even the savage is bound by a mass of tribal customs and transmitted beliefs that modify his original nature, and it is these acquired habits that make it so difficult to transform him into a civilized human being.

The revolutionary radical, on the other hand, overlooks the force of engrained habits. He is right, in my opinion, about the indefinite plasticity of human nature. But he is wrong in thinking that patterns of desire, belief, and purpose do not have a force comparable to the momentum of physical objects once they are set in motion, and comparable to the inertia, the resistance to movement, possessed by these same objects when they are at rest. Habit, not original human nature, keeps things moving most of the time, about as they have moved in the past.

If human nature is unchangeable, then there is no such thing as education and all our efforts to educate are doomed to failure. For the very meaning of education is modification of native human nature in formation of those new ways of thinking, of feeling, of desiring, and of believing that are foreign to raw human nature. If the latter were unalterable, we might have training but not education. For training, as distinct from education, means simply the acquisition of certain skills. Native gifts can be trained to a point of higher efficiency without that development of new attitudes and dispositions which is the goal of education. But the result is mechanical. It is like supposing that while a musician may acquire by practice greater technical ability, he cannot rise from one plane of musical appreciation and creation to another.

The theory that human nature is unchangeable is thus the most depressing and pessimistic of all possible doctrines. If it were carried out logically, it would mean a doctrine of predestination from birth that would outdo the most rigid of theological doctrines. For according to it, persons are what they are at birth and nothing can be done about it, beyond the kind of training that an acrobat might give to the muscular system with which he is originally endowed. If a person is born with criminal tendencies, a criminal he will become and remain. If a person is born with an excessive amount of greed, he will become a person living by predatory activities at the expense of others; and so on. I do not doubt at all the existence of differences in natural endowment. But what I am questioning is the notion that they doom individuals to a fixed channel of expression. It is difficult indeed to make a silk purse out of a sow's ear. But the particular form which say, a natural musical endowment will take depends upon the social influences to which he is subjected. Beethoven in a savage tribe would doubtless have been outstanding as a musician, but he would not have been the Beethoven who composed symphonies.

The existence of almost every conceivable kind of social institution at some time and place in the history of the world is evidence of the plasticity of human nature. This fact does not prove that all these different social systems are of equal value, materially, morally, and culturally. The slightest observation shows that such is not the case. But the fact in proving the changeability of human nature indicates the attitude that should be taken toward proposals for social changes. The question is primarily whether they, in special cases, are desirable or not. And the way to answer that question is to try to discover what their consequences would be if they were adopted. Then if the conclusion is that they are desirable, the further question is how they can be accomplished with a minimum of waste, destruction, and needless dislocation.

In finding the answer to this question, we have to take into account the force of existing traditions and customs; of the patterns of action and belief that already exist. We have to find out what forces already at work can be reinforced so that they move toward the desired change and how the conditions that oppose change can be gradually weakened. Such questions as these can be considered on the basis of fact and reason.

The assertion that a proposed change is impossible because of the fixed constitution of human nature diverts attention from the question of whether or not a change is desirable and from the other question of how it shall be brought about. It throws the question into the arena of blind emotion and brute force. In the end, it encourages those who think that great changes can be produced offhand and by the use of sheer violence.

When our sciences of human nature and human relations are anything like as developed as are our sciences of physical nature, their chief concern will be with the problem of how human nature is most effectively modified. The question will not be whether it is capable of change, but of how it is to be changed under given conditions. This problem is ultimately that of education in its widest sense. Consequently, whatever represses and distorts the processes of education that might bring about a change in human dispositions with the minimum of waste puts a premium upon the forces that bring society to a state of deadlock, and thereby encourages the use of violence as a means of social change.

12

Epilogue

ARISTOTLE, KANT, AND MILL

ARISTOTLE. I left Athens so as not to repeat the fate of Socrates. Now I stand once again before these Macedonian mountains so like brows knitted in meditation, while behind me, what was Greece is no more. Nor shall I think more about those things which feed the mind only with pain, but shall henceforth dwell upon contemplation itself, thinking upon thinking, absorbed in that which is purest, most unalloyed activity, and as my inquiries converge upon one another, united with the structure of all that is natural. This will be the happiness which earlier I had tasted only momentarily and fitfully; it will be the summer of consummation like all the world's swallows brought together. Let these talkative fellows pass; they need not see me.

KANT. No question about it, Plato was quite right to feel responsibility for establishing the intellectual foundations of Western civilization. I, too, lived at the end of a period of enlightenment, whose moral framework was threatening to collapse. I conceived my task to be the preservation of the moral heritage of the West.

MILL. What you sought to do was as commendable as it was bold, although I never concealed my dislike for your position as I understood it. It seems to me that in ethics, for example, you were much more concerned to preserve the Hebraic-Christian emphasis upon obedience than you were to keep alive the Greek respect for rationality. Wasn't this so?

KANT. Obedience, yes, but obedience to reason! What could be more Greek than that?

ARISTOTLE. I had thought to let you pass, but your remarks about the Greeks cannot go uncorrected. Don't you understand that the less the Greeks practised rationality, the more they idealized it? It's for the same reason that both of you worshipped freedom—because you enjoyed it so seldom. But we (I never know whether to say "we" or "they" in talking about the Greeks) would never use a phrase such as "obedience to reason." Reason was not an end in itself for us; we saw it rather as the best available means of achieving the highest of all goods: happiness in life.

KANT. Of course we all want happiness: that's only natural. But the fact that we all want it doesn't make it the supreme good.

MILL. Besides, happiness is simply pleasure.

ARISTOTLE. The supreme good is distinguished by two criteria: first, it must be always an end and never a means: second, it must be discoverable in every specific instance of goodness. Happiness fulfills both of these requirements. As for your remark that happiness is nothing but pleasure, surely there are intellectual and aesthetic gratifications that transcend mere pleasure!

MILL. All you're saying is that there are intellectual and aesthetic pleasures.

KANT. Let's get back to what you were talking about before, Mill—freedom and rationality. Now, my passion for freedom was no mere exercise in rhetoric. The American and French revolutions I welcomed with enthusiasm. After all, what is freedom but the dutiful carrying out of self-imposed, rational rules? If I demanded that men be obedient, it wasn't obedience to tyrants—or to any kind of irrational authority—that I had in mind, but obedience to the laws which men would rationally produce and impose upon themselves.

MILL. Yet I have the distinct impression that, according to you, one is free so long as he respectfully obeys—no matter how blindly, mind you!—the laws produced by human reason. However, I can't help feeling that a person is unfree precisely to the degree to which he obeys blindly, no matter how reasonable may be the laws themselves which he obeys.

KANT. Please—you must try to understand that there are two distinct processes of decision-making. There is the process by which we decide rules or laws, and there is the process by which we make decisions as to particular acts. These different processes require different decision-making agencies. When it comes to deciding what the moral law must be, the agency is man's *reason*. But when it's the specific case of a particular individual who must make a moral choice in a particular situation, then it is not reason but moral *character* which guides the virtuous man into doing his duty purely out of respect for the moral law. These particular choices cannot be entrusted to reason, for in such cases reason degenerates into a mere strategy of self-interest—an exercise in cunning.

ARISTOTLE. You're right about moral character: it's quite essential to moral conduct. But one does not get to engage in virtuous acts by first possessing a virtuous character. It's rather that one develops a virtuous character through more and more habitually engaging in virtuous acts.

KANT. I'm not talking about the origin of moral character, but its function. A virtuous person is one who commits himself wholeheartedly and without reservation to the moral law. Moral obedience cannot be a matter of calculation or of guile. From Paul and Augustine and Luther, I learned how feeble is reason without commitment, while from Hume I learned how futile reason is without experience. But put these components together—reason, experience, and commitment—and a disclplined freedom becomes possible.

MILL. A "disciplined" freedom?

KANT. Well, as you know, I don't believe ideal freedom can be proven. We can postulate it, of course, but we can't demonstrate it. Nevertheless there's a practical sense in which we can be said to be free: when we live as we ought to live—in accordance with the laws of reason, itself the most noble aspect of our nature. We must forego excuses and compel ourselves to live here and now, in this wretched society, as virtuously as we would in a world of perfectly upright men. But this takes discipline. Just as there can be no pressure without a counter-pressure, there can be no moral freedom without regulation and constraint, nor can there be creativity without control. That hawk over there, wheeling in the sky—could he stay aloft at all if he didn't spread his wings so that the air beneath pressed up against him? Or take a soap bubble that a child has blown—how delicate a combination it is of inner forces seeking to push their way out, contained and balanced by the filmy sphere of soap, ever threatening to burst or collapse! Our civilization is like that bubble, precariously balanced as it floats through time, shimmering, fragile and lovely. But weaken the moral order, the moral integument of the civilization, and it will collapse. Or weaken the character, the moral integument of the individual, and he collapses too.

MILL. So you felt it your task to set forth the ideal conditions of morality. Yet why did you deny that science could provide knowledge of those conditions?

KANT. Science tells us how people do in fact behave everywhere in the world. But this is anthropology, not ethics. We can never go from such descriptions of how people *do* in fact behave to how they *ought* to behave.

ARISTOTLE. I fail to see the problem which you seem to find so monumental. Surely it is a fact that men naturally have certain needs and desires. Surely it is a fact that men seek the happiness that accompanies the achievement of those desires and needs. And surely it is no less a fact that there is no better guarantee of arriving at well-being than by living reasonably. Therefore a virtuous man is none other than one who excels in guiding his life in a reasonable manner. Once we know what the function of something is—say, an axe—science can determine what is a good thing of that kind. A good axe is one that chops well, and a good man is one who performs the human function well, of living in accordance with reason. How can you possibly maintain that science cannot tell us anything about moral value?

KANT. Granted, the facts you cite tell us not merely how men *do* live, but also how they *can* live. But such facts still can never tell us how men *ought* to live; only reason can do that.

MILL. I must say, Kant, that I most vehemently object to your notion that any action discovered by reason to be universalizable is thereby a right action. Now if this were so, there would be no contradiction in the adoption by all the world of the most outrageously immoral rules of conduct. And you get yourself into this predicament by your concentration upon *rules* and *motives* rather than upon *results*. For instance, if a man saves my life, what do I care what his motive was? What do I care whether or not he was being dutiful to the moral law as he conceived it? All that matters to me is that the effects of his act were generally pleasurable effects. This is the only justification for calling his action "virtuous."

KANT. You seem to think that the fundamental question of ethics is whether we should follow rules or anticipated results. But that's not it at all. Rather, we must decide between the results of our following rules consistently and the results of our not doing so. Our positions, you see, are not so much contradictory as complementary. Certainly we're both very much concerned with the liberation of the individual and the full development of his powers. It was my hope that my writing would advance man toward a higher level of maturity than anything he had previously known or envisaged.

MILL. Well, I was in full rebellion against the stuffiness and callousness of mid-nineteenth-century England—the forces making for conformity, the encroachments upon privacy, the arbitrary refusal of those in power to be responsive to those they ruled. I detested the nasty hypocrisies by which women were deprived of their political rights, and by which the liberty of thought and expression among all citizens was ruthlessly violated or insufferably hedged about. As you see, I'm still indignant.

KANT. And rightly so. To me, these were the puerilities, indeed, the infantilisms, of the culture of our era. I felt that in time, and not without great effort on our part, we would slough off these pathetic symptoms of the childhood of mankind, and rise to our full stature, in a world where each would accept his moral responsibility for all.

MILL. Whenever you intimate that each of us must legislate for all, I become uneasy. But obviously your concern for humanity and mine for human individuality do reinforce each other. In fact, nothing in your writing impresses me more than your insistence that men must treat each other as ends, never as means.

KANT. Had I realized the Industrial Revolution was taking place as I wrote, I would have been even more insistent on that point. Men had always made use of one another, but never so systematically.

That men should be mere instruments or things, tools for other men's purposes, that they should literally *employ* one another—and come to find this acceptable—this I now see is not so much barbaric as depraved.

ARISTOTLE. It's so easy to be wise—once one has hindsight. I used to sit at Plato's feet and listen to him talk about Socrates, and more than once it crossed my mind that they were a pair of fools, however clever they might have been in conversation. I pitted my knowledge and my logic against their brilliance, and I seriously believed for a time that I had corrected their countless errors. But I hadn't allowed for their wisdom, comparable to none before or since. Let me leave these two now, before I make the same mistake again.

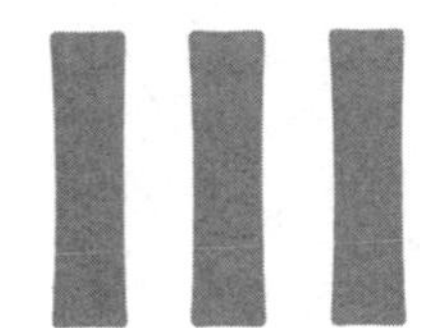

THE RELIGIOUS POINT OF VIEW

13

Introduction

Why must there be a philosophy of religion (or for that matter, a philosophy of science, or a philosophy of art)? Theorists in such fields—for example, theologians in the field of religion—often maintain that they are objective enough and critical enough to examine their disciplines impartially and expertly. Thus many of them argue that there is little need for philosophical treatments of these subject-areas. But philosophers have generally been dissatisfied with such contentions. They have tended to maintain that scientists are not always prepared to examine their own presuppositions, and that adherents of religion are not without reluctance to analyze the concepts and assumptions from which their own thinking proceeds.

Those who have lived through a particular experience, however vivid it may have been, are not necessarily in the best position to analyze or explain how it came about or how it might be interpreted. In this sense, philosophers suspect that proponents of religion and art and science may have commitments to their specialties that prevent them from being wholly self-critical. Hence the call for a philosophical approach —such as the philosophy of religion—not necessarily committed to the values that appear essential to those already engaged in the discipline to be investigated.

It is often noted, with respect to observations made by scientists, that such observations are guided by and conditioned by the general theories upon which such scientists operate, with the result that scientific perceptions are not theory-free, but are very much "theory-laden." In like manner, a philosopher may find it difficult to consider an account of religion by a proponent of religion—or by an antagonist of religion—without being struck by the degree to which such descriptions are "belief-laden," down to the styles of prose in which such descriptions are couched.

To many a philosopher of religion, the hinge or turning-point upon the entire discussion of religion is pinioned is the "problem of evil." This problem can be briefly summarized by saying that there appears to be unmerited suffering in the world. If there is a God, then He has failed to prevent such suffering because He is too weak to do so, too evil to do so, or both. Such a contention dramatizes very vividly the sharply conflicting views of those who are to be found wrestling with the problem of religious belief. Perhaps we can take our first steps into this area by considering a few of these conflicting perspectives.

1. One view, held by sceptics about religion, is an elaboration of the argument just alluded to, in which it is maintained that unmerited suffering characterizes a very great part of human life. Such injustice can be nothing but evil. Towards suffering itself we may be stoic or callous, but it is evident that the vast bulk of such suffering is utterly undeserved: the countless children born maimed and deformed, the botching of the hopes and lives of young people due to poverty and disease, the destruction of millions of victims in absurd wars and insane massacres, the traumatic shock of discovering that one's skin color disqualifies one from equal access to many of the goods of life, the endless round of despair and frustration that typifies so much the lives of innocent human beings who, having been brought unasked into the world, must then live as though being unspeakably punished for unspeakable, unmentionable crimes. Divine justice cannot be compatible with the sufferings of the innocent. Therefore, divine justice must be ruled out—and for some who hold to this position this likewise rules out any possibility of belief in God's existence.

2. Defenders of religion have utilized a variety of arguments in seeking to come to grips with the problem of evil. Some have contended that no suffering is unmerited, while others have argued that no suffering is real. Some have taken the position that unmerited suffering is God's way of putting man to the test, of trying his faith. Others have argued that the evil in the world is the aesthetic complement to the good in the world—together they form a *chiaroscuro* that is eminently pleasing in the sight of God. Still others have said that God's ways are simply incomprehensible to man, but such inscrutability on God's part is no justification of men's losing their faith in Him. Yet another response has been that God is indeed wholly good, but his goodness is so far removed from human goodness (which apparently involves not hurting others unnecessarily) as to be of a different order entirely.

3. Other defenders of religion have not remained so undaunted by the problem of evil. Abandoning the belief in the supernatural, they

have retreated to and retrenched themselves in more humanistic or more naturalistic conceptions. Many have sought to redefine their conceptions of religion—as the experience of the holy, as reverence for the sacred, as ultimate concern, as respect for the intrinsic worth of any object or being, as enchantment with the mystery and creativity of existence, and so on. And not a few, echoing Kant, have suggested that, while traditional religion was seen as the source of ethics, a more rational and humanistic approach would see ethics as the source of religion.

Among the writers included in this section, Hume, Nietzsche, and Hanson have views in common with those set forth as position (1) above, St. Thomas and Kierkegaard express the more traditional perspective depicted in (2), and Tillich's views are among those alluded to in (3). Obviously, these three approaches do not exhaust the spectrum of ways in which religion may be viewed. But it may not be amiss to refer to yet a fourth point of view, which is an effort to consider the entire dialogue concerning religion from a historical metalevel outside the arena of the conflict itself, and to portray the discussion as inevitably endless but not unrewarding:

4. From this perspective, every new generation seeks to discover the meaning of its own experience, in however broad a context it can locate such experience. Thus, every new generation is a new beginning. The young, surrounded by silences, painfully aware at every point of emptiness and meaninglessness, begin casting about for significant relationships, objects in which faith and trust might be reposed. They pay attention to details often previously overlooked, and find grounds here and there for joy and hope. The horrors of their parents' world have not been forgotten, for they were never learned; they are not of the young, but of a world the young would prefer to ignore and leave behind. So, like a phoenix reborn of its own ashes, religion steps forward fresh and attractive to every rising generation, and can be recognized as the protagonist in an endless series of such declines and startling reemergences, of defeats following hard upon victories, and victories following hard upon defeats.

It is on the basis of so perennial a recurrence that the theses and antitheses of philosophical discussions of religion are founded. It is for these reasons that discussions of religious experience and religious language, of God and immortality, in one sense get nowhere, and are yet in another sense inexhaustible. In a world in which nothing is final or absolute, the quest for the absolute is guaranteed a perpetual existence, and will always have, therefore, a powerful effect upon the minds and hearts, the hopes and dreams of mankind.

From this metalevel, the fact of religion would appear to be as painful to philosophy as the fact of evil is to religion. If evil is the rock upon which the frail vessel of religious understanding must sooner or later come aground, then religion may also be a rock endangering the frail vessel of philosophical understanding. For philosophy constantly seeks to make religion over into its own image—to interpret it as plausible analogy or as conceivable possibility. Philosophy, it has been said, frequently busies itself with a quest for the grounds of religious belief, as though, if the belief *had* grounds, it would still be religious rather than scientific. It seeks to replace the rapture that transcends understanding with the ecstasy that comes with understanding, not realizing that the one can never adequately substitute for the other. Religion can hardly be content with such meager categories as possibility and actuality, though these be the daily diet of the metaphysician. It soars beyond actuality and possibility alike on wings of paradox and self-contradiction, defies logic, transcends rationality, and thumbs its nose at its philosophical detractors. Hence the paradox that its own death is its own rebirth, its quixotic absurdity is its crowning glory, and its tattered rationalizations of evil struggle to unmask themselves as daring glimpses of the infinite.

It would be unjust to Santayana to suggest that this fourth alternative is a characterization of his views, but it may not be inappropriate to suggest that the questions raised in this perspective are among those with which Santayana seeks to cope in the essay that concludes this section.

St. Thomas's "proofs" may not have been intended as proofs in the usual sense, but only as ways of explaining to the devout a rational basis for their beliefs. The simplicity and succinctness of these formulations deprive them of the more elaborate and detailed considerations that St. Thomas devoted elsewhere to the issues involved. But the demonstrations put in evidence the dialectical approach he employed, beginning with a statement of the view to be rejected, then considering alternative but unsatisfactory forms of rejecting the "incorrect" view, and finally offering his own formulation of the matter. Each of Thomas's own arguments raises serious logical issues that succeeding thinkers have not failed to point out. But as Hume himself suggests, such "proofs" as these can be surprisingly resilient, and may retain a certain plausibility long after their critics have been content to point out their futility through purely logical demonstrations.

Hume's criticism is aimed at eighteenth-century versions of Thomas's fifth proof, the so-called "Argument from Design." What Hume seeks to show is that such arguments claim to be scientific because they rest upon analogy and because scientific induction likewise rests upon analogy. Such an inference, however, is quite invalid. The principle of analogy applies only where there have been comparable situations: where similar terms are compared under similar conditions. Without the experience of similar universes, Hume argues, we cannot reasonably infer the divine creation of this one.

Hume's attack is not upon religion as such, but only upon arguments by spokesmen for religion, which are presented as being scientific demonstrations. For Hume is equally concerned to disparage rationalistic claims to universal understanding. He sees no final explanation possible—not only of the world in general, but of each and every particular event as well. Therefore, if the miraculous is to be understood as the inexplicable, then every occurrence is an incomprehensible miracle whose mysterious irruption into the world must arouse our awe and reverence, as it must strengthen our perplexity and wonderment.

Kierkegaard sees the development of the human individual—every human individual—as embracing sensuous needs and impulses, rational obligations to society, and ultimate realization of one's own individuality. The life of pleasure, as guided by aesthetic taste, is attractive to the individual, as is the life of reason, as guided by moral rules and conventions. However, the individual discovers that neither the moral nor the aesthetic life is sufficient. The life of pleasure turns out to be self-defeating. Moreover, the individual finds that he is incapable of living up to the moral law, and is filled with a sense of guilt. The resolution of the paradox can be found only in the religious life—or, more precisely, in God. But God is not objectively knowable; all efforts to prove His existence through logical or scientific demonstration are quite futile. God is not object, but Subject, and can be known only subjectively. Thus, just as the true being of each individual person is not his objective, scientifically knowable being, but his own authentic self which only he himself experiences directly and yet subjectively, so the truth of all existence is the subjectivity of God. Man's reason cannot take him to such a God; the abyss between God and man is one that only faith can overleap, and since there are no guarantees, one risks everything in attempting to discover that which yields itself only to an inward rather than to an outward understanding.

Nietzsche sees religion as one of those crippling yet creative institutions that have turned man from a bold savage to a domesticated, civilized animal. Without religion, man would probably be still more violent, less ingeniously refined. Nevertheless it is religion that contrives the moralities by which men live out their lives of tedious routine, having forsaken the glorious adventures of savagery. But man, to fulfill his potentialities, cannot rest halfway up the ladder of evolution. He must brave every challenge, invite dangers, ignore suffering, act always upon his strengths rather than his needs, and drive on to an undreamed-of excellence. In short, Nietzsche champions an end to self-effacement, self-disparagement, and guilt, the very means by which religion, in his view, seeks to intimidate man into respectability. He espouses instead, at least for a small, elite minority, a self-imposed regimen in which each individual demands the utmost of himself, and in which he assumes responsibility for his actions, instead of seeking to blame them on the social, historical, or environmental conditions under which he lives. The fate and future of man as a species therefore rests upon these daringly creative individuals who achieve unprecedented forms of greatness while yet respecting and treasuring the greatness of their predecessors.

The classic selections in the beginning of this section offer only a hint of the unending struggle among religious thinkers over whether or not gods exist. To Tillich, such contention is utterly futile. Once God is permitted to become an object of inquiry, once the discussion is phrased in terms of God's "existing or not existing," religious understanding becomes impossible. Or rather, Tillich contends, the loss of a sense of depth, the flattening-out of all human experience into the narrowest of dimensions, is precisely what causes us to raise such a pointless question, and what precludes even the possibility of our finding a meaningful answer.

The Argument from Purpose or Design, which we encountered in St. Thomas, surfaces again in Smart's essay, in which he seeks to employ evolutionary accounts of the cosmos as arguments for God's existence. The notion of creativity, he suggests, offers us a non-scientific but intelligible explanation both of the emergence of human beings, and of the growth of human awareness of the divine.

Whereas many naturalists—Santayana in particular comes to mind here—are concerned to translate traditional religious terms and concepts into naturalistic language, Simone Weil makes a fervent plea for the religious significance of such traditionally philosophical notions as the true and the beautiful. Her claim that children naively believe adults mean them no harm, and that such trust goes to the very heart of what is sacred, is a moving (although equally dogmatic) denial of Hobbes's contention that what is most characteristic of mankind is its brutality, and is a subtle rephrasing of Rousseau's claim that human beings are born prepared to do good in the world.

In his discussion of the language of religious discourse, Ricoeur presents a rich and elaborate analysis of the hermeneutical (as opposed to an analytical) approach to a religious text, through a rediscovery of the conditions of its origin, and through a discovery of the life-possibilities that such a text opens to its reader. The Santayana selection is a boldly speculative interpretation of religion, and has been called one of the most brilliant and profound essays of the twentieth century. In it Santayana moves from scepticism to affirmation, not of the intelligibility of Spinoza's divine Nature, but of its "omnificence"—its awesomely, infinitely profuse makings, doings, and performings. Certainly it would be difficult to find a statement of naturalism in which religious piety and spirituality had been defended more eloquently or more persuasively.

14

The Grounding of Belief

ST. THOMAS AQUINAS

(1225?–1274)

Born near Naples, Italy, St. Thomas was educated at Monte Cassino, the University of Naples, and the University of Paris. He had become a member of the Dominican Order, but so strongly did his family object to this affiliation that he was actually shut up and guarded for a time. Later, in Paris and in Rome, he taught and defended the rights of his Order. He became a regular professor of theology in 1256 at the University of Paris, but returned to Italy three years later, and for the next decade taught in various Italian cities. In 1274 he was summoned by Pope Gregory X to participate in the Council of Lyons, but he died on his way there. Forty-nine years later he was canonized as a saint. No other theologian has had greater influence upon the theological thought of the Western church.

St. Thomas is best known for his two treatises, the Summa Theologica *(a Summary of Theology) and the* Summa contra Gentiles *(A Summary against the Gentiles. By "Gentiles" in the latter work is apparently meant the heathen—specifically, those Mohammedans whose outlook was naturalistic. The* Summa Theologica *was written for novices engaged in learning the rudiments of theology. While largely theological, it does contain some portions that are more strictly philosophical in character.*

Proving God's Existence

WHETHER GOD EXISTS?

We proceed thus to the Third Article:

Objection 1. It seems that God does not exist; because if one of two contraries be infinite, the other would be altogether destroyed. But the word "God" means that He is infinite goodness. If, therefore, God existed, there would be no evil discoverable; but there is evil in the world. Therefore God does not exist.

Obj. 2. Further, it is superfluous to suppose that what can be accounted for by a few principles has been produced by many. But it seems that everything we see in the world can be accounted for by other principles, supposing God did not exist. For all natural things can be reduced to one principle, which is nature; and all voluntary things can be reduced to one principle, which is human reason, or will. Therefore there is no need to suppose God's existence.

On the contrary, It is said in the person of God: *I am Who am* (Exod. iii. 14).

I answer that, The existence of God can be proved in five ways.

The first and more manifest way is the argument from motion. It is certain, and evident to our senses, that in the world some things are in motion. Now whatever is in motion is put in motion by another, for nothing can be in motion except it is in potentiality to that towards which it is in motion; whereas a thing moves inasmuch as it is in act. For motion is nothing else than the reduction of something from potentiality to actuality. But nothing can be reduced from potentiality to actuality, except by something in a state of actuality. Thus that which is actually hot, as fire, makes wood, which is potentially hot, to be actually hot, and thereby moves and changes it. Now it is not possible that the same thing should be at once in actuality and potentiality in the same respect, but only in different respects. For what is actually hot cannot simultaneously be potentially hot; but it is simultaneously potentially cold. It is therefore impossible that in the same respect and in the same way a thing should be both mover and moved, *i.e.,* that it should move itself. Therefore, whatever is in motion must be put in motion by another. If that by which it is put in motion be itself put in motion, then this also must needs be put in motion by another, and that by another again. But this cannot go on to infinity, because then there would be no first mover, and, consequently, no other mover; seeing that subsequent movers move only inasmuch as they are put in motion by the first mover; as the staff moves only because

From the Summa Theologica, *Part 1, Vol. 1, Benziger Bros. and Burns & Oates Ltd. (1947).*

it is put in motion by the hand. Therefore it is necessary to arrive at a first mover, put in motion by no other; and this everyone understands to be God.

The second way is from the nature of the efficient cause. In the world of sense we find there is an order of efficient causes. There is no case known (neither is it, indeed, possible) in which a thing is found to be the efficient cause of itself; for so it would be prior to itself, which is impossible. Now in efficient causes it is not possible to go on to infinity, because in all efficient causes following in order, the first is the cause of the intermediate cause, and the intermediate is the cause of the ultimate cause, whether the intermediate cause be several, or one only. Now to take away the cause is to take away the effect. Therefore, if there be no first cause among efficient causes, there will be no ultimate, nor any intermediate cause. But if in efficient causes it is possible to go on to infinity, there will be no first efficient cause, neither will there be an ultimate effect, nor any intermediate efficient causes; all of which is plainly false. Therefore it is necessary to admit a first efficient cause, to which everyone gives the name of God.

The third way is taken from possibility and necessity, and runs thus. We find in nature things that are possible to be and not to be, since they are found to be generated, and to corrupt, and consequently, they are possible to be and not to be. But it is impossible for these always to exist, for that which is possible not to be at some time is not. Therefore, if everything is possible not to be, then at one time there could have been nothing in existence. Now if this were true, even now there would be nothing in existence, because that which does not exist only begins to exist by something already existing. Therefore, if at one time nothing was in existence, it would have been impossible for anything to have begun to exist; and thus even now nothing would be in existence—which is absurd. Therefore, not all beings are merely possible, but there must exist something the existence of which is necessary. But every necessary thing either has its necessity caused by another, or not. Now it is impossible to go on to infinity in necessary things which have their necessity caused by another, as has been already proved in regard to efficient causes. Therefore we cannot but postulate the existence of some being having of itself its own necessity, and not receiving it from another, but rather causing in others their necessity. This all men speak of as God.

The fourth way is taken from the gradation to be found in things. Among beings there are some more and some less good, true, noble, and the like. But "more" and "less" are predicated of different things, according as they resemble in their different ways something which is the maximum, as a thing is said to be hotter according as it more nearly resembles that which is hottest; so that there is something which is truest, something best, something noblest, and, consequently, something which is uttermost being; for those things that are greatest in truth are greatest in being, as it is written in *Metaph*. ii. Now the maximum in any genus is the cause of all in that genus; as fire, which is the maximum of heat, is the cause of all hot things. Therefore there must also be something which is to all beings the cause of their being, goodness, and every other perfection; and this we call God.

The fifth way is taken from the governance in the world. We see that things which lack intelligence, such as natural bodies, act for an end, and this is evident from their acting always, or nearly always, in the same way, so as to obtain the best result. Hence it is plain that not fortuitously, but designedly, do they achieve their end. Now whatever lacks intelligence cannot move towards an end, unless it be directed by some being endowed with knowledge and intelligence; as the arrow is shot to its mark by the archer. Therefore some intelligent being exists by whom all natural things are directed to their end; and this being we call God.

Reply Obj. 1. As Augustine says *(Enchir.* xi.*): Since God is the highest good, He would not allow any evil to exist in His works, unless His omnipotence and goodness were such as to bring good even out of evil.* This is part of the infinite goodness of God, that He should allow evil to exist, and out of it produce good.

Reply Obj. 2. Since nature works for a determinate end under the direction of a higher agent, whatever is done by nature must needs be traced back to God, as to its first cause. So also whatever is done voluntarily must also be traced back to some higher cause other than human reason or will, since these can change and fail; for all things that are changeable and capable of defect must be traced back to an immovable and self-necessary first principle, as was shown in the body of the *Article*.

DAVID HUME

(1711–1776)

One of the major figures in British philosophy, David Hume was born in Edinburgh, and attended the University of Edinburgh. In 1739 he published the Treatise of Human Nature, *but was disappointed by its failure to create a stir. He revised the work however, and it appeared in 1748 as the* Enquiry into Human Understanding. *His opinions were considered unacceptable by the universities of Edinburgh and Glasgow, so that he failed to receive the academic appointments for which he had hoped. In 1763 he became secretary to the British embassy in France, and was able to savor the French admiration for his work. With Rousseau, his friend for a time, he returned to England in 1765, and the next year was made Undersecretary of State for Scotland. In 1775, knowing that he did not have long to live, he wrote his autobiography. His* Dialogues Concerning Natural Religion *was published posthumously in 1779, Hume having been induced to hold the work back during his lifetime because of the sceptical views it contained.*

THE LOGIC OF SCEPTICISM

I must own, Cleanthes, said Demea, that nothing can more surprise me, than the light, in which you have, all along, put this argument. By the whole tenor of your discourse, one would imagine that you were maintaining the Being of a God, against the cavils of Atheists and Infidels; and were necessitated to become a champion for that fundamental principle of all religion. But this, I hope, is not by any means a question among us. No man; no man, at least, of common sense, I am persuaded, ever entertained a serious doubt with regard to a truth so certain and self-evident. The question is not concerning the being, but the nature of God. This I affirm, from the infirmities of human understanding, to be altogether incomprehensible and unknown to us. The essence of that supreme mind, his attributes, the manner of his existence, the very nature of his duration; these and every particular, which regards so divine a Being, are mysterious to men. Finite, weak, and blind creatures, we ought to humble ourselves in his august presence, and, conscious of our frailties, adore in silence his infinite perfections, which eye hath not seen, ear hath not heard, neither hath it entered into the heart of man to conceive. They are covered in a deep cloud from human curiosity: It is profaneness to attempt penetrating through these sacred obscurities: And next to the impiety of denying his existence, is the temerity of prying into his nature and essence, decrees and attributes.

But lest you should think that my *piety* has here got the better of my *philosophy*, I shall support my opinion, if it needs any support, by a very great authority. I might cite all the divines almost, from the foundation of Christianity, who have ever treated of this or any other theological subject: But I shall confine myself, at present, to one equally celebrated for piety and philosophy. It is Father Malebranche, who, I remember, thus expresses himself. "One ought not so much (says he) to call God a spirit, in order to express positively what he is, as in order to signify that he is not matter. He is a Being infinitely perfect: Of this we cannot doubt. But in the same manner as we ought not to imagine, even supposing him corporeal, that he is clothed with a human body, as the Anthropomorphites asserted, under color that that figure was the most perfect of any; so neither ought we to imagine, that the Spirit of God has human ideas, or bears any resemblance to our spirit; under color that we know nothing more perfect than a human mind. We ought rather to believe, that as he comprehends also the perfections of matter without being material . . . he comprehends also the perfections of created spirits, without being spirit, in the manner we conceive spirit: That his true name is, *He that is,* or, in other words, Being without restriction, All Being, the Being infinite and universal."

From Dialogues concerning Natural Religion *(1779), as edited by Green and Grose, pp. 389–400, 411–415.*

After so great an authority, Demea, replied Philo, as that which you have produced, and a thousand more, which you might produce, it would appear ridiculous in me to add my sentiment, or express my approbation of your doctrine. But surely, where reasonable men treat these subjects, the question can never be concerning the *Being*, but only the *Nature* of the Deity. The former truth, as you well observe, is unquestionable and self-evident. Nothing exists without a cause; and the original cause of this universe (whatever it be) we call God; and piously ascribe to him every species of perfection. Whoever scruples this fundamental truth deserves every punishment which can be inflicted among philosophers, to wit, the greatest ridicule, contempt and disapprobation. But as all perfection is entirely relative, we ought never to imagine that we comprehend the attributes of this divine Being, or to suppose, that his perfections have any analogy or likeness to the perfections of a human creature. Wisdom, Thought, Design, Knowledge; these we justly ascribe to him; because these words are honourable among men, and we have no other language or other conceptions, by which we can express our adoration of him. But let us beware, lest we think, that our ideas any wise correspond to his perfections, or that his attributes have any resemblance to these qualities among men. He is infinitely superior to our limited view and comprehension; and is more the object of worship in the temple, than of disputation in the schools.

In reality, Cleanthes, continued he, there is no need of having recourse to that affected sceptism, so displeasing to you, in order to come at this determination. Our ideas reach no farther than our experience: We have no experience of divine attributes and operations: I need not conclude my syllogism. You can draw the inference yourself. And it is a pleasure to me (and I hope to you too) that just reasoning and sound piety here concur in the same conclusion, and both of them establish the adorably mysterious and incomprehensible nature of the Supreme Being.

Not to lose any time in circumlocutions, said Cleanthes, addressing himself to Demea, much less in replying to the pious declamations of Philo; I shall briefly explain how I conceive this matter. Look round the world: contemplate the whole and every part of it: You will find it to be nothing but one great machine, subdivided into an infinite number of lesser machines, which again admit of subdivisions, to a degree beyond what human senses and faculties can trace and explain. All these various machines, and even their most minute parts, are adjusted to each other with an accuracy which ravishes into admiration all men who have ever contemplated them. The curious adapting of means to ends, throughout all nature, resembles exactly, though it much exceeds, the productions of human contrivance; of human designs, thought, wisdom, and intelligence. Since therefore the effects resemble each other, we are led to infer, by all the rules of analogy, that the causes also resemble; and that the Author of Nature is somewhat similar to the mind of man; though possessed of much larger faculties, proportioned to the grandeur of the work, which he has executed. By this argument *a posteriori*, and by this argument alone, do we prove at once the existence of a Deity, and his similarity to human mind and intelligence.

I shall be so free, Cleanthes, said Demea, as to tell you, that from the beginning, I could not approve of your conclusion concerning the similarity of the Deity to men; still less can I approve of the mediums, by which you endeavour to establish it. What! No demonstration of the Being of a God! No abstract arguments! No proofs *a priori*! Are these, which have hitherto been so much insisted on by philosophers, all fallacy, all sophism? Can we reach no farther in this subject than experience and probability? I will not say, that this is betraying the cause of a Deity: But surely, by this affected candor, you give advantage to Atheists, which they never could obtain, by the mere dint of argument and reasoning.

What I chiefly scruple in this subject, said Philo, is not so much, that all religious arguments are by Cleanthes reduced to experience, as that they appear not to be even the most certain and irrefragable of that inferior kind. That a stone will fall, that fire will burn, that the earth has solidity, we have observed a thousand and a thousand times; and when any new instance of this nature is presented, we draw without hesitation the accustomed inference. The exact similarity of the cases gives us a perfect assurance of a similar event; and a stronger evidence is never desired nor sought after. But wherever you depart, in the least, from the similarity of the cases, you diminish proportionably the evidence; and may at last bring it to a very weak *analogy*, which is confessedly liable to error and uncertainty. After having experienced the circulation of the blood in human creatures, we make no doubt that it takes place in Titius and Mævius: but from its circulation in frogs and fishes, it is only a presumption, though a strong one, from analogy, that it takes place in men and other animals. The analogical reasoning is much weaker, when we infer the circulation of the sap in vegetables from our experience, that the blood circulates in animals; and those, who hastily followed that imperfect analogy, are found, by more accurate experiments, to have been mistaken.

If we see a house, Cleanthes, we conclude, with the greatest certainty, that it had an architect or builder; because this is precisely that species of effect, which we have experienced to proceed from that species of cause. But surely you will not affirm, that the universe bears such a resemblance to a house, that we can with the same certainty infer a similar cause, or that the analogy is here entire and perfect. The dissimilitude is so striking, that the utmost you can here pretend to is a guess, a conjecture, a presumption concerning a similar cause; and how that pretension will be received in the world, I leave you to consider.

It would surely be very ill received, replied Cleanthes; and I should be deservedly blamed and detested, did I allow, that the proofs of a Deity amounted to no more than a guess or conjecture. But is the whole adjustment of means to ends in a house and in the universe so slight a resemblance? The economy of final causes? The order, proportion, and arrangement of every part? Steps of a stair are plainly contrived, that human legs may use them in mounting; and this inference is certain and infallible. Human legs are also contrived for walking and mounting; and this inference, I allow, is not altogether so certain, because of the dissimilarity which you remark; but does it, therefore, deserve the name only of presumption or conjecture?

Good God! cried Demea, interrupting him, where are we? Zealous defenders of religion allow, that the proofs of a Deity fall short of perfect evidence! And you, Philo, on whose assistance I depended, in proving the adorable mysteriousness of the Divine Nature, do you assent to all these extravagant opinions of Cleanthes? For what other name can I give them? Or why spare my censure, when such principles are advanced, supported by such an authority, before so young a man as Pamphilus?

You seem not to apprehend, replied Philo, that I argue with Cleanthes in his own way; and by showing him the dangerous consequences of his tenets, hope at last to reduce him to our opinion. But what sticks most with you, I observe, is the representation which Cleanthes has made of the argument *a posteriori*; and finding, that that argument is likely to escape your hold and vanish into air, you think it so disguised, that you can scarcely believe it to be set in its true light. Now, however much I may dissent, in other respects, from the dangerous principles of Cleanthes, I must allow, that he has fairly represented that argument; and I shall endeavour so to state the matter to you, that you will entertain no farther scruples with regard to it.

Were a man to abstract from every thing which he knows or has seen, he would be altogether incapable, merely from his own ideas, to determine what kind of scene the universe must be, or to give the preference to one state or situation of things above another. For as nothing which he clearly conceives could be esteemed impossible or implying a contradiction, every chimera of his fancy would be upon an equal footing; nor could he assign any just reason, why he adheres to one idea or system, and rejects the others, which are equally possible.

Again; after he opens his eyes, and contemplates the world, as it really is, it would be impossible for him, at first, to assign the cause of any one event; much less, of the whole of things or of the universe. He might set his Fancy a rambling; and she might bring him in an infinite variety of reports and representations. These would all be possible; but being all equally possible, he would never, of himself, give a satisfactory account for his preferring one of them to the rest. Experience alone can point out to him the true cause of any phenomenon.

Now, according to his method of reasoning, Demea, it follows (and is, indeed, tacitly allowed by Cleanthes himself) that order, arrangement, or the adjustment of final causes is not, of itself, any proof of design; but only so far as it has been experienced to proceed from that principle. For aught we can know *a priori*, matter may contain the source or spring of order originally, within itself, as well as mind does; and there is no more difficulty in conceiving that the several elements, from an internal unknown cause, may fall into the most exquisite arrangement, than to conceive that their ideas, in the great, universal mind, from a like internal, unknown cause, fall into that arrangement. The equal possibility of both these suppositions is allowed. But by experience we find, (according to Cleanthes) that there is a difference between them. Throw several pieces of steel together, without shape or form; they will never arrange themselves so as to compose a watch: Stone, and mortar, and wood, without an architect, never erect a house. But the ideas in a human mind, we see, by an unknown, inexplicable economy, arrange themselves so as to form the plan of a watch or house. Experience, therefore, proves, that there is an original principle of order in mind, not in matter. From similar effects we infer similar causes. The adjustment of means to ends is alike in the universe, as in a machine of human contrivance. The causes, therefore, must be resembling.

I was from the beginning scandalised, I must own, with this resemblance, which is asserted, between the Deity and human creatures; and must conceive it to imply such a degradation of the Supreme Being as no sound Theist could endure. With your assistance, therefore, Demea, I shall endeavour to defend what you justly called the adorable mysteriousness of the Divine Nature, and shall refute this reasoning of Cleanthes, provided he allows that I have made a fair representation of it.

When Cleanthes had assented, Philo, after a short pause, proceeded in the following manner.

That all inferences, Cleanthes, concerning fact, are founded on experience, and that all experimental reasonings are founded on the supposition, that similar causes prove similar effects, and similar effects similar causes; I shall not, at present, much dispute with you. But observe, I entreat you, with what extreme caution all just reasoners proceed in the transferring of experiments to similar cases. Unless the cases be exactly similar, they repose to perfect confidence in applying their past observation to any particular phenomenon. Every alteration of circumstances occasions a doubt concerning the event; and it requires new experiments to prove certainly, that the new circumstances are of no moment or importance. A change in bulk, situation, arrangement, age, disposition of the air, or surrounding bodies; any of these particulars may be attended with the most unexpected consequences: And unless the objects be quite familiar to us, it is the highest temerity to expect with assurance, after any of these changes, an event similar to that which before fell under our observation. The slow and deliberate steps of philosophers, here, if any where, are distinguished from the precipitate march of the vulgar, who, hurried on by the smallest similitude, are incapable of all discernment or consideration.

But can you think, Cleanthes, that your usual phlegm and philosophy have been preserved in so wide a step as you have taken, when you compared to the universe houses, ships, furniture, machines; and from their similarity in some circumstances inferred a similarity in their causes? Thought, design, intelligence, such as we discover in men and other animals, is no more than one of the springs and principles of the universe, as well as heat or cold, attraction or repulsion, and a hundred others, which fall under daily observation. It is an active cause, by which some particular parts of nature, we find, produce alterations on other parts. But can a conclusion, with any propriety, be transferred from parts to the whole? Does not the great disproportion bar all comparison and inference? From observing the growth of a hair, can we learn any thing concerning the generation of a man? Would the manner of a leaf's blowing, even though perfectly known, afford us any instruction concerning the vegetation of a tree?

But allowing that we were to take the *operations* of one part of nature upon another for the foundation of our judgement concerning the *origin* of the whole (which never can be admitted) yet why select so minute, so weak, so bounded a principle as the reason and design of animals is found to be upon this planet? What peculiar privilege has this little agitation of the brain which we call *thought*, that we must thus make it the model of the whole universe? Our partiality in our own favour does indeed present it on all occasions; but sound philosophy ought carefully to guard against so natural an illusion.

So far from admitting, continued Philo, that the operations of a part can afford us any just conclusion concerning the origin of the whole, I will not allow any one part to form a rule for another part, if the latter be very remote from the former. Is there any reasonable ground to conclude, that the inhabitants of other planets possess thought, intelligence, reason, or any thing similar to these faculties in men? When Nature has so extremely diversified her manner of operation in this small globe; can we imagine, that she incessantly copies herself throughout so immense a universe? And if thought, as we may well suppose, be confined merely to this narrow corner, and has even there so limited a sphere of action; with what propriety can we assign it for the original cause of all things? The narrow view of a peasant, who makes his domestic economy the rule for the government of kingdoms, is in comparison a pardonable sophism.

But were we ever so much assured, that a thought and reason, resembling the human, were to be found throughout the whole universe, and were its activity elsewhere vastly greater and more commanding than it appears in this globe; yet I cannot see, why the operations of a world, constituted, arranged, adjusted, can with any propriety be extended to a world, which is in its embryo state, and is advancing towards that constitution and arrangement. By observation, we know somewhat of the economy, action, and nourishment of a finished animal; but we must transfer with great caution that observation to the growth of a fœtus in the womb, and still more, in the formation of an animalcule in the loins of its male parent. Nature, we find, even from our limited experience, possesses an infinite number of springs and principles, which incessantly discover themselves on every change of her position and situation. And what new and unknown principles would actuate her in so new and unknown a situation as that of the formation of a universe, we cannot, without the utmost temerity, pretend to determine.

A very small part of this great system, during a very short time, is very imperfectly discovered to us: and do we then pronounce decisively concerning the origin of the whole?

Admirable conclusion! Stone, wood, brick, iron, brass, have not, at this time, in this minute globe of earth, an order or arrangement without human art and contrivance: therefore the universe could not originally attain its order and arrangement, without something similar to human art. But is a part of nature a rule for another part very wide of the former? Is it a rule for the whole? Is a very small part a rule for the universe? Is nature in one situation, a certain rule for nature in another situation, vastly different from the former?

And can you blame me, Cleanthes, if I here imitate the prudent reserve of Simonides, who, according to the noted story, being asked by Hiero, *What God was?* desired a day to think of it, and then two days more; and after that manner continually prolonged the term, without ever bringing in his definition or description? Could you even blame me, if I had answered at first *that I did not know*, and was sensible that this subject lay vastly beyond the reach of my faculties? You might cry out sceptic and rallier as much as you pleased: but having found, in so many other subjects, much more familiar, the imperfections and even contradictions of human reason, I never should expect any success from its feeble conjectures, in a subject, so sublime, and so remote from the sphere of our observation. When two *species* of objects have always been observed to be conjoined together, I can *infer*, by custom, the existence of one wherever I *see* the existence of the other: and this I call an argument from experience. But how this argument can have place, where the objects, as in the present case, are single, individual, without parallel, or specific resemblance, may be difficult to explain. And will any man tell me with a serious countenance, that an orderly universe must arise from some thought and art, like the human; because we have experience of it? To ascertain this reasoning, it were requisite, that we had experience of the origin of worlds; and it is not sufficient surely, that we have seen ships and cities arise from human art and contrivance. . . .

Philo was proceeding in this vehement manner, somewhat between jest and earnest, as it appeared to me; when he observed some signs of impatience in Cleanthes, and then immediately stopped short. What I had to suggest, said Cleanthes, is only that you would not abuse terms, or make use of popular expressions to subvert philosophical reasonings. You know, that the vulgar often distinguish reason from experience, even where the question relates only to matter of fact and existence; though it is found, where that *reason* is properly analyzed, that it is nothing but a species of experience. To prove by experience the origin of the universe from mind is not more contrary to common speech than to prove the motion of the earth from the same principle. And a caviller might raise all the same objections to the Copernican system, which you have urged against my reasonings. Have you other earths, might he say, which you have seen to move? Have . . .

Yes! cried Philo, interrupting him, we have other earths. Is not the moon another earth, which we see to turn round its centre? Is not Venus another earth, where we observe the same phenomenon? Are not the revolutions of the sun also a confirmation, from analogy, of the same theory? All the planets, are they not earths, which revolve about the sun? Are not the satellites moons, which move round Jupiter and Saturn, and along with these primary planets, round the sun? These analogies and resemblances, with others, which I have not mentioned, are the sole proofs of the Copernican system: and to you it belongs to consider, whether you have any analogies of the same kind to support your theory.

In reality, Cleanthes, continued he, the modern system of astronomy is now so much received by all enquirers, and has become so essential a part even of our earliest education, that we are not commonly very scrupulous in examining the reasons upon which it is founded. It is now become a matter of mere curiosity to study the first writers on that subject, who had the full force of prejudice to encounter, and were obliged to turn their arguments on every side, in order to render them popular and convincing. But if we peruse Galileo's famous Dialogues concerning the system of the world, we shall find, that that great genius, one of the sublimest that ever existed, first bent all his endeavours to prove, that there was no foundation for the distinction commonly made between elementary and celestial substances. The schools, proceeding from the illusions of sense, had carried this distinction very far; and had established the latter substances to be ingenerable, incorruptible, unalterable, impassible; and had assigned all the opposite qualities to the former. But Galileo, beginning with the moon, proved its similarity in every particular to the earth; its convex figure, its natural darkness when not illuminated, its density, its distinction into solid and liquid, the variations of its phases, the mutual illuminations of the earth and moon, their mutual eclipses, the inequalities of the lunar surface, etc. After many instances of this kind, with regard to all the planets, men plainly saw, that these bodies became proper objects of experience; and that the similarity of their nature enabled us to extend the same arguments and phenomena from one to the other.

In this cautious proceeding of the astronomers, you may read your own condemnation, Cleanthes; or rather may see, that the subject in which you are engaged exceeds all human reason and enquiry. Can you pretend to show any such similarity between the fabric of a house, and the generation of a universe? Have you ever seen nature in any such situation as resembles the first arrangement of the elements? Have worlds ever been formed under your eye? and have you had leisure to observe the whole progress of the phenomenon, from the first appearance of order to its final consummation? If you have, then cite your experience, and deliver your theory.

But to show you still more inconveniencies, continued Philo, in your Anthropomorphism; please to take a new survey of your principles. *Like effects prove like causes.* This is the experimental argument; and this, you say too, is the sole theological argument. Now it is certain, that the liker the effects are, which are seen, and the liker the causes, which are inferred, the stronger is the argument. Every departure on either side diminishes the probability, and renders the experiment less conclusive. You cannot doubt of the principle: neither ought you to reject its consequences. . . .

Now, Cleanthes, said Philo, with an air of alacrity and triumph, mark the consequences. *First,* By this method of reasoning, you renounce all claim to infinity in any of the attributes of the Deity. For as the cause ought only to be proportioned to the effect, and the effect, so far as it falls under our cognizance, is not infinite; what pretensions have we, upon your suppositions, to ascribe that attribute to the divine Being? You will still insist, that, by removing him so much from all similarity to human creatures, we give in to the most arbitrary hypothesis, and at the same time weaken all proofs of his existence.

Secondly, You have no reason, on your theory, for ascribing perfection to the Deity, even in his finite capacity; or for supposing him free from every error, mistake, or incoherence in his undertakings. There are many inexplicable difficulties in the works of Nature, which, if we allow a perfect author to be proved *a priori*, are easily solved, and become only seeming difficulties, from the narrow capacity of man, who cannot trace infinite relations. But according to your method of reasoning, these difficulties become all real; and perhaps will be insisted on, as new instances of likeness to human art and contrivance. At least, you must acknowledge, that it is impossible for us to tell, from our limited views, whether this system contains any great faults, or deserves any considerable praise, if compared to other possible, and even real systems. Could a peasant, if the Æneid were read to him, pronounce that poem to be absolutely faultless, or even assign to it its proper rank among the productions of human wit; he, who had never seen any other production?

But were this world ever so perfect a production, it must still remain uncertain, whether all the excellences of the work can justly be ascribed to the workman. If we survey a ship, what an exalted idea must we form of the ingenuity of the carpenter, who framed so complicated, useful, and beautiful a machine? And what surprise must we feel, when we find him a stupid mechanic, who imitated others, and copied an art, which, through a long succession of ages, after multiplied trials, mistakes, corrections, deliberations, and controversies, had been gradually improving? Many worlds might have been botched and bungled, throughout an eternity, ere this system was struck out: much labor lost: many fruitless trials made: and a slow, but continued improvement carried on during infinite ages in the art of world making. In such subjects, who can determine, where the truth; nay, who can conjecture where the probability, lies; amidst a great number of hypotheses which may be proposed, and a still greater number which may be imagined?

And what shadow of an argument, continued Philo, can you produce, from your hypothesis, to prove the unity of the Deity? A great number of men join in building a house or ship, in rearing a city, in framing a commonwealth: why may not several deities combine in contriving and framing a world? This is only so much greater similarity to human affairs. By sharing the work among several, we may so much further limit the attributes of each, and get rid of that extensive power and knowledge, which must be supposed in one deity, and which, according to you, can only serve to weaken the proof of his existence. And if such foolish, such vicious creatures as man can yet often unite in framing and executing one plan; how much more those deities or dæmons, whom we may suppose several degrees more perfect!

To multiply causes, without necessity, is indeed contrary to true philosophy: but this principle applies not to the present case. Were one deity antecedently proved by your theory, who were possessed of every attribute, requisite to the production of the universe; it would be needless, I own (though not absurd) to suppose any other deity existent. But while it is still a question, Whether all these attributes are united in one subject, or dispersed among several independent beings: by what phenomena in nature can we pretend to decide the controversy? Where we see a body raised in a scale, we are sure that there is in the opposite scale, however concealed from sight, some counterpoising weight equal to it: but it is still allowed to doubt, whether that weight be an aggregate of several distinct bodies, or one uniform united mass. And if the weight requisite very much exceeds any thing which we have ever seen conjoined in any single body, the former supposition becomes still more probable and natural. An intelligent being of such vast power and capacity, as is necessary to produce the universe, or, to speak in the language of ancient philosophy, so prodigious an animal, exceeds all analogy, and even comprehension.

But further, Cleanthes; men are mortal, and renew their species by generation; and this is common to all living creatures. The two great sexes of male and female, says Milton, animate the world. Why must this circumstance, so universal, so essential, be excluded from those numerous and limited deities? Behold then the theogony of ancient times brought back upon us.

And why not become a perfect Anthropomorphite? Why not assert the deity or deities to be corporeal, and to have eyes, a nose, mouth, ears, etc.? Epicurus maintained, that no man had ever seen reason but in a human figure; therefore the gods must have a human figure. And this argument, which is deservedly so much ridiculed by Cicero, becomes, according to you, solid and philosophical.

In a word, Cleanthes, a man, who follows your hypothesis, is able, perhaps, to assert, or conjecture, that the universe, sometime, arose from something like design: but beyond that position he cannot ascertain one single circumstance, and is left afterwards to fix every point of this theology, by the utmost license of fancy and hypothesis. This world, for aught he knows is very faulty and imperfect, compared to a superior standard; and was only the first rude essay of some infant deity, who afterwards abandoned it, ashamed of his lame performance: it is the work only of some dependent, inferior deity; and is the object of derision to his superiors: it is the production of old age and dotage in some superannuated deity; and ever since his death, has run on at adventures, from the first impulse and active force, which it received from him. You justly give signs of horror, Demea, at these strange suppositions: but these, and a thousand more of the same kind, are Cleanthes's suppositions, not mine. From the moment the attributes of the Deity are supposed finite, all these have place. And I cannot, for my part, think, that so wild and unsettled a system of theology is, in any respect, preferable to none at all.

SØREN KIERKEGAARD

(1813–1855)

It is sometimes said that Søren Kierkegaard was the first existentialist of philosophical significance. Certainly he must be considered one of the founders of modern existentialism, and a figure of considerable importance in the history of Protestant Christianity as well. Between 1830 and 1840, Kierkegaard was a student of theology at Copenhagen University. Although he published voluminously in his lifetime, much of his work appeared under curious pseudonyms. His writings, sometimes brilliant, sometimes despairing, sometimes humorous, sometimes ironic, reflect a profoundly troubled cast of thought. Kierkegaard seems to have been concerned always to unsettle established opinion, whether that opinion be liberal or conservative. He was deeply concerned with his personal relationship to religion, and yet defiant of all that would encroach upon his individuality. Among his books are The Concept of Irony *(1841),* Either/Or; A Fragment of Life *(1843),* Fear and Trembling *(1843),* The Concept of Dread *(1846),* Concluding Unscientific Postscript *(1846), and* Philosophical Fragments *(1849)*

THE UNCHANGING GOD

God is unchangeable. In His omnipotence He created this visible world—and made Himself invisible. He clothed Himself in the visible world as in a garment; He changes it as one who shifts a garment—Himself unchanged. Thus in the world of sensible things. In the world of events He is present everywhere in every moment; in a truer sense than we can say of the most watchful human justice that it is present everywhere, God is omnipresent, though never seen by any mortal; present everywhere, in the least event as well as in the greatest, in that which can scarcely be called an event and in that which is the only event, in the death of a sparrow and in the birth of the Saviour of mankind. In each moment every actuality is a possibility in His almighty hand; He holds all in readiness, in every instant prepared to change everything: the opinions of men, their judgments, human greatness and human abasement; He changes all, Himself unchanged. When everything seems stable (for it is only in appearance that the external world is for a time unchanged, in reality it is always in flux) and in the overturn of all things, he remains equally unchanged; no change touches Him, not even the shadow of a change; in unaltered clearness He, the father of lights, remains eternally unchanged. In unaltered clearness—aye, this is precisely why He is unchanged, because He is pure clearness, a clarity which betrays no trace of dimness, and which no dimness can come near. With us men it is not so. We are not in this manner clear, and precisely for this reason we are subject to change: now something becomes clearer in us, now something is dimmed, and we are changed; now changes take place about us, and the shadow of these changes glides over us to alter us; now there falls upon us from the surroundings an altering light, while under all this we are again changed within ourselves.

This thought *is terrifying, all fear and trembling*. This aspect of it is in general perhaps less often emphasized: we complain of men and their mutability, and of the mutability of all temporal things; but God is unchangeable, this is our consolation, an entirely comforting thought—so speaks even frivolity. Aye, God is in very truth unchangeable.

But first and foremost, do you also have an understanding with God? Do you earnestly consider and sincerely strive to understand—and this is God's eternally unchangeable will for you as for every human being, that you should sincerely strive to attain this understanding—what God's will for you may be? Or do you live your life in such a fashion that this thought has never so much as entered your mind? How terrifying then that He is eternally unchangeable! For with this immutable will you

From the English edition of For Self-Examination and Judge for Yourselves, *trans. by David F. Swenson. This essay was originally delivered by Kierkegaard, in the form of a sermon, in 1851. By permission of the Oxford University Press.*

must nevertheless some time, sooner or later, come into collision—this immutable will, which desired that you should consider this because it desired your welfare; this immutable will, which cannot but crush you if you come into hostile collision with it.

In the second place, you who have some degree of understanding with God, do you also have a good understanding with Him? Is your will unconditionally His will, your wishes, each one of them, His commandments, your thoughts, first and last, His thoughts? If not, how terrifying that God is unchangeable, everlastingly, eternally, unchangeable! Consider but in this connection what it means to be at odds merely with a human being. But perhaps you are the stronger, and console yourself with the thought that the other will doubtless be compelled to change his attitude. But now if he happens to be the stronger—well, perhaps you think to have more endurance. But suppose it is an entire contemporary generation with which you are at odds; and yet, in that case you will perhaps say to yourself: seventy years is no eternity. But when the will is that of one eternally unchangeable—if you are at odds with this will it means an eternity: how terrifying!

Imagine a wayfarer. He has been brought to a standstill at the foot of a mountain, tremendous, impassable. It is this mountain—no, it is not his destiny to cross it, but he has set his heart upon the crossing; for his wishes, his longings, his desires, his very soul, which has an easier mode of conveyance, are already on the other side; it only remains for him to follow. Imagine him coming to be seventy years old; but the mountain still stands there, unchanged, impassable. Let him become twice seventy years; but the mountain stands there unalterably blocking his way, unchanged, impassable. Under all this he undergoes changes, perhaps; he dies away from his longings, his wishes, his desires; he now scarcely recognizes himself. And so a new generation finds him, altered, sitting at the foot of the mountain, which still stands there, unchanged, impassable. Suppose it to have happened a thousand years ago: the altered wayfarer is long since dead, and only a legend keeps his memory alive; it is the only thing that remains—aye, and also the mountain, unchanged, impassable. And now think of Him who is eternally unchangeable, for whom a thousand years are but as one day—ah, even this is too much to say, they are for Him as an instant, as if they did not even exist—consider then, if you have in the most distant manner a will to walk a different path than that which He wills for you: how terrifying!

True enough, if your will, if my will, if the will of all these many thousands happens to be not so entirely in harmony with God's will: things nevertheless take their course as best they may in the hurly-burly of the so-called actual world; it is as if God did not pay any attention. It is rather as if a just man—if there were such a man!—contemplating this world, a world which, as the Scriptures say, is dominated by evil, must needs feel disheartened because God does not seem to make Himself felt. But do you believe on that account that God has undergone any change? Or is the fact that God does not seem to make Himself felt any the less a terrifying fact, as long as it is nevertheless certain that He is eternally unchangeable? To me it does not seem so. Consider the matter, and then tell me which is the more terrible to contemplate: the picture of one who is infinitely the stronger, who grows tired of letting himself be mocked, and rises in his might to crush the refractory spirits—a sight terrible indeed, and so represented when we say that God is not mocked, pointing to the times when His annihilating punishments were visited upon the human race—but is this really the most terrifying sight? Is not this other sight still more terrifying: one infinitely powerful, who—eternally unchanged!—sits quite still and sees everything without altering a feature, almost as if He did not exist; while all the time, as the just man must needs complain, lies achieve success and win to power, violence and wrong gain the victory, to such an extent as even to tempt a better man to think that if he hopes to accomplish anything for the good he must in part use the same means; so that it is as if God were being mocked, God the infinitely powerful, the eternally unchangeable, who none the less is neither mocked nor changed—is not this the most terrifying sight? For why, do you think, is He so quiet? Because He knows with Himself that He is eternally unchangeable. Anyone not eternally sure of Himself could not keep so still, but would rise in his strength. Only one who is eternally immutable can be in this manner so still.

He gives men time, and He can afford to give them time, since He has eternity and is eternally unchangeable. He gives time, and that with premeditation. And then there comes an accounting in eternity, where nothing is forgotten, not even a single one of the improper words that were spoken; and He is eternally unchanged. And yet, it may be also an expression for His mercy that men are thus afforded time, time for conversion and betterment. But how fearful if the time is not used for this purpose! For in that case the folly and frivolity in us would rather have Him straightway ready with His punishment, instead of thus giving men time, seeming to take not cognizance of the wrong, and yet remaining eternally unchanged.

Ask one experienced in bringing up children—and in relation to God we are all more or less as children; ask one who has had to do with transgressors—and each one of us has at least once in his life gone astray, and goes astray for a longer or a shorter time, at longer or shorter intervals: you will find him ready to confirm the observation that for the frivolous it is a great help, or rather, that it is a preventive of frivolity (and who dares wholly acquit himself of frivolity!) when the punishment follows if possible instantly upon the transgression, so the memory of the frivolous may acquire the habit of associating the punishment immediately with the guilt. Indeed, if transgression and punishment were so bound up with one another that, as in a double-barreled shooting weapon, the pressure on a spring caused the punishment to follow instantly upon the seizure of the forbidden fruit, or immediately upon the commitment of the transgression—then I think that frivolity might take heed. But the longer the interval between guilt and punishment (which when truly understood is an expression for the gravity of the case), the greater the temptation to frivolity; as if the whole might perhaps be forgotten, or as if justice itself might alter and acquire different ideas with the passage of time, or as if at least it would be so long since the wrong was committed that it will become impossible to make an unaltered presentation of it before the bar of justice. Thus frivolity changes, and by no means for the better. It comes to feel itself secure; and when it has become secure it becomes more daring; and so the years pass, punishment is withheld, forgetfulness intervenes, and again the punishment is withheld, but new transgressions do not fail, and the old evil becomes still more malignant. And then finally all is over; death rolls down the curtain—and to all this (it was only frivolity!) there was an eternally unchangeable witness: is this also frivolity? One eternally unchangeable, and it is with this witness that you must make your reckoning. In the instant that the minute-hand of time showed seventy years, and the man died, during all that time the clock of eternity has scarcely moved perceptibly: to such a degree is everything present for the eternal, and for Him who is unchangeable.

And therefore, whoever you may be, take time to consider what I say to myself, that for God there is nothing significant and nothing insignificant, that in a certain sense the significant is for Him insignificant, and in another sense even the least significant is for Him infinitely significant. If then your will is not in harmony with His will, consider that you will never be able to evade Him. Be grateful to Him if through the use of mildness or of severity He teaches you to bring your will into agreement with His—how fearful if He makes no move to arrest your course, how fearful if in the case of any human being it comes to pass that he almost defiantly relies either upon the notion that God does not exist, or upon His having been changed, or even upon His being too great to take note of what we call trifles! For the truth is that God both exists and is eternally unchangeable; and His infinite greatness consists precisely in seeing even the least thing, and remembering even the least thing. Aye, and if you do not will as He wills, that He remembers it unchanged for an eternity!

There is thus sheer fear and trembling, for us frivolous and inconstant human beings, in this thought of God's unchangeableness. Oh, consider it well! Whether God makes Himself immediately felt or not, He is eternally unchangeable. He is eternally unchangeable, consider this, if as we say you have any matter outstanding with Him: He is unchangeable. You have perhaps promised Him something, obligated yourself in a sacred pledge—but in the course of time you have undergone a change, and now you rarely think of God—now that you have grown older, have you perhaps found more important things to think about? Or perhaps you now have different notions about God, and think that He does not concern Himself with the trifles of your life, regarding such beliefs as childishness. In any case you have just about forgotten what you promised Him; and thereupon you have proceeded to forget that you promised Him anything; and finally, you have forgotten, forgotten—aye, forgotten that He forgets nothing, since He is eternally unchangeable, forgotten that it is precisely the inverted childishness of mature years to imagine that anything is insignificant for God, or that God forgets anything, He who is eternally unchangeable!

In human relationships we so often complain of inconstancy, one party accuses the other of having changed. but even in the relationship between man and man, it is sometimes the case that the constancy of one party may come to seem like a tormenting affliction for the other. A man may, for example, have talked to another person about himself. What he said may have been merely a little childish, pardonably so. But perhaps, too, the matter was more serious than this: the poor foolish vain heart was tempted to speak in lofty tones of its enthusiasm, of the constancy of its feelings, and of its purposes in this world. The other man listened calmly; he did not even smile, or interrupt the speech; he let him speak on to the end, listened and kept silence; only he promised, as he was asked to do, not to forget what had been said. Then some time elapsed, and the first man had long since forgotten all this; only the other had not forgotten. Aye, let us suppose something still stranger: he had permitted himself to be moved inwardly by the thoughts that the first man had expressed under the influence of his mood, when he poured out, so to speak, his momentary feeling; he had in sincere endeavor shaped his life in accordance with these ideas. What torment in this unchanged remembrance by one who showed only too clearly that he had retained in his memory every last detail of what had been said in that moment!

And now consider Him, who is eternally unchangeable—and this human heart! O this human heart, what is not hidden in your secret recesses, unknown to others—and that is the least of it—but sometimes almost unknown to the individual himself! When a man has lived a few years it is almost as if it were a burial-plot, this human heart! There they lie buried in forgetfulness: promises, intentions, resolutions, entire plans and fragments of plans, and God knows what—aye, so say we men, for we rarely think about what we say; we say: there lies God knows what. And this we say half in a spirit of frivolity, and half weary of life—and it is so fearfully true that God does know what to the last detail, knows what you have forgotten, knows what for your recollection has suffered alteration, knows it all unchanged. He does not remember it merely as having happened some time ago, nay, He remembers it as if it were today. He knows whether, in connection with any of these wishes, intentions, resolutions, something so to speak was said to Him about it—and He is eternally unchanged and eternally unchangeable. Oh, if the remembrance that another human being carries about with him may seem as it were a burden to you—well, this remembrance is after all not always so entirely trustworthy, and in any case it cannot endure for an eternity: sometime I may expect to be freed from this other man and his remembrance. But an omniscient witness and an eternally unchangeable remembrance, one from which you can never free yourself, least of all in eternity: how fearful!

No, in a manner eternally unchanged, everything is for God eternally present, always equally before Him. No shadow of variation, neither that of morning nor of evening, neither that of youth or of old age, neither that of forgetfulness nor of excuse, changes Him; for Him there is no shadow. If we human beings are mere shadows, as is sometimes said, He is eternal clearness in eternal unchangeableness. If we are shadows that glide away—my soul, look well to thyself; for whether you will it or not, you go to meet eternity, to meet Him, and He is eternal clearness. Hence it is not so much that He keeps a reckoning, as that He is Himself the reckoning. It is said that we must render up an account, as if we perhaps had a long time to prepare for it, and also perhaps as if it were likely to be cluttered up with such an enormous mass of detail as to make it impossible to get the reckoning finished: O my soul, the account is every moment complete! For the unchangeable clearness of God is the reckoning, complete to the last detail, preserved by Him who is eternally unchangeable, and who has forgotten nothing of the things that I have forgotten, and who does not, as I do, remember some things otherwise than they really were.

There is thus sheer fear and trembling in this thought of the unchangeableness of God, almost as if it were far, far beyond the power of any human being to sustain a relationship to such an unchangeable power; aye, as if this thought must drive a man to such unrest and anxiety of mind as to bring him to the verge of despair.

But then it is also true that *there is rest and happiness in this thought*. It is really true that when, wearied with all this human inconstancy, this temporal and earthly mutability, and wearied also of your own inconstancy, you might wish to find a place where rest may be found for your weary head, your weary thoughts, your weary spirit, so that you might rest and find complete repose: Oh, in the unchangeableness of God there is rest! When you therefore permit this unchangeableness to serve you according to His will, for your own welfare, your eternal welfare; when you submit yourself to discipline, so that your selfish will (and it is from this that the change chiefly comes, more than from the outside) dies away, the sooner the better—and there is no help for it, you must whether willing or resisting, for think how vain it is for your will to be at odds with an eternal immutability; be therefore as the child when it profoundly feels that it has over against itself a will in relation to which nothing avails except obedience—when you submit to be disciplined by His unchangeable will, so as to renounce inconstancy and changeableness and caprice and self-will: then you will steadily rest more and more securely, and more and more blessedly, in the unchangeableness of God.

For that the thought of God's unchangeableness is a blessed thought—who can doubt it? But take heed that you become of such a mind that you can rest happily in this immutability! Oh, as one is wont to speak who has a happy home, so speaks such an individual. He says: my home is eternally secure, I rest in the unchangeableness of God. This is a rest that no one can disturb for you except yourself; if you could become completely obedient in invariable obedience, you would each and every moment, with the same necessity as that by which a heavy body sinks to the earth or a light body moves upward, freely rest in God.

And as for the rest, let all things change as they do. If the scene of your activity is on a larger stage, you will experience the mutability of all things in greater measure; but even on a lesser stage, or on the smallest stage of all, you will still experience the same, perhaps quite as painfully. You will learn how men change, how you yourself change; sometimes it will even seem to you as if God Himself changed, all of which belongs to the upbringing. On this subject of the mutability of all things one older than I would be able to speak in better fashion, while perhaps what I could say might seem to someone very young as if it were new. But this we shall not further expound, leaving it rather for the manifold experiences of life to unfold for each one in particular, in a manner intended especially for him, that which all other men have experienced before him. Sometimes the changes will be such as to call to mind the saying that variety is a pleasure—an indescribable pleasure! There will also come times when you will have occasion to discover for yourself a saying which the language has suppressed, and you will say to yourself: "Change is not pleasant—how could I ever have said that variety is a pleasure!" When this experience comes to you, you will have especial occasion (though you will surely not forget this in the first case either) to seek Him who is unchangeable.

My hearer, this hour is now soon past, and the discourse. Unless you yourself will it otherwise, this hour and its discourse will soon be forgotten. And unless you yourself will it otherwise, the thought of God's unchangeableness will also soon be forgotten in the midst of life's changes. But for this He will surely not be responsible, He who is unchangeable! But if you do not make yourself guilty of forgetfulness with respect to it, you will in this thought have found a sufficiency for your entire life, aye, for eternity.

Imagine a solitary wayfarer, a desert wanderer. Almost burned by the heat of the sun, languishing with thirst, he finds a spring. O refreshing coolness! Now God be praised, he says—and yet it was merely a spring he found; what then must not he say who found God! and yet he too must say: "God be praised, I have found God—now I am well provided for. Your faithful coolness, O beloved well-spring, is not subject to any change. In the cold of winter, if winter visited this place, you would not become colder, but would preserve the same coolness unchanged, for the waters of the spring do not freeze! In the midday heat of the summer sun you preserve precisely the same coolness, for the waters of the spring do not become lukewarm!" There is nothing untrue in what he says, no false exaggeration in his eulogy. (And he who chooses a spring as subject for his eulogy chooses in my opinion no ungrateful theme, as anyone may better understand the more he knows what the desert signifies, and solitude.) However, the life of our wanderer took a turn otherwise than he had thought; he lost touch with the spring, and went astray in the wide world. Many years later he returned to the same place. His first thought was of the spring—but it was not, it had run dry. For a moment he stood silent in grief. Then he gathered himself together and said: "No, I will not retract a single word of all that I said in your praise; it was all true. And if I praised your refreshing coolness while you were still in being, O beloved well-spring, let me now also praise it when you have vanished, in order that there may be some proof of unchangeableness in a human breast. Nor can I say that you deceived me; had I found you, I am convinced that your coolness would have been quite unchanged—and more you had not promised."

But Thou O God, who are unchangeable, Thou art always and invariably to be found, and always to be found unchanged. Whether in life or in death, no one journeys so far afield that Thou art not to be found by him, that Thou are not there, Thou who art everywhere. It is not so with the well-springs of earth, for they are to be found only in special places. And besides—overwhelming security!—Thou dost not remain, like the spring, in a single place, but Thou dost follow the traveller on his way. Ah, and no one ever wanders so far astray that he cannot find the way back to Thee, Thou who are not merely as a spring that may be found—how poor and inadequate a description of what Thou art!—but rather as a spring that itself seeks out the thirsty traveller, the errant wanderer: who has ever heard the like of any spring! Thus Thou art unchangeably always and everywhere to be found. And whenever any human being comes to Thee, of whatever age, at whatever time of the day, in whatever state: if he comes in sincerity he always finds Thy love equally warm, like the spring's unchanged coolness, O Thou who art unchangeable! Amen!

FRIEDRICH NIETZSCHE

(1844–1900)

Friedrich Wilhelm Nietzsche was born in the Prussian province of Saxony, and received his education at Naumburg and Bonn. Although a theology student at first, reading the philosophy of Schopenhauer caused him to give up his religious beliefs, and he began to concentrate upon philology instead. At this time he was strongly influenced by the music and thought of Richard Wagner. When Nietzsche's study of Greek artistic achievement, The Birth of Tragedy, *appeared in 1870–71, it was severely condemned by academic scholars. He later broke with Wagner and, in 1879, as his health began to fail, Nietzsche resigned his professorship at Basle, in Switzerland, and spent the remainder of his life in Northern Italy and on the French Riviera. The next decade was a highly productive one for him.* Thus Spake Zarathustra *was written in 1883–85,* Beyond Good and Evil *in 1885–86, and* The Genealogy of Morals *in 1887. But the emotional turmoil of his life was unendurable, and in 1888 he began to suffer from mental illness, never to recover.*

GUILT AND THE FORGING OF BELIEF

I can no longer postpone giving tentative expression to my own hypothesis concerning the origin of "bad conscience." It is one that may fall rather strangely on our ears and that requires close meditation. I take bad conscience to be a deep-seated malady to which man succumbed under the pressure of the most profound transformation he ever underwent—the one that made him once and for all a sociable and pacific creature. Just as happened in the case of those sea creatures who were forced to become land animals in order to survive, these semi-animals, happily adapted to the wilderness, to war, free roaming, and adventure, were forced to change their nature. Of a sudden they found all their instincts devalued, unhinged. They must walk on legs and carry themselves, where before the water had carried them: a terrible heaviness weighed upon them. They felt inapt for the simplest manipulations, for in this new, unknown world they could no longer count on the guidance of their unconscious drives. They were forced to think, deduce, calculate, weigh cause and effect—unhappy people, reduced to their weakest, most fallible organ, their consciousness! I doubt that there has ever been on earth such a feeling of misery, such a leaden discomfort. It was not that those old instincts had abruptly ceased making their demands; but now their satisfaction was rare and difficult. For the most part they had to depend on new, covert satisfactions. All instincts that are not allowed free play turn inward. This is what I call man's interiorization; it alone provides the soil for the growth of what is later called man's *soul*. Man's interior world, originally meager and tenuous, was expanding in every dimension, in proportion as the outward discharge of his feelings was curtailed. The formidable bulwarks by means of which the polity protected itself against the ancient instincts of freedom (punishment was one of the strongest of these bulwarks) caused those wild, extravagant instincts to turn in upon man. Hostility, cruelty, the delight in persecution, raids, excitement, destruction all turned against their begetter. Lacking external enemies and resistances, and confined within an oppressive narrowness and regularity, man began rending, persecuting, terrifying himself, like a wild beast hurling itself against the bars of its cage. This languisher, devoured by nostalgia for the desert, who had to turn *himself* into an adventure, a torture chamber, an insecure and dangerous wilderness—this fool, this pining and desperate prisoner, became the inventor of "bad conscience." Also the generator of the greatest and most disastrous of maladies, of which humanity has not to this day been cured: his sickness of himself, brought on by the violent severance from his animal past, by his sudden leap and fall into new layers and conditions of existence, by his declaration of war against the old instincts that had hitherto been the foundation of his power, his joy, and his awesomeness. Let me hasten to add that the phenomenon of an animal soul turning in upon itself, taking arms against itself, was so novel, profound, mysterious, contradictory, and pregnant with possibility, that the whole complexion of the universe was changed thereby. This spectacle (and the end of it is not yet in sight) required a divine audience to do it justice. It was a spectacle too sublime and paradoxical to pass unnoticed on some trivial planet. Henceforth man was to figure among the most unexpected and breathtaking throws in the game of dice played by Heracleitus' great "child," be he called Zeus or Chance. Man now aroused an interest, a suspense, a hope, almost a conviction—as though in him something were heralded, as though he were not a goal but a way, an interlude, a bridge, a great promise. . . .

My hypothesis concerning the origin of bad conscience presupposes that this change was neither gradual nor voluntary, that it was not an organic growing into new conditions but rather an abrupt break, a leap, a thing compelled, an ineluctable disaster, which could neither be struggled against nor even resented. It further presupposes that the fitting of a hitherto unrestrained and shapeless populace into a tight mold, as it had begun with an act of violence, had to be brought to conclusion by a series of violent acts; that the earliest commonwealth constituted a terrible despotism, a ruthless, oppressive machinery for not only kneading and suppling a brutish populace but actually shaping it. I have used the word "commonwealth," but it should be clearly understood what I mean: a pack of savages, a race of conquerors, themselves organized for war and able to organize others, fiercely dominating a population perhaps vastly superior in numbers yet amorphous and nomadic. Such was the beginning of the human polity; I take it we have got over that sentimentalism that would have it begin with a contract. What do men who can command, who are born rulers, who evince power in act and deportment, have to do with contracts? Such beings are unaccountable; they come like destiny, without rhyme or reason, ruthlessly, bare of pretext. Suddenly they are here, like a stroke of lightning, too terrible, convincing, and "different" for hatred even. Their work is an instinctive imposing of forms. They are the most spontaneous, most unconscious artists that exist. They appear, and presently something entirely new has arisen, a live dominion whose parts and functions are delimited and interrelated, in which there is room for nothing that has not previously received its meaning from the whole. Being natural organizers, these men know nothing of guilt, responsibility, consideration. They are actuated by the terrible egotism of the artist, which is justified by the work he must do, as the mother by the child she will bear. Bad conscience certainly did not originate with these men, yet, on the other hand, that unseemly growth could not have developed *without* them, without their hammer blows, their artist's violence, which drove a great quantity of freedom out of sight and made it latent. In its earliest phase bad conscience is nothing other than the instinct of freedom forced to become latent, driven underground, and forced to vent its energy upon itself.

We should guard against taking too dim a view of this phenomenon simply because it is both ugly and painful. After all the same will to power which in those violent artists and organizers created politics, in the "labyrinth of the hearts"—more pettily, to be sure, and in inverse direction—created negative ideals and humanity's bad conscience. Except that now the material upon which this great natural force was employed was man himself, his old animal self—and not, as in that grander and more spectacular phenomenon—his fellow man. This secret violation of the self, this artist's cruelty, this urge to impose on recalcitrant matter a form, a will, a distinction, a feeling of contradiction and contempt, this sinister task of a soul divided against itself, which makes itself suffer for the pleasure of suffering, this most energetic "bad conscience"—has it not given birth to a wealth of strange beauty and affirmation? Has it not given birth to beauty itself? Would beauty exist if ugliness had not first taken cognizance of itself, not said to itself, "I am ugly"? This hint will serve, at any rate, to solve the riddle of why contradictory terms such as *selflessness, self-denial, self-sacrifice* may intimate an ideal, a beauty. Nor will the reader doubt henceforth that the *joy* felt by the self-denying, self-sacrificing, selfless person was from the very start a *cruel* joy.—So much for the origin of altruism as a moral value. Bad conscience, the desire for self-mortification, is the well-spring of all altruistic values.

There can be no doubt that bad conscience is a sickness, but so, in a sense, is pregnancy. We shall presently describe the conditions which carried that "sickness" to its highest and most terrible peak. But first let us return for a moment to an earlier consideration. The civil-law relationship of debtor to creditor has been projected into yet another context, where we find it even more difficult to understand today, namely into the relationship between living men and their forebears. Among primitive tribes, each new generation feels toward the preceding ones, and especially toward the original founders of the tribe, a *juridical* obligation (rather than an *emotional* obligation, which seems to be of relatively recent origin). Early societies were convinced that their continuance was guaranteed solely by the sacrifices and achievements of their ancestors and that these sacrifices and achievements required to be paid back. Thus a debt was acknowledged which continued to increase, since the ancestors, surviving as powerful spirits, did not cease to provide the tribe with new benefits out of their store. Gratuitously? But nothing was gratuitous in those crude and "insensitive" times. Then how could they be repaid? By burnt offerings (to provide them with food), by rituals, shrines, customs, but above all, by obedience—for all rites, having been established by the forebears, were also permanently enjoined by them. But could they ever be *fully* repaid? An anxious doubt remained and grew steadily, and every so often there occurred some major act of "redemption," some gigantic repayment of the creditor (the famous sacrifice of the first-born, for example; in any case blood, human blood). Given this primitive logic, the fear of the ancestor and his power and the consciousness of indebtedness increase in direct proportion as the power of the tribe itself increases, as it becomes more successful in battle, independent, respected and feared. Never the other way round. Every step leading to the degeneration of the tribe, every setback, every sign of imminent dissolution, tends to diminish the fear of the ancestral spirits, to make them seem of less account, less wise, less provident, less powerful. Following this kind of logic to its natural term, we arrive at a situation in which the ancestors of the most powerful tribes have become so fearful to the imagination that they have receded at last into a numinous shadow: the ancestor becomes a god. Perhaps this is the way all gods have arisen, out of *fear*. . . . And if anyone should find it necessary to add, "But also out of piety," his claim would scarcely be justified for the longest and earliest period of the human race. But it would certainly hold true for that intermediate period during which the noble clans emerged, of whom it may justly be said that they paid back their ancestors (heroes or gods) with interest all those noble properties which had since come to reside abundantly in themslves. We shall have an opportunity later on of dealing with this "ennoblement" of the ancestral spirits (which is not the same thing as their "consecration"), but first, let us bring to a conclusion the story of man's consciousness of guilt.

Man's firm belief that he was indebted to the gods did not cease with the decline of tribal organization. Just as man has inherited from the blood aristocracies the concepts *good* and *bad*, together with the psychological penchant for hierarchies, so he has inherited from the tribes, together with the tribal gods, a burden of outstanding debt and the desire to make final restitution. (The bridge is provided by those large populations of slaves and serfs, who, either perforce or through servile mimicry, had adopted the cults of their overlords. The heritage spreads out from them in all directions.) The sense of indebtedness to the gods continued to grow through the centuries, keeping pace with the evolution of man's concept of the deity. (The endless tale of ethnic struggle, triumph, reconciliation, and fusion, in short, whatever precedes the final hierarchy of racial strains in some great synthesis, is mirrored in the welter of divine genealogies and legends dealing with divine battles, victories, and reconciliations. Every progress toward universal empire has also been a progress toward a universal pantheon. Despotism, by overcoming the independent nobles, always prepares the way for some form of monotheism.) The advent of the Christian god, the "highest potency" god yet conceived by man, has been accompanied by the widest dissemination of the sense of indebtedness, guilt. If we are right in assuming that we have now entered upon the inverse development, it stands to reason that the steady decline of belief in a Christian god should entail a commensurate decline in man's guilt consciousness. It also stands to reason—doesn't it?—that a complete and definitive victory of atheism might deliver mankind altogether from its feeling of being indebted to its beginnings, its *causa prima*. Atheism and a kind of "second innocence" go together.

So much, for the moment, about the connection of "guilt" and "duty" with religious presuppositions. I have deliberately left on one side the "moralization" of these terms (their pushing back into conscience, the association of the notion of bad conscience with a deity), and even wrote at the end of the last paragraph as though such a moralization had never taken place; as though with the notion of a divine creditor falling into disuse those notions too were doomed. Unfortunately this is far from being the case. The modern moralization of the ideas of guilt and duty—their relegation to a purely subjective "bad conscience"—represents a determined attempt to invert the normal order of development, or at least to stop it in its tracks. The object now is to close the prospect of final deliverance and make man's gaze rebound from an iron barrier; to force the ideas of guilt and duty to face about and fiercely turn on—whom? Obviously on the "debtor," first of all, who, infested and eaten away by bad conscience, which spreads like a polyp, comes to view his debt as unredeemable by any act of atonement (the notion of "eternal penance"). But eventually the "creditor" too is turned on in the same fashion. Now the curse falls upon man's *causa prima* ("Adam," "original sin," the "bondage of the will"); or upon nature, which gave birth to man and which is now made the repository of the evil principle (nature as the instrument of the devil); or upon universal existence, which now appears as absolute nonvalue (nihilistic turning away from life, a longing for nothingness or for life's "opposite," for a different sort of "being"—Buddhism, etc.). Then suddenly we come face to face with that paradoxical and ghastly expedient which brought temporary relief to tortured humanity, that most brilliant stroke of Christianity: God's sacrifice of himself for man. God makes himself the ransom for what could not otherwise be ransomed; God alone has power to absolve us of a debt we can no longer discharge; the creditor offers himself as a sacrifice for his debtor out of sheer love (can you believe it?), out of love for his debtor. . . .

By now the reader will have guessed what has really been happening behind all these façades. Man, with his need for self-torture, his sublimated cruelty resulting from the cooping up of his animal nature within a polity, invented bad conscience in order to hurt himself, after the blocking of the more natural outlet of his cruelty. Then this guilt-ridden man seized upon religion in order to exacerbate his self-torment to the utmost. The thought of being in God's debt became his new instrument of torture. He focused in God the last of the opposites he could find to his true and inveterate animal instincts, making these a sin against God (hostility, rebellion against the "Lord," the "Father," the "Creator"). He stretched himself upon the contradiction "God" and "Devil" as on a rack. He projected all his denials of self, nature, naturalness out of himself as affirmations, as true being, embodiment, reality, as God (the divine Judge and Executioner), as transcendence, as eternity, as endless torture, as hell, the infinitude of guilt and punishment. In such psychological cruelty we see an insanity of the *will* that is without parallel: man's will to find himself guilty, and unredeemably so; his will to believe that he might be punished to all eternity without ever expunging his guilt; his will to poison the very foundation of things with the problem of guilt and punishment and thus to cut off once and for all his escape from this labyrinth of obsession; his will to erect an ideal (God's holiness) in order to assure himself of his own absolute unworthiness. What a mad, unhappy animal is man! What strange notions occur to him; what perversities, what paroxysms of nonsense, what bestialities of idea burst from him, the moment he is prevented ever so little from being a beast of action! . . . All this is exceedingly curious and interesting, but dyed with such a dark, somber, enervating sadness that one must resolutely tear away one's gaze. Here, no doubt, is sickness, the most terrible sickness that has wasted man thus far. And if one is still able to hear—but how few these days have ears to hear it!—in this night of torment and absurdity the cry *love* ring out, the cry of rapt longing, of redemption in love, he must turn away with a shudder of invincible horror. . . . Man harbors too much horror; the earth has been a lunatic asylum for too long.

15

Religion in Contemporary Perspective

PAUL TILLICH

(1886–1965)

Paul Tillich came to the United States in 1933 from Germany, where he had taught theology at various universities. From 1933 to 1954 he was professor of philosophy and theology at Union Theological Seminary, after which he became University Professor at Harvard. A prolific and influential author, his major writings include The Shaking of the Foundations *(1948),* The Protestant Era *(1948),* Systematic Philosophy *(3 vols., 1951–1963),* The Courage to Be *(1952),* Dynamics of Faith *(1956), and* Theology of Culture *(1959).*

THE LOST DIMENSION

The decisive element in the predicament of Western man in our period is his loss of the dimension of depth. Of course, "dimension of depth" is a metaphor. It is taken from the spatial realm and applied to man's spiritual life. What does it mean?

It means that man has lost an answer to the question: What is the meaning of life? Where do we come from, where do we go to? What shall we do, what should we become in the short stretch between birth and death? Such questions are not answered or even asked if the "dimension of depth" is lost. And this is precisely what has happened to man in our period of history. He has lost the courage to ask such questions with an infinite seriousness—as former generations did—and he has lost the courage to receive answers to these questions, wherever they may come from.

I suggest that we call the dimension of depth the religious dimension in man's nature. Being religious means asking passionately the question of the meaning of our existence and being willing to receive answers, even if the answers hurt. Such an idea of religion makes religion universally human, but it certainly differs from what is usually called religion. It does not describe religion as the belief in the existence of gods or one God, and as a set of activities and institutions for the sake of relating oneself to these beings in thought, devotion and obedience. No one can deny that the religions which have appeared in history are religions in this sense. Nevertheless, religion in its innermost nature is more than religion in this narrower sense. It is the state of being concerned about one's own being and being universally.

There are many people who are ultimately concerned in this way who feel far removed, however, from religion in the narrower sense, and therefore from every historical religion. It often happens that such people take the question of the meaning of their life infinitely seriously and reject any historical religion just for this reason. They feel that the concrete regions fail to express their profound concern adequately. They are religious while rejecting the religions. It is this experience which forces us to distinguish the meaning of religion as living in the dimension of depth from particular expressions of one's ultimate concern in the symbols and institutions of a concrete religion. If we now turn to the concrete analysis of the religious situation of our time, it is obvious that our key must be the basic meaning of religion and not any particular religion, not even Christianity. What does this key disclose about the predicament of man in our period?

From "The Lost Dimension in Religion," (New York: Alfred A. Knopf; Reprinted from the June 14, 1968, issue of The Saturday Evening Post, *with permission of* The Saturday Evening Post, © 1958 The Curtis Publishing Company.

If we define religion as the state of being grasped by an infinite concern we must say: Man in our time has lost such infinite concern. And the resurgence of religion is nothing but a desperate and mostly futile attempt to regain what has been lost.

How did the dimension of depth become lost? Like any important event, it has many causes, but certainly not the one which one hears often mentioned from ministers' pulpits and evangelists' platforms—namely, that a widespread impiety of modern man is responsible. Modern man is neither more pious nor more impious than man in any other period. The loss of the dimension of depth is caused by the relation of man to his world and to himself in our period, the period in which nature is being subjected scientifically and technically to the control of man. In this period, life in the dimension of depth is replaced by life in the horizontal dimension. The driving forces of the industrial society of which we are a part go ahead horizontally and not vertically. In popular terms this is expressed in phrases like "better and better," "bigger and bigger," "more and more." One should not disparage the feeling which lies behind such speech. Man is right in feeling that he is able to know and transform the world he encounters without a foreseeable limit. He can go ahead in all directions without a definite boundary.

A most expressive symbol of this attitude of going ahead in the horizontal dimension is the breaking through of the space which is controlled by the gravitational power of the earth into the world-space. It is interesting that one calls this world-space simply "space" and speaks, for instance, of space travel, as if every trip were not travel into space. Perhaps one feels that the true nature of space has been discovered only through our entering into indefinite world-space. In any case, the predominance of the horizontal dimension over the dimension of depth has been immensely increased by the opening up of the space beyond the space of the earth.

If we now ask what does man do and seek if he goes ahead in the horizontal dimension, the answer is difficult. Sometimes one is inclined to say that the mere movement ahead without an end, the intoxication with speeding forward without limits, is what satisfies him. But this answer is by no means sufficient. For on his way into space and time man changes the world he encounters. And the changes made by him change himself. He transforms everything he encounters into a tool; and in doing so he himself becomes a tool. But if he asks, a tool for what, there is no answer.

One does not need to look far beyond everyone's daily experience in order to find examples to describe this predicament. Indeed our daily life in office and home, in cars and airplanes, at parties and conferences, while reading magazines and watching television, while looking at advertisements and hearing radio, are in themselves continuous examples of a life which has lost the dimension of depth. It runs ahead, every moment is filled with something which must be done or seen or said or planned. But no one can experience depth without stopping and becoming aware of himself. Only if he has moments in which he does not care about what comes next can he experience the meaning of this moment here and now and ask himself about the meaning of his life. As long as the preliminary, transitory concerns are not silenced, no matter how interesting and valuable and important they may be, the voice of the ultimate concern cannot be heard. This is the deepest root of the loss of the dimension of depth in our period—the loss of religion in its basic and universal meaning.

If the dimension of depth is lost, the symbols in which life in this dimension has expressed itself must also disappear. I am speaking of the great symbols of the historical religions in our Western world, of Judaism and Christianity. The reason that the religious symbols became lost is not primarily scientific criticism, but it is a complete misunderstanding of their meaning; and only because of this misunderstanding was scientific critique able, and even justified, in attacking them. The first step toward the non-religion of the Western world was made by religion itself. When it defended its great symbols, not as symbols, but as literal stories, it had already lost the battle. In doing so the theologians (and today many religious laymen) helped to transfer the powerful expressions of the dimension of depth into objects or happenings on the horizontal plane. There the symbols lose their power and meaning and become an easy prey to physical, biological and historical attack.

If the symbol of creation which points to the divine ground of everything is transferred to the horizontal plane, it becomes a story of events in a removed past for which there is no evidence, but which contradicts every piece of scientific evidence. If the symbol of the Fall of Man, which points to the tragic estrangement of man and his world from their true being is transferred to the horizontal plane, it becomes a story of a human couple a few thousand years ago in what is now present-day Iraq. One of the most profound psychological descriptions of the general human predicament becomes an absurdity on the horizontal plane. If the symbols of the Saviour and the salvation through Him which point to the healing power in history and personal life are transferred to the horizontal plane, they become stories of a half-divine being coming from a heavenly place and returning to it. Obviously, in this form, they have no meaning whatsoever for people whose view of the universe is determined by scientific astronomy.

If the idea of God (and the symbols applied to Him) which expresses man's ultimate concern is transferred to the horizontal plane, God becomes a being among others whose existence or nonexistence is a matter of inquiry. Nothing, perhaps, is more symptomatic of the loss of the dimension of depth than the permanent discussion about the existence or nonexistence of God—a discussion in which both sides are equally wrong, because the discussion itself is wrong and possible only after the loss of the dimension of depth.

When in this way man has deprived himself of the dimension of depth and the symbols expressing it, he then becomes a part of the horizontal plane. He loses his self and becomes a thing among things. He becomes an element in the process of manipulated production and manipulated consumption. This is now a matter of public knowledge. We have become aware of the degree to which everyone in our social structure is managed, even if one knows it and even if one belongs himself to the managing group. The influence of the gang mentality on adolescents, of the corporation's demands on the executives, of the conditioning of everyone by public communication, by propaganda and advertising under the guidance of motivation research, et cetera, have all been described in many books and articles.

Under these pressures, many can hardly escape the fate of becoming a thing among the things he produces, a bundle of conditioned reflexes without a free, deciding and responsible self. The immense mechanism, set up by man to produce objects for his use, transforms man himself into an object used by the same mechanism of production and consumption.

But man has not ceased to be man. He resists this fate anxiously, desperately, courageously. He asks the question, for what? And he realizes that there is no answer. He becomes aware of the emptiness which is covered by the continuous movement ahead and the production of means for ends which become means again without an ultimate end. Without knowing what has happened to him, he feels that he has lost the meaning of life, the dimension of depth.

Out of this awareness the religious question arises and religious answers are received or rejected. Therefore, in order to describe the contemporary attitude toward religion, we must first point to the places where the awareness of the predicament of Western man in our period is most sharply expressed. These places are the great art, literature and, partly at least, the philosophy of our time. It is both the subject matter and the style of these creations which show the passionate and often tragic struggle about the meaning of life in a period in which man has lost the dimension of depth. This art, literature, philosophy is not religious in the narrower sense of the word; but it asks the religious question more radically and more profoundly than most directly religious expressions of our time.

It is the religious question which is asked when the novelist describes a man who tries in vain to reach the only place which could solve the problem of his life, or a man who disintegrates under the memory of a guilt which persecutes him, or a man who never had a real self and is pushed by his fate without resistance to death, or a man who experiences a profound disgust of everything he encounters.

It is the religious question which is asked when the poet opens up the horror and the fascination of the demonic regions of his soul, or if he leads us into the deserts and empty places of our being, or if he shows the physical and moral mud under the surface of life, or if he sings the song of transitoriness, giving words to the ever-present anxiety of our hearts.

It is the religious question which is asked when the playwright shows the illusion of a life in a ridiculous symbol, or if he lets the emptiness of a life's work end in self-destruction, or if he confronts us with the inescapable bondage to mutual hate and guilt, or if he leads us into the dark cellar of lost hopes and slow disintegration.

It is the religious question which is asked when the painter breaks the visible surface into pieces, then reunites them into a great picture which has little similarity with the world at which we normally look, but which expresses our anxiety and our courage to face reality.

It is the religious question which is asked when the architect, in creating office buildings or churches, removes the trimmings taken over from past styles because they cannot be considered an honest expression of our own period. He prefers the seeming poverty of a purpose-determined style to the deceptive richness of imitated styles of the past. He knows that he gives no final answer, but he does give an honest answer.

The philosophy of our time shows the same hiddenly religious traits. It is divided into two main schools of thought, the analytic and the existentialist. The former tries to analyze logical and linguistic forms which are always used and which underlie all scientific research. One may compare them with the painters who dissolve the natural forms of bodies into cubes, planes and lines; or with those architects who want the structural "bones" of their buildings to be conspicuously visible and not hidden by covering features. This self-restriction produces the almost monastic poverty and seriousness of this philosophy. It is religious—without any contact with religion in its method—by exercising the humility of "learned ignorance."

In contrast to this school the existentialist philosophers have much to say about the problems of human existence. They bring into rational concepts what the writers and poets, the painters and architects, are expressing in their particular material. What they express is the human predicament in time and space, in anxiety and guilt and the feeling of meaninglessness. From Pascal in the seventeenth century to Heidegger and Sartre in our time, philosophers have emphasized the contrast between human dignity and human misery. And by doing so, they have raised the religious question. Some have tried to answer the question they have asked. But if they did so, they turned back to past traditions and offered to our time that which does not fit our time. Is it possible for our time to receive answers which are born out of our time?

Answers given today are in danger of strengthening the present situation and with it the questions to which they are supposed to be the answers. This refers to some of the previously mentioned major representatives of the so-called resurgence of religion, as for instance the evangelist Billy Graham and the counseling and healing minister, Norman Vincent Peale. Against the validity of the answers given by the former, one must say that, in spite of his personal integrity, his propagandistic methods and his primitive theological fundamentalism fall short of what is needed to give an answer to the religious question of our period. In spite of all his seriousness, he does not take the radical questions of our period seriously.

The effect that Normal Peale has on large groups of people is rooted in the fact that he confirms the situation which he is supposed to help overcome. He heals people with the purpose of making them fit again for the demands of the competitive and conformist society in which we are living. He helps them to become adapted to the situation which is characterized by the loss of the dimension of depth. Therefore, his advice is valid on this level; but it is the validity of this level that is the true religious question of our time. And this question he neither raises nor answers.

In many cases the increase of church membership and interest in religious activities does not mean much more than the religious consecration of a state of things in which the religious dimension has been lost. It is the desire to participate in activities which are socially strongly approved and give internal and a certain amount of external security. This is not necessarily bad, but it certainly is not an answer to the religious question of our period.

Is there an answer? There is always an answer, but the answer may not be available to us. We may be too deeply steeped in the predicament out of which the question arises to be able to answer it. To acknowledge this is certainly a better way toward a real answer than to bar the way to it by deceptive answers. And it may be that in this attitude the real answer(within available limits) is given. The real answer to the question of how to regain the dimension of depth is not given by increased church membership or church attendance, nor by conversion or healing experiences. But it is given by the awareness that we have lost the decisive dimension of life, the dimension of depth, and that there is no easy way of getting it back. Such awareness is in itself a state of being grasped by that which is symbolized in the term, dimension of depth. He who realizes that he is separated from the ultimate source of meaning shows by this realization that he is not only separated but also reunited. And this is just our situation. What we need above all—and partly have—is the radical realization of our predicament, without trying to cover it up by secular or religious ideologies. The revival of religious interest would be a creative power in our culture if it would develop into a movement of search for the lost dimension of depth.

This does not mean that the traditional religious symbols should be dismissed. They certainly have lost their meaning in the literalistic form into which they have been distorted, thus producing the critical reaction against them. But they have not lost their genuine meaning—namely, of answering the question which is implied in man's very existence in powerful, revealing and saving symbols. If the resurgence of religion would produce a new understanding of the symbols of the past and their relevance for our situation, instead of premature and deceptive answers, it would become a creative factor in our culture and a saving factor for many who live in estrangement, anxiety and despair. The religious answer has always the character of "in spite of." In spite of the loss of dimension of depth, its power is present, and most present in those who are aware of the loss and are striving to regain it with ultimate seriousness.

NINIAN SMART

(b. 1927)

Roderick Ninian Smart, who since 1961 has been Professor of Theology at the University of Birmingham, is the son of the renowned astronomer, William Marshall Smart. Educated at Glasgow Academy and at Oxford, he has been teaching since 1952, first at the University College of Wales, then as lecturer in the History of Philosophy of Religion at Kings College, University of London. He has been a visiting professor at Yale and at the University of Wisconsin. Among his publications are Reasons and Faiths *(1958),* A Dialogue of Religions *(1960),* Philosophers and Religious Truth *(1964),* Doctrine and Argument in Indian Philosophy *(1964), and* The Teacher and Christian Belief *(1966).*

CREATIVITY AND TRANSCENDENCE

Life is both strange and commonplace. But for most of the time it is commonplace, and we are not surprised that the world is as it is, for we have no experience of any other mode of existence. The surprises that come our way are only surprises within an unsurprising framework. It may astonish us that Henry has suddenly entered a monastery or that the government of France has been overthrown, but Henry and monasteries and governments and France are part of the order of things. Yet every so often the whole set-up may suddenly strike us as strange. We find ourselves in a universe containing, among other things, France and monasteries: but why should there be a universe at all? Why should it contain conscious, rational beings like ourselves? And what is the world really like? Are the things we see around us really as they seem to be—bathed in colour and light and shade? Or is this only an appearance that our brains and minds foist upon them? Such questions arise from, and themselves also supply, the sense of strangeness that can sometimes afflict us. The universe is our home; and yet now and then we look around uneasily, wondering whether all the time it is a stranger's house. Out of this unease and strangeness and wonder, science and philosophy spring. Men who feel this strangeness are no longer immersed in the flow of life: they are beginning to contemplate it and to try to understand its secrets.

From Philosophers and Religious Truth *(1964), SCM Press Ltd., pp. 11–14, 144–150, 164–166.*

In the new light of such contemplation, everything comes under scrutiny. We may, for instance, have been brought up to worship God, to be pious in our religious duties. Even this solemn and central feature of life is, to the person who does not reflect, and who remains immersed in the flow of existence, commonplace. That God reveals himself to men, that some men respond to this and go to church, that you shut your eyes when you pray—these facts seem quite normal. This is how things are. But as soon as the philosophical sense of strangeness begins to afflict us, all these commonplaces take on a new and uncanny look. Philosophy brings religion under scrutiny, just as it questions the other facets of life and of existence.

In relation to religious truth, philosophy is ambiguous. It is at once a menace and an ally. It is a menace, because the sense of wonder issues in the question "Why should things be so?" More particularly, why should revelation or ecclesiastical authority be accepted? How can anyone claim to know the mysteries of God? Perhaps the pretensions of faith all rest upon illusion. In such ways, philosophy is menacing to revelation and piety. For as soon as we ask questions of this kind, simple faith, and sometimes even sophisticated faith, is seen to be inadequate. Of course, it would be silly to suppose that therefore simple folk cannot be good Christians, or that you have to be something of a philosopher to have spiritual respectability. Still, if you become aware of these questions, if they bite into you so that you cannot shake yourself free from them, then it is no use trying to hide from this particular form of your destiny and to take refuge in simple faith. Unfortunately there are many who in effect have done just this. Profoundly disturbed by the questions, and by the unnerving impact of modern science upon traditional beliefs, they throw away their intellects. They cling to the literal inerrancy of scripture or to some other clearcut authority, and build a wall in their minds to keep out science and philosophy from the domain of faith. One can well understand this: and indeed one can sympathize with their predicament. But it is not a happy destiny, nor is it a fully human one. The universe must be faced, and the truth about reality cannot in this simple way be prejudged. So if the philosophical fate is your fate, then it is as well to be clear that it is, as far as faith goes, a menacing one. But, as I said, philosophy is ambiguous. The questioning attitude of mind can, paradoxically, also be an ally of the religious spirit.

If God is just a commonplace, religious devotion and understanding can be merely superficial. Perhaps this is why saintliness and doubts often go together. A God who is accepted simply as an unsurprising part of reality, and as a Person who quite as a matter of course supplies a revelation, has no real majesty, mystery or depth. He is anthropomorphic—an invisible man writ large. But if the world strikes us in all its strangeness, then suddenly religion acquires a new significance. It really is most odd, how men bow down and worship, how they perform bizarre rituals. It seems like a kind of madness to talk to God, to search for the unseen. The madness, though, may be the madness of genius, and the invisible reality may have an uncanny glory, once we penetrate beyond the commonplace attitudes of piety. The philosophical spirit, by liberating us from a humdrum view of life, may bring depth to our understanding of faith. In such a way, for all its menace, it can be an ally.

But it would not be philosophical to predict in advance how things will turn out in the pursuit of truth. Of course, there is room for hunches: maybe we feel at the outset that truth must be like this or that. Nevertheless, once we are committed by our intellectual destiny to asking certain sorts of questions, to asking the uncomfortable questions about the truth of religion, then it would be wrong to tame the menace by laying it down that in the end everything will be all right. . . .

A radical questioning of the validity of religious experience should not overlook the fact that religion constitutes a dynamic and central part of the history of men. Therefore, good reasons ought to be given for being sceptical of the tradition that men can gain some insight in experience into the nature of the transcendent. It is not just blind conservatism which holds that it would be strange indeed if all such visions and experiences were entirely delusory. It is therefore reasonable to approach the matter in a rather cautious way. It would be wrong to follow the example of, say, Freud, and base the view that religion is illusory on speculative ideas in psychology and a grossly distorted account of prehistory. Are the walls of Jericho to tumble at such a weak and homemade trumpet?

A further important point of method is this. If we are mainly looking at revelation as religious experience, we are necessarily concerned centrally with the deliverances of the more important figures of religious history, with the Jeremiahs, the Pauls, the Buddhas. We are not basing important truths of religion on my feeble intuitions or my neighbour's faltering visions. These may be personally important. But we are not either so presumptuous or democratic as to suppose that God must reveal himself in an intense and illuminating way in each individual heart. Necessarily, then, ours is a rather "aristocratic" approach. This is the only realistic way of tackling the problem, by looking to the focal points in religious histories. We are more in the position of critics than of artists, ordinary people who may recognize revelation, but are not the immediate recipients of it. I am not, of course, in the comparison with artists suggesting that people like Jeremiah themselves, as religious geniuses, *created* the revelation: for was it not a feature of such explosively numinous experiences that they seemed to come spontaneously and, as it were, from "outside"?

But the word "outside" raises some acute philosophical problems. We may believe that a perception is in part caused by the object perceived, and that an experience which does not have such an outside source is illusory. For instance, the alcoholic who sees pink rats is suffering from an hallucination precisely because outside there in the room there are no pink rats. What causes his hallucination comes from "inside" him (whisky may be the cause, but only on condition that it first gets inside him!). Likewise, it may be argued that if a perception of the divine Being is to be genuine, it must be in part caused by something lying outside the individual, namely by God. But here the real trouble starts. For the daffodil I perceive is literally outside me: it is at a different point in space from me. But God is not in space, and so cannot be literally outside me. There is another trouble, too: for the rather naïve view that the cause of a true perception lies outside me raises difficulties about me. If I include my body, then it is false that true perceptions must have part-causes outside me. I can truly perceive, through certain organs of feeling, that there is a lot of food in my stomach. But my stomach is inside me. But if we mean by me the mind, then there is a difficulty in speaking of things being literally inside or outside my mind, since the mind is not a spatial object in the ordinary sense.

Consequently, we must refine our ideas about the causes of perception. Perhaps as follows: by saying that for a perception to be genuine, the object of my perception, that is, the thing which I believe myself to be perceiving, must be part-cause of my experience. Thus, for instance, if we introduced some pink rats into the alcoholic's room, but if, too, he would have seen pink rats anyway, we would be somewhat reluctant to say that he really saw the real pink rats. By analogy, we may want to say that if an experience is a genuine experience of God, God must be part-cause at least of that experience.

But this in turn raises other problems. For if God is creator of the whole cosmos, then he is certainly part-cause of any supposed experience of him. The condition is automatically fulfilled. But this does not seem satisfactory as an answer to our problem. For if, it may well be held, an experience of God is entirely caused by prior causes in the world—mundane causes—then it is suspect. If a vision has psychological causes (we may think) then it can be written off. Rather, we want assurance that at least some religious experiences are in some sense directly caused by God.

The phrase "at least some" is important. For it may be objected to the whole line of approach in this discussion that you can have genuine knowledge without its being directly caused by its object. For instance, a piece of mathematical knowledge is not mysteriously caused by numbers existing outside the individual. Similarly, if a person at a service finds, in the ceremony and the fellowship, a heightened awareness of God's grace, isn't this something genuine, even if we do not think that there is some kind of direct intervention by God? Or if a theologian reaches a correct conclusion about a matter of doctrine, is this not genuine knowledge? Yet, nevertheless, surely it is supposed in the great religions that the "aristocratic" experiences are somehow specially caused by God. Moreover, we must distinguish between knowledge *that* and knowledge *of*. I can know that such and such is the case: but this is not some kind of perceptual experience. But knowledge of a person, encountering him, does directly involve perceptual experience. The theologian knows *that* such-and-such is the case; but this does not imply that the theologian must necessarily have had any direct knowledge *of* God. And in talking of religious experience it is knowledge *of* that we are chiefly concerned with.

Perhaps part of the solution of our problem will come to us if we consider religious experience in the first instance simply from the human side. Bearing in mind our earlier conclusions about creativity, could we think of the great religious deliverances, for instance those of the Old Testament prophets, as examples of creative novelty? Certainly the same sort of conditions are present as in the case of scientific and artistic discovery. For there is a certain range of experience and activity (religion) and within this pattern of conscious response to the numinous there breaks in something which goes beyond what was before. The vivid and powerful awareness of something supremely holy which the prophets displayed goes beyond earlier ideas and responses. Similarly, that religion itself which the prophets did so much to shape was later transcended in the work and teaching of Christ. In both cases, there was in existence already a body of tradition which was necessary to the later developments which in part rendered the body of tradition obsolete. Here, then, in the sphere of religious experience there is something like the creative novelty which we can find elsewhere in human progress.

So far we are looking at the matter simply from the human side. But already we have some intimation that it may be quite wrong to think that a causal account of the great experiences of religion can be given. But still (it will be objected), how are we to know whether these creative developments are not *merely* human? It may be that, as well as having a genius in the arts, men also have a genius for the numinous. Every so often sudden uprushes of religious feeling take on a creative form and supersede what went before. But so what?

The critic might indeed go further. If men can have a creative genius for fiction, why not also have a genius for making myths about a transcendent world? It may be that religion is a superbly elaborate kind of self-deception. And if men can be creative in good, remember, too, that they can be creative in evil: and both the discovery of truth and the creation of falsehood are human gifts.

But we can reply: to what end does the deception take place? It is true that priests have often manipulated sacred knowledge for their own benefit, and that it often looks as though certain doctrines play a role in keeping society together in a certain form. And there is no doubt that some myths are the product of deep psychological urges. But even when all this is taken into account, it still remains a fact that religion does involve its own kind of experiences and inner logic, and these still have to be accounted for. If the numinous experience, for example, is distinct from other forms of human consciousness, then how can it simply be derived from them, on the assumption that numinous creativity is a kind of self-deception? For if it arises to deal with psychological or social problems, no doubt in an unconscious way, then why does it have its own peculiar character?

Of course, if one has already made up one's mind that the universe has no transcendent source and no transcendent side to it, that the only reality is the observable cosmos, then no doubt it will be easier to think that religion arises out of psychological and other urges, even though the special character of numinous experience so far remains unaccounted for. It is something of a gamble either way: it is a leap to believe in the transcendent, and it is a leap to believe that somehow in theory religious experience could be given some kind of natural explanation. But all this underlines once again the importance of natural theology, for in giving us some hint that the cosmos is created, even if such a hint is in no sense a proof, it does provide some rational ground for refusing to see the cosmos as the whole of reality.

But then, once the leap is made, towards some kind of belief in the transcendent, the importance of religious experience is bound to strike us powerfully. For it is not as though the prophets' experiences can be merely regarded as a form of human creativity, since it is implicit in their visions, their awareness of the holy, that they should ascribe them to an "outside" source. Moreover, this "outside" source is outside in a strange way, for it (or he) lies somehow beyond or behind the objects in the environment of the prophet. The holy Being is "present" as though in the environment of the prophet, and yet somehow also it is concealed by the environment. This suggestion that the holy Being is "beyond" what is seen in space and time fits in with the metaphysical idea of a creator "outside" the cosmos. But it would be wrong to think that our thinking need operate only in this direction—beginning with the metaphysical idea and then, on that basis, seeing the validity of religious experience: equally we might move the other way, and judge metaphysics by the yardstick of religious experience. Suffice it to say that the two approaches fit together, and that they lend each other mutual support.

We can now draw together the threads of our whole argument up to now, and see what kind of picture of the world it presents. Both in regard to miracles, and in regard to free will, we argued against a rigidly "closed" view of reality, as though everything needs to be governed by causal regularities. At least the theoretical possibility of God's miraculous intervention in the world must be allowed: and a proper explanation of free will may mean that we use some such idea as that of creativity. This in turn renews hope in the possibility of arguing for God's existence. For if there is to be an explanation of the existence of the cosmos, it must be non-scientific, and yet at the same time intelligible. The idea of human creativity fulfils both these requirements, so that we can think of the Cause of the cosmos by analogy with the way in which humanity sometimes transcends the regularities in which it is embedded. Once we make this leap of explanation, we can also make use of the facts to which the Teleological Argument draws attention, for the comparative orderliness of the cosmos does indeed look significant when we see that it is sufficient to allow the evolution of conscious and rational beings, who thereby confer value upon what otherwise would be dead and meaningless. Nevertheless, such solutions to the problems thrown up by the existence and orderliness of the cosmos remain rather thin unless they are joined to belief in revelation. The mistake of some philosophers, and notably Kant, is to ignore this possibility of an encounter with the transcendent. Religious experience has to be examined. We then went on to give reasons for thinking that this may provide a valid avenue of knowledge about reality, and to see how theism can be defended in the context of the world's religions.

Our total picture has been an evolutionary one: of the world as being created as a theatre for the production of human and other values, an arena for the exercise of creativity. But the possibility of a genuine encounter between men and God through God's self-revelation gives this evolutionary picture a deeper significance. For it is as if men's knowledge of God is itself evolutionary. From dim beginnings, men have struggled upward towards this higher knowledge; and the struggle is not finished yet.

SIMONE WEIL

(1909–1943)

Paris-born, Simone Weil obtained her baccalaureate degree with honors at the age of fifteen, and proceeded to major in philosophy, studying under La Senne and Alain. Thereafter she taught the subject from 1931 to 1935. But she wanted to share the experience of peasants and laborers, and during the summer months she would work in the fields of the Jura; and later, in spite of her delicate health, she took on a demanding job in the Renault autoworks. Her articles on the fatiguing life of the French worker, written during this period, are profoundly sensitive and moving documents. The Spanish Civil War engaged her attention, and she spent some time with the Republican Army on the Catalonian front, involving herself in a struggle in which she devoutly believed, and encountering directly the calamity of the war and the devastation and misery it brought. When World War II broke out, she went from France to New York City for a brief time, then returned to England to serve under the French provisional government. She wrote extensively on politics, and increasingly, on the subject of religion. Though she was physically exhausted, she refused extra nourishment in order that her diet be no better than that of her compatriots in the occupied zone of France. Her insistence upon exposing herself to the hardships and sufferings of her fellow men aggravated her illness, from which she died at the age of thirty-four. Among her works (for the most part posthumous) are Waiting for God, Gravity and Grace, *and* The Need for Roots.

WHAT IS SACRED?

At the bottom of the heart of every human being, from earliest infancy until the tomb, there is something that goes on indomitably expecting, in the teeth of all experience of crimes committed, suffered, and witnessed, that good and not evil will be done to him. It is this above all that is sacred in every human being.

The good is the only source of the sacred. There is nothing sacred except the good and what pertains to it.

This profound and childlike and unchanging expectation of good in the heart is not what is involved when we agitate for our rights. The motive which prompts a little boy to watch jealously to see if his brother has a slightly larger piece of cake arises from a much more superficial

From Selected Essays *1934–1943, translated from the French by Sir Richard Rees, published by Oxford University Press, pp. 10–11, 22–34. Reprinted by permission of A D Peters & Co Ltd.*

level of the soul. The word justice means two very different things according to whether it refers to the one or the other level. It is only the former one that matters.

Every time that there arises from the depths of a human heart the childish cry which Christ himself could not restrain, "Why am I being hurt?", then there is certainly injustice. For if, as often happens, it is only the result of a misunderstanding, then the injustice consists in the inadequacy of the explanation.

Those people who inflict the blows which provoke this cry are prompted by different motives according to temperament or occasion. There are some people who get a positive pleasure from the cry; and many others simply do not hear it. For it is a silent cry, which sounds only in the secret heart.

These two states of mind are closer than they appear to be. The second is only a weaker mode of the first; its deafness is complacently cultivated because it is agreeable and it offers a positive satisfaction of its own. There are no other restraints upon our will than material necessity and the existence of the other human beings around us. Any imaginary extension of these limits is seductive, so there is a seduction in whatever helps us to forget the reality of the obstacles. That is why upheavals like war and civil war are so intoxicating; they empty human lives of their reality and seem to turn people into puppets. That is also why slavery is so pleasant to the masters. . . .

So far from its being his person, what is sacred in a human being is the impersonal in him.

Everything which is impersonal in man is sacred, and nothing else.

In our days, when writers and scientists have so oddly usurped the place of priests, the public acknowledges, with a totally unjustified docility, that the artistic and scientific faculties are sacred. This is generally held to be self-evident, though it is very far from being so. If any reason is felt to be called for, people allege that the free play of these faculties is one of the highest manifestations of the human personality.

Often it is, indeed, no more than that. In which case it is easy to see how much it is worth and what can be expected from it.

One of its results is the sort of attitude which is summed up in Blake's horrible saying: "Sooner murder an infant in its cradle than nurse unacted desires," or the attitude which breeds the idea of the "gratuitous act." Another result is a science in which every possible standard, criterion, and value is recognized except truth.

Gregorian chant, Romanesque architecture, the *Iliad*, the invention of geometry were not, for the people through whom they were brought into being and made available to us, occasions for the manifestation of personality.

When science, art, literature, and philosophy are simply the manifestation of personality they are on a level where glorious and dazzling achievements are possible, which can make a man's name live for thousands of years. But above this level, far above, separated by an abyss, is the level where the highest things are achieved. These things are essentially anonymous.

It is pure chance whether the names of those who reach this level are preserved or lost; even when they are remembered they have become anonymous. Their personality has vanished.

Truth and beauty dwell on this level of the impersonal and the anonymous. This is the realm of the sacred; on the other level nothing is sacred, except in the sense that we might say this of a touch of color in a picture if it represented the Eucharist.

What is sacred in science is truth; what is sacred in art is beauty. Truth and beauty are impersonal. All this is too obvious.

If a child is doing a sum and does it wrong, the mistake bears the stamp of his personality. If he does the sum exactly right, his personality does not enter into it at all.

Perfection is impersonal. Our personality is the part of us which belongs to error and sin. The whole effort of the mystic has always been to become such that there is no part left in his soul to say "I."

But the part of the soul which says "We" is infinitely more dangerous still. . . . There is a natural alliance between truth and affliction, because both of them are mute suppliants, eternally condemned to stand speechless in our presence.

Just as a vagrant accused of stealing a carrot from a field stands before a comfortably seated judge who keeps up an elegant flow of queries, comments, and witticisms while the accused is unable to stammer a word, so truth stands before an intelligence which is concerned with the elegant manipulation of opinions.

It is always language that formulates opinions, even when there are no words spoken. The natural faculty called intelligence is concerned with opinion and language. Language expresses relations; but it expresses only a few, because its operation needs time. When it is confused and vague, without precision or order, when the speaker or listener is deficient in the power of holding a thought in his mind, then language is empty or almost empty of any real relational content. When it is perfectly clear, precise, rigorous, ordered, when it is addressed to a mind which is capable of keeping a thought present while it adds a third, and so on, then in such a case language can hold a fairly rich content of relations. But like all wealth, this relative wealth is abject poverty compared with the perfection which alone is desirable.

At the very best, a mind enclosed in language is in prison. It is limited to the number of relations which words can make simultaneously present to it; and remains in ignorance of thoughts which involve the combination of a greater number. These thoughts are outside language, they are unformulable, although they are perfectly rigorous and clear and although every one of the relations they involve is capable of precise expression in words. So the mind moves in a closed space of partial truth, which may be larger or smaller, without ever being able so much as to glance at what is outside.

If a captive mind is unaware of being in prison, it is living in error. If it has recognized the fact, even for the tenth of a second, and then quickly forgotten it in order to avoid suffering, it is living in falsehood. Men of the most brilliant intelligence can be born, live, and die in error and falsehood. In them, intelligence is neither a good, nor even an asset. The difference between more or less intelligent men is like the difference between criminals condemned to life imprisonment in smaller or larger cells. The intelligent man who is proud of his intelligence is like a condemned man who is proud of his large cell.

A man whose mind feels that it is captive would prefer to blind himself to the fact. But if he hates falsehood, he will not do so and in that case he will have to suffer a lot. He will beat his head against the wall until he faints. He will come to again and look with terror at the wall, until one day he begins afresh to beat his head against it; and once again he will faint. And so on endlessly and without hope. One day he will wake up on the other side of the wall.

Perhaps he is still in a prison, although a larger one. No matter. He has found the key; he knows the secret which breaks down every wall. He has passed beyond what men call intelligence, into the beginning of wisdom. . . .

By the power of words we always mean their power of illusion and error. But, thanks to a providential arrangement, there are certain words which possess, in themselves, when properly used, a virtue which illumines and lifts up towards the good. These are the words which refer to an absolute perfection which we cannot conceive. Since the proper use of these words involves not trying to make them fit any conception, it is in the words themselves, as words, that the power to enlighten and draw upward resides. What they express is beyond our conception.

God and *truth* are such words; also *justice, love,* and *good.*

It is dangerous to use words of this kind. They are like an ordeal. To use them legitimately one must avoid referring them to anything humanly conceivable and at the same time one must associate with them ideas and actions which are derived solely and directly from the light which they shed. Otherwise, everyone quickly recognizes them for lies.

They are uncomfortable companions. Words like *right, democracy* and *person* are more accommodating and are therefore naturally preferred by even the best intentioned of those who assume public functions. Public functions have no other meaning except the possibility of doing good to men, and those who assume them with good intentions do in fact want to procure good for their contemporaries; but they usually make the mistake of thinking they can begin by getting it at bargain prices.

Words of the middle region, such as *right, democracy, person,* are valid in their own region, which is that of ordinary institutions. But for the sustaining inspiration of which all institutions are, as it were, the projection, a different language is needed.

The subordination of the person to the collectivity is in the nature of things, like the inferiority of a gram to a kilogram on the scales. But there can be a scales on which the gram outweighs the kilogram. It is only necessary for one arm to be more than a thousand times as long as the other. The law of equilibrium easily overcomes an inequality of weight. But the lesser will never outweigh the greater unless the relation between them is regulated by the law of equilibrium.

In the same way, there is no guarantee for democracy, or for the protection of the person against the collectivity, without a disposition of public life relating it to the higher good which is impersonal and unrelated to any political form.

It is true that the word person is often applied to God. But in the passage where Christ offers God himself as an example to men of the perfection which they are told to achieve, he uses not only the image of a person but also, above all, that of an impersonal order: "That ye may be like the children of your Father which is in heaven; for he maketh his sun to rise on the evil and on the good, and sendeth rain on the just and on the unjust."

Justice, truth, and beauty are the image in our world of this impersonal and divine order of the universe. Nothing inferior to them is worthy to be the inspiration of men who accept the fact of death.

Above those institutions which are concerned with protecting rights and persons and democratic freedoms, others must be invented for the purpose of exposing and abolishing everything in contemporary life which buries the soul under injustice, lies, and ugliness.

They must be invented, for they are unknown, and it is impossible to doubt that they are indispensable.

16

Interpretations of Religious Experience

PAUL RICOEUR

(b. 1913)

Paul Ricoeur, born in France in 1913, received his Doctorat es Lettres from the University of Paris in 1950, and has since received honorary degrees from Basel, Chicago, Montreal, and Ohio State universities. After teaching at the University of Strasbourg, he became Professor of Philosophy at the University of Paris in 1957, and has since taught also at the University of Chicago. Since 1945, he has been publisher of the French magazine Esprit, *and he is the author of* History and Truth *(1955),* Philosophy of the Will *(1950–1961, 3 vols.),* Fallible Man *(1965), and* Freud and Philosophy.

PHILOSOPHY AND RELIGIOUS LANGUAGE

My title expresses in a few words a certain number of assumptions that it will be my task to clarify as far as is possible in the space of an hour.

The first assumption is that, for a philosophical inquiry, a religious faith may be identified through its language, or, to speak more accurately, as a kind of discourse. This first contention does not say that language, that linguistic expression, is the only dimension of the religious phenomenon; nothing is said—either pro or con—concerning the controversial notion of religious experience, whether we understand experience in a cognitive, a practical, or an emotional sense. What is said is only this: whatever ultimately may be the nature of the so-called religious experience, it comes to language, it is articulated in a language, and the most appropriate place to interpret it on its own terms is to inquire into its linguistic expression.

The second assumption is that this kind of discourse is not senseless, that it is worthwhile to analyze it, because something is said that is not said by other kinds of discourse—ordinary, scientific, or poetic, or, to put it into more positive terms, that it is meaningful at least for the community of faith which uses it either for the sake of self-understanding or for the sake of communication with others exterior to the faith community.

My third presupposition is that philosophy is implied in this inquiry because this kind of discourse does not merely claim to be meaningful, but also to be true. This claim must be understood on its own terms. It implies that we do not yet recognize the truth value of this kind of language if we do not put in question the criteria of truth which are borrowed from other spheres of discourse, mainly the scientific one, whether we invoke a criterion of verification, or a criterion of falsification. The presupposition here is that philosophy is confronted by a mode of discourse which displays claims both to meaningfulness and to fulfilment such that new dimensions of reality and truth are disclosed, and that a new formulation of truth is required.

Such are the main presuppositions implied in my title, "Philosophy and Religious Language" (or discourse).

My intention is to clarify these presuppositions one after the other by using the specific approach of a theory of interpretation, or, in more technical terms, of a philosophical hermeneutics.

Let me introduce this method by contrasting it with Anglo-

From The Journal of Religion, *1971, pp. 71–73, 74–75, 76–78, 80–83, 84–85. Used by permission of The University of Chicago Press and of the author.*

American linguistic analysis on the issues raised by the three assumptions I just outlined.

I should say that hermeneutics and linguistic analysis equally share the first assumption, namely that religious faith or experience may be identified on the basis of the language used. We shall see later, however, that hermeneutics qualifies this first assumption in a way which is proper to it. Nevertheless, this first assumption furnishes the common basis for a fruitful dialogue between the two approaches.

The second assumption, it seems to me, is common to a certain extent to both hermeneutics and linguistic analysis, at least to that brand of linguistic analysis which, with Austin and Wittgenstein, does not want to measure meaningfulness by the canons of artificial languages, or of ordinary language as reformulated according to logical rules, but which rather seeks to analyze the functioning of the different language games according to their own rules. Here too, we shall see how hermeneutics understands this methodological principle, that is, the requirement that the meaningfulness of a kind of discourse be measured by its own criteria of meaningfulness.

The main discrepancy between linguistic analysis and hermeneutics concerns without a doubt the third assumption. Linguistic analysis is so heavily determined by the history of the principles of verification and falsification that it is very difficult for this school of thought to conceive of a concept of truth which would not be taken for granted and defined a priori as *adequation*. The idea that each mode of fulfilment develops its own criteria of truth and that truth may mean not *adequation* but *manifestation* seems to be alien to the main thesis of linguistic analysis and more typical of hermeneutics, more or less influenced by Heideggerian philosophy. Nevertheless there are hints of this feeling concerning a necessary revision of the basic concept of truth in the work of Ian Ramsey and Frederick Ferré. But whatever may be the difference in approach, I do not think that it is too inaccurate to say that even this third assumption may become, if not a common presupposition, at least a common issue.

My purpose is not to refute the methodology of linguistic analysis, but merely to *clarify* the three assumptions of a philosophy of religious language following a hermeneutical method.

I

As I just said, the first assumption is common to both linguistic analysis and to hermeneutics. Both approach religious faith as *expressed in language*. But the difference of approach starts already at this level. Linguistic analysis readily starts with *statements* such as God exists, or God is immutable, all-powerful, and so forth—that is, from statements which clearly constitute a very sophisticated type of expression and which belong to a second-order discourse, that of theology. At this level religious discourse is reinterpreted in conceptual terms with the help of speculative philosophy. A hermeneutical philosophy, on the contrary, will try to get as close as possible to the most *originary* expressions of a community of faith, to those expressions through which the members of this community have interpreted their experience for the sake of themselves or for others' sake.

These documents of faith do not primarily contain theological statements, in the sense of metaphysical speculative theology, but expressions embedded in such modes of discourse as narratives, prophecies, legislative texts, proverbs and wisdom sayings, hymns, prayers, and liturgical formulas. These are the ordinary expressions of religious faith. The first task of any hermeneutic is to identify these originary modes of discourse through which the religious faith of a community comes to language. . . .

The main implication of this for hermeneutics would concern the new specific kinds of *distanciation* linked to the production of discourse as a work. A poem is a good example. But a narrative would serve the same purpose. A work of discourse, as a the work of art, is an autonomous object at a distance from the authorial intention, from its initial situation (its *Sitz im Leben*), and from its primitive audience. For this very reason it is open to an infinite range of interpretations. There is room for interpretation because the recovery of the initial event of discourse takes the form of a reconstruction starting from the structure and the inner organization of the specific modes of discourse. In other words, if hermeneutics is always an attempt to overcome a distance, it has to use distanciation as both the obstacle and the instrument in order to reenact the initial event of discourse in a new event of discourse which will claim to be both faithful and creative.

Such is the hermeneutical way of treating our first assumption, namely that the religious faith of a community has to be identified through its language. In hermeneutical terms this means that the first task of a biblical hermeneut is to identify the different modes of discourse which, taken together, constitute the finite field of interpretation within the boundaries of which religious language may be understood. This task precedes that of a linguistic analysis applied to theological statements which have lost their rooting in these primary expressions of religious faith and which proceed from a reformulation of these primary expressions in a conceptual language of the same order as that of a speculative philosophy.

II

If we assume the hermeneutical formulation of our first thesis—namely that religious experience comes to language through specific modes of discourse—we are prepared to clarify our second thesis according to the same line of thought.

It is not enough to say that religious language is meaningful, that it is not senseless, that it makes sense, that it has a meaning of its own, and so forth. We have to say that its meanings are ruled and guided by the modes of articulation specific to each mode of discourse. Here I reach the fundamental point of my lecture, which I will formulate in the following way.

The "confession of faith" which is expressed in the biblical documents is inseparable from the *forms* of discourse, by which I mean the narrative structure; for example, the Pentateuch and the Gospels, the oracular structure of the prophecies, the parables, the hymn, and so forth. Not only does each form of discourse give rise to a style of confession of faith, but also the confrontation of these forms of discourse gives rise to tensions and contrasts, within the confessions of faith itself, which are theologically significant. The opposition between narration and prophecy, so fundamental for the mentality of the Old Testament, is perhaps only one of the pairs of structures whose opposition contributes to engendering the global shape of its meaning. We shall speak later of other contrasting pairs at the level of literary genres. Perhaps we should even go so far as to consider the closing of the canon as a fundamental structural act which delimits the space for the interplay of forms of discourse and determines the finite configuration within which each form and each pair of forms unfolds its signifying function.

There are thus three problems to consider under the aegis of forms of biblical discourse: (1) the affinity between a form of discourse and a certain modality of the confession of faith; (2) the relation between a certain pair of structures (for example, narration and prophecy) and the corresponding tension in the theological message; and finally (3) the relation between the configuration of the whole of the literary corpus and what one might correlatively call the space of interpretation opened by all the forms of discourse taken together. . . .

Perhaps an exhaustive enquiry, if one were possible, would disclose that all these forms of discourse together constitute a circular system and that the theological content of each one of them receives its signification from the total constellation of forms of discourse. Religious language would then appear as a polyphonic language sustained by the circularity of the forms. But perhaps this hypothesis is unverifiable and confers on the closing of the canon a sort of necessity which would not be appropriate to what should perhaps remain a historical accident of the text. At least this hypothesis is coherent with the central theme of this analysis, that the finished work which we call the Bible is a limited space for interpretation in which the theological significations are correlatives of forms of disclosure. It is no longer possible to interpret the significations without making the long detour through a structural explication of the forms.

III

Let me now say something about the third presupposition of a philosophy of religious language, namely, that it develops specific claims to truth measured by *criteria* appropriate to this kind of discourse. Here too, a philosophical hermeneutics paves the way to a more specific treatment of religious expressions, documents, and texts.

The category which has to be introduced here is that of *the world of the text*. This notion prolongs—but at the level of complex works of discourse—what I earlier called the reference of discourse. Let me remind you of the distinction introduced by Gottlob Frege at the level of simple propositions between the sense and the reference. The sense or the meaning is the ideal object which is intended. This meaning is purely immanent to discourse. The reference is the truth value of the proposition, its claim to reach reality. Through this character discourse is opposed to language which has no relationship with reality. Words refer to other words in the round without end of the dictionary. Only discourse, we say, intends things, is applied to reality, expresses the world.

The new question that arises is the following. What happens to the reference when discourse becomes a text? It is here that writing and above all the structure of the work alter the reference to the point of rendering it entirely problematic. In oral discourse the problem is ultimately resolved by the ostensive function of discourse. In other words, the reference is resolved by the power of showing a reality common to the interlocuters. Or if we cannot show the thing being talked about, at least we can situate it in relation to a unique spatial-temporal network to which the interlocuters also belong. It is this network, here and now determined by the discourse situation, which furnishes the ultimate reference of all discourse.

With writing, things begin to change. There is no longer a common situation between the writer and the reader. And at the same time, the concrete conditions for the act of pointing something out no longer exist. Without a doubt it is this abolition of the demonstrative or denotative characteristics of reference which makes possible the phenomenon which we call literature, where every reference to the given reality may be abolished. But it is essentially with the appearance of certain literary genres, generally tied to writing, but not necessarily so, that this abolition of reference to the given world is led to its most extreme conditions. It is the role of most of our literature, it would seem, to destroy this world. This is true of fictional literature—fairy tales, myths, novels, drama—but also of all literature which we can call poetic literature, where the language seems to glorify itself without depending on the referential function of ordinary discourse.

And yet if such fictional discourse does not rejoin ordinary reality, it still refers to another more fundamental level than that attained by descriptive, assertive, or didactic discourse which we call ordinary language. My thesis here is that the abolition of first-order reference, an abolition accomplished by fiction and poetry, is the condition of possibility for the liberation of a second order of reference which reaches the world not only at the level of manipulable objects, but at the level Husserl designated by the expression *Lebenswelt,* and which Heidegger calls being-in-the-world.

It is this referential dimension, which is absolutely original with fictional and poetic works which, for me, poses the most fundamental hermeneutical problem. If we can no longer define hermeneutics as the search for another person and psychological intentions which hide behind the text, and if we do not want to reduce interpretation to the identification of structures, what remains to be interpreted? My response is that to interpret is to explicate the sort of being-in-the-world unfolded in front of the text.

Here we rejoin Heidegger's suggestion about the meaning of *Verstehen*. It will be remembed that, in *Being and Time*, the theory of understanding is not tied to the comprehension of others, but becomes a structure of being-in-the-world. More precisely, it is a structure which is examined after the structure of *Befindlichkeit*, state of mind, has been introduced. The moment of understanding responds dialectically to being in a situation, as the projection of our ownmost possibilities in those situations where we find ourselves. I want to take this idea of the "projection of our ownmost possibilities" from his analysis and apply it to the theory of the text. In effect, what is to be interpreted in a text is a proposed world, a world that I might inhabit and wherein I might project my ownmost possibilities. This is what I call the world of the text, the world probably belonging to this unique text.

The world of the text of which we are speaking is not therefore the world of everyday language. In this sense it constitutes a new sort of distanciation which we can call a distanciation of the real from itself. It is this distanciation that fiction introduces into our apprehension of reality. A story, a fairy tale, or a poem does not lack a referent. Through fiction and poetry new possibilities of being-in-the-world are opened up within everyday reality. Fiction and poetry intend being, but not through the modality of givenness, but rather through the modality of possibility. And in this way everyday reality is metamorphosed by means of what we would call the imaginative variations that literature works on the real. . . .

We can now see in what sense this biblical hermeneutics is at once a particular case of the sort of general hermeneutics described here and at the same time a unique case. It is a particular case of a more general enterprise because the new being of which the Bible speaks is not to be sought anywhere but in the word of this text which is one text among others. It is a unique case because all the partial discourses are referred to a name which is the point of intersection and the index of incompleteness of all our discourse about God, and because this name has become bound up with the *meaning-event* preached as Resurrection. But biblical hermeneutics can only claim to say something unique if this unique thing speaks as the world of the text which is addressed to us, as the issue of the text.

To conclude this lecture I should like to make a suggestion concerning the concept of religious faith which we have not considered in itself, but through its linguistic and literary expressions. For a hermeneutical philosophy, faith never appears as an immediate experience, but always as mediated by a certain language which articulates it. For my part I should link the concept of faith to that of *self-understanding* in the face of the text. Faith is the attitude of one who accepts being interpreted at the same time that he interprets the world of the text. Such is the hermeneutical constitution of the biblical faith.

In thus recognizing the hermeneutical constitution of the biblical faith, we are resisting all psychologizing reductions of faith. This is not to say that faith is not authentically an *act* which cannot be reduced to linguistic treatment. In this sense, faith is the limit of all hermeneutics and the nonhermeneutical origin of all interpretation. The ceaseless movement of interpretation begins and ends in the risk of a response which is neither engendered nor exhausted by commentary. It is in taking account of this prelinguistic or hyperlinguistic characteristic that faith could be called "ultimate concern," which speaks of the laying hold of the necessary and unique thing from whose basis I orient myself in all my choices. It has also been called a "feeling of absolute dependence" to underscore the fact that it responds to an initiative which always precedes me. Or it could be called "unconditional trust" to say that it is inseparable from a movement of hope which makes its way in spite of the contradictions of experience and which turns reasons for despair into reasons for hope according to the paradoxical laws of a logic of superabundance. In all these traits the thematic of faith escapes from hermeneutics and testifies to the fact that the latter is neither the first nor the last word.

But hermeneutics reminds us that biblical faith cannot be separated from the movement of interpretation which elevates it into language. "Ultimate concern" would remain mute if it did not receive the power of a word of interpretation ceaselessly renewed by signs and symbols which have, we might say, educated and formed this concern over the centuries. The feeling of absolute dependence would remain a weak and inarticulated sentiment if it were not the response to the proposition of a new being which open new possibilities of existence for me. Hope, unconditional trust, would be empty if it did not rely on a constantly renewed interpretation of sign-events reported by the writings, such as the Exodus in the Old Testament and the Resurrection in the New Testament. These are the events of deliverance which open and disclose the utmost possibilities of my own freedom and thus become for me the Word of God. Such is the properly hermeneutical constitution of faith.

GEORGE SANTAYANA

(1863–1952)

Late in his life, Santayana was to remark, "The dismay that has fallen of late upon so many minds has not touched me. I have never had any illusions about the world's being rationally guided or true to any ideals; reason and ideals arise in doing well something that at bottom there was no reason for doing. This is naturalism, as I understand it. . . . I am not a believer in any religion, literally understood; but I am a man of priestly disposition and think that it is possible to live nobly in this world only if we live in another world ideally." Santayana, born in Spain, came to the United States in 1869, and was educated at Harvard, where he remained to teach philosophy until 1912. He spent much of the remainder of his life in Rome. Among his major works are The Life of Reason *(5 vols., 1905–1906),* Scepticism and Animal Faith *(1923),* Dialogues in Limbo *(1925), and* Realms of Being *(1928–1937). He was also a poet and novelist, and remains one of the most eminent figures in naturalistic American philosophy.*

ULTIMATE RELIGION

Before this chosen audience, in this consecrated place, I may venture to pass over all subsidiary matters and come at once to the last question of all: What inmost allegiance, what ultimate religion, would be proper to a wholly free and disillusioned spirit? The occasion invites us to consider this question, and to consider it with entire frankness. Great as you and I may feel our debt to be to Spinoza for his philosophy of nature, there is, I think, something for which we owe him an even greater debt; I mean, the magnificent example he offers us of philosophic liberty, the courage, firmness, and sincerity with which he reconciled his heart to the truth. Any clever man may sometimes see the truth in flashes; any scientific man may put some aspect of the truth into technical words; yet all this hardly deserves the name of philosophy so long as the heart remains unabashed, and we continue to live like animals lost in the stream of our impressions, not only in the public routine and necessary cares of life, but even in our silent thoughts and affections.

"Ultimate Religion" is reprinted by permission of Charles Scribner's Sons from Obiter Scripta *by George Santayana, edited by Justus Buchler and Benjamin Schwartz. Copyright 1936 Charles Scribner's Sons. Pp. 368–377. This essay was written in commemoration of the 300th anniversary of Spinoza's birth.*

Many a man before Spinoza and since has found the secret of peace: but the singularity of Spinoza, at least in the modern world, was that he facilitated this moral victory by no dubious postulates. He did not ask God to meet him half way: he did not whitewash the facts, as the facts appear to clear reason, or as they appeared to the science of his day. He solved the problem of the spiritual life after stating it in the hardest, sharpest, most cruel terms. Let us nerve ourselves today to imitate his example, not by simply accepting his solution, which for some of us would be easy, but by exercising his courage in the face of a somewhat different world, in which it may be even more difficult for us than it was for him to find a sure foothold and a sublime companionship.

There is a brave and humorous saying of Luther's, which applies to Spinoza better, perhaps, than to Luther himself. When asked where, if driven out of the Church, he would stand, he replied: "Under the sky." The sky of Luther was terribly clouded: there was a vast deal of myth tumbling and thundering about in it: and even in the clear sky of Spinoza there was perhaps something specious, as there is in the blue vault itself. The sun, he tells us, seemed to be about two hundred feet away: and if his science at once corrected this optical illusion, it never undermined his conviction that all reality was within easy reach of his thought. Nature was dominated, he assumed, by unquestionable scientific and dialectical principles; so that while the forces of nature might often put our bodily existence in jeopardy, they always formed a decidedly friendly and faithful object for the mind. There was no essential mystery. The human soul from her humble station might salute the eternal and the infinite with complete composure and with a certain vicarious pride. Every man had a true and adequate idea of God: and this saying, technically justified as it may be by Spinoza's definitions of terms, cannot help surprising us: it reveals such a virgin sense of familiarity with the absolute. There could not but be joy in the sweep of an intelligence that seemed so completely victorious, and no misgivings could trouble a view of the world that explained everything.

Today, however, we can hardly feel such assurance: we should be taking shelter in a human edifice which the next earthquake might shake down. Nor is it a question really of times or temperaments: anyone anywhere, if he does not wish to construct a plausible system, but to challenge his own assumptions and come to spiritual self-knowledge, must begin by abstention from all easy faith, lest he should be madly filling the universe with images of his own reason and his own hopes. I will therefore ask you today, provisionally, for an hour, and without prejudice to your ulterior reasonable convictions, to imagine the truth to be as unfavourable as possible to your desires and as contrary as possible to your natural presumptions; so that the spirit in each of us may be drawn away from its accidental home and subjected to an utter denudation and supreme trial. Yes, although the dead cannot change their minds, I would respectfully beg the shade of Spinoza himself to suspend for a moment that strict rationalism, that jealous, hard-reasoning, confident piety which he shared with the Calvinists and Jansenists of his day, and to imagine—I do not say to admit—that nature may be but imperfectly formed in the bosom of chaos, and that reason in us may be imperfectly adapted to the understanding of nature. Then, having hazarded no favourite postulates and invoked no cosmic forces pledged to support our aspirations, we may all quietly observe what we find; and whatever harmonies may then appear to subsist between our spirits and the nature of things will be free gifts to us and, so far as they go, unchallengeable possessions. We shall at last be standing unpledged and naked, under the open sky.

In what I am about to say, therefore, I do not mean to prejudge any cosmological questions, such as that of free will or necessity, theism or pantheism. I am concerned only with the sincere confessions of a mind that has surrendered every doubtful claim and every questionable assurance. Of such assurances or claims there is one which is radical and comprehensive: I mean, the claim to existence and to directing the course of events. We say conventionally that the future is uncertain: but if we withdrew honestly into ourselves and examined our actual moral resources, we should feel that what is insecure is not merely the course of particular events but the vital presumption that there is a future coming at all, and a future pleasantly continuing our habitual experience. We rely in this, as we must, on the analogies of experience, or rather on the clockwork of instinct and presumption in our bodies; but existence is a miracle, and, morally considered, a free gift from moment to moment. That it will always be analogous to itself is the very question we are begging. Evidently all interconnections and sequences of events, and in particular any consequences which we may expect to flow from our actions, are really entirely beyond our spiritual control. When our will commands and seems, we know not how, to be obeyed by our bodies and by the world, we are like Joshua seeing the sun stand still at his bidding; when we command and nothing happens, we are like King Canute surprised that the rising tide should not obey him: and when we say we have executed a great work and re-directed the course of history, we are like Chanticleer attributing the sunrise to his crowing.

What is the result? That at once, by a mere act of self-examination and frankness, the spirit has come upon one of the most important and radical of religious perceptions. It has perceived that though it is living, it is powerless to live; that though it may die, it is powerless to die; and that altogether, at every instant and in every particular, it is in the hands of some alien and inscrutable power.

Of this felt power I profess to know nothing further. To me, as yet, it is merely the counterpart of my impotence. I should not venture, for instance, to call this power almighty, since I have no means of knowing how much it can do: but I should not hesitate, if I may coin a word, to call it *omnificent*: it is to me, by definition, the doer of everything that is done. I am not asserting the physical validity of this sense of agency or cause: I am merely feeling the force, the friendliness, the hostility, the unfathomableness of the world. I am expressing an impression; and it may be long before my sense of omnipresent power can be erected, with many qualifications, into a theological theory of the omnipresence of God. But the moral presence of power comes upon a man in the night, in the desert, when he finds himself, as the Arabs say, alone with Allah. It re-appears in every acute predicament, in extremities, in the birth of a child, or in the face of death. And as for the unity of this power, that is not involved in its sundry manifestations, but rather in my own solitude; in the unity of this suffering spirit overtaken by all those accidents. My destiny is single, tragically single, no matter how multifarious may be the causes of my destiny. As I stand amazed, I am not called upon to say whether, if I could penetrate into the inner workings of things, I should discover omnificent power to be simple or compound, continuous or spasmodic, intentional or blind. I stand before it simply receptive, somewhat as, in Rome, I might stand before the great fountain of Trevi. There I see jets and cascades flowing in separate streams and in divers directions. I am not sure that a single Pontifex Maximus designed it all, and led all those musical waters into just those channels. Some streams may have dried up or been diverted since the creation; some rills may have been added today by fresh rains from heaven; behind one of those artificial rocks some little demon, of his own free will, may even now be playing havoc with the conduits; and who knows how many details, in my image, may not have been misplaced or multiplied by optical tricks of my own? Yet here, for the spirit, is one total marvellous impression, one thunderous force, confronting me with this theatrical but admirable spectacle.

Yet this is not all. Power comes down upon me clothed in a thousand phenomena; and these manifestations of power open to me a new spiritual resource. In submitting to power, I learn its ways; from being passive my spirit becomes active; it begins to enjoy one of its essential prerogatives. For like a child the spirit is attracted to facts by the mere assault of their irrational presence and variety. It watches all that happens or is done with a certain happy excitement, even at the most fearful calamities. Although the essence of spirit may be merely to think, yet some intensity and progression are essential to this thinking; thinking is a way of living, and the most vital way. Therefore all the operations of universal power, when they afford themes for perception, afford also occasions for intellectual delight. Here will and intellect, as Spinoza tells us, coincide: for omnificent power flows in part through our persons; the spirit itself is a spark of that fire, or rather the light of that flame: it cannot have an opposite principle of motion. With health a certain euphoria, a certain alacrity and sense of mastery are induced in the spirit; and a natural effect of perspective, the pathos of nearness, turns our little spark for us into a central sun. The world moves round us, and we move gladly with the world. What if the march of things be destined to overwhelm us? It can not destroy the joy we had in its greatness and in its victory. There may even be some relief in passing from the troubled thought of ourselves to the thought of something more rich in life, yet in its own sphere ard progression, untroubled: and it may be easier for me to understand the motion of the heavens and to rejoice in it than to understand or rejoice in my own motions. My own eclipse, my own vices, my own sorrows, may become a subject to me for exact calculation and a pleasing wonder. The philosophical eye may compose a cosmic harmony out of these necessary conflicts, and an infinite life out of these desirable deaths.

Does it not begin to appear that the solitude of a naked spirit may be rather well peopled? In proportion as we renounce our animal claims and commitments, do we not breathe a fresher and more salubrious air? May not the renunciation of everything disinfect everything and return everything to us in its impartial reality, at the same time disinfecting our wills also, and rendering us capable of charity? This charity will extend, of course, to the lives and desires of others, which we recognize to be no less inevitable than our own; and it will extend also to their ideas, and by a curious and blessed consequence, to the relativity and misery of our own minds. Yet this intellectual charity, since it is inspired by respect for the infinite, will by no means accept all views passively and romantically, as if they were equal and not subject to correction; but doing better justice to the holy aspiration which animates them in common, it will rise from them all, and with them all, to the conception of eternal truth.

Here we touch the crown of Spinoza's philosophy, that intellectual love of God in which the spirit was to be ultimately reconciled with universal power and universal truth. This love brings to consciousness a harmony intrinsic to existence: not an alleged harmony such as may be posited in religions or philosophies resting on faith, but a harmony which, as far as it goes, is actual and patent. In the realm of matter, this harmony is measured by the degree of adjustment, conformity, and cooperation which the part may have attained in the whole; in a word, it is measured by *health*. In the realm of truth, the same natural harmony extends as far as do capacity and pleasure in understanding the truth: so that besides health we may possess *knowledge*. And this is no passive union, no dead peace; the spirit rejoices in it; for the spirit, being, according to Spinoza, an essential concomitant of all existence, shares the movement, the *actuosa essentia* of the universe: so that we necessarily *love* health and knowledge, and *love* the things in which health and knowledge are found. In so far as omnificent power endows us with health, we necessarily love that power whose total movement makes for our own perfection; and in so far as we are able to understand the truth, we necessarily love the themes of an intense and unclouded vision, in which our imaginative faculty reaches its perfect function.

Of this religion of health and understanding Spinoza is a sublime prophet. By overcoming all human weaknesses, even when they seemed kindly or noble, and by honouring power and truth, even if they should slay him, he entered the sanctuary of an unruffled superhuman wisdom, and declared himself supremely happy, not because the world as he conceived it was flattering to his heart, but because the gravity of his heart disdained all flatteries, and with a sacrificial prophetic boldness uncovered and relished his destiny, however tragic his destiny might be. And presently peace descended; this keen scientific air seemed alone fit to breathe, and only this high tragedy worthy of a heroic and manly breast. Indeed the truth is a great cathartic and wonderfully relieves the vital distress of existence. We stand as on a mountaintop, and the spectacle, so out of scale with all our petty troubles, silences and overpowers the heart, expanding it for a moment into boundless sympathy with the universe.

Nevertheless, the moral problem is not solved. It is not solved for mankind at large, which remains no less distracted than it was before. Nor is it solved even for the single spirit. There is a radical and necessary recalcitrancy in the finite soul in the face of all this cosmic pomp and all this cosmic pressure: a recalcitrancy to which Spinoza was less sensitive than some other masters of the spiritual life, perhaps because he was more positivistic by temperament and less specifically religious. At any rate many a holy man has known more suffering than Spinoza found in the long work of salvation, more uncertainty, and also, in the end, a more lyrical and warmer happiness. For in the first place, as I said in the beginning, a really naked spirit cannot assume that the world is thoroughly intelligible. There may be surds, there may be hard facts, there may be dark abysses before which intelligence must be silent, for fear of going mad. And in the second place, even if to the intellect all things should prove perspicuous, the intellect is not the whole of human nature, nor even the whole of pure spirit in man. Reason may be the differentia of man; it is surely not his essence. His essence, at best, is animality qualified by reason. And from this animality the highest flights of reason are by no means separable. The very life of spirit springs from animal predicaments: it moves by imposing on events a perspective and a moral urgency proper to some particular creature or some particular interest.

Good, as Spinoza would tell us, is an epithet which we assign to whatsoever increases our perfection. Such a doctrine might seem egotistical, but is simply biological; and on its moral side, the maxim is a greater charter of liberty and justice than ever politician framed. For it follows that every good pursued is genuinely good, and the perfection of every creature equally perfection. Every good therefore is a good forever to a really clarified, just, and disinterested spirit; such a spirit cannot rest in the satisfaction of any special faculty, such as intelligence, nor of any special art, such as philosophy. That the intellect might be perfectly happy in contemplating the truth of the universe, does not render the universe good to every other faculty; good to the heart, good to the flesh, good to the eye, good to the conscience or the sense of justice. Of all systems an optimistic system is the most oppressive. Would it not be a bitter mockery if, in the words of Bradley, this were the best of possible worlds, and everything in it a necessary evil? The universal good by which the spirit, in its rapt moments, feels overwhelmed, if it is not to be a mystical illusion, cannot fall short of being the sum of all those perfections, infinitely various, to which all living things severally aspire. A glint or symbol of this universal good may be found in any moment of perfect happiness visiting any breast; but it is impossible unreservedly to love or worship anything, be it the universe or any part of it, unless we find in the end that this thing is completely good: I mean, unless it is perfect after its kind and a friend to itself, and unless at the same time it is beneficent universally, and a friend to everything else. Pure spirit would be lame and evidently biassed by some biological accident, if it did not love every good loved anywhere by anybody. These varied perfections are rivals and enemies in the press of the world, where there seems not to be matter or time enough for everything: but to impartial spirit no good can render another good odious. Physically, one good may exclude another: nature and natural morality must choose between them, or be dissolved into chaos: but in eternity the most opposite goods are not enemies; rather little brothers and sisters, as all odd creatures were to St. Francis. And that all these various perfections are not actually attainable is a material accident, painful but not confusing to a free spirit. Their contrariety increases sorrow but does not diminish love; the very pain is a fresh homage to the beauty missed, and a proof of loyalty; so that the more the spirit suffers the more clearly, when it unravels its suffering, it understands what it loves. Every perfection then shines, washed and clear, separate and uncontaminated: yet all compatible, each in its place, and harmonious. To love things spiritually, that is to say, intelligently and disinterestedly, means to love the love in them, to worship the good which they pursue, and to see them all prophetically in their possible beauty. To love things as they are would be a mockery of things: a true lover must love them as they would wish to be. For nothing is quite happy as it is, and the first act of true sympathy must be to move with the object of love towards its happiness.

Universal good, then, the whole of that to which all things aspire, is some thing merely potential; and if we wish to make a religion of love, after the manner of Socrates, we must take universal good, not universal power, for the object of our religion. This religion would need to be more imaginative, more poetical, than that of Spinoza, and the word God, if we still used it, would have to mean for us not the universe, but the good of the universe. There would not be a universe worshipped, but a universe praying; and the flame of the whole fire, the whole seminal and generative movement of nature, would be the love of God. This love would be erotic; it would be really love and not something wingless called by that name. It would bring celestial glimpses not to be retained, but culminating in moments of unspeakable rapture, in a union with all good, in which the soul would vanish as an object because, as an organ, it has found its perfect employment.

For there is a mystery here, the mystery of seeming to attain emotionally the logically unattainable. Universal good is something dispersed, various, contrary to itself in its opposite embodiments; nevertheless, to the mystic, it seems a single living object, the One Beloved, a good to be embraced all at once, finally and for ever, leaving not the least shred of anything good outside. Yet I think this mystery may be easily solved. Spirit is essentially synthetic; and just as all the known and unknown forces of nature make, in relation to experience and destiny, one single omnificent power; and just as all facts and all the relations between facts compose for the historical and prophetic mind one unalterable realm of truth; so exactly, for the lover, all objects of love form a single ineffable good. He may say that he sees all beauties in a single face, that all beauties else are nothing to him; yet perhaps in this hyperbole he may be doing his secret heart an injustice. Beauty here may be silently teaching him to discern beauty everywhere, because in all instances of love only the sheer love counts in his eyes: and in the very absoluteness of his love he may feel an infinite promise. His ecstasy, which passes for a fulfilment, remains a sort of agony: and though itself visionary, it may, by its influence, free his heart from trivial or accidental attachments and lead it instead to a universal charity. Beggars in Catholic and Moslem countries used to beg an alms, sometimes, for the love of God. It was a potent appeal; because God, according to the Socratic tradition, was the good to which all creation moved; so that anyone who loved deeply, and loved God, could not fail, by a necessary inclusion, to love the good which all creatures lived by pursuing, no matter how repulsive these creatures might be to natural human feeling.

Thus the absolute love of anything involves the love of universal good; and the love of universal good involves the love of every creature.

Such, in brief, seems to me the prospect open to a mind that examines its moral condition without any preconceptions. Perhaps an empirical critic, strictly reducing all objects to the functions which they have in experience, might see in my meagre inventory all the elements of religion. Mankind, he might say, in thinking of God or the gods have always meant the power in events: as when people say: *God willing*. Sometimes they have also meant the truth, as when people say: *God knows*. And perhaps a few mystics may have meant the good, or the supreme object of love, union with whom they felt would be perfect happiness. I should then have merely changed the language of traditional religion a little, translated its myths into their pragmatic equivalents, and reduced religion to its true essence. But no: I make no such professions: they would be plainly sophistical. The functions which objects have in experience no doubt open to us different avenues to those objects: but the objects themselves, if they exist, are not mere names for those functions. They are objects of faith and the religion of mankind, like their science, has always been founded on faith. Now there is no faith invoked in the examination of conscience which I have made before you this evening:and therefore, properly speaking, what I come to is not religion. Nor is it exactly philosophy, since I offer no hypotheses about the nature of the universe or about the nature of knowledge. Yet to be quite sincere, I think that in this examination of conscience there is a sort of secret or private philosophy perhaps more philosophical than the other: and while I set up no gods, not even Spinoza's infinite *Deus sive Natura* [God or Nature], I do not consider on what subjects and to what end we might consult those gods, if we found that they existed: and surely the aspiration that would prompt us, in that case, to worship the gods, would be our truest heart-bond and our ultimate religion.

If then any of us who are so minded should ever hear the summons of a liturgical religion calling to us: *Sursum corda, Lift up your hearts*, we might sincerely answer, *Habemus ad Dominum, Our hearts by nature are addressed to the Lord*. For we recognize universal power, and respect it, since on it we depend for our existence and fortunes. We look also with unfeigned and watchful allegiance towards universal truth, in which all the works of power are eternally defined and recorded; since in so far as we are able to discover it, the truth raises all things for us into the light, into the language of spirit. And finally, when power takes on the form of life, and begins to circle about and pursue some type of perfection, spirit in us necessarily loves these perfections, since spirit is aspiration become conscious, and they are the goals of life: and in so far as any of these goals of life can be defined or attained anywhere, even if only in prophetic fancy, they become glory, or become beauty, and spirit in us necessarily worships them: not the troubled glories and brief perfections of this world only, but rather that desired perfection, that eternal beauty, which lies sealed in the heart of each living thing.

17

Epilogue

ST. THOMAS, HUME, AND NIETZSCHE

THOMAS. Start, I say, from that which is at hand. Start with the things we see and hear and touch, the things and movements of this world, with all that is changing, developing, flaring up, and dying down. Start with things swift, slow, sweet, sour, "adazzle, original, spare, strange." Start with—as this fine English poet I quote has it—"Landscapes plotted and pieced—fold, fallow, and plow," and you'll be able to comprehend and to contemplate how all things God "fathers forth," how all things, of which He is First Cause, praise Him.

HUME. I can neither begin where you begin, nor reason as you reason: and it is most certain that I cannot end where you end. You say to begin with what is observed to happen in the world, and from there you proceed by a baffling kind of logic to the conclusion that God exists. But "the world out there" is not something we *can* begin with, for it is something men have constructed, not discovered. What we begin with are our own private sense impressions. What we end with are also impressions. I fail to see how this testimony of the senses can be used to demonstrate the existence of something which is evidently not perceivable by sense.

NIETZSCHE. It's hard to guess which of these droll fellows is more mad. One declares that from statements about what goes on in the world, he can deduce the existence of a supernatural being. The other claims not only to be unconvinced of the existence of a supernatural God, but to know nothing of the "external world" itself, since all *he* ever encounters are his own impressions. They seem not to realize that they're merely playing scholarly games, trying to rationalize their pet obsessions. Yet on they go, on and on with these pointless charades, these witless pretentions to sanity. But that's man, of course—the plausible animal! There, now, they're at it again!

THOMAS. All the universe is arranged choir-like, in an ascending order of beings, and all things are animated by the same energy, which is as it must be, for the love of God's perfection surges through everything. And every being, moved by that love, is driven towards its own perfection. How marvellous and yet, how utterly rational it is!

NIETZSCHE. These dreary exchanges between sceptics and saints! All this prattle and claptrap by this believing Thomas about God! What is God, that he is mindful of Him? These arrogant philosophers—as if man were not vain enough already. . . . If the chisel of Michelangelo could speak, what an egoist it would turn out to be: "I did the David! I did the Moses! I did Lorenzo!" So with man. . . . Nature's the hammer, man's the chisel, the chiseled—and the chiseler too? Ha!

HUME. From Princes Street, just off which I lived, I could see Edinborough castle high up, glistening in the morning light, while the dark fog on which it seemed to float enveloped everything below. The castle in its majesty was clearly visible, everything else was obscure. From what you say, on the contrary, the world is tangible and many-colored and bright, but the transcendent God is nowhere to be perceived. Can you blame me for finding only the perceivable castle a credible object of knowledge?

THOMAS. I haven't the least desire to blame you, of course, but neither can I praise you while you continue to confuse categories as you now do. God's existence is not in the same category as that of His creatures, and one cannot apply the same criteria of existence to the one category as to the other. Your castle has a specific location in time and space; God certainly does not. Your castle is perceivable; God is not. Why should these things seem so strange to you? God's modes of being and of relating are not the same as man's. He has no specific location, yet He relates uniquely to each human soul. Consequently in divine space, if I may speak in such fashion (for that, and not natural space, is what medieval artists depicted), all perspective lines converge upon us as individual beholders, and radiate outward from us to God. Such is the unique secret of our medieval perspective. The theological counterpart of this mode of understanding was the conviction that each Christian soul is a center for the love of God. The scientific counterpart was the medieval belief that the entire universe was centered upon the earth.

HUME. You have a way of exploring the diverse charming alleys that lead off philosophy—poetry, theology, art, science. . . . Shouldn't we get back to the main road, to philosophy proper, and consider these arguments which you presume to prove God's existence?

KIERKEGAARD. Oh no, not again! Not another rational demonstration of that which is undemonstrable—I couldn't take it! Nietzsche, why do you torment yourself by listening to them?

NIETZSCHE. Out of their idiocies, a marvellous beauty is born, as the noblest virtues emerge out of the rankest decadence and bestiality.

Let us confront once for all the utter absurdity of existence and the pointlessness of human life. Let us boldly confront it, and there shall be an end to despair. We shall laugh and sing, we shall be glorious and adventurous, and we shall transmute the vast, dreary emptiness around us into the gold of art and civilization. If the ape could turn himself into a man, then man could turn himself into—.

Kierkegaard. A god? No, don't say it. Let us rise up like men to confront Him. Let us deal with Him face to face, one to one. No more going through bureaucratic channels—face to face! Beyond the natural, if not beyond the human, we shall yet encounter Him in all of His individuality and in all of our own. In this world in which everything changes, in which everything evolves and decays, what a delight it will be to find that which is totally immutable, totally changeless and unchangeable, eternally and forever the same, utterly reliable, absolutely identical with Himself and with nothing else! Let us cease our own vacillations and be like Him in His mild, unruffled, eternally unchangeable serenity. Ah, listen—they begin again.

Thomas. I must warn you that I didn't write these demonstrations for the edification of philosophers. Rather they were intended as study guides for novices in the monasteries. I never thought them useful to convert the nonbeliever, but I did think they might serve to show the believer that a logic did indeed correspond with his faith.

Hume. But what kind of logic is it that permits the assertion that there cannot be an infinite regress of causes, because there would then be no first cause? Isn't it a most palpable violation of logic to assume antecedently that which one is seeking to prove? I don't mind your defining God as First Cause; you're free to define him as you like. But why does the existence of a series give you the right to assume that such an existence had a beginning? Look, permit me to illustrate the difficulty I find with your procedure. You suggest that moving backwards in time from today (if we could do this) would lead us eventually to some point at which the world began. But if from today we were to move forward in time, would we necessarily encounter an end to the series of possible days? Of course not. Tomorrow is one day from now, the next is two, the next is three, and so on, to infinity. Similarly, yesterday was one day ago, the day before yesterday was two, the day before that was three, and so backwards infinitely. So you see, from a truly logical point of view, the world *need* not have had any beginning at all. Surely Aristotle made you aware of this.

Thomas. Having read Aristotle scrupulously, I'm quite aware of the naturalistic arguments which seek to show that the world has always existed. But even Aristotle, you'll recall, spoke of a First Cause, although I'll admit he conceived of such a First Cause as quite compatible with a world having neither beginning nor end. And in any case, even if I had accepted such a position, would it really have made matters any less difficult to understand? There's much that puzzles me about the Creation, but I fail to see how matters would be any less mysterious if we were to believe in God's coexistence with a temporal, historical world.

HUME. That's just it—I quite agree! There's mystery either way. There is no ultimate understanding and there are no ultimate answers. Not for the universe, and not for any specific event within the universe. To explain anything is to relate it causally to its context. But nature as a whole has no context; hence it is inexplicable, as is all within it. Its ultimate principles, if there are such, will remain forever hidden from us. And if by "miracle" you mean an inexplicable happening, then each and every occurrence, no matter how regularly or how frequently it occurs, in the last analysis is totally inexplicable and miraculous.

NIETZSCHE. There they go—one illogical, both irrational. I should have burst upon them, savage and brilliant, devastating their arguments, compelling them to recognize the audacity of my views. I'd have shown them that man is that incredible curiosity, a wild creature who has brutally tamed and domesticated himself. Just as one tames a bear with whips and scourges and heated irons, so man has destroyed his own passions. Instead of turning his natural powers upon others, he has turned them inwards upon himself. But the true diabolical genius of the human creature, his most marvellous cunning, his most magnificent inspiration, all were then employed in his hitherto incomprehensible invention of religion and the gods as *instruments* (like those whips and scourges) by which man could become cultivated, civilized, and refined. The history of religion is a history of blood and torture, piously, patiently reducing the stronger individuals (the healthy ones who felt no guilt about their natural instincts) into the pitiful weaklings who were destined to inherit the earth. But why go on? They would smile, saint and sceptic alike; they would shrug and turn away, as though slightly embarrassed about me. Too long sane in the madhouse; one almost begins to long for adjustment. . . .

KIERKEGAARD. Come away, come away. When it comes to the doctors of science and the doctors of the church, there's little or nothing that poor, forked fellows like ourselves can do, except to heap our scorn upon their heads—

NIETZSCHE.—and to perfect the use of irony!

KIERKEGAARD. Ah, irony, there you have it—what a remorseless weapon of destruction! But now, gently, come away. . . .

KNOWING, PERCEIVING, AND EXPERIENCING

18

Introduction

Nothing is more ordinary than to be asked (having made some comment or other), "How do you know?" A simple question indeed, but a rich and disturbing one.

"How do you know?" may mean, "By what method have you found this out?" Or it may mean, "How can you be sure?" Or it could mean, "How is this fact to be explained?" Or again, "What makes you think so?" or "How can you tell?"

You may think that the observation you made is utterly common and unsurprising. You noted, let us say, that you "have a body." Well, and do not all people have bodies? What could be more obvious?

Yet you are questioned. First on the level of language. The very terms you used in your remark are scrutinized. "I have a body." To what does the word "I" refer? What does personal identity consist in? The word "have" is examined. What is it to have, to possess? Do you have your body or does it have you? And what is meant by "a body?" Is it a thing, an object? Or an object that can be subject?

Bewildering? Yes, but this is not all. As you attempt to offer explanations of how you know, you assume that you can take for granted what an explanation is. Nothing so simple. Without the concept of an explanation, and without standards indicating what an adequate explanation might be, it would not be possible to tell if your answer constituted a satisfactory answer or not.

You might try to explain your statement, "I have a body," by testifying to certain sensations you have, like the feeling of the weight and mass of your body. But your questioner, loath to give off tormenting you, may insist upon a theory of perception in addition to a theory of language and a theory of explanation. Or he may ask why you cite the feeling of weight as confirming the statement "I have a body," and you may find yourself at this point more perplexed than ever.

Perplexities such as these are the stock-in-trade of that branch of philosophy known as "epistemology" or "the theory of knowledge." The epistemologist inquires into the nature of knowledge and may devise theories of the various processes involved in knowing, such as experiencing, perceiving, explaining, understanding, thinking, and so on. He may also devise criteria aimed at determining what counts for an adequate explanation, or how perception is to be distinguished from sensation, or at what point knowledge can be taken to be knowledge of the truth.

How does one know? How can one be sure? It was questions such as these that tantalized Descartes, and led him to a pioneering role in the theory of knowledge. Let us begin our quest for certainty, Descartes suggests, by asking what we can take for granted (for example, can we take our own bodies for granted?). Knowing can be compared with seeing: a person with normal vision sees what is there to be seen, and sees it clearly and distinctly. Likewise with the mind: if it grasps its ideas with clarity and distinctness, it can proceed with the assurance that it knows what is knowable. These intuitively certain truths can then serve as a basis for further deductions that, if valid, will provide us with an entire system of truths about the world, without having had to rely upon the vagaries of sense experience. By doubting methodically, we can rid our minds of false notions, and by reasoning methodically we can stock our minds with true ones. If we allow mathematics and geometry to serve as our models of reliable knowledge, we must conclude that the system of true knowledge has reference only to that which is measurable. Hence, external reality must be some measurable, extended substance. But color, sound, taste, and odor are not extended in the world: they are only mental after-images consequent upon external events. Descartes thereby arrives at a dualistic theory of knowledge, in which the mind is in perfect touch with reality, but a reality denuded of virtually all the values and qualities by which we would normally recognize it.

Descartes' conception of the world provided Locke with the starting point of his representational or "copy" theory of knowledge, in which he maintained that our ideas of things are probably copies of the primary qualities of things—those qualities, such as shape and size, that Locke believed exist even when not perceived. But, Berkeley argues, isn't it self-contradictory to claim that things exist unperceived, if the only evidence we have of their existence is that we perceive them? Berkeley thus advocates a rejection of the copy theory of knowledge, and a return to a direct or presentational epistemology. At the same time, Berkeley contends that matter is a totally unprovable notion and should be dispensed with. If the mind can know only its own ideas, as Locke had thought, then the mind can never know that something "outside the mind" exists at all. By affirming that only mental qualities are real, Berkeley claims, we can once again assert the reality of a world of directly perceived colors and tastes, odors and sounds. The denial of material substance is a small enough price to pay to get rid of the copy theory of knowledge, the correspondence theory of truth (that our ideas are true when they correspond to that which they refer to in the world), and the obnoxious dualism between mind and matter. Berkeley's radical attack thus lay the groundwork for both the positivism and the pragmatism of the next two centuries.

One version of such pragmatism is to be found in James. James concurs with Berkeley's insight into the intimate relationship between knowledge and perception. On the other hand, James is sharply critical of the way in which Berkeley and other British thinkers took it for granted that our experience is composed of bits of sensation or atomistic perceptions, that the things we encounter in the world are nothing other than clusters or bundles of such sensations. Is it the case that an apple is merely a patchwork collection of taste, shape, texture, color, and odor? James contends that experience is more likely to be composed of wholes or totalities that are subsequently broken down by reflective analysis into discrete components. To think things are made up of such components simply because our inquiries decompose them into simple qualities is to commit the gross mistake of confusing categories of method with categories of subject-matter. Even if we can discern different orders within experience, such as the mental and the physical, this does not preclude the possibility that such orders simple *intersect*, so that a single object could be in both a mental and a physical order at the same moment, rather than that there be two objects, one physical and real, the other a merely apparent mental copy.

To be introduced to the thought of Descartes, of Berkeley, and of James is to make the acquaintance of three significantly different ways of understanding the nature of human knowledge. In some ways, each of these men is characteristic of some broader philosophical perspective—Descartes of rationalism, Berkeley of empirical idealism, and James of pragmatism. But at the same time, each has his own texture of thought and combines the strands of his reasoning in complex and novel ways, so that to take him to be representative of a broad, widely-shared philosophical outlook could have its hazards. Thus it would not be accurate to take Berkeley as typical of empiricists, even though he insists that he trusts his senses completely, for his empiricism must be understood in the light of his idealism—a position that holds that Reality is essentially spiritual.

The ideal of a wholly perfect, error-free knowledge has long been attractive to philosophers, and is what some of them have identified as "truth." It is often assumed that the truth of such ideal and complete knowledge can be detached from the general system of ideas, and can be seen as a property of individual ideas, taken as independent entities. Thus there have developed those theories of truth that prescribe the conditions under which particular ideas are to be taken as true. One, the correspondence theory, takes ideas to be true if they correspond to some external reality; a second, the coherence theory, assumes ideas to be true that are consistent with the body of ideas already accepted as true; the third, the pragmatic theory, is willing to call those ideas true that function successfully in the removal of doubt, and only for so long as they do.

Traditional epistemological theory had always articulated the criteria that knowledge would have to possess in order to be excellent: that it be capable of formulation, consistent, reliable, verifiable, publicly ascertainable, supported by suitable evidence, and capable of validation by fitting into generally accepted frameworks of understanding. But in recent years, increasing attention has been given to an examination of the criteria of evidence, to the nature of scientific discovery, to a critique of the notion of "appearance," to study of the *a priori* element in knowledge, to criticism of the traditionally accepted notion that experience is reducible to atomic sensations which are basic, indivisible and irreducible, and to the role of language in the formulation of knowledge.

As we become more and more aware of the linguistic, psychological, and cultural conditions of knowledge, these conditions can be better taken into account, and the knowledge then formulated will be more objective than it would have been if these conditions had remained unspecified. The dichotomy between knowledge and experience therefore diminishes as we recognize that the meanings of the terms we employ are dependent upon the contexts in which we employ them, the usages to which they have habitually been put, and the practical bearings they have for us in terms of experienceable consequences.

Among the contemporary selections, Ayer discusses the possibility that knowing is a cluster of activities that are only loosely connected, just as members of a family may only loosely resemble one another. But he finds Wittgenstein's notion of family membership unacceptable when applied to different forms of knowing. His conclusion is that we *know* when we have a *right* to be sure, and *are* sure, of the truth of what we say—and when what we say happens also to be *true*. Yolton's essay, more a survey of the field and its contemporary representatives, is useful for understanding the stages of awareness out of which knowledge develops, as well as the individual mental processes—such as remembering, predicting, and expecting—that knowing involves. It also helps us to understand why the search for criteria is so crucial to the definition of knowledge.

Popper sketches a theory of scientific explanation in which he criticizes naive empiricism—the passive absorption of sense impressions—and insists instead that the question or the hypothesis must precede the observation. Moreover, Popper asserts, we are more in touch with reality when our theories are falsified than when we merely find further evidence to support what we already believe.

Quine sees progress in language theory commencing with the shift of focus from ideas to words. Word usage is a matter of overt, observable behavior, from which mental life is subsequently inferred. Quine thus defends a behavioristic empiricism, arguing that "there is nothing in meaning that is not in behavior." But Black raises probing questions about Quine's subordination of philosophy to science and about Quine's assertion that mental life is merely inferred. We may indeed have to infer *other* people's mental lives, Black suggests; but we hardly are limited to inference when it is our own thoughts that are at issue.

In his reflections on perception, Ryle concentrates upon making two points—that attacks on the testimony of certain sense experiences necessarily presuppose the reliability of other sense experiences (an obvious rejection of Platonism and Cartesianism), and that language treats perception not as a process but as the end of a process. The latter point may be merely a charming idiosyncrasy, but the first is of a significance that Hamlyn acknowledges. However, Hamlyn suggests that the citation of unreliable sense testimony does not necessarily imply the existence of reliable testimony from sense experience. It merely points to the existence of criteria for "what might count as knowledge." Thus, Ryle and Hamlyn are to be found in disagreement as to whether the standard of reliability is discoverable within sense experience or independently of sense experience. Their dispute recalls to us that the controversy is a long-standing one, and was once summed up by Plato, in *The Statesman*, with the remark that we "jumble together two widely different things, relation to one another, and to a standard. . . ."

The Buchler selection is suggestive of the scope and amplitude of his overall philosophical system, a system that has established him, along with Peirce, Dewey, and Whitehead, as a significant contributor to the fashioning of contemporary metaphysical theory. Students concerned to discover a broad philosophical context in which to locate the more technical issues to which most philosophy is devoted may well find that Buchler's analysis of human experience in terms of three major modes of judgment—acting, asserting, and arranging—ushers them into a philosophical world-view of unusual comprehensiveness and richness.

19

The Thought World

RENÉ DESCARTES

(1596–1650)

The most influential philosopher of his century, Descartes was educated at the Jesuit school at La Flèche, in France. While in military service with the Dutch army, he concentrated on mathematics and discovered analytical geometry. In 1628 he settled in Holland, which was an artistic and scientific center of the Western world. In 1637 he published the Discourse on Method, *and in 1641 the* Meditations. *His* Principles, *published in 1644, was dedicated to one of his admirers, the Princess Elizabeth of Bohemia. He died in Sweden while serving as a consultant to the Swedish queen, Christina.*

THE THINKING THING AND THE PIECE OF WAX

The Meditation of yesterday has filled my mind with so many doubts, that it is no longer in my power to forget them. Nor do I see, meanwhile, any principle on which they can be resolved; and, just as if I had fallen all of a sudden into very deep water, I am so greatly disconcerted as to be made unable either to plant my feet firmly on the bottom or sustain myself by swimming on the surface. I will, nevertheless, make an effort, and try anew the same path on which I had entered yesterday, that is, proceed by casting aside all that admits of the slightest doubt, not less than if I had discovered it to be absolutely false; and I will continue always in this track until I shall find something that is certain, or at least, if I can do nothing more, until I shall know with certainty that there is nothing certain. Archimedes, that he might transport the entire globe from the place it occupied to another, demanded only a point that was firm and immovable; so also, I shall be entitled to entertain the highest expectations, if I am fortunate enough to discover only one thing that is certain and indubitable.

I suppose, accordingly, that all the things which I see are false (fictitious); I believe that none of those objects which my fallacious memory represents ever existed; I suppose that I possess no senses; I believe that body, figure, extension, motion, and place are merely fictions of my mind. What is there, then, that can be esteemed true? Perhaps this only, that there is absolutely nothing certain.

But how do I know that there is not something different altogether from the objects I have now enumerated, of which it is impossible to entertain the slightest doubt? Is there not a God, or some being, by whatever name I may designate him, who causes these thoughts to arise in my mind? But why suppose such a being, for it may be I myself am capable of producing them? Am I, then, at least not something? But I before denied that I possessed senses or a body; I hesitate, however, for what follows from that? Am I so dependent on the body and the senses that without these I cannot exist? But I had the persuasion that there was absolutely nothing in the world, that there was no sky and no earth, neither minds nor bodies; was I not, therefore, at the same time, persuaded that I did not exist? Far from it; I assuredly existed, since I was persuaded. But there is I know not what being, who is possessed at once of the highest power and the deepest cunning, who is constantly employing all his ingenuity in deceiving me. Doubtless, then, I exist, since I am deceived; and, let him deceive me as he may, he can never bring it about that I am

From Meditations, *Part II.*

nothing, so long as I shall be conscious that I am something. So that it must, in fine, be maintained, all things being maturely and carefully considered, that this proposition (*pronunciatum*) I am, I exist, is necessarily true each time it is expressed by me, or conceived in my mind.

But I do not yet know with sufficient clearness what I am, though assured that I am, and hence, in the next place, I must take care, lest perchance I inconsiderately substitute some other object in room of what is properly myself, and thus wander from truth, even in that knowledge (cognition) which I hold to be of all others the most certain and evident. For this reason, I will now consider anew what I formerly believed myself to be, before I entered on the present train of thought; and of my previous opinion I will retrench all that can in the least be invalidated by the grounds of doubt I have adduced, in order that there may at length remain nothing but what is certain and indubitable. What then did I formerly think I was? Undoubtedly I judged that I was a man. But what is a man? Shall I say a rational animal? Assuredly not; for it would be necessary forthwith to inquire into what is meant by animal, and what by rational, and thus, from a single question, I should insensibly glide into others, and these more difficult than the first; nor do I now possess enough of leisure to warrant me in wasting my time amid subtleties of this sort. I prefer here to attend to the thoughts that sprung up of themselves in my mind, and were inspired by my own nature alone, when I applied myself to the consideration of what I was. In the first place, then, I thought that I possessed a countenance, hands, arms, and all the fabric of members that appears in a corpse, and which I called by the name of body. It further occurred to me that I was nourished, that I walked, perceived, and thought, and all those actions I referred to the soul; but what the soul itself was I either did not stay to consider, or, if I did, I imagined that it was something extremely rare and subtile, like wind, or flame, or ether, spread through my grosser parts. As regarded the body, I did not even doubt of its nature, but thought I distinctly knew it, and if I had wished to describe it according to the notions I then entertained, I should have explained myself in this manner: By body I understand all that can be terminated by a certain figure; that can be comprised in a certain place, and so fill a certain space as therefrom to exclude every other body; that can be perceived either by touch, sight, hearing, taste, or smell; that can be moved in different ways, not indeed of itself, but by something foreign to it by which it is touched [and from which it receives the impression]; for the power of self-motion, as likewise that of perceiving and thinking, I held as by no means pertaining to the nature of body; on the contrary, I was somewhat astonished to find such faculties existing in some bodies.

But [as to myself, what can I now say that I am], since I suppose there exists an extremely powerful, and, if I may so speak, malignant being, whose whole endeavours are directed towards deceiving me? Can I affirm that I possess any one of all those attributes of which I have lately spoken as belonging to the nature of body? After attentively considering them in my own mind, I find none of them that can properly be said to belong to myself. To recount them were idle and tedious. Let us pass, then, to the attributes of the soul. The first mentioned were the powers of nutrition and walking; but, if it be true that I have no body, it is true likewise that I am capable neither of walking nor of being nourished. Perception is another attribute of the soul; but perception too is impossible without the body: besides, I have frequently, during sleep, believed that I perceived objects which I afterwards observed I did not in reality perceive. Thinking is another attribute of the soul; and here I discover what properly belongs to myself. This alone is inseparable from me. I am—I exist: this is certain; but how often? As often as I think; for perhaps it would even happen, if I should wholly cease to think, that I should at the same time altogether cease to be. I now admit nothing that is not necessarily true: I am therefore, precisely speaking, only a thinking thing, that is, a mind (*mens sive animus*), understanding, or reason—terms whose signification was before unknown to me. I am, however, a real thing, and really existent; but what thing? The answer was, a thinking thing. The question now arises, am I aught besides? I will stimulate my imagination with a view to discover whether I am not still something more than a thinking being. Now it is plain I am not the assemblage of members called the human body; I am not a thin and penetrating air diffused through all these members, or wind, or flame, or vapour, or breath, or any of all the things I can imagine; for I supposed that all these were not, and, without changing the supposition, I find that I still feel assured of my existence.

But it is true, perhaps, that those very things which I suppose to be non-existent, because they are unknown to me, are not in truth different from myself whom I know. This is a point I cannot determine, and do not now enter into any dispute regarding it. I can only judge of things that are known to me: I am conscious that I exist, and I who know that I exist inquire into what I am. It is, however, perfectly certain that the knowledge of my existence, thus precisely taken, is not dependent on things, the existence of which is as yet unknown to me: and consequently it is not dependent on any of the things I can feign in imagination. Moreover, the phrase itself, I frame an image (*effingo*), reminds me of my error; for I should in truth frame one if I were to imagine myself to be anything, since to imagine is nothing more than to contemplate the figure or image of a corporeal thing; but I already know that I exist, and that it is possible at the same time that all those images, and in general all that relates to the nature of body, are merely dreams [or chimeras]. From this I discover that it is not more reasonable to say, I will excite my imagination that I may know more distinctly what I am, than to express myself as follows: I am now awake, and perceive something real; but because my perception is not sufficiently clear, I will of express purpose go to sleep that my dreams may represent to me the object of my perception with more truth and clearness. And, therefore, I know that nothing of all that I can embrace in imagination belongs to the knowledge which I have of myself, and that there is need to recall with the utmost care the mind from this mode of thinking, that it may be able to know its own nature with perfect distinctness.

But what, then, am I? A thinking thing, it has been said. But what is a thinking thing? It is a thing that doubts, understands [conceives], affirms, denies, wills, refuses, that imagines also, and perceives. Assuredly it is not little, if all these properties belong to my nature. But why should they not belong to it? Am I not that very being who now doubts of almost everything; who, for all that, understands and conceives certain things, who affirms one alone as true, and denies the others; who desires to know more of them, and does not wish to be deceived; who imagines many things, sometimes even despite his will; and is likewise percipient of many, as if through the medium of the senses. Is there nothing of all this as true as that I am, even although I should be always dreaming, and although he who gave me being employed all his ingenuity to deceive me? Is there also any one of these attributes that can be properly distinguished from my thought, or that can be said to be separate from myself? For it is of itself so evident that it is I who doubt, I who understand, and I who desire, that it is here unnecessary to add anything by way of rendering it more clear. And I am as certainly the same being who imagines; for, although it may be (as I before supposed) that nothing I imagine is true, still the power of imagination does not cease really to exist in me and to form part of my thoughts. In fine, I am the same being who perceives, that is, who apprehends certain objects as by the organs of sense, since, in truth, I see light, hear a noise, and feel heat. But it will be said that these presentations are false, and that I am dreaming. Let it be so. At all events it is certain that I seem to see light, hear a noise, and feel heat; this cannot be false, and this is what in me is properly called perceiving (*sentire*), which is nothing else than thinking. From this I begin to know what I am with somewhat greater clearness and distinctness than heretofore.

But, nevertheless, it still seems to me, and I cannot help believing, that corporeal things, whose images are formed by thought [which fall under the senses], and are examined by the same, are known with much greater distinctness than that I know not what part of myself which is not imaginable; although, in truth, it may seem strange to say that I know and comprehend with greater distinctness things whose existence appears to me doubtful, that are unknown, and do not belong to me, than others of whose reality I am persuaded, that are known to me, and appertain to my proper nature; in a word, than myself. But I see clearly what is the state of the case. My mind is apt to wander, and will not yet submit to be restrained within the limits of truth. Let us therefore leave the mind to itself once more, and, according to it every kind of liberty [permit it to consider the objects that appear to it from without], in order that, having afterwards withdrawn it from these gently and opportunely [and fixed it on the consideration of its being and the properties it finds in itself], it may then be the more easily controlled.

Let us now accordingly consider the objects that are commonly thought to be [the most easily, and likewise] the most distinctly known, viz., the bodies we touch and see; not, indeed, bodies in general, for these general notions are usually somewhat more confused, but one body in particular. Take, for example, this piece of wax; it is quite fresh, having been but recently taken from the beehive; it has not yet lost the sweetness of the honey it contained; it still retains somewhat of the odour of the flowers from which it was gathered; its colour, figure, size, are apparent (to the sight); it is hard, cold, easily handled; and sounds when struck upon with the finger. In fine, all that contributes to make a body as distinctly known as possible, is found in the one before us. But, while I am speaking, let it be placed near the fire—what remained of the taste exhales, the smell evaporates, the colour changes, its figure is destroyed, its size increases, it becomes liquid, it grows hot, it can hardly be handled, and, although struck upon, it emits no sound. Does the same wax still remain after this change? It must be admitted that it does remain; no one doubts it, or judges otherwise. What, then, was it I knew with so much distinctness in the piece of wax? Assuredly, it could be nothing of all that I observed by means of the senses, since all the things that fell under taste, smell, sight, touch, and hearing are changed, and yet the same wax remains. It was perhaps what I now think, viz., that this wax was neither the sweetness of honey, the pleasant odour of flowers, the whiteness, the figure, nor the sound, but only a body that a little before appeared to me conspicuous under these forms, and which is now perceived under others. But, to speak precisely, what is it that I imagine when I think of it in this way? Let it be attentively considered, and, retrenching all that does not belong to the wax, let us see what remains. There certainly remains nothing, except something extended, flexible, and movable. But what is meant by flexible and movable? Is it not that I imagine that the piece of wax, being round, is capable of becoming square, or of passing from a square into a triangular figure? Assuredly such is not the case, because I conceive that it admits of an infinity of similar changes; and I am, moreover, unable to compass this infinity by imagination, and consequently this conception which I have of the wax is not the product of the faculty of imagination. But what now is this extension? Is it not also unknown? for it becomes greater when the wax is melted, greater when it is boiled, and greater still when the heat increases; and I should not conceive [clearly and] according to truth, the wax as it is, if I did not suppose that the piece we are considering admitted even of a wider variety of extension than I ever imagined. I must, therefore, admit that I cannot even comprehend by imagination what the piece of wax is, and that it is the mind alone (*mens*, Lat.; *entendement*, F.) which perceives it. I speak of one piece in particular; for, as to wax in general, this is still more evident. But what is the piece of wax that can be perceived only by the [understanding of] mind? It is certainly the same which I see, touch, imagine; and, in fine, it is the same which, from the beginning, I believed it to be. But (and this it is of moment to observe) the perception of it is neither an act of sight, of touch, nor of imagination, and never was either of these, though it might formerly seem so, but is simply an intuition (*inspectio*) of the mind, which may be imperfect and confused, as it formerly was, or very clear and distinct, as it is at present, according as the attention is more or less directed to the elements which it contains, and of which it is composed.

But, meanwhile, I feel greatly astonished when I observe [the weakness of my mind, and] its proneness to error. For although, without at all giving expression to what I think, I consider all this in my own mind, words yet occasionally impede my progress, and I am almost led into error by the terms of ordinary language. We say, for example, that we see the same wax when it is before us, and not that we judge it to be the same from its retaining the same colour and figure: whence I should forthwith be disposed to conclude that the wax is known by the act of sight, and not by the intuition of the mind alone, were it not for the analogous instance of human beings passing on in the street below, as observed from a window. In this case I do not fail to say that I see the men themselves, just as I say that I see the wax; and yet what do I see from the window beyond hats and cloaks that might cover artificial machines, whose motions might be determined by springs? But I judge that there are human beings from these appearances, and thus I comprehend, by the faculty of judgment alone which is in the mind, what I believed I saw with my eyes.

The man who makes it his aim to rise to knowledge superior to the common, ought to be ashamed to seek occasions of doubting from the vulgar forms of speech: instead, therefore, of doing this, I shall proceed with the matter in hand, and inquire whether I had a clearer and more perfect perception of the piece of wax when I first saw it, and when I thought I knew it by means of the external sense itself, or, at all events, by the common sense (*sensus communis*), as it is called, that is, by the imaginative faculty; or whether I rather apprehend it more clearly at present, after having examined with greater care, both what it is, and in what way it can be known. It would certainly be ridiculous to entertain any doubt on this point. For what, in that first perception, was there distinct? What did I perceive which any animal might not have perceived? But when I distinguish the wax from its exterior forms, and when, as if I had stripped it of its vestments, I consider it quite naked, it is certain, although some error may still be found in my judgment, that I cannot, nevertheless, thus apprehend it without possessing a human mind.

But, finally, what shall I say of the mind itself, that is, of myself? for as yet I do not admit that I am anything but mind. What, then! I who seem to possess so distinct an apprehension of the piece of wax,—do I not know myself, both with greater truth and certitude, and also much more distinctly and clearly? For if I judge that the wax exists because I see it, it assuredly follows, much more evidently, that I myself am or exist, for the same reason: for it is possible that what I see may not in truth be wax, and that I do not even possess eyes with which to see anything; but it cannot be that when I see, or, which comes to the same thing, when I think I see, I myself who think am nothing. So likewise, if I judge that the wax exists because I touch it, it will still also follow that I am; and if I determine that my imagination, or any other cause, whatever it be, persuades me of the existence of the wax, I will still draw the same conclusion. And what is here remarked of the piece of wax is applicable to all the other things that are external to me. And further, if the [notion or] perception of wax appeared to me more precise and distinct, after that not only sight and touch, but many other causes besides, rendered it manifest to my apprehension, with how much greater distinctness must I now know myself, since all the reasons that contribute to the knowledge of the nature of wax, or of any body whatever, manifest still better the nature of my mind? And there are besides so many other things in the mind itself that contribute to the illustration of its nature, that those dependent on the body, to which I have here referred, scarcely merit to be taken into account.

But, in conclusion, I find I have insensibly reverted to the point I desired; for, since it is now manifest to me that bodies themselves are not properly perceived by the senses nor by the faculty of imagination, but by the intellect alone; and since they are not perceived because they are seen and touched, but only because they are understood [or rightly comprehended by thought], I readily discover that there is nothing more easily or clearly apprehended than my own mind. But because it is difficult to rid one's self so promptly of an opinion to which one has been long accustomed, it will be desirable to tarry for some time at this stage, that, by long continued meditation, I may more deeply impress upon my memory this new knowledge.

GEORGE BERKELEY

(1685—1753)

Berkeley was educated at Trinity College, Dublin, and became a fellow there in 1707. Two years later he published his Essay towards a New Theory of Vision, *a theory still of much interest to the psychology and philosophy of perception. The following year, his* Treatise concerning the Principles of Human Knowledge, *Part I, appeared, the ideas of which were later elaborated in his* Three Dialogues between Hylas and Philonous *(1713). The second part of the* Treatise *was never published. Berkeley lost the manuscript during his travels in Italy, and commented many years later that "I never had leisure since to do so disagreeable a thing as writing twice on the same subject."*

He visited Rhode Island from 1728 to 1731, during which time he had hopes of establishing a college in the Bermudas, but his plans did not materialize due to lack of funds. Two years after publishing Alciphron *(1732), a dialogue written in Rhode Island, he was made Bishop of Cloyne, in his native Ireland, and spent his last twenty years attending to his diocese. In this period he wrote* Siris, *in which he again takes up the metaphysical and theological themes that characterize much of his work.*

NOTHING UNPERCEIVED EXISTS

It is evident to any one who takes a survey of the objects of human knowledge, that they are either ideas actually imprinted on the senses, or else such as are perceived by attending to the passions and operations of the mind, or lastly ideas formed by help of memory and imagination, either compounding, dividing, or barely representing those originally perceived in the aforesaid ways. By sight I have the ideas of light and colors with their several degrees and variations. By touch I perceive, for example, hard and soft, heat and cold, motion and resistance, and of all these more and less either as to quantity or degree. Smelling furnishes me with odors; the palate with tastes; and hearing conveys sounds to the mind in all their variety of tone and composition. And as several of these are observed to accompany each other, they come to be marked by one name, and so to be reputed as one thing. Thus, for example, a certain color, taste, smell, figure and consistence having been observed to go together, are accounted one distinct thing, signified by the name *apple*. Other collections of ideas constitute a stone, a tree, a book, and the like sensible things; which, as they are pleasing or disagreeable, excite the passions of love, hatred, joy, grief, and so forth.

But besides all that endless variety of ideas or objects of knowledge, there is likewise something which knows or perceives them, and exercises divers operations, as willing, imagining, remembering about them. This perceiving, active being is what I call *mind, spirit, soul* or *my self*. By which words I do not denote any one of my ideas, but a thing entirely distinct from them, wherein they exist, or, which is the same thing, whereby they are perceived; for the existence of an idea consists in being perceived.

That neither our thoughts, nor passions, nor ideas formed by the imagination, exist without the mind, is what every body will allow. And it seems no less evident that the various sensations or ideas imprinted on the sense, however blended or combined together (that is, whatever objects they compose) cannot exist otherwise than in a mind perceiving them. I think an intuitive knowledge may be obtained of this, by any one that shall attend to what is meant by the term *exist* when applied to sensible things. The table I write on, I say, exists, that is, I see and feel it; and if I were out of my study I should say it existed, meaning thereby that if I was in my study I might perceive it, or that some other spirit actually does perceive it. There was an odor, that is, it was smelled; there was a sound, that is to say, it was heard; a color or figure, and it was perceived by sight or touch. This is all that I can understand by these and the like

From "A Treatise Concerning the Principles of Human Knowledge," in The Works of George Berkeley, *Vol. 2 (1734), edited by T. E. Jessop, Thomas Nelson & Sons, Ltd., Publishers, pp.41–59 and 69–70.*

expressions. For as to what is said of the absolute existence of unthinking things without any relation to their being perceived, that seems perfectly unintelligible. Their *esse* is *percipi*, nor is it possible that they should have any existence out of the minds or thinking things which perceive them.

It is indeed an opinion strangely prevailing amongst men, that houses, mountains, rivers, and in a word all sensible objects have an existence natural or real, distinct from their being perceived by the understanding. But with how great an assurance and acquiescence soever this principle may be entertained in the world; yet whoever shall find in his heart to call it in question, may, if I mistake not, perceive it to involve a manifest contradiction. For what are the forementioned objects but the things we perceive by sense, and what do we perceive besides our own ideas or sensations; and is it not plainly repugnant that any one of these or any combination of them should exist unperceived?

If we thoroughly examine this tenet, it will, perhaps, be found at bottom to depend on the doctrine of *abstract ideas*. For can there be a nicer strain of abstraction than to distinguish the existence of sensible objects from their being perceived, so as to conceive them existing unperceived? Light and colors, heat and cold, extension and figures, in a word the things we see and feel, what are they but so many sensations, notions, ideas or impressions on the sense; and is it possible to separate, even in thought, any of these from perception? For my part I might as easily divide a thing from itself. I may indeed divide in my thoughts or conceive apart from each other those things which, perhaps, I never perceived by sense so divided. Thus I imagine the trunk of a human body without the limbs, or conceive the smell of a rose without thinking on the rose itself. So far I will not deny I can abstract, if that may properly be called *abstraction*, which extends only to the conceiving separately such objects, as it is possible may really exist or be actually perceived asunder. But my conceiving or imagining power does not extend beyond the possibility of real existence or perception. Hence as it is impossible for me to see or feel anything without an actual sensation of that thing, so is it impossible for me to conceive in my thoughts any sensible thing or object distinct from the sensation or perception of it.

Some truths there are so near and obvious to the mind, that a man need only open his eyes to see them. Such I take this important one to be, to wit, that all the choir of heaven and furniture of the earth, in a word all those bodies which compose the mighty frame of the world, have not any subsistence without a mind, that their being is to be perceived or known; that consequently so long as they are not actually perceived by me, or do not exist in my mind or that of any other created spirit, they must either have no existence at all, or else subsist in the mind of some eternal spirit: it being perfectly unintelligible and involving all the absurdity of abstraction, to attribute to any single part of them an existence independent of a spirit. To be convinced of which, the reader need only reflect and try to separate in his own thoughts the being of a sensible thing from its being perceived.

From what has been said, it follows, there is not any other substance than *spirit*, or that which perceives. But for the fuller proof of this point, let it be considered, the sensible qualities are color, figure, motion, smell, taste, and such like, that is, the ideas perceived by sense. Now for an idea to exist in an unperceiving thing, is a manifest contradiction; for to have an idea is all one as to perceive: that therefore wherein color, figure, and the like qualities exist, must perceive them; hence it is clear there can be no unthinking substance or *substratum* of those ideas.

But say you, though the ideas themselves do not exist without the mind, yet there may be things like them whereof they are copies or resemblances, which things exist without the mind, in an unthinking substance. I answer, an idea can be like nothing but an idea; a color or figure can be like nothing but another color or figure. If we look but ever so little into our thoughts, we shall find it impossible for us to conceive a likeness except only between our ideas. Again, I ask whether those supposed originals or external things, of which our ideas are the pictures or representations, be themselves perceivable or no? If they are, then they are ideas, and we have gained our point; but if you say they are not, I appeal to anyone whether it be sense, to assert a color is like something which is invisible; hard or soft, like something which is intangible; and so of the rest.

Some there are who make a distinction betwixt *primary* and *secondary* qualities: by the former, they mean extension, figure, motion, rest, solidity or impenetrability and number: by the latter they denote all other sensible qualities, as colors, sounds, tastes, and so forth. The ideas we have of these they acknowledge not to be the resemblances of any thing existing without the mind or unperceived; but they will have our ideas of the primary qualities to be patterns or images of things which exist without the mind, in an unthinking substance which they call *matter*. By matter therefore we are to understand an inert, senseless substance, in which extension, figure, and motion do actually subsist. But it is evident from what we have already shewn, that extension, figure and motion are only ideas existing in the mind, and that an idea can be like nothing but another idea, and that consequently neither they nor their archetypes can exist in an unperceiving substance. Hence it is plain, that the very notion of what is called *matter* or *corporeal substance*, involves a contradiction in it.

They who assert that figure, motion, and the rest of the primary or original qualities do exist without the mind, in unthinking substances, do at the same time acknowledge that colors, sounds, heat, cold, and such like secondary qualities, do not, which they tell us are sensations existing in the mind alone, that depend on and are occasioned by the different size, texture and motion of the minute particles of matter. This they take for an undoubted truth, which they can demonstrate beyond all exception. Now if it be certain, that those original qualities are inseparably united with the other sensible qualities, and not, even in thought, capable of being abstracted from them, it plainly follows that they exist only in the mind. But I desire any one to reflect and try, whether he can by any abstraction of thought, conceive the extension and motion of a body, without all other sensible qualities. For my own part, I see evidently that it is not in my power to frame an idea of a body extended and moved, but I must withal give it some color or other sensible quality which is acknowledged to exist only in the mind. In short, extension, figure, and motion, abstracted from all other qualities, are inconceivable. Where therefore the other sensible qualities are, there must these be also, to wit, in the mind and nowhere else. . . .

But say you, surely there is nothing easier than to imagine trees, for instance, in a park, or books existing in a closet, and no body by to perceive them. I answer, you may so, there is no difficulty in it: but what is all this, I beseech you, more than framing in your mind certain ideas which you call *books* and *trees*, and at the same time omitting to frame the idea of any one that may perceive them? But do not you yourself perceive or think of them all the while? This therefore is nothing to the purpose: it only shows you have the power of imagining or forming ideas in your mind; but it doth not shew that you can conceive it possible, the objects of your thought may exist without the mind: to make out this, it is necessary that you conceive them existing unconceived or unthought of, which is a manifest repugnancy. When we do our utmost to conceive the existence of external bodies, we are all the while only contemplating our own ideas. But the mind taking no notice of itself, is deluded to think it can and doth conceive bodies existing unthought of or without the mind; though at the same time they are apprehended by or exist in itself. A little attention will discover to any one the truth and evidence of what is here said, and make it unnecessary to insist on any other proofs against the existence of material substance.

It is very obvious, upon the least inquiry into our own thoughts, to know whether it be possible for us to understand what is meant, by the *absolute existence of sensible objects in themselves, or without the mind*. To me it is evident those words mark out either a direct contradiction, or else nothing at all. And to convince others of this, I know no readier or fairer way, than to entreat they would calmly attend to their own thoughts: and if by this attention, the emptiness or repugnancy of those expressions does appear, surely nothing more is requisite for their conviction. It is on this therefore that I insist, to wit, that the absolute existence of unthinking things are words without a meaning, or which include a contradiction. This is what I repeat and inculcate, and earnestly recommend to the attentive thoughts of the reader.

All our ideas, sensations, or the things which we perceive, by whatsoever names they may be distinguished, are visibly inactive, there is nothing of power or agency included in them. So that one idea or object of thought cannot produce, or make any alteration in another. To be satisfied of the truth of this, there is nothing else requisite but a bare observation of our ideas. For since they and every part of them exist only in the mind, it follows that there is nothing in them but what is perceived. But whoever shall attend to his ideas, whether of sense or reflexion, will not perceive in them any power or activity; there is therefore no such thing contained in them. A little attention will discover to us that the very being of an idea implies passiveness and inertness in it, insomuch that it is impossible for an idea to do anything, or, strictly speaking, to be the cause of anything: neither can it be the resemblance or pattern of any active being, as is evident from *Sect.* 8. Whence it plainly follows that extension, figure and motion cannot be the cause of our sensations. To say therefore, that these are the effects of powers resulting from the configuration, number, motion, and size of corpuscles, must certainly be false.

We perceive a continual succession of ideas, some are anew excited, others are changed or totally disappear. There is therefore some cause of these ideas whereon they depend, and which produces and changes them. That this cause cannot be any quality or idea or combination of ideas, is clear from the preceding section. It must therefore be a substance; but it has been shewn that there is no corporeal or material substance: it remains therefore that the cause of ideas is an incorporeal active substance or spirit.

WILLIAM JAMES

(1842–1910)

The early schooling of William James and his brother Henry (who later became a major novelist) was irregular and lacking in discipline. William at first studied art, then turned to medicine. Illness cut short his medical studies in Germany, and though he received the degree of M.D. from Harvard in 1869, he remained a semi-invalid until 1872. He then began teaching at Harvard—first physiology, then physiological psychology. A new vigor and zest became noticeable in his personality and in his writing. His monumental and definitive textbook, The Principles of Psychology, *appeared in 1891. With the completion of this work, James turned from psychology to philosophy, and in particular to the fields of ethics and religion. There followed a series of books on these topics, most noteworthy being* The Will to Believe *(1897) and* The Varieties of Religious Experience *(1902). Meanwhile, inspired by the work of Charles Peirce, who had developed a theory of philosophic method called Pragmatism, James proceeded to develop the theory in the light of his own experience. He expressed his views, with characteristic energy and vitality, in the writings of his final period. These include* Pragmatism *(1907),* A Pluralistic Universe *(1909),* The Meaning of Truth *(1909), and (posthumously)* Essays in Radical Empiricism *(1912).*

DOES "CONSCIOUSNESS" EXIST?

To deny plumply that "consciousness" exists seems so absurd on the face of it—for undeniably "thoughts" do exist—that I fear some readers will follow me no farther. Let me then immediately explain that I mean only to deny that the word stands for an entity, but to insist most emphatically that it does stand for a function. There is, I mean, no aboriginal stuff or quality of being, contrasted with that of which material objects are made, out of which our thoughts of them are made; but there is a function in experience which thoughts perform, and for the performance of which this quality of being is invoked. That function is *knowing*. "Consciousness" is supposed necessary to explain the fact that things not only are, but get reported, are known. Whoever blots out the notion of consciousness from his list of first principles must still provide in some way for that function's being carried on.

I

My thesis is that if we start with the supposition that there is only one primal stuff or material in the world, a stuff of which everything is composed, and if we call that stuff "pure experience," then knowing can easily be explained as a particular sort of relation toward one another into which portions of pure experience may enter. The relation itself is a part of pure experience; one of its "terms" becomes the subject or bearer of the knowledge, the knower,[1] the other becomes the object known. This will need much explanation before it can be understood. The best way to get it understood is to contrast it with the alternative view; and for that we may take the recentest alternative, that in which the evaporation of the definite soul-substance has proceeded as far as it can go without being yet complete. If neo-Kantism has expelled earlier forms of dualism, we shall have expelled all forms if we are able to expel neo-Kantism in its turn.

For the thinkers I call neo-Kantian, the word consciousness today does no more than signalize the fact that experience is indefeasibly dualistic in structure. It means that not subject, not object, but object-plus-subject is the minimum that can actually be. The subject-object distinction meanwhile is entirely different from that between mind and matter, from that between body and soul. Souls were detachable, had

From the Journal of Philosophy, Psychology and Scientific Method, *Vol. 1, No. 18 (Sept. 1, 1904), pp. 477–491.*

---

[1]In my *Psychology* I have tried to show that we need no knower other than the "passing thought." (*Principles of Psychology*, vol. I, pp. 338 ff.)

separate destinies; things could happen to them. To consciousness as such nothing can happen, for, timeless itself, it is only a witness of happenings in time, in which it plays no part. It is, in a word, but the logical correlative of "content" in an Experience of which the peculiarity is that *fact comes to light* in it, that *awareness of content* takes place. Consciousness as such is entirely impersonal—"self" and its activities belong to the content. To say that I am self-conscious, or conscious of putting forth volition, means only that certain contents, for which "self" and "effort of will" are the names, are not without witness as they occur.

Thus, for these belated drinkers at the Kantian spring, we should have to admit consciousness as an "epistemological" necessity, even if we had no direct evidence of its being there.

But in addition to this, we are supposed by almost every one to have an immediate consciousness of consciousness itself. When the world of outer fact ceases to be materially present, and we merely recall it in memory, or fancy it, the consciousness is believed to stand out and to be felt as a kind of impalpable inner flowing, which, once known in this sort of experience, may equally be detected in presentations of the outer world. "The moment we try to fix our attention upon consciousness and to see *what*, distinctly, it is," says a recent writer, "it seems to vanish. It seems as if we had before us a mere emptiness. When we try to introspect the sensation of blue, all we can see is the blue; the other element is as if it were diaphanous. Yet it *can* be distinguished, if we look attentively enough, and know that there is something to look for."[2] "Consciousness" (*Bewusstheit*), says another philosopher, "is inexplicable and hardly describable, yet all conscious experiences have this in common that what we call their content has this peculiar reference to a centre for which 'self' is the name, in virtue of which reference alone the content is subjectively given, or appears. . . . While in this way consciousness, or reference to a self, is the only thing which distinguishes a conscious content from any sort of being that might be there with no one conscious of it, yet this only ground of the distinction defies all closer explanations. The existence of consciousness, although it is the fundamental fact of psychology, can indeed be laid down as certain, can be brought out by analysis, but can neither be defined nor deduced from anything but itself."

"Can be brought out by analysis," this author says. This supposes that the consciousness is one element, moment, factor—call it what you like—of an experience of essentially dualistic inner constitution, from which, if you abstract the content, the consciousness will remain revealed to its own eye. Experience, at this rate, would be much like a paint of which the world pictures were made. Paint has a dual constitution, involving, as it does, a menstruum (oil, size or what not) and a mass of content in the form of pigment suspended therein. We can get the pure menstruum by letting the pigment settle, and the pure pigment by pour-

---

[2]G. E. Moore, *Mind*, vol. XII, N. S. (1903), p. 450.

ing off the size or oil. We operate here by physical subtraction; and the usual view is, that by mental subtraction we can separate the two factors of experience in an analogous way—not isolating them entirely, but distinguishing them enough to know that they are two.

II

Now my contention is exactly the reverse of this. *Experience, I believe, has no such inner duplicity; and the separation of it into consciousness and content comes, not by way of subtraction, but by way of addition*—the addition, to a given concrete piece of it, of other sets of experiences, in connection with which severally its use or function may be of two different kinds. The paint will also serve here as an illustration. In a pot in a paint shop, along with other paints, it serves in its entirety as so much salable matter. Spread on a canvas, with other paints around it, it represents, on the contrary, a feature in a picture and performs a spiritual function. Just so, I maintain, does a given undivided portion of experience, taken in one context of associates, play the part of a knower, of a state of mind, of "consciousness"; while in a different context the same undivided bit of experience plays the part of a thing known, of an objective "content." In a word, in one group it figures as a thought, in another group as a thing. And, since it can figure in both groups simultaneously we have every right to speak of it as subjective and objective both at once. The dualism connoted by such double-barreled terms as "experience," "phenomenon," "datum," "*Vorfindung*"—terms which, in philosophy at any rate, tend more and more to replace the single-barreled terms of "thought" and "thing"—that dualism, I say, is still preserved in this account, but reinterpreted, so that, instead of being mysterious and elusive, it becomes verifiable and concrete. It is an affair of relations, it falls outside, not inside, the single experience considered, and can always be particularized and defined.

The entering wedge for this more concrete way of understanding the dualism was fashioned by Locke when he made the word "idea" stand indifferently for thing and thought, and by Berkeley when he said that what common sense means by realities is exactly what the philosopher means by ideas. Neither Locke nor Berkeley thought his truth out into perfect clearness, but it seems to me that the conception I am defending does little more than consistently carry out the "pragmatic" method which they were the first to use.

If the reader will take his own experiences, he will see what I mean. Let him begin with a perceptual experience, the "presentation," so called, of a physical object, his actual field of vision, the room he sits in, with the book he is reading as its center; and let him for the present treat this complex object in the commonsense way as being "really" what it seems to be, namely, a collection of physical things cut out from an environing world of other physical things with which these physical things have actual or potential relations. Now at the same time it is just *those selfsame things* which his mind, as we say, perceives; and the whole philosophy of perception from Democritus' time downward has been just one long wrangle over the paradox that what is evidently one reality should be in two places at once, both in outer space and in a person's mind. "Representative" theories of perception avoid the logical paradox, but on the other hand they violate the reader's sense of life, which knows no intervening mental image but seems to see the room and the book immediately just as they physically exist.

The puzzle of how the one identical room can be in two places is at bottom just the puzzle of how one identical point can be on two lines. It can, if it be situated at their intersection; and similarly, if the "pure experience" of the room were a place of intersection of two processes, which connected it with different groups of associates respectively, it could be counted twice over, as belonging to either group, and spoken of loosely as existing in two places, although it would remain all the time a numerically single thing.

Well, the experience is a member of diverse processes that can be followed away from it along entirely different lines. The one self-identical thing has so many relations to the rest of experience that you can take it in disparate systems of association, and treat it as belonging with opposite contexts. In one of these contexts it is your "field of consciousness"; in another it is "the room in which you sit," and it enters both contexts in its wholeness, giving no pretext for being said to attach itself to consciousness by one of its parts or aspects, and to outer reality by another. What are the two processes, now, into which the room-experience simultaneously enters in this way?

One of them is the reader's personal biography, the other is the history of the house of which the room is part. The presentation, the experience, the *that* in short (for until we have decided *what* it is it must be a mere *that*) is the last term of a train of sensations, emotions, decisions, movements, classifications, expectations, etc., ending in the present, and the first term of a series of similar "inner" operations extending into the future, on the reader's part. On the other hand, the very same *that* is the *terminus ad quem* of a lot of previous physical operations, carpentering, papering, furnishing, warming, etc., and the *terminus a quo* of a lot of future ones, in which it will be concerned when undergoing the destiny of a physical room. The physical and the mental operations form curiously incompatible groups. As a room, the experience has occupied that spot and had that environment for thirty years. As your field of consciousness it may never have existed until now. As a room, attention will go on to discover endless new details in it. As your mental state merely, few new ones will emerge under attention's eye. As a room, it will take an earthquake, or a gang of men, and in any case a certain amount of time, to destroy it. As your subjective state, the closing of your eyes, or any instantaneous play of your fancy will suffice. In the real world, fire will consume it. In your mind, you can let fire play over it without effect. As an outer object, you must pay so much a month to inhabit it. As an inner content, you may occupy it for any length of time rent free. If, in short, you follow it in the mental direction, taking it along with events of personal biography solely, all sorts of things are true of it which are false, and false of it which are true if you treat it as a real thing experienced, follow it in the physical direction, and relate it to associates in the outer world. . . .

The room thus again gets counted twice over. It plays two different rôles, being *Gedanke* and *Gedachtes*, the thought-of-an-object, and the object-thought-of, both in one; and all this without paradox or mystery, just as the same material thing may be both low and high, or small and great, or bad and good, because of its relations to opposite parts of an environing world.

As "subjective" we say that the experience represents; as "objective" it is represented. What represents and what is represented is here numerically the same; but we must remember that no dualism of being represented and representing resides in the experience per se. In its pure state, or when isolated, there is no self-splitting of it into consciousness and what the consciousness is "of". Its subjectivity and objectivity are functional attributes solely, realized only when the experience is "taken," i.e., talked-of, twice, considered along with its two differing contexts respectively, by a new retrospective experience, of which that whole past complication now forms the fresh content.

The instant field of the present is at all times what I call the "pure" experience. It is only virtually or potentially either object or subject as yet. For the time being, it is plain, unqualified actuality, or existence, a simple *that*. In this *naïf* immediacy it is of course *valid*; it is *there*, we *act* upon it; and the doubling of it in retrospection into a state of mind and a reality intended thereby, is just one of the acts. The "state of mind," first treated explicitly as such in retrospection, will stand corrected or confirmed, and the retrospective experience in its turn will get a similar treatment; but the immediate experience in its passing is always "truth," practical truth, *something to act on*, at its own movement. If the world were then and there to go out like a candle, it would remain truth absolute and objective, for it would be "the last word," would have no critic, and no one would ever oppose the thought in it to the reality intended.

I think I may now claim to have made my thesis clear. Consciousness connotes a kind of external relation, and does not denote a special stuff or way of being. *The peculiarity of our experiences, that they not only are, but are known, which their "conscious" quality is invoked to explain, is better explained by their relations—these relations themselves being experiences—to one another. . . .*

VI

The next objection is more formidable, in fact it sounds quite crushing when one hears it first.

"If it be the selfsame piece of pure experience, taken twice over, that serves now as thought and now as thing"—so the objection runs—"how comes it that its attributes should differ so fundamentally in the two takings. As thing, the experience is extended; as thought, it occupies no space or place. As thing, it is red, hard, heavy; but who ever heard of a red, hard or heavy thought? Yet even now you said that an experience is made of just what appears, and what appears is just such adjectives. How can the one experience in its thing-function be made of them, consist of them, carry them as its own attributes, while in its thought-function it disowns them and attributes them elsewhere? There is a self-contradiction here from which the radical dualism of thought and thing is the only truth that can save us. Only if the thought is one kind of being can the adjectives exist in it 'intentionally' (to use the scholastic term); only if the thing is another kind, can they exist in it, constitutively and energetically. No simple subject can take the same adjectives and at one time be qualified by it, and at another time be merely 'of' it, as of something only meant or known."

The solution insisted on by this objector, like many other common-sense solutions, grows the less satisfactory the more one turns it in one's mind. To begin with, *are* thought and thing as heterogeneous as is commonly said?

No one denies that they have some categories in common. Their relations to time are identical. Both, moreover, may have parts (for psychologists in general treat thoughts as having them); and both may be complex or simple. Both are of kinds, can be compared, added and subtracted and arranged in serial orders. All sorts of adjectives qualify our thoughts which appear incompatible with consciousness, being as such a bare diaphaneity. For instance, they are natural and easy, or laborious. They are beautiful, happy, intense, interesting, wise, idiotic, focal, marginal, insipid, confused, vague, precise, rational, casual, general, particular, and many things besides. Moreover, the chapters on "Perception" in the psychology books are full of facts that make for the essential homogeneity of thought with thing. How, if "subject" and "object" were separated "by the whole diameter of being," and had no attributes in common, could it be so hard to tell, in a presented and recognized material object, what part comes in through the sense organs and what part comes "out of one's own head"? Sensations and apperceptive ideas fuse here so intimately that you can no more tell where one begins and the other ends, than you can tell, in those cunning circular panoramas that have lately been exhibited, where the real foreground and the painted canvas join together.

Descartes for the first time defined thought as the absolutely unextended, and later philosophers have accepted the description as correct. But what possible meaning has it to say that, when we think of a foot rule or a square yard, extension is not attributable to our thought? Of every extended object the *adequate* mental picture must have all the extension of the object itself. The difference between objective and subjective extension is one of relation to a context solely. In the mind the various extents maintain no necessarily stubborn order relatively to each other, while in the physical world they bound each other stably, and, added together, make the great enveloping Unit which we believe in and call real Space. As "outer," they carry themselves adversely, so to speak, to one another, exclude one another and maintain their distances; while, as "inner," their order is loose, and they form a *durcheinander* in which unity is lost.[3] But to argue from this that inner experience is absolutely inextensive seems to me little short of absurd. The two worlds differ, not by the presence or absence of extension, but by the relations of the extensions which in both worlds exist.

Does not this case of extension now put us on the track of truth in the case of other qualities? It does; and I am surprised that the facts should not have been noticed long ago. Why, for example, do we call a fire hot, and water wet, and yet refuse to say that our mental state, when it is "of" these objects, is either wet or hot? "Intentionally," at any rate, and when the mental state is a vivid image, hotness and wetness are in it just as much as they are in the physical experience. The reason is this, that, as the general chaos of all our experiences gets sifted, we find that there are some fires that will always burn sticks and always warm our bodies, and that there are some waters that will always put out fires; while there are other fires and waters that will not act at all. The general group of experiences that *act,* that do not only possess their natures intrinsically, but wear them adjectively and energetically, turning them against one another, comes inevitably to be contrasted with the group whose members, having identically the same natures, fail to manifest them in the "energetic" way. I make for myself now an experience of blazing fire; I place it near my body; but it does not warm me in the least. I lay a stick upon it, and the stick either burns or remains green, as I please. I call up water, and pour it on the fire, and absolutely no difference ensues. I account for all such facts by calling this whole train of experiences unreal, a mental train. Mental fire is what won't burn real sticks; mental water is what won't necessarily (though of course it may) put out even a mental fire. Mental knives may be sharp, but they won't cut real wood. Mental triangles are pointed, but their points won't wound. With "real" objects, on the contrary, consequences always accrue; and thus the real experiences get sifted from the mental ones, the things from our thoughts of them, fanciful or true, and precipitated together as the stable part of the whole experience-chaos, under the name of the physical world. Of this our perceptual experiences are the nucleus, they being the originally *strong* experiences. We add a lot of conceptual experiences to them, making these strong also in imagination, and building out the remoter parts of the physical world by their means; and around this core of reality the world of laxly connected fancies and mere rhap-

---

[3]I speak here of the complete inner life in which the mind plays freely with its materials. Of course the mind's free play is restricted when it seeks to copy real things in real space.

sodical objects floats like a bank of clouds. In the clouds, all sorts of rules are violated which in the core are kept. Extensions there can be indefinitely located; motion there obeys no Newton's laws.

20

Knowledge and Explanation

A. J. AYER

(b. 1910)

Alfred Jules Ayer has been Wykeham Professor of Logic in the University of Oxford since 1959, and has sometimes been described as the "most representative" of present-day English philosophers. Educated at Eton and Christ Church College, Oxford, he obtained his B.A. degree in 1932, and his M.A. in 1936. The same year saw the publication of his first book, Language, Truth and Logic, *a manifesto of the logical positivist views of the Vienna Circle. His second book,* The Foundations of Empirical Knowledge, *appeared in 1940. During World War II, Ayer served as an attaché of the British embassy in Paris. In 1946 he became Grote Professor of the Philosophy of Mind and Logic at London University. He has since published* Philosophical Essays *(1954),* The Problem of Knowledge *(1956), and* The Concept of a Person *(1963). Ayer has been a visiting professor at New York University and at the College of the City of New York. In 1952 he became a fellow of the British Academy, and in 1963 was made an honorary member of the American Academy of Arts and Sciences.*

TRUTH AS ACCREDITED KNOWLEDGE

Let us begin with the question whether the various sorts of knowing have any one thing in common, and the suggestion that this common feature is a mental state or act.

COMMON FEATURES OF KNOWLEDGE

Except where a word is patently ambiguous, it is natural for us to assume that the different situations, or types of situation, to which it applies have a distinctive common feature. For otherwise why should we use the same word to refer to them? Sometimes we have another way of describing such a common feature; we can say, for example, that what irascible people have in common is that they are all prone to anger. But very often we have no way of saying what is common to the things to which the same word applies except by using the word itself. How else would we describe the distinctively common feature of red things except by saying that they are all red? In the same way, it might be said that what the things that we call "games" have in common is just that they are games; but here there seems to be a difference. Whereas there is a simple and straightforward resemblance between the things whose color we call "red," the sort of resemblance that leads us naturally to talk of their having an identical quality, there is no such simple resemblance between the things that we call "games." The *Oxford English Dictionary* defines a game as "a diversion of the nature of a contest, played according to rules, and decided by superior skill, strength, or good fortune." But not all games are diversions, in the sense of being played for fun; games of patience are hardly contests, though they are decided by skill and luck; children's games are not always played according to rules; acting games need not be decided. Wittgenstein,[1] from whom I have taken this example, concludes that we cannot find anything common to all games, but only a "complicated network of similarities" which "overlap and crisscross" in the same way as the resemblances between people who belong to the same family. " 'Games' " he says, "form a family."

This is a good analogy, but I think that Wittgenstein is wrong to infer from it that games do not have any one thing in common. His doing so suggests that he takes the question whether things have something in common to be different from the question whether there are resemblances between them. But surely the difference is only one of

From The Problem of Knowledge, *Penguin Books Ltd. (1956), pp. 10–14, 31–35. Reprinted by permission of Penguin Books Ltd.*

---

[1]L. Wittgenstein, *Philosophical Investigations* (Oxford, 1953), 1, 66, 67, pp. 31–32.

formulation. If things resemble one another sufficiently for us to find it useful to apply the same word to them, we are entitled to say, if it pleases us, that they have something in common. Neither is it necessary that what they have in common should be describable in different words, as we saw in the case of "red." It is correct, though not all enlightening, to say that what games have in common is their being games. The point which Wittgenstein's argument brings out is that the resemblance between the things to which the same word applies may be of different degrees. It is looser and less straightforward in some cases than in others.

Our question then becomes whether the different sorts of cases in which we speak of something's being known resemble one another in some straightforward fashion like the different instances of the color red, or whether they merely have what Wittgenstein would call a family resemblance. Another possibility is that they share a common factor the possession of which is necessary to their being instances of knowledge, even though it is not sufficient. If knowledge were always knowledge that something is the case, then such a common factor might be found in the existence of a common relation to truth. For while what is true can be believed, or disbelieved, or doubted, or imagined, or much else besides being known, it is, as we have already noted, a fact of ordinary usage that what is known, in this sense, cannot but be true.

But can it reasonably be held that knowledge is always knowledge that something is the case? If knowing that something is the case is taken to involve the making of a conscious judgement, then plainly it cannot. A dog knows its master, a baby knows its mother, but they do not know any statements to be true. Or if we insist on saying that there is a sense in which they do know statements to be true, that the dog which knows its master knows the fact that this is his master, we must allow that what we call knowing facts may sometimes just be a matter of being disposed to behave in certain appropriate ways; it need not involve any conscious process of judging, or stating, that such and such is so. Indeed, we constantly recognize objects without troubling to describe them, even to ourselves. No doubt, once we have acquired the use of language, we can always describe them if we choose, although the descriptions that we have at our command may not always be the descriptions that we want. "I know that tune," I say, though its name escapes me and I cannot remember where I heard it before; "I know that man," though I have forgotten who he is. But at least I identify him as a man, and as a man that I have met somewhere or other. There is a sense in which knowing something, in this usage of the term, is always a matter of knowing what it is; and in this sense it can perhaps be represented as knowing a fact, as knowing that something is so.

Much the same applies to the cases where knowing is a matter of knowing how. Certainly, when people possess skills, even intellectual skills, like the ability to act or teach, they are not always consciously aware of the procedures which they follow. They use the appropriate means to attain their ends, but the fact that these means are appropriate may never be made explicit by them even to themselves. There are a great many things that people habitually do well, without remarking how they do them. In many cases they could not say how they did them if they tried. Nor does this mean that their performances are unintelligent. As Professor Ryle has pointed put,[2] the display of intelligence lies in the manner of the performance, rather than in its being accompanied or preceded by any conscious recognition of the relevant facts. The performer does not need to tell himself that if such and such things are done, then such and such will follow. He may, indeed, do so, but equally he may not: and even when he does it is not because of this that his performance is judged to be intelligent. This point is convincingly established by Professor Ryle. But once again, if we are prepared to say that knowing facts need not consist in anything more than a disposition to behave in certain ways, we can construe knowing how to do things as being, in its fashion, a matter of knowing facts. Only by this time we shall have so extended our use of the expression "knowing facts" or "knowing that something is the case" that it may well become misleading. It may be taken to imply that the resemblances between the different ways of having, or manifesting, knowledge are closer and neater than they really are. . . .

KNOWING AS HAVING THE RIGHT TO BE SURE

The answers which we have found for the questions we have so far been discussing have not yet put us in a position to give a complete account of what it is to know that something is the case. The first requirement is that what is known should be true, but this is not sufficient; not even if we add to it the further condition that one must be completely sure of what one knows. For it is possible to be completely sure of something which is in fact true, but yet not to know it. The circumstances may be such that one is not entitled to be sure. For instance, a superstitious person who had inadvertently walked under a ladder might be convinced as a result that he was about to suffer some misfortune; and he might in fact be right. But it would not be correct to say that he knew that this was going to be so. He arrived at his belief by a process of reasoning which would not be generally reliable; so, although his prediction came true, it was not a case of knowledge. Again, if someone were fully persuaded of a mathematical proposition by a proof which could be shown to be invalid, he would not, without further evidence, be said to know the proposition, even though it was true. But while it is not hard to find examples of true and fully confident beliefs which in some ways fail to meet the standards required for knowledge, it is not at all easy to determine exactly what these standards are.

---

[2]G. Ryle, *The Concept of Mind* (London, 1949), ch. 2.

One way of trying to discover them would be to consider what would count as satisfactory answers to the question How do you know? Thus people may be credited with knowing truths of mathematics or logic if they are able to give a valid proof of them, or even if, without themselves being able to set out such a proof, they have obtained this information from someone who can. Claims to know empirical statements may be upheld by a reference to perception, or to memory, or to testimony, or to historical records, or to scientific laws. But such backing is not always strong enough for knowledge.

Whether it is so or not depends upon the circumstances of the particular case. If I were asked how I knew that a physical object of a certain sort was in such and such a place, it would, in general, be a sufficient answer for me to say that I could see it; but if my eyesight were bad and the light were dim, this answer might not be sufficient. Even though I was right, it might still be said that I did not really know that the object was there. If I have a poor memory and the event which I claim to remember is remote, my memory of it may still not amount to knowledge, even though in this instance it does not fail me. If a witness is unreliable, his unsupported evidence may not enable us to know that what he says is true, even in a case where we completely trust him and he is not in fact deceiving us. In a given instance it is possible to decide whether the backing is strong enough to justify a claim to knowledge. But to say in general how strong it has to be would require our drawing up a list of the conditions under which perception, or memory, or testimony, or other forms of evidence are reliable. And this would be a very complicated matter, if indeed it could be done at all.

Moreover, we cannot assume that, even in particular instances, an answer to the question How do you know? will always be forthcoming. There may very well be cases in which one knows that something is so without its being possible to say how one knows it. I am not so much thinking now of claims to know facts of immediate experience, statements like "I know that I feel pain," which raise problems of their own into which we shall enter later on. In cases of this sort it may be argued that the question how one knows does not arise. But even when it clearly does arise, it may not find an answer. Suppose that someone were consistently successful in predicting events of a certain kind, events, let us say, which are not ordinarily thought to be predictable, like the results of a lottery. If his run of successes were sufficiently impressive, we might very well come to say that he knew which number would win, even though he did not reach this conclusion by any rational method, or indeed by any method at all. We might say that he knew it by intuition, but this would be to assert no more than that he did know it but that we could not say how. In the same way, if someone were consistently successful in reading the minds of others without having any of the usual sort of evidence, we might say that he knew these things telepathically. But in default of any further explanation this would come down to saying merely that he did know them, but not by an ordinary means. Words like "intuition" and "telepathy" are brought in just to disguise the fact that no explanation has been found.

But if we allow this sort of knowledge to be even theoretically possible, what becomes of the distinction between knowledge and true belief? How does our man who knows what the results of the lottery will be differ from one who only makes a series of lucky guesses? The answer is that, so far as the man himself is concerned, there need not be any difference. His procedure and his state of mind, when he is said to know what will happen, may be exactly the same as when it is said that he is only guessing. The difference is that to say that he knows is to concede to him the right to be sure, while to say that he is only guessing is to withhold it. Whether we make this concession will depend upon the view which we take of his performance. Normally we do not say that people know things unless they have followed one of the accredited routes to knowledge. If someone reaches a true conclusion without appearing to have any adequate basis for it, we are likely to say that he does not really know it. But if he were repeatedly successful in a given domain, we might very well come to say that he knew them. We should grant him the right to be sure, simply on the basis of his success. This is, indeed, a point on which people's views might be expected to differ. Not everyone would regard a successful run of predictions, however long sustained, as being by itself a sufficient backing for a claim to knowledge. And here there can be no question of proving that this attitude is mistaken. Where there are recognized criteria for deciding when one has the right to be sure, anyone who insists that their being satisfied is still not enough for knowledge may be accused, for what the charge is worth, of misusing the verb "to know." But it is possible to find, or at any rate to devise, examples which are not covered in this respect by any established rule of usage. Whether they are to count as instances of knowledge is then a question which we are left free to decide.

It does not, however, matter very greatly which decision we take. The main problem is to state and assess the grounds on which these claims to knowledge are made, to settle, as it were, the candidate's marks. It is a relatively unimportant question what titles we then bestow upon them. So long as we agree about the marking, it is of no great consequence where we draw the line between pass and failure, or between the different levels of distinction. If we choose to set a very high standard, we may find ourselves committed to saying that some of what ordinarily passes for knowledge ought rather to be described as probable opinion. And some critics will then take us to task for flouting ordinary usage. But the question is purely one of terminology. It is to be decided, if at all, on grounds of practical convenience.

One must not confuse this case, where the markings are agreed upon, and what is in dispute is only the bestowal of honours, with the case where it is the markings themselves that are put in question. For this second case is philosophically important, in a way in which the other is not. The sceptic who asserts that we do not know all that we think we know, or even perhaps that we do not strictly know anything at all, is not suggesting that we are mistaken when we conclude that the recognized criteria for knowing have been satisfied. Nor is he primarily concerned with getting us to revise our usage of the verb "to know," any more than one who challenges our standards of value is trying to make us revise our usage of the word "good." The disagreement is about the application of the word, rather than its meaning. What the sceptic contends is that our markings are too high; that the grounds on which we are normally ready to concede the right to be sure are worth less than we think; he may even go so far as to say that they are not worth anything at all. The attack is directed, not against the way in which we apply our standards of proof, but against these standards themselves. It has, as we shall see, to be taken seriously because of the arguments by which it is supported.

I conclude then that the necessary and sufficient conditions for knowing that something is the case are first that what one is said to know be true, secondly that one be sure of it, and thirdly that one should have the right to be sure. This right may be earned in various ways; but even if one could give a complete description of them it would be a mistake to try to build it into the definition of knowledge, just as it would be a mistake to try to incorporate our actual standards of goodness into a definition of good. And this being so, it turns out that the questions which philosophers raise about the possibility of knowledge are not all to be settled by discovering what knowledge is. For many of them reappear as questions about the legitimacy of the title to be sure. They need to be severally examined; and this is the main concern of what is called the theory of knowledge.

JOHN W. YOLTON

(b.1921)

Yolton is an American philosopher, well known for his works in the theory of knowledge, particularly his 1962 work, Thinking and Perceiving. *He has taught at Johns Hopkins, Princeton, and the University of Maryland. Since 1963 he has been at York University, where he was president from 1973 to 1974. Among his other publications are* Locke and the Compass of Human Understanding *(1970),* Metaphysical Analysis *(1968), and* Locke and Education *(1971).*

DESCRIPTIVE AND NORMATIVE EPISTEMOLOGY

The study of the history of philosophy discloses, what the label itself suggests, that what has come to be called "theory of knowledge" (also "philosophy of knowledge" and "epistemology") marks a concern with questions about knowing and knowledge. A companion label is "theory of reality," a designation for concerns with questions about the nature of the world and of man. This area of theory of reality (usually termed "metaphysics"), it is sometimes said, is the more fundamental of the two. Aristotle called it the study of "being *qua* being," that is, the study of what there is and of the properties of what there is. But of course, any account of the world or of man ought to have some backing; the metaphysician writing fantasy or the scientist composing science fiction does not command our attention. We would like to have their credentials to enable us to judge the worth of what they say about man and the world. Questions about knowing and knowledge arise at this point: Can the account of the world and of man be defended as a knowledge-claim? How, in fact, do we come to know anything at all?

If I say "I know that the table is made of oak," I am advancing a claim for which you expect me to have reasons which I ought to be able to defend and explain. Such a claim states more than the locution, "I believe the desk is made of oak," though the belief-claim too has some grounds and some defense. Theory of knowledge is in part concerned with the relations between claims and reasons, with the different sorts of reasons which can serve to back up any knowledge-claim or belief-claim. The interest in the claims and reasons for claiming what we do claim constitute what I am calling the *normative* or *justificatory* aspects of theory of knowledge. To know requires not only that I have reasons which will justify my knowing and my claim; it requires as well that I be aware, that I have perceived, understood, inferred, weighed evidence, etc. The analysis of these various sorts of mental operations—of perceiving, understanding, inferring, etc.—comprises what I am calling *descriptive* epistemology. . . .

Part I—*Descriptive Epistemology*, being the interest in describing how awareness first arises and what mental operations unfold in leading us to knowlege. The concern here is also with characterizing these operations as *mental*.

Part II—*Some Forms of Cognition*, being an analysis of particular processes, e.g., of believing, remembering, and of making predictions, as instances of mental operations requisite for knowledge. The essays in this part will be found to be both descriptive and normative, though more the latter than the former.

Part III—*Normative Epistemology*, being the attempt to find criteria of knowledge which cannot be questioned, as well as the attempt to reject the possibility of such criteria.

PART I–DESCRIPTIVE EPISTEMOLOGY

Aristotle reminds us that all men by nature desire to know. He then proceeds to indicate the various stages in awareness which lead up to and make knowledge possible. Obviously, one of the conditions for knowledge is a sentient organism, with an intact brain and nervous system. It is not these conditions for knowledge, however, that Aristotle talks about. His analysis ignores neurophysiology and concentrates upon the mental operations of knowing. He saw a development and progress in these operations, a development both genetic and logical. Thus, we find him insisting upon the order: sensation, memory, experience, art, and reasoning. Just as we would today distinguish between the physical processes in the brain and nervous system and stimuli for those processes, so Aristotle distinguished between the mental processes and their contents, their objects. Correlated with the scale of mental operations of sensing, remembering, etc., he cited three types of objects: sense-impressions, particular objects like tables and chairs, and universals or class properties shared by many particular objects. Knowledge proper for him has to do with universals, class characteristics, e.g., "man," not "this particular man." Aristotle's teacher, Plato, made similar distinctions between mental processes and the objects or contents of these processes; his account was set forth in the divided-line and cave analogies in his *Republic*.

Locke also talked in genetic terms about the emergence and growth of awareness. What he called the "plain, historical method" attempted to characterize how, in fact, sensing, perceiving, attending, judging, and considering function in supplying the mind with the data for knowledge. Locke was also careful to distinguish the physical processes leading up to awareness (causal operations by tiny corpuscles) from the resulting awareness. He left the details of the causal processes to science. His *Essay Concerning Human Understanding* was a detailed account of our mental processes. Locke did argue that all mental processes, and all the objects of these processes, were derived from sensation and reflection. He was confuting what he took to be a false doctrine, one which claimed that some mental contents were innate, not derived from the physical world via sensation. His concern to refute such a doctrine led him to give most of his attention to sensation and reflection, though, in his accounts of these processes and their contents, Locke relied heavily upon many other mental operations.

An important aspect of all such mental operations and their contents is the factor of *significance,* or *meaning*. When we respond to our friend's request to do this or that, when we follow traffic signals and signs in driving, when we guide ourselves through a forest, we are reacting to stimuli. But so are we reacting to stimuli (or stimuli are being reacted to) when our eyes blink at oncoming objects. The processes within our bodies are also reactions to stimuli, e.g., when light waves are translated into electrical impulses in the nerve tissue of eye and brain. The differences between these various stimuli and reactions to them (e.g., light as an electromagnetic radiation and light as sensed in our awareness) have not always been emphasized. The importance of these differences emerges when we wish to give an account of those responses to stimuli which not only are learned responses—very few reponses are unaffected by learning—but which require attention, understanding, and conscious awareness. The epistemologist interested in describing knowing in the broad sense of conscious awareness frequently finds himself meeting the psychologist attempting to deal with similar topics. Before the explicit development of a discipline called "psychology," the philosopher had to work alone in his attempts at describing the cognitive processes. Even so, many philosophers did not stress the importance of meaning and significance in the cognitive response.

The notion of meaning can, of course, be employed in such a way that the differences between the eye-blink, the activities of neurons, my unselfconscious reactions to stimuli as I move about, and my responses to oral requests and to the written word are blurred or denied. The epistemologist will follow this course only at great risk, for in doing so he is close to denying cognition entirely, or to interpreting cognition in terms of some electronic or mechanical model. There is room for argument here, to be sure; but before the advantage of a common model for all reactions to stimuli overpowers us with its explanatory force, it is wise to examine carefully the case for differences in kind. Not only does Cassirer draw a sharp line between electronic, mechanical, and physical reactions to stimuli but he also insists, even more strongly, upon the difference in kind between animal and human behavior. His analysis of the learning experiences of Helen Keller gives a forceful case for singling out man's psychological responses as unique.

In one sense the difference is obvious, though many philosophers and psychologists often talk as if they were denying or underplaying the difference. Cassirer is careful to present the development of awareness from physiological to psychological response. . . . He has termed his analysis "philosophical anthropology." Another more recent label for the sort of analysis he offers is "philosophical psychology." Descriptive epistemology leads to such overlapping of disciplines just because it is concerned with exploring the nature and operations of mental processes. The overlap, however, of philosophy and psychology is not so marked as it might seem. One of the more important issues in contemporary theory of knowledge is the question of whether we can or should talk at all about mental processes. Philosophers and psychologists have recently tended to ignore the mental aspects of knowing. Psychologists concentrate upon behavior or neurophysiology, primarily because the physical processes of the body (both overt and internal) can be observed, experiments can be devised, and conclusions can be checked by approved scientific methods. Philosophers have been caught in a bind. Recognizing that they can add little by way of information to the study of man and his world, pressed on all sides by the advance of particular sciences, the contemporary philosopher has found a way of talking about the world in an indirect fashion. He talks about the world by talking about language, about the use of words, just those words essential for talking about thinking, knowing, believing, etc. An analysis of the language of morals, for instance, still talks about traditional problems of ethics, but what is said is said via an examination of ethical speech, by watching the roles of such words as "good," "right," "duty."[1] Another important contemporary book, *The Concept of Mind*, by G. Ryle, talks about mind, thinking, and perceiving by analyzing mental conduct words and giving what Ryle calls their "logical geography," i.e., locating them in relation to other kinds of words which behave in other ways.

Concern with being very scientific on the one hand, and concern to avoid being scientific at all on the other, have tended to lead psychologist and philosopher respectively to overlook the analysis of thinking, believing, knowing, etc., as cognitive processes. Some of the more traditional philosophers, not affected by this contemporary dispute, have attempted to address themselves to the substantive questions here. Contemporary philosophical psychology is just beginning to return to those questions.

PART II–SOME FORMS OF COGNITION

While a major problem in descriptive epistemology is that of characterizing the differences and connections between physiological

---

[1]R. M. Hare, *The Language of Morals* (New York: Oxford University Press, 1952).

and psychological reactions to stimuli, another important task is that of distinguishing the various sorts of mental processes at work in cognition, and getting clear about their order. Two orders have been followed by philosophers of knowledge. The one order is genetic and chronological; the philosopher must be aided here by science. There are difficulties, inherent in the subject matter of such genetic analysis, which introduce an element of speculation into the account, namely, the difficulties of knowing what awareness is like for the early infant or for primitive man. Contributions to such genetic analysis have been made by biologists, neurologists, animal psychologists, psychoanalysts, learning theorists, and philosophers. The philosopher is more inclined to resort to the second order of cognition, the logical order. For this order, he takes the sophisticated theories and claims of science as the terminus, or goal, of other modes of cognition. Clearly, the infant does not theorize. Likewise, it is reasonable to observe that sensing and the use of memory must precede the use of judgment. There are, in short, some obvious priorities in chronology which fit into a logical ordering. Some forms of cognition are necessary for other forms.

A philosopher's attention to the particular forms of cognition slides easily between a descriptive and a normative interest; which interest is paramount in some particular writer is not always obvious. But usually, when a philosopher gives an analysis of some form of cognition, he has purposes in mind other than that of describing that form of cognition. Thus, Russell's interest in perception arises not only from what seems an obvious point—that knowledge of a physical world must come through our sensory organs—but also from Russell's belief about the nature of the physical world which he wishes to protect in his account of perception. Russell's analysis of perception is also controlled by criteria he accepts for knowledge, criteria of certainty which were voiced by Descartes. The theory of knowledge and the theory of reality are especially intertwined in Russell's account of perception. He is not unique in this respect. Philosophers of knowledge have frequently been obsessed with saying what there is; they have tried to move from knowing to being. Thus we find proofs for an external world based upon the features of sensing or perception, proofs for other minds constructed upon what we know in our own case and what we are aware of beyond ourselves. The philosopher has sometimes rushed through his analysis of knowing in order to see what, on the basis of that analysis, we are justified in saying there is. Some of the controversy in theory of knowledge has arisen because one of the parties to the dispute has failed to notice that the other is talking on the justificatory, not the factual level. Disputes over the analysis of perception are noteworthy in this respect. What some perception theorists say is not what *in fact* we see, but rather what, given specific criteria of knowledge and belief about reality, we are *entitled to say* we see. That is, the philosopher of knowledge is not concerned with the facts of perception or learning, with adding to our stock of information about these processes. Even when he is engaged in what I am calling descriptive epistemology, the philosopher's goal is not just the description of such processes; he frequently describes only as a means of dealing with some normative problem. Readers are sometimes astonished at the things philosophers write; often this astonishment can be dissipated if they understand this distinction between what there is and what we can say there is.

To the reader approaching Russell for the first time, it may seem ludicrous for Russell to say we do not see physical objects. What it is we are said to see, and the way in which such seeing is related to the world which Russell wants to say is there, are important points typical of the philosophical analysis of perception. The normative control enters in the way in which the account of perception is a function of prior commitments to a criterion of knowledge and a theory of reality. To know, in *that* sense, that sort of world, requires *that* sort of account of perception. . . .

Not only do we make claims about the past, we also have expectations about the future and we predict events yet to occur. A justificatory question arises here also: What right do we have for trusting our predictions? Our predictions are based upon the regularities we have found. Some regularities are obvious and taken for granted, like chairs supporting our weight; others have to be carefully discovered, like those in astronomy. Because we have found events in the past standing in significant correlations, we are naturally led to expect those correlations to occur again. We would be shocked, for example, if we went up in the air when we stepped down the stairs. Our world, even our awareness is built upon such regularities. The philosopher does not deny these expectations of future regularities, but he does ask about the justification of such expectations. As in the case of memory-knowledge, so in that of inductive-knowledge, two different questions arise. The one question concerns our everyday inferences from past experience to present generalizations or predictions about future events. The other question seeks for a justification, in general, for so inferring and predicting. More specifically, Hume wants to know whether the principle that the future will be like the past can be justified. This question is tied in with what is meant by "justification." Hume says that a cause is not necessary for every event because it is possible to conceive of some event now occurring without also conceiving of a cause for that event. What Hume seems to understand by "conceive" is not a psychological, but a logical operation. In brief, the possibility of an event not having a cause, the possibility of the future not being like the past, are logical possibilities: we can deny causes of events and we can deny that the future will be like the past without involving ourselves in a logical contradiction. That is, the statement "X is an event without a cause" and the statement "the sun will not rise tomorrow" are not self-contradictory statements as "Jones is a bachelor and married" is self-contradictory.

To justify induction might mean to show that statements of this sort (about specific future events) or statements of the more general sort ("the future will be like the past") are logical truths whose denial is self-contradictory. But such an interpretation of "justify" would be much too stringent. Another possible meaning for the phrase "to justify induction" would be to show that there are deductive relations between statements about past regularities and statements about future regularities. While this claim is less stringent than the preceding one, it seems a hopeless claim, since at best only a person with omniscient knowledge would be in a position to make *deductions* of future events from past events. Still a third way of explaining Hume's remarks about induction is to say he showed that we cannot *know* that the future will be like the past, we can only *believe* it will be. He *was* much occupied with belief, his analysis of induction and causation is made in close connection with his analysis of belief. Hume was one of the first philosophers to call attention to the importance of belief for theory of knowledge. . . .

PART III–NORMATIVE EPISTEMOLOGY

Knowledge, as opposed to conjecture or belief, has had a particular fascination for the philosopher. Frequently he claims access to a special sort of knowing which gives him insight into the nature of the world. The history of philosophy has many examples of philosophers recommending various sorts of formulae for achieving the special insight which they identify with knowledge. Sometimes the formula calls for intuition, preceded by special training; at other times knowledge is seen as arising through aesthetic experiences. Other writers, being more inclined toward reason than toward intuition, have claimed that reason itself can, when properly employed, lead to special insights into the world. The partisan of reason insists upon criteria for knowledge which are not as subjective as are appeals to intuition, to the "natural light of reason," or to innate truths.[2]

If I am working in an apple orchard and I am told by the foreman to sort these apples into eating apples and cider apples (those to be pressed into juice), the criteria I am to use may be obvious. But the foreman, in order to be sure of my performance, may call my attention to the characteristics of cider apples. I could carry out his instruction by watching carefully for the cider apple characteristics. When I begin work, I do not know the difference between eating apples and cider apples. With a knowledge of the criteria of the latter sort, I now know the difference. Are we ever in a similar situation about knowledge itself, such that ignorance is replaced by knowledge in virtue of our being supplied with criteria?

Descartes tried to search for knowledge by feigning ignorance of everything save a criterion of knowledge. His criterion was not clearly formulated until after he had, through doubt, discovered a statement which could not be doubted; but the implicit criterion for determining

---

[2]The appeal to intuition, to the "natural light of reason," and to innate truths was common in the sixteenth and seventeenth centuries.

when a statement or belief could not be doubted was a logical criterion. Certain knowledge, a statement which cannot be doubted, would be such that its denial would be self-contradictory. He then proceeded to examine various candidates purporting to satisfy this criterion. There is much debate about whether Descartes did produce an instance of certain knowledge: he thought that the proposition "I am, I exist" was a proposition whose truth is certain when one utters that proposition. To say (and mean it) "I do not exist" is, if not self-contradictory, at least odd. Descartes was unable to obtain any further truths without adding dubious assumptions to the "I am, I exist" proposition. It is very doubtful whether anything more than the proposition about one's own existence can be obtained by means of Descartes' experiment in doubt, although there is a parallel example found in Russell's essay, the certainty of immediate awareness. Chisholm's "non-comparative appear statements" embody a similar certainty. These propositions of immediate awareness can be given various formulations, the safest being something like "I am being appeared to in a table-like way." When we separate what *is* from what *appears to be*, we can then assert, with a certainty akin to that of Descartes' proposition, a proposition about appearances to a subject. But just as Descartes cannot make any other moves without extra assumptions, so Russell's starting point of an indubitable proposition about appearances can serve no epistemological function by itself: it must be helped out by *ad hoc* assumptions.

The ideal of a knowledge whose certainty is such that we cannot be in error about it has served as a standard for many in theory of knowledge. Even philosophers like Locke and Hume who urge us to derive all cognitive claims from sense experience, measured such sensory knowledge by the standard of deductive, logically certain knowledge. Those who have confronted Descartes' claim of having solved the problem of the criterion by establishing criteria from the very experience which produced an instance satisfying the criterion, have reacted in several different ways. There are three main reactions: (1) there is Chisholm's rejection, not of criteria, but of the stringent Cartesian criteria and of the way such criteria were established; (2) there is Arner's rejection of the legitimacy of asking for criteria at all; and (3) there is the sceptic's rejection of the possibility of justifying knowledge, of finding instances which satisfy the knowledge criteria.

In one sense, Chisholm denies that there can be a criterion, a mark of evidence which, prior to having any evidence, will indicate when we come across some evidence, when we do have some knowledge. Chisholm questions the propriety of asking "what is knowledge?" while pretending we do not have in our possession bits of knowledge. If we do not already know what counts as knowledge, how can we recognize the knowing which is knowledge? There are parallels in ethics. If we do not already know, in some sense of "know," which actions are morally right and wrong, we are hardly in a position to go out in the world looking for right actions. Aristotle's answer to the moral question "how do we learn which actions are right?" is that we acquire such "knowledge" through habit and custom instilled by our family and society. Chisholm's solution to the problem of the criterion runs along similar lines: we "know" beforehand what the marks of evidence are, what we take as valid knowledge-claims. As he remarks in his book on perception, "when we set out to solve the problem of the criterion, we already knew which propositions are the ones that are evident; we knew in advance that skepticism with regard to the senses is mistaken."[3] The task for theory of knowledge is then to formulate these marks, to make them explicit. . . . Chisholm attempts to formulate a satisfactory criterion for our perceptual knowledge, what he calls 'the sensibly taking criterion." The decision as to what sort of criterion to formulate was made by considering what it is we want to say we know in perception; "I see a cat on the roof" becomes the paradigm for perceptual claims.

Opposed to the quest for criteria which will delineate knowledge, no matter where or when it is found, Arner stresses the contextual nature of knowledge-claims.[4] As he says . . . "What counts as conclusive evidence is a matter of tacit, continuing agreement among the users of the language." The philosopher cannot stand apart from society and proclaim special earmarks of knowledge in general. What we claim to know must be so, but the grounds for making the claim are found in the context of assertion, in the subject matter and circumstances. The grounds for scientific claims differ from those for more ordinary, less technical claims. Arner agrees with Chisholm that there cannot be a mark of evidence for evidence; the authorities for knowledge-claims cannot be queried indefinitely.

Another feature of Arner's essay worth noticing is the way he catches the sceptic using the logical criteria of knowledge. Like the philosopher who claims a special sort of insight, the sceptic uses the word "knowledge" to designate a very special type of cognition, a type which cannot be wrong, which lacks even the possibility of being wrong. The sceptic assumes that before we can know that S is P it must be impossible that S is not P, and "impossible" is used in the logical sense employed by Descartes and Hume. That is, something is "possible" if its denial is not self-contradictory; "impossible" if it is self-contradictory. The sceptic offers still other kinds of considerations designed to cast doubt upon any knowledge-claim. Sometimes the sceptic has in mind the fact that further experiences may force us to revise our claims, but always the unattainable ideal of knowledge which is logically sound in all its phases hovers in the background of the sceptic's case.

---

[3]Roderick M. Chisholm, *Perceiving: A Philosophical Study* (Ithaca, N. Y.: Cornell University Press, 1957), p. 102.

[4]Douglas G. Arner, "On Knowing," *The Philosophical Review,* LXVIII, No. 1, Jan., 1959.

KARL POPPER

(b. 1902)

Sir Karl Popper was born in Vienna. Between 1949 and 1969, he was Professor of Logic and Scientific Method at London University, and between 1945 and 1966 he served as Head of the Department of Philosophy, Logic and Scientific Method at the London School of Economics. Among his many books are The Open Society and Its Enemies, The Poverty of Historicism, The Logic of Scientific Discovery, Conjectures and Refutations, *and* Objective Knowledge.

THE BUCKET AND THE SEARCHLIGHT: TWO THEORIES OF KNOWLEDGE

The purpose of this paper is to criticize a widely held view about the aims and methods of the natural sciences, and to put forward an alternative view.

I

I shall start with a brief exposition of the view I propose to examine, which I will call *'the bucket theory of science'* (or *'the bucket theory of the mind'*). The starting point of this theory is the persuasive doctrine that before we can know or say anything about the world, we must first have had perceptions—sense experiences. It is supposed to follow from this doctrine that our knowledge, our experience, consists either of accumulated perceptions (naïve empiricism) or else of assimilated, sorted, and classified perceptions (a view held by Bacon and, in a more radical form, by Kant).

The Greek atomists had a somewhat primitive notion of this process. They assumed that atoms break loose from the objects we perceive, and penetrate our sense organs, where they become perceptions; and

A lecture delivered (in German) at the European Forum of the Austrian College, Alpbach, Tyrol, in August 1948, and first published, in German, under the title 'Naturgesetze und theoretische Systeme' *in* Gesetz und Wirklichkeit, *edited by Simon Moser, 1949. [Textual additions made in this translation are put into square brackets, or indicated in the footnotes.] From* Objective Knowledge *by Karl R. Popper, pp. 341–343, 345–352, 359–361.*

out of these, in the course of time, our knowledge of the external world fits itself together [like a self-assembling jigsaw puzzle]. According to this view, then, our mind resembles a container—a kind of bucket—in which perceptions and knowledge accumulate. (Bacon speaks of perceptions as 'grapes, ripe and in season' which have to be gathered, patiently and industriously, and from which, if pressed, the pure wine of knowledge will flow.)

Strict empiricists advise us to interfere as little as possible with this process of accumulating knowledge. True knowledge is pure knowledge, uncontaminated by those prejudices which we are only too prone to add to, and mix with, our perceptions; these alone constitute experience pure and simple. The result of these additions, of our disturbing and interfering with the process of accumulating knowledge, is error. Kant opposes this theory: he denies that perceptions are ever pure, and asserts that our experience is the result of a process of assimilation and transformation—the combined product of sense perceptions and of certain ingredients added by our minds. The perceptions are the raw material, as it were, which flows from outside into the bucket, where it undergoes some (automatic) processing—something akin to digestion, or perhaps to systematic classification—in order to be turned in the end into something not so very different from Bacon's 'pure wine of experience'; let us say, perhaps, into fermented wine.

I do not think that either of these views suggests anything like an adequate picture of what I believe to be the actual process of acquiring experience, or the actual method used in research or discovery. Admittedly, Kant's view might be so interpreted that it comes much nearer to my own view than does pure empiricism. I grant, of course, that science is impossible without experience (but the notion of 'experience' has to be carefully considered). Though I grant this, I nevertheless hold that perceptions do not constitute anything like the raw material, as they do according to the 'bucket theory', out of which we construct either 'experience' or 'science'.

II

In science it is *observation* rather than perception which plays the decisive part. But observation is a process in which we play an intensely *active* part. An observation is a perception, but one which is planned and prepared. We do not 'have' an observation [as we may 'have' a sense experience] but we 'make' an observation. [A navigator even 'works' an observation.] An observation is always preceded by a particular interest, a question, or a problem—in short, by something theoretical.[1] After all,

[1]By the word 'theoretical' I do not mean here the opposite of 'practical' (since our interest might very well be a practical one) it should rather be understood in the sense of 'speculative' [as with a speculative interest in a pre-existing problem] in contrast to 'perceptive'; or 'rational' as opposed to 'sensual'.

we can put every question in the form of a hypothesis or conjecture to which we add: 'Is this so? Yes or no?' Thus we can assert that every observation is preceded by a problem, a hypothesis (or whatever we may call it); at any rate by something that interests us, by something theoretical or speculative. This is why observations are always selective, and why they presuppose something like a principle of selection. . . .

IV

Let us now return to the problem of observation. An observation always presupposes the existence of some system of expectations. These expectations can be formulated in the form of queries; and the observation will be used to obtain either a confirming or a correcting answer to expectations thus formulated.

My thesis that the question, or the hypothesis, must precede the observation may at first have seemed paradoxical; but we can see now that it is not at all paradoxical to assume that expectations—that is, dispositions to react—must precede every observation and, indeed, every perception: for certain dispositions or propensities to react are innate in all organisms whereas perceptions and observations clearly are not innate. And although perceptions and, even more, observations, play an important part in the process of *modifying* our dispositions or propensities to react, some such dispositions or propensities must, of course, be present first, or they could not be modified.

These biological reflections are by no means to be understood as implying my acceptance of a behaviourist position. I do not deny that perceptions, observations, and other states of consciousness occur, but I assign to them a role very different from the one they are supposed to play according to the bucket theory. Nor are these biological reflections to be regarded as forming in any sense an assumption on which my arguments will be based. But I hope that they will help towards a better understanding of these arguments. The same may be said of the following reflections, which are closely connected with these biological ones.

At every instant of our pre-scientific or scientific development we are living in the centre of what I usually call a '*horizon of expectations*'. By this I mean the sum total of our expectations, whether these are subconscious or conscious, or perhaps even explicitly stated in some language. Animals and babies have also their various and different horizons of expectations though no doubt on a lower level of consciousness than, say, a scientist whose horizon of expectations consists to a considerable extent of linguistically formulated theories or hypotheses.

The various horizons of expectations differ, of course, not only in their being more or less conscious, but also in their content. Yet in all these cases the horizon of expectations plays the part of a frame of reference: only their setting in this frame confers meaning or significance on our experiences, actions, and observations.

Observations, more especially, have a very peculiar function within this frame. They can, under certain circumstances, destroy even the frame itself, if they clash with certain of the expectations. In such a case they can have an effect upon our horizon of expectations like a bombshell. This bombshell may force us to reconstruct, or rebuild, our whole horizon of expectations; that is to say, we may have to correct our expectations and fit them together again into something like a consistent whole. We can say that in this way our horizon of expectations is raised to and reconstructed on a higher level, and that we reach in this way a new stage in the evolution of our experience; a stage in which those expectations which have not been hit by the bomb are somehow incorporated into the horizon, while those parts of the horizon which have suffered damage are repaired and rebuilt. This has to be done in such a manner that the damaging observations are no longer felt as disruptive, but are integrated with the rest of our expectations. If we succeed in this rebuilding, then we shall have created what is usually known as an *explanation* of those observed events [which created the disruption, the problem].

As to the question of the temporal relation between observation on the one hand and the horizon of expectations or theories on the other, we may well admit that a new explanation, or a new hypothesis, is generally preceded in time by *those* observations which destroyed the previous horizon of expectations and thus were the stimulus to our attempting a new explanation. Yet this must not be understood as saying that observations generally precede expectations or hypotheses. On the contrary, each observation is preceded by expectations or hypotheses; by those expectations, more especially, which make up the horizon of expectations that lends those observations their significance; only in this way do they attain the status of real observations.

The question, 'What comes first, the hypothesis *(H)* or the observation *(O)*?' reminds one, of course, of that other famous question: 'What came first, the hen *(H)* or the egg *(O)*?' Both questions are soluble. The bucket theory asserts that [just as a primitive form of an egg *(O)*, a unicellular organism, precedes the hen *(H)*] observation *(O)* always precedes every hypothesis *(H)*; for the bucket theory regards the latter as arising from observations by generalization, or association, or classification. By contrast, we can now say that the hypothesis (or expectation, or theory, or whatever we may call it) precedes the observation, even though an observation that refutes a certain hypothesis may stimulate a new (and therefore a temporally later) hypothesis.

All this applies, more especially, to the formation of scientific hypotheses. For we learn only from our hypotheses what kind of observations we ought to make: whereto we ought to direct our attention; wherein to take an interest. Thus it is the hypothesis which becomes our guide, and which leads us to new observational results.

This is the view which I have called the '*searchlight theory*' (in contradistinction to the '*bucket theory*'. [According to the searchlight theory, observations are secondary to hypotheses.] Observations play, however, an important role as *tests* which a hypothesis must undergo in the course of our [critical] examination of it. If the hypothesis does not pass the examination, if it is falsified by our observations, then we have to look around for a new hypothesis. In this case the new hypothesis will come after those observations which led to the falsification or rejection of the old hypothesis. Yet what made the observations interesting and relevant and what altogether gave rise to our undertaking them in the first instance, was the earlier, the old [and now rejected] hypothesis.

In this way science appears clearly as a straightforward continuation of the pre-scientific repair work on our horizons of expectations. Science never starts from scratch; it can never be described as free from assumptions; for at every instant it presupposes a horizon of expectations—yesterday's horizon of expectations, as it were. Today's science is built upon yesterday's science [and so it is the result of yesterday's searchlight]; and yesterday's science, in turn, is based on the science of the day before. And the oldest scientific theories are built on pre-scientific myths, and these, in their turn, on still older expectations. Ontogenetically (that is, with respect to the development of the individual organism) we thus regress to the state of the expectations of a newborn child; phylogenetically (with respect to the evolution of the race, the phylum) we get to the state of expectations of unicellular organisms. (There is no danger here of a vicious infinite regress—if for no other reason than that every organism is born with *some* horizon of expectations.) There is, as it were, only one step from the amoeba to Einstein.

Now if this is the way science evolves, what can be said to be the characteristic step which marks the transition from pre-science to science? . . .

XII

I hope that some of my formulations which at the beginning of this lecture may have seemed to you far-fetched or even paradoxical will now appear less so.

There is no road, royal or otherwise, which leads of necessity from a 'given' set of specific facts to any universal law. What we call 'laws' are hypotheses or conjectures which always form a part of some larger system of theories [in fact, of a whole horizon of expectations] and which, therefore, can never be tested in isolation. The progress of science consists in trials, in the elimination of errors, and in further trials guided by the experience acquired in the course of previous trials and errors. No particular theory may ever be regarded as absolutely certain: every theory may become problematical, no matter how well corroborated it may seem now. No scientific theory is sacrosanct or beyond criticism. This fact has often been forgotten, particularly during the last century, when we were impressed by the often repeated and truly magnificent corroborations of certain mechanical theories, which eventually came to be regarded as indubitably true. The stormy development of physics since the turn of the century has taught us better; and we have now come to see that it is the task of the scientist to subject his theory to ever new tests, and that no theory must be pronounced final. Testing proceeds by taking the theory to be tested and combining it with all possible kinds of initial conditions as well as with other theories, and then comparing the resulting predictions with reality. If this leads to disappointed expectations, to refutations, then we have to rebuild our theory.

The disappointment of some of the expectations with which we once eagerly approached reality plays a most significant part in this procedure. It may be compared with the experience of a blind man who touches, or runs into, an obstacle, and so becomes aware of its existence. *It is through the falsification of our suppositions that we actually get in touch with 'reality'*. It is the discovery and elimination of our errors which alone constitute that 'positive' experience which we gain from reality.

It is of course always possible to save a falsified theory by means of supplementary hypotheses [like those of epicycles]. But this is not the way of progress in the sciences. The proper reaction to falsification is to search for new theories which seem likely to offer us a better grasp of the facts. Science is not interested in having the last word if this means shutting off our minds from falsifying experiences, but rather in learning from our experience; that is, in learning from our mistakes.

There is a way of formulating scientific theories which points with particular clarity to the possibility of their falsification: we can formulate them in the form of prohibitions [or *negative existential statements*] such as, for example, 'There does not exist a closed physical system, such that energy changes in one part of it without compensating changes occurring in another part' (first law of thermodynamics). Or, 'There does not exist a machine which is 100 per cent efficient' (second law). It can be shown that universal statements and negative existential statements are logically equivalent. This makes it possible to formulate all universal laws in the manner indicated; that is to say, as prohibitions. However, these are prohibitions intended only for the technicians and not for the scientist. They tell the former how to proceed if he does not want to squander his energies. But to the scientist they are a challenge to test and to falsify; they stimulate him to try to discover those states of affairs whose existence they prohibit, or deny.

Thus we have reached a point from which we can see science as a magnificent adventure of the human spirit. It is the invention of ever new theories, and the indefatigable examination of their power to throw light on experience. The principles of scientific progress are very simple. They demand that we give up the ancient idea that we may attain certainty [or even a high degree of 'probability' in the sense of the probability calculus] with the propositions and theories of science (an idea which derives from the association of science with magic and of the scientist with the magician): the aim of the scientist is not to discover absolute certainty, but to discover better and better theories [or to invent more and more powerful searchlights] capable of being put to more and more severe tests [and thereby leading us to, and illuminating for us, ever new experiences]. But this means that these theories must be falsifiable: it is through their falsification that science progresses.

21

Language

W. V. QUINE

(b.1908)

Willard Van Orman Quine has taught philosophy at Harvard since 1936, and has been Edgar Pierce professor of philosophy there since 1955. Quine was educated at Oberlin, Harvard, and Oxford. His many books and articles, especially in logic and mathematics, have been widely read and cited. Among his better known works are From a Logical Point of View *(1953),* Word and Object *(1961),* The Ways of Paradox *(1966),* Ontological Relativity *(1969),* The Web of Belief *(1970), and* The Roots of Reference *(1973).*

PHILOSOPHICAL PROGRESS IN LANGUAGE THEORY

Philosophy, or what appeals to me under that head, is continuous with science. It is a wing of science in which aspects of method are examined more deeply, or in a wider perspective than elsewhere. It is also a wing in which the objectives of a science receive more than average scrutiny, and the significance of the results receives special appreciation. The man who does this philosophical sort of work may be a philosopher in point of professional affiliation, but a philosopher with an interest in the special science concerned; or again, he may be an affiliate of the special science, but philosophical in attitude and motivation. Einstein was in this latter category. His empirical critique of the concept of simultaneity is a philosophical paradigm. Bohr's infusion of epistemology into quantum mechanics makes him another example. Further philosophical spirits in professional physics are the cosmologists, such as Bondi and Hoyle. For that matter, surely what has drawn most theoretical physicists to physics is a philosophical quest for the inner nature of reality.

Thus I picture the professional physicist and the professional philosopher as impelled alike, by philosophical curiosity, into physics and its philosophical wing. This picture strikes me as truer than the picture which depicts a general-utility philosophical reservoir as tapped now and again by physics or other sciences. True, empiricism and idealism are full-width philosophies, and Einstein and Bohr are sometimes regarded as funneling the one or the other into physics. On the other hand empiricism itself, surely, is no less justly seen as science's gift to philosophy. It is, at any rate, the separation that I am against. The relation between philosophy and science is not best seen even in terms of give and take. Philosophy, or what appeals to me under that head, is an aspect of science.

Rather than speak of applications of philosophy to a science, therefore, or even of progress in the philosophy of the science, I would speak of philosophical progress *in* the science. What I am to speak of more particularly is philosophical progress in language theory.

This progress is characterized, of course, by scrupulous empirical method. But we must notice in empiricism a curious opposition of currents which, in relation to language theory, can make all the difference between black and white. On the one hand, it is in the empiricist tradition to take subjective sense impressions as the starting point and to try to reduce all talk of external objects to this basis. On the other hand, the

Reprinted from Language, Belief and Metaphysics, *edited by Howard E. Kiefer and Milton K. Munitz, pp. 3–6, by permission of the State University of New York Press.*

method of introspection is often condemned by empirical scientists as the very antithesis of empirical method.

This latter trend, the externalizing of empiricism, comes from a heightened appreciation of the role of language in knowledge. If I were to set an initial date, I might take 1786. That year saw the publication of a sort of declaration of independence. The author of the declaration was the philologist John Horne Tooke, who wrote in part as follows: "The greatest part of Mr. Locke's essay, that is, all which relates to what he calls the abstraction, complexity, generalization, relation, etc. of ideas, does indeed merely concern language."[1] With Tooke, and with his younger contemporary Jeremy Bentham, the theory of language was on its way to becoming independent of the theory of ideas. Ideas dropped to a subordinate status, as adjuncts of words. They stayed on as meanings or intensions or connotations of words.

Once the focus had shifted thus from ideas to language, the externalizing of empiricism was assured. For language, unlike the idea, is conspicuously external. Language is a social art, acquired on evidence of social usage.

The learning not just of language but of anything, at the level where learning is best understood, is of course external in one respect: it is a conditioning of responses to external stimulation. Even the old empiricists appreciated this point, in their way; *nihil in intellectu quod non prius in sensu*. But the learning of language, in particular, is an external affair also in a further respect—because of the social character of language. It is not just that we learn language by a conditioning of overt responses to external stimulation. The more special point is that verbal behavior is determined by what people can observe of one another's responses to what people can observe of one another's external stimulations. In learning language, all of us, from childhood on, are amateur students of behavior, and, simultaneously, subjects of amateur studies of behavior. Thus, consider the typical learning of a word, at its simplest: you are confronted by the object of the word in the presence of your teacher. Part of the plan is that he knows that you see the object and you know that he does. This feature is equally in point on the later occasion when the teacher approves or disapproves of your use of the word. The natural consequence is that the clearest words, or at least the words that are learned first and used more consistently, tend to be words not for sense impressions but for conspicuous external objects.

Thus it is that the declaration of independence precipitated a revolution, a Copernican flip. There are, we see, two factors: first, the philosophical shift of focus from idea to word; second, the linguistic fact that the words in sharpest focus are mainly words for external objects. For empiricism as thus reoriented, the focus of understanding is outside us. Our mental life settles into an inferential status. The internal looks now for its legitimation to external evidence. The ghost, in Ryle's phrase,

---

[1]John Horne Tooke, "Επεα πτεροέντα; or, *the Diversions of Purley*. 2 Vols. (London, 1786, 1805, 1829). First American edition, 1806, p. 32.

is exorcised from the machine.[2] This is behaviorism. It has not become everyone's philosophy, nor even every empiricist's philosophy. The revolution has been, for empiricism, less a turning point than a splitting point.

Even those who have not embraced behaviorism as a philosophy are, however, obliged to adhere to behavioristic method within certain scientific pursuits; and language theory is such a pursuit. A scientist of language is, insofar, a behaviorist ex officio. Whatever the best eventual theory regarding the inner mechanism of language may turn out to be, it is bound to conform to the behavioral character of language learning: the dependence of verbal behavior on observation of verbal behavior. A language is mastered through social emulation and social feedback, and these controls ignore any idiosyncrasy in an individual's imagery or associations that is not discovered in his behavior. Minds are indifferent to language insofar as they differ privately from one another; that is, insofar as they are behaviorally inscrutable.

Thus, though a linguist may still esteem mental entities philosophically, they are pointless or pernicious in language theory. This point was emphasized by Dewey in the twenties, when he argued that there could not be, in any serious sense, a private language.[3] Wittgenstein also, years later, came to appreciate this point. Linguists have been conscious of it in increasing measure; Bloomfield to a considerable degree, Harris fully.

Earlier linguistic theory operated in an uncritical mentalism. An irresponsible semantics prevailed, in which words were related to ideas much as labels are related to the exhibits in a museum. To switch languages was to switch the labels. The uncritical mentalism and irresponsible semantics were, of course, philosophical too. I do not limit the role of philosophy in language theory to Tooke, Bentham, Dewey, and behaviorism; but I am speaking of philosophical *progress* in language theory.

It should be noted that the contrast between behaviorism and mentalism has little to do with the contrast in early empiricism between the learned and the innate. Any behaviorist account of the learning process is openly and emphatically committed to innate beginnings. The behaviorist recognizes the indispensability, for any kind of learning, of prior biases and affinities. Without these there could be no selective reinforcements or extinctions of responses, since all discriminable stimulations would count as equally dissimilar. There must be innate inequalities in our qualitative spacing, so to speak, of stimulations. This much applies to men and other animals equally, insofar as the conditioning of responses is to be possible at all.[4]

Moreover, it has long been recognized that our innate endowments for language learning go yet further than the mere spacing of qualities.

---

[2]Gilbert Ryle, *The Concept of Mind* (Hutchinson's University Library, London, 1949).

[3]John Dewey, *Experience and Nature* (W. W. Norton, New York, 1925), pp. 170, 178,185.

[4]See my *Word and Object* (M.I.T. Press, Cambridge, 1960), pp. 83ff.

Otherwise we should expect other animals to learn language; and also, as Chomsky has lately stressed, we should expect our own learning to take longer than it does. Two generations ago, the supplementary innate endowment that got the main credit was an instinct for mimicry. One generation ago, a babbling instinct moved to first place; the infant babbles at random and the parent reinforces these utterances selectively. Currently, the babbling instinct is losing favor and the instinct for mimicry is back in the ascendancy. I expect that both of these innate aids are there, and also of course the innate spacing of qualities, as well as some further innate apparatus which has not yet been identified.

Clearly the innate aids to language are extensive, whatever their details. I stress this because I have sensed of late a mistaken notion that there is a strain between behaviorism and innate dispositions. Nothing could be farther from the truth, since conditioning itself rests on innate spacing of qualities. I suppose the mistaken notion arises from first associating behaviorism with empiricism, which is right, and then associating empiricism with Locke's repudiation of innate ideas, which is as may be, and finally associating innate ideas with innate dispositions.

This chain of associations neglects the externalization of empiricism, which, I said earlier, makes all the difference between black and white. Before externalization, ideas were the stock in trade. Locke and his predecessors Hobbes and Gassendi, having to state empiricist standards in ideational terms, drew the line between ideas rooted in sensation and innate ideas; *nihil in intellectu quod non prius in sensu*. When empiricism is externalized, however, talk of ideas goes by the board. If any of it is to be dredged back up, it must be made sense of in terms of dispositions to overt behavior. It is this insistence on making sense in terms of dispositions to overt behavior that characterizes empiricism after externalization; and there is nothing unempirical, in this sense, about innate dispositions to overt behavior. . . .

MAX BLACK

(b. 1909)

Max Black has written frequently in the area of logic, and the philosophies of language and science. Since 1946, he has been S. L. Sage Professor of Philosophy at Cornell. A native of Russia, Black studied philosophy at Cambridge and the University of London, becoming an American citizen in 1948. Among his publications are Models and Metaphors *(1962),* The Labyrinth of Language *(1968) and* Margin of Precision *(1970).*

PHILOSOPHICAL PITFALLS IN LANGUAGE THEORY

I cannot do justice in a short time to Professor Quine's rich and far-ranging paper. I shall, therefore, confine myself to saying a few things about some of the points which most interested me, choosing especially those that I may have misunderstood.

Let me start with Quine's preliminary remarks concerning the relations between philosophy and science. He has told us that philosophy "is continuous with science"; he also said philosophy is both a wing of science and an aspect of it. Quine's topography of the scientific mansion is somewhat confusing. I presume each branch of science has its own "wing," with still another, for the philosophy of probability and induction, to serve them all. Should there perhaps also be a place, however humble, for art and the humanities? The intended design is hard to grasp.

Again, it seems to me somewhat difficult to think of a "part" of science as "continuous" with the whole. Even if philosophy were continuous with science, it might be clearly distinguishable from it. Continuity is, of course compatible with striking difference—as, say, red is continuous with yellow, but different from it.

Altogether, I am not clear about how Quine conceives of philosophy. I conjecture that he is really thinking of it as a part of science. He says, for example, that "philosophical progress in language theory" must

Reprinted from Language, Belief and Metaphysics, *edited by Howard E. Kiefer and Milton K. Munitz, pp. 19–24, by permission of the State University of New York Press.*

use "scrupulous empirical method." Well, much depends on how one understands empirical method or the science to which it ministers. If by science Quine means something like *episteme*, or *Wissenschaft* in the German sense, then there is no reason to disagree. Philosophy does aim at knowledge, among other things, and can be so far "scientific." But if Quine means science in the special sense of the word that has been current for only a century, his claim is less plausible. I recall that the great Lord Rutherford once defined science as "physics—and stamp collecting." And I think this is how Quine, too, really thinks of science. For him, it seems fair to say, science is or ought to be modeled on physics.

Consider how Quine uses "behavior." The word is not intended to apply to such obvious examples as smiling, gritting one's teeth, recognizing another person, or being angry—all of which might reasonably be called examples of "observable behavior." Such ordinary-language descriptions could, however, have no role in physics. For Quine, as for other behaviorists, "behavior" is typically the kind of thing that could be recorded and classified by some inanimate physical instrument.

I may be wrong about this. One thing that leads me to suspect so is Quine's surprising apposition of physics with "a philosophical quest for the inner nature of reality." That sound astonishingly metaphysical for a radical empiricist.

At any rate, it seems clear to me that Quine is not practising science in this paper. Whatever else he may be doing, he is offering a persuasive definition of "science"—and I wonder whether we *should* be persuaded that all the questions arising in connection with a science can be assimilated under "empirical methods." My own opinion is that in this paper Quine is not even trying to be severely "empirical," but is rather offering us a kind of picture or perspective. Whether to accept the picture or not seems to me not really a straightforwardly scientific question.

I shall turn now to the central theme of the "externalizing of empiricism," as Quine has called it. I remind you that he describes this as "a shift of focus from ideas to words," with a heightened appreciation of the relation of the "linguistic fact that the words in sharpest focus are mainly words for external objects." For empiricism thus rejuvenated, Quine says, "Our mental life settles into an inferential status." And, finally, "This is behaviorism."

Let me say, first, that I was a little surprised to see Horne Tooke and Bentham so prominently featured. These two writers, whatever their merits, have had negligible influence on the development of linguistics. On the other hand, outstanding linguists like De Saussure and Sapir have rarely been behaviorists or radical empiricists, but often some kind of unsystematic idealists.

But after all, I suspect, Quine is not offering us serious historical remarks. He *is* presenting a specific conception of language learning: words as learned in the presence of the object, of the word, and of the teacher. This is, of course, a drastically over-simplified picture. Taken quite literally, the recommended picture of learning to speak would be something like this: another person exclaims "rabbit" when a rabbit appears; hearing the word so used in such episodes, a bystander then learns the meaning of "rabbit" by induction. But this kind of episode, if it ever occurs, is surely exceptional. If one is really to learn any language or any part of it, one has to know a good deal about the teaching situation and has to assume that one's partner shares this knowledge. Indeed, Quine himself brings this out in a number of remarks. "Part of the plan is that he, the teacher, knows that you see the object and you know that he does." Quite so. But now we are a long way away from the simple stimulus-response paradigm. The stimulus, if it is still to be called that, must now include the relevant background knowledge. And similarly for the case of the field-linguist, trying to learn from native informants what they mean when they use certain words. What puzzles me is that, according to the view under discussion, the "externalization of empiricism," it is supposed to follow that mental life is an inference—"our mental life settles into an inferential status." And so a good empiricist is advised to reject "mental entities" as "pointless or pernicious." We are, indeed, picturesquely warned against "the slough of ideas."

I am puzzled on two counts. First, why the inference, if it occurs, should cast doubt upon the status of the thing inferred: you can hardly infer to something unless it exists. Even in the case of learning the meaning of "cat," as Quine emphasizes, inference is present, on his principles. Why should he not say, therefore, that the existence of cats is as much a matter of inference as the existence of minds and warn us against the "slough" occupied by felines? On the other hand, if he really means that references to *my own* pains, thoughts, and so on, are based upon inference, then, so far as I can see, he is plainly wrong. When I say that I can feel my thumb now, I am certainly not inferring, and yet I am clearly talking about something which, in Quine's terminology, is part of my mental life. (Perhaps he means that only references to the mental occurrence of *others* involve inference, which would, of course, be much more plausible.)

22

Perception and Experience

GILBERT RYLE

(b. 1900) –1976)

Oxford-educated, Ryle returned in 1945 to become Waynflete Professor of Metaphysical Philosophy. His most well-known work is The Concept of Mind, *and other works of his include* Dilemmas *(1954) and* Plato's Progress *(1966). For many years, he was editor of the influential periodical* Mind, *and in some quarters he is regarded as the most distinguished British philosopher of his generation.*

PERCEIVING

How could anything be more familiar to us than seeing things, hearing things, smelling, tasting and touching things? We have our ordinary verbs of perceptual detection, discrimination and exploration under very good control long before we leave the nursery. Nor do we need to get much sophistication before we are pretty familiar with many of the more prevalent abnormalities of perception. We soon find out about seeing double, hearing the sounds of the sea in sea-shells, losing the senses of smell and taste; about rainbows, reflections and echoes; about magnifying glasses, mirrors and megaphones. We soon get the notions of blindness, deafness, numbness; of long sight, short sight and dazzlement; and having learned that these are connected with interference, damage or deficiency in the appropriate sense-organs, we are not surprised to find that spectacles make differences to what we see, but not to what we hear or taste, or that it is for the medical profession to find the causes of personal defects of perception and the remedies for them.

At the start we say and follow things said *with* verbs of perception where we are not yet talking *about* perceiving but about the things that we perceive or fail to perceive. At a later stage we learn, for example, to tell the oculist or ear-doctor the things that he wants to know, not facts about the clock we hear ticking or about the birds we see on the lawn, but facts about the way they sound and look to us. Already used to the idea that sometimes things are not as they look or sound to be, we soon get interested in such questions as why the distant bat sounds as if it strikes the ball quite a long time after it does strike, why the note of the engine's whistle drops as it passes us, and what makes the mountains look much nearer on some days than on others. We begin to talk about the conditions governing different classes of sights, felt temperatures and heard sounds.

There are hosts of notorious generalities about the limitations and fallibilities of our senses. The conjuror reminds us—of course in vain—that the quickness of the hand deceives the eye; proverbs remind us that all that glitters is not gold; and Æsop's story of the greedy dog reminds us that the reflections of bones can be mistaken for bones until it comes to eating them.

Thinkers who wish to maintain the pre-eminence of mathematical knowledge over other beliefs, and thinkers who wish to depreciate mundane beliefs in favour of supra-mundane beliefs have often argued from these notorious facts of illusion, delusion and imprecision in sense-perception to the sweeping conclusion that we can never find out anything for certain by using our eyes, ears and noses. What is sometimes fraudulent may be always fraudulent. Where we have relied and been

From Dilemmas *(London: Cambridge University Press, 1966), pp. 93–102.*

disappointed we should cease to rely. Even if there are some genuine articles, still they are stamped with no hall-marks. There is never anything to tell us that *this* is one of the genuine articles.

I do not want to spend long in examining the arguments for this general depreciation of sense-perception or the intellectual motives for denying all credentials to sense-perception in order to enhance those of calculation, demonstration or religious faith. I want to get quickly to the much thornier briar-patch, the place, namely, where scientific accounts of perception seem to issue in the consequential doctrine that observers, including the physiologists and psychologists themselves, never perceive what they naïvely suppose themselves to perceive. But as there is some cross-trading between the two firms, I must say a little about the quite general argument from the notorious limitations and fallibilities of our senses to the impossibility of our getting to know anything at all by looking, listening and touching.

A country which had no coinage would offer no scope to counterfeiters. There would be nothing for them to manufacture or pass counterfeits of. They could, if they wished, manufacture and give away decorated discs of brass or lead, which the public might be pleased to get. But these would not be false coins. There can be false coins only where there are coins made of the proper materials by the proper authorities.

In a country where there is a coinage, false coins can be manufactured and passed; and the counterfeiting might be so efficient that an ordinary citizen, unable to tell which were false and which were genuine coins, might become suspicious of the genuineness of any particular coin that he received. But however general his suspicions might be, there remains one proposition which he cannot entertain, the proposition, namely, that it is possible that all coins are counterfeits. For there must be an answer to the question 'Counterfeits of what?' Or a judge, who has found all too many witnesses in the past inaccurate and dishonest, may be right to expect today's testimonies to break down under examination; but he cannot declare that there are no such things as accuracy and sincerity in testifying. Even to consider whether this witness has been insincere or inaccurate involves considering what would be the honest or precise thing to say. Ice could not be thin if ice could not be thick.

But more than this. You and I know the general truth that we could be taken in by a counterfeit coin or a confidence-trickster; and in a particular contingency, though aware of the danger, we might still be without any conclusive or even worth-while acid tests or lie-detectors by means of which to decide between the sham and the genuine. But our situation is not always like this. You and I sometimes make mistakes in counting, adding and multiplying, and we may remind ourselves of this general liability in the very same breath with making one of these mistakes. So, at first sight, it looks as though we ought to surrender and say that we can never find out by counting the number of chairs in a room and never find out by adding or multiplying the right answers to our arithmetical problems. Yet we do not surrender. For here we have in our possession all the acid tests and lie-detectors that we need. Namely we can count again, quite carefully, and compute again, quite carefully. Nor will this care be merely a useless, anxious watchfulness against nothing in particular. It will be vigilance for just those specific slips which we and our associates have made before and detected and corrected before. In this case we know by experience both what it is like to miscount and miscalculate and what it is like to avoid, detect and correct those miscalculations or miscountings. But still our precautions may not be sufficient. Perhaps we count three times, once fast and twice slowly, and not always starting in the same place; but still we miscount. Or perhaps we add, first going down from top to bottom, and then going up from bottom to top; but still we miscalculate. Very good—but how is the mistake exposed? By someone counting correctly or by someone adding correctly. The thing was doable; the thing was done. We did not do it, but we know all that went to the doing of it. We could have done it ourselves. So far from our thinking that perhaps nothing can ever be found out by counting or adding, we realize not only that things can be so found out but also that among the things that can be thus found out are mistakes in counting and adding.

Compare with these human fallibilities the fallibility of a proof-reader. He has to find the misprints, if any, on a printed page, and his only way of finding them, if they are there, is by seeing them. Perhaps he signals three and misses two. One of the three that he signals is not a misprint but an alternative legitimate spelling. He is told this and takes care not to make that mistake again, though this does not rule out all possibility of his making it again. What of the two misprints that he does find and the one that he misses? The two that he finds are there, and he found them by seeing them. So it was some good using his eyes. The one that he missed was, perhaps, found by someone else who found it by using his eyes. So it was some good his using his eyes too. Moreover, the proof-corrector himself admits in retrospect that he had overlooked that misprint, namely the misprint that he now sees when it is pointed out to him.

Using one's eyes is the only way of finding misprints and proof-readers with good or normal eyesight, who have had plenty of practice and who employ the techniques of their craft, can be relied on to find out nearly, though not quite all the misprints that are there to be found. The chances of mistakes and oversights never dwindle to nil; but they can and often do dwindle to negligible dimensions. But the proof-reader's candid confession 'It is always possible that I have missed a misprint' does not amount to the lament 'It is possible that I always miss all misprints', or to the despairing suggestion that perhaps everything printed in every book is misprinted, though quite undiscoverably misprinted.

For future purposes we should notice that while sometimes a proof-reader fails to see a misprint until it is pointed out to him, when he sees it well enough, sometimes he cannot see it even when it is pointed out to him—and there are different sorts of obstacles which prevent him from doing so. He cannot see misprints when he has a cataract; when the light is bad; when the page is several feet from his eyes. But also he may be unable to see it because he is flustered or hurried; or because he has not learned the language or the orthography of the misprinted word; or because he was himself the author of the passage and therefore knows so well what should be on the page that, without taking special precautions, he does not see that what is printed on the page is not what he meant to have there; or else he is thinking too much about the topic dealt with in the passage to think enough about how it is printed. He will reproach himself for having been the victim of some of these liabilities, but for others, like his cataract or the bad illumination, he will express regret but not remorse. That is, some of the explanations that he will give for some of his mistakes and failures will be of the same sort as the explanations he would give for his mistakes and failures in counting or multiplying, but some will be of quite different sorts, like the explanations that he couches in the terms of elementary ophthalmology or optics.

But even when his mistakes and failures are to be explained in ophthalmological or optical terms, this fact does not by itself prove the disheartening general proposition that nobody's eyes are ever any good for anything, with its tacitly implied rider that no proof-readers can really find out for certain whether there are misprints on a page or not. The existence of disabilities is evidence against and not in favour of the non-existence of abilities.

It makes all the difference whether the imputation of general fraudulence to the senses is made to rest on the existence of disabilities, like colour-blindness, or on the existence of inefficiencies in the exercises of our abilities. We can fail to spot misprints, though we see them quite well when they are pointed out to us; but so we can fail to detect fallacies in arguments, though we recognize them when they are pointed out to us. We can mistake a shadow for a snake, a mirage for a puddle, or a swarm of bees for a trail of smoke; but so we can give 54 as the product of 8 and 7. We can, but we need not. We know how not to make such mistakes, or if we do not yet know, we can still learn. We make these mistakes, not because there is anything wrong with our eyes but because we are still ignorant, or we are impetuous or indolent or the victims of rigid habits. We do not use our eyes as well as we might or as well as some other people do. Lapses of this kind are of a piece with lapses in counting, calculating, translating and reasoning. The fact that we can and often do go astray does not prove that we are forced astray, or that we cannot keep straight. On the contrary, we reprobate going astray by contrast with keeping straight and we only establish that someone has gone astray by going straight ourselves. Only paths that can be kept can be strayed from.

But the argument for the general fraudulence of the senses hinges, very often, not on the quite general facts that we are not always careful or always well educated, but on the much more special facts that our eyes, ears and noses are themselves subject to chronic or occasional impairments. It is not for want of trying or for want of training that the colour-blind cannot distinguish colours which the rest of us can distinguish. The fact that dogs can smell smells and hear shrill whistles which are out of our range reveals limitations in our equipment, not in our efficiency in using it. There certainly are hosts of facts of this general kind, many well known to everybody, many known only to specialists. But in so far as they go to show that there is much that we are not equipped to perceive, they do not, as yet, go any way towards showing that there is nothing that we are equipped to perceive. There are many things that are too big and many that are too small for me to handle with my hands or to chew with my teeth, but it does not follow and it is not true that I cannot handle pens or chew biscuits. We have excellent reasons for thinking that dogs, bats and moths can detect things that men cannot detect; but these, by themselves, are no reasons for doubting whether men can detect anything at all. We can, in fact, see and hear, among other things, how dogs, bats and moths behave.

Before moving on from this line of disparagement of the senses to the next and much more important line, I want just to give a warning against taking too literally certain pervasive figures of speech. When we speak of our eyes deceiving us, or of the testimony of our noses being suspect, we are talking as if we and our eyes are two parties in a dispute, or as if our noses are in the witness-box while we ourselves are sitting down in the midst of our fellow jurymen. Harm need not come from employing these figures of speech, but it can do so. An athlete might picturesquely lament that his ankle had betrayed him or that his wrist had gone on strike; and if such modes of speech acquired a wide vogue, we might now and then fall into the trap of supposing that we and our limbs are related in the way in which employers are related to their employees. We might start to talk seriously of cricketers being well advised to dismiss their limbs and to try to get on without them.

The notion that our eyes, ears and noses are foreign correspondents who send us messages, which, on examination, turn out often and perhaps always to be fabrications, does enjoy a wide vogue. I think that I need not labour the point that, when taken seriously, it is an attempt to fit familiar generalities about perception, delusions, misestimates, deafness, etc., into an unsuitable conceptual harness, namely that of some political or social fabric, like that of a police-court or the head-office of a newspaper.

People make mistakes, are confused, fail to make things out, overlook things, and so on, in looking about them as they do in calculating, translating, demonstrating and playing games. But only misleadingly can these troubles be described as the outcomes of false or ambiguous messages from reporters. For reporters are themselves good or bad observers, and the critical or uncritical recipients of information from others. So to liken our eyes to reporters is simply to push back the question of the sources of error by one stage—as if there would be some advantage in getting the answer that they were sent false information by *their* eyes and ears or by *their* undisciplined imaginations.

D. W. HAMLYN

(b. 1924)

Since 1964, Hamlyn has been Professor of Philosophy at Birkbeck College, University of London. He was educated at Oxford, and has been editor of Mind *since 1972. His publications include* The Psychology of Perception *(1957),* Sensation and Perception *(1961), and* The Theory of Knowledge *(1970).*

IS SCEPTICISM ABOUT PERCEPTION POSSIBLE?

The question that I ask here is whether skepticism is a possible position at all when it becomes wholesale and universal. It is of course possible to be skeptical about particular claims to knowledge or even about whole provinces or fields of so-called knowledge, e.g., about astrology. Indeed, skepticism is right and proper over many claims to knowledge, for there will be reasons for doubt in the fields in question, and thus reasons for refusing to admit the claims to knowledge. Could there be similar reasons for doubt whether knowledge is possible at all? If not, the skeptic may be disarmed; for if he can have no reasons for his wholesale doubt, such doubts become empty and otiose. In such a situation we need pay no further attention to him, especially if there are prima facie reasons in favor of the position that we do have knowledge, sometimes, at any rate. . . . It may be noted now that to say that wholesale skepticism is empty and otiose is not to say that it is an impossible position in itself; it is merely to say that there are no grounds for its acceptance. The suggestions, already noted, that skepticism is an impossible position if wholesale, must have a different and firmer basis if they are to be valid.

There are two arguments that have been used recently that attempt to provide such a basis. There is in a way a certain affinity between these two arguments. They are, respectively, the argument from polar concepts, and the paradigm-case argument; they both depend on considerations about meaning The first argument turns on the fact that certain terms or concepts come in pairs such that a given member of any pair is somehow essentially contrasted with the other; indeed, it gets its sense by way of this contrast. These pairs are polar in this way. It was pointed out by Norman Malcolm that real/unreal, knowledge/belief, and many other examples are polar in this sense.[1] The sense in question has been discussed critically by Colin Grant.[2] It is sufficient to say here that in claiming that a pair of concepts is polar, it is maintained not only that there is an exclusion between instances of the concepts but also that one of the concepts can be understood only if the other is understood also. . . . A further point, which is not directly relevant perhaps to the present issue, is that it might be argued that one of the pair of polar concepts is in some way prior to the other, and it has been argued by J. L. Austin that in the case of "real" and "unreal" it is "unreal" that is really prior; as he puts it, it is "unreal" that wears the trousers[3]. This kind of point is relevant to the question where the onus of justification lies; it could thus be used to put the onus on the skeptic to prove his case rather than demanding that his opponents should prove theirs. But the central point of the argument from polar concepts is not this but the claim that if there are to be instances of one member of the polar pair there must be instances of the other. If there is to be mere supposition, there must also be knowledge; hence the skeptic cannot demolish knowledge in favor of mere supposition.

One of the best expositions of this argument is to be found in Gilbert Ryle's *Dilemmas*,[4] where Ryle uses it to argue against the supposition that all perception may be illusory or nonveridical. His argument in effect takes the form of a series of analogies to bring out the same point. He argues that there cannot be counterfeit coins unless there are genuine ones, and that ice could not be thin unless there were thick ice. Similarly, there could not be illusory perception if there were not veridical perception. Ryle's analogies are scarcely convincing in themselves. In the first place, "thick" and "thin" are relative notions. Of course, given knowledge of the range of thicknesses that ice can take, it is possible to say that a certain piece of ice is thick or thin by the standards of ice; and it may be argued that given this knowledge, and given that we wish to discriminate thicknesses of ice, we can infer that there must be pieces of ice of varying thicknesses that can be described as thick or thin. But the assumptions are necessary; for it might be that we had no interest in the varying thicknesses of ice, that we had no interest in speaking of "thick or

[1] N. Malcolm, "Moore and Ordinary Language" in *The Philosophy of G. E. Moore*, ed. P. Schilpp (Evanston, Illinois,1942), pp. 343ff.

[2] C. K. Grant, "Polar Concepts and Metaphysical Arguments," *Proc. Arist. Soc.* (1955-56), pp. 83ff.

[3] J. L. Austin, *Sense and Sensibilia* (Oxford, 1962),pp. 70-71.

[4] G. Ryle, *Dilemmas* (Cambridge, 1954), p.94.

thin by the standards of ice." In that case ice might be judged by other standards and thus might always be considered thin. There would then be no case whatever for saying that if ice is thin it must also be thick. It remains true, of course (and this is a point made by Grant), that the fact that we might not apply "thick" to ice has no implications for the question of whether it is possible to apply "thick" to other things. The point that does emerge is that if there is a thin *X* there need not be a thick *X* unless we mean "thin" or "thick" *by the standard of X's*. For example, are not razor blades always thin?

Ryle's other example is subject to similar objections. The supposition is that genuine coins must actually exist if there are to be counterfeit ones. But it seems conceivable that in a country where there were a large number of counterfeit coins the genuine ones might go out of circulation or be melted down, leaving only the counterfeit ones. Indeed, it is perhaps conceivable that there might not have been any genuine ones in the first place; the pattern for genuine coins might have been laid down but none minted, and from negligence or some other motive the authorities may never have taken steps to prevent circulation of the counterfeit coins. These were manufactured by forgers, anxious perhaps to obtain foreign currency. So there seems to be no necessity that genuine noncounterfeit coins should exist if there are to be counterfeit ones. On the other hand, the point about the pattern is important; in order to speak of counterfeit coins at all it must be possible to know what they are counterfeit of, what sort of thing would count as a genuine coin if there were any. In other words, it must be possible to know what it is for something to be a genuine coin if it is to make sense to speak of counterfeit coins. Not that one must actually know this. One must of course know it if one is to be *justified* in saying that any given coin is counterfeit; but its making sense to speak of counterfeit coins and our being justified in saying that any given coin is counterfeit are two quite different things. In sum, where two concepts, *A* and *B*, are polar, in order for it to make sense to speak of things being *A* it must make sense to speak of things being *B*; hence, if there are things that are *A*, it must make sense to speak of things being *B*; it must be *possible* for things to be *B*, whether or not there *are* any *B* things. Hence, if the skeptic casts doubt on our ordinary claims to knowledge, saying that they are only supposition, we can at least ask him what it is to know something. He can quite properly *claim* that there are no cases of knowledge, as long as he gives some sense to the concept of knowledge. Without this his claim is truly senseless, but nothing follows from this as to whether there are any actual cases of knowledge.

JUSTUS BUCHLER

(b. 1913)

Justus Buchler is presently Distinguished Professor of Philosophy at the State University of New York at Stony Brook. Previously, from 1959 to 1971, he had been Johnsonian Professor of Philosophy at Columbia University. He was educated at City College of New York and at Columbia, and is the author of a number of outstanding philosophical works, including Charles Peirce's Empiricism *(1939),* Toward a General Theory of Human Judgment *(1951),* Nature and Judgment *(1955),* The Concept of Method *(1961),* Metaphysics of Natural Complexes *(1966), and* The Main of Light *(1974).*

THREE MODES OF JUDGMENT

Man is unavoidably a taker of positions. And the way in which his positions are rendered discoverable is through his products, that is, his acts, his contrivances, and his verbal combinations. The product, being a product of the individual, actualizes a relation between the individual and some natural complex, but a relation consummated *by* him. It is an utterance or judgment. It defines a place where he stands. Collectively, a man's judgments constitute the record of all the places where he stands—meaning, all that he does, makes, and says. We must go on to ask in greater detail what it means to have an attitude or take a position; whether products are indeed the form taken by these positions; whether it is justifiable to regard products as judgments; what judgment is; and what the philosophic implications or advantages of this approach are. Since the answers to these questions are closely intertwined, we need not consider each in isolation from the rest.

Why does an individual do, make, or say anything? The impulse to answer, half-facetiously and half-evasively, that it all depends on who the individual is and what motivates him, is fair enough and does not suppress the universality of the conclusion at which we would arrive. To produce is to manifest the natural commitments of a self, and to apply in a fresh instance the cumulative resultant of these commitments. The man who takes a short cut on his walk home is *ipso facto* making a judg-

From Nature and Judgment *(New York: Columbia University Press, 1955), pp. 10–14, 20–31.*

ment, and a judgment of a rather complex sort, with respect to means that fulfill his habits, desires, or needs. He is devising or applying a technique that arises out of what he is and what he has been. To say that in taking the short cut he is making a judgment does not mean that he is asserting to himself what goals the action will accomplish. It is his action that is the judgment. He may, in addition to his action, represent the action verbally. But whether he does so or not, the action subserves the same function. It is as much an expression by him as the assertion. (We shall distinguish "expression 'by' " from "expression 'of.' ") It is of course customary, both popularly and philosophically, to apply the term "judgment" to the assertion. "He judged the shortest way home" is supposed to mean "He said to himself, this is the shortest way home." But to limit the usage is to limit the analysis. If the man walking home were completely preoccupied with other matters and took the shortest path automatically, this habitual action would still, fully as much as the verbal representation, embody a policy relating him to his environment and to his own past history, and characterize the existences among which he is located.

When a man carves in stone, determines his wardrobe, composes music, or arranges dinnerware on a table, when, in short, he makes, he is ordering materials in accordance with an established or an evolved disposition. He is judging a natural complex by contriving its structure or by modifying an existing structure within it. He is adopting one order and ignoring or discarding another. What he makes is one mode of defining where he stands and what he is in a given set of circumstances. He may, in addition, assert "this is good," "that belongs here," "those I like." The judgment consisting in the assertion may supplement, accompany, precede, or be fused with the judgment consisting in the contrivance. How a man orders materials, no less than what he describes them to be, reflects the direction of his self and defines the character of something in his world.

Every judgment is at the least a pronouncement on some phase of the individual's world. Painting pictures is a pronouncement on the characteristics of what is envisaged, and composing music is a pronouncement on the traits of sound-combinations. Cowering in fear is a pronouncement on the dangers of the immediate environment. Taking the shortest route epitomizes many facts and relations: the time it takes to get home, the allocation of personal energy, the properties of movement. Taking the shortest route not habitually but once, or for the first time, or whimsically, or at random, are all judgments but different ones, and, depending on the full circumstances of each, conceivably very different ones, differently defining properties of the individual's world. To call every judgment a pronouncement is not to imply that acting and making are alternative ways of asserting. Persistence in the narrow usage of "pronouncement" is as stultifying philosophically as persistence in the narrow usage of "judgment" itself. To pronounce is to apply an attitude or to bring a natural complex within the orbit of an attitude. The properties of things are defined by being brought into relation to us. We bring things into relation to us, we render them more determinate in a given respect, by doing something to them, *or* by making something out of them, or by saying something about them. We pronounce on an object when we eye it with interest, when we mold it into a round shape, or when we call it "red". The proverb that actions speak louder than words would be a tolerable recognition of the fact that other than verbal products are judgments or utterances, did it not suggest that an act is a covert form of speech. There are better bases of recognition in established usage. In one of his stories Hawthorne, referring to the look of weariness and scorn on a character's face, speaks of "the moral deformity of which it was the utterance." Yet even in the broader usage of "utterance" there remains the danger of narrow interpretation, as we must note presently.

Judgment is as much appraisal as it is pronouncement. To separate appraisal and pronouncement is impossible. In pronouncing upon traits we are appraising their status in relation to our traits. Every instance of making, saying, or doing rests on a tacit appraisal of some traits as relevant and some as irrelevant. To run from a situation is, indifferently, to pronounce it as dangerous or to appraise it as dangerous. To describe an object as red is, indifferently, to pronounce on the presence or absence of a given color, or to appraise a color as deserving or not deserving a given predicate. The ubiquity of appraisal is obscured by such distinctions as that between "prizing" and "appraising." Supposedly, prizing is a direct behavioral act; appraising, an "act that involves comparison." Appraisal is made out to be the intellectualized level of estimation. But "comparison," and therefore appraisal, is present on any level of estimation. Comparison can take the form either of deliberation and criticism on the one hand or of unmeditated discrimination on the other. Both are appraisive, the former through systematic production, the latter merely through production as such. Discrimination or selection from alternatives is present in the simplest products; it helps to explain the product as judgment. Like "appraisal," "discrimination" can be intellectualized to the exclusion of its essential meaning; it is so often made synonymous with "keen discrimination" or "wise discrimination" that the rudimentary factors in it are overlooked. Similarly, "indiscriminateness," which implies the absence of wisdom in discrimination, is made synonymous with the absence of the process itself. . . .

The three modes of human production, doing, making, and saying, are three modes of judgment which may be designated respectively as active, exhibitive, and assertive judgment. Each of these, neither more nor less than the other two, defines the traits of a natural complex in a given perspective. Each emerges from the intersection of various processes. One of these processes is an individual history, within which the judgment is an event, and from which it draws some of the materials and some of the nuances of its character. Another is the persistent impress of nature at large, which has placed the individual from the outset in a state of relative urgency, to be thenceforth mitigated by judgments.

A third is the process of social communication, which largely determines the external form of judgments, contributes to their matter, and transmits through its own media the specific influences of nature.

The most familiar guise of the assertion is of course the declarative sentence. Assertions usually occur in some form of symbolism which has syntactical structure. But it is an error to suppose that assertive judgment or either of the two other modes can be identified exclusively by a set of physical characters. "Saying" and "asserting" may suggest writing, talking, and images of words, very much as "courage" incurably suggests warfare. "Acting" and "doing" may suggest the image of a man in rapid motion or wrestling with levers. And "making" may suggest the image of a man kneading clay or fitting boards together. But an assertion may be made without using words at all, for instance, by the act of nodding in answer to a question. Nodding as such could be considered an active judgment which, in this context, also functions assertively. The ostensibly auxiliary function may be of greater importance in communication and experience than the act as such. In another context, nodding may be an act of lamentation, or a distracted utterance of grief; and in such cases the assertive function may be negligible or absent. A poem consists of words, but ordinarily it is an exhibitive judgment, primarily a shaping or molding. It may assume assertive import for one person or another. Its exhibitive function may be small in value and its status as an active judgment magnified—for example, if it stimulates patriotic sentiment or wins a prize or violates a statute on obscenity. An assertive judgment, for example a lecture, may be regarded as a work of art, and, in so far, exhibitively. So may an action, such as a dance. Doing, making, and saying, then, the three modes of judgment, are functional rather than structural distinctions, despite the fact that custom associates them respectively with movement, with sensuous or visible forms, and with the use of words.

The principal distinguishing mark of an assertive judgment is the applicability to it of the predicates "true" and "false," as well as those predicates commonly regarded as derivative from or dependent upon some epistemic state of a user, "probable," "likely," "doubtful." Conversely, when questions of truth or falsity or probability, or, in general, questions of evidential status, are asked about a product, that product is being used as an assertive judgment. Assertive judgment is distinguished also by the fact that it lends itself, with great elasticity, to socially accepted forms of ellipsis; most of the assertions made in everyday discourse are elliptical and even utterly disguised. In practice, assertive and nonassertive judgments are bound up all together in amorphous masses. Human communication, being fully as interrogative as it is contributive in character, often concerns itself with the resolution of the ellipses in assertions. "What do you mean?" is most often the demand for the formalization of an apparently indeterminate expression, expectantly assertive. It is the signal for the transformation of that product into a product conventionally tractable. By the layman it is applied to works of art as well as to assertions—to cases where translation may violate a product rather than resolve an assumed indeterminacy. And it is applied, with less incongruity but often with equal unreasonableness, to products of formal inquiry, such as scientific or philosophic works, which can translate within limits, and which can (always in the case of science, at least) translate assertively, but not necessarily into familiar modes of formulation. "Common-sensist" and positivist philosophers, who perforce are content not to lock horns with the procedures of science, apply their methodological naïveté to philosophic judgments, exorcising both individual expressions and entire conceptual structures which are not translated into assertions of preconceived types.

It is a temptation to say that assertive judgment is the mode of utterance by which men record their institutions, their situations, and the events of nature; that it is the unique instrument by which natural process is taken hold of or made, as we say, intelligible. We "record" in the sense that we appropriate something for possession, or preserve it in relatively unchanging form. But this is what we may be said to do also when we shape materials in a work of art. What we exhibit may be "representational" or it may not; and in either case, we preserve or record as well as array discovered or produced traits. Among all types of products, what seems intrinsically unfitted to be a vehicle of record is the act. And yet written history, the deliberative record of the past, or "artificial memory" as Santayana calls it, is a compound of action, contrivance, and formulation. It achieves possession by seeking and sifting remains and evoking testimony (all these through action), by ordering (exhibitively) what it has thus garnered, and by describing (asserting) what it has thus ordered.

An individual judges his world, and judges it exhibitively, whenever he rearranges materials within it into a constellation that is regarded or assimilated as such. This identification of the exhibitive judgment is not redundant. The rearrangement, the specifiability of materials, the constellation, and the emphasis on the constellation are distinguishable factors, all essential. For rearrangement, first of all, is insufficient. By an action which influences the lives of other persons, an individual may effect important rearrangements. His active judgment is potentially, but not through the action alone, also exhibitive. In thus effecting rearrangements, he is manipulating complexes in so far as they are existences rather than in so far as they are materials. In an exhibitive utterance we order or shape what are specifiable as materials; it is not enough, metaphorically, to "shape" the course of existence. Such materials include conventional or devised signs of all kinds. And the product of the rearrangement may be "sensuously" and "affectively" available or "intellectually" available. But the third of the essential factors is not yet necessarily implied. When metal tools (materials) are assembled (rearranged) for the purpose of opening a safe, we may not properly speak of an exhibitive judgment. The materials are not ordered into a constellation or structure, unless it be temporarily or instrumentally. But what, now, of a verbal assertion? May it not be said to be typically an ordering of materials (words) into a constellation, and is not the constellation essential in determining the import of the assertion? We require the fourth of the conditions for exhibitive judgment, that aspect of the ordering which most directly warrants the use of the term "exhibitive." To contrive a structure is to be concerned in some sense with its character or quality as a structure. This is not to say that such concern need be of lifelong duration; it may be fleeting. Nor is it to say that such concern or such involvement need be momentous; it may be casual. In every instance the pronouncement inherent in the product relates to ordered natural traits as traits, or to traits in just that order. The sentence, in so far as it functions no more than assertively, is a constellation of materials but is not emphasized or regarded primarily as such. Depending on the presence of this condition, the use of the voice in speech. of the body in motion, of words in written sequence, of bricks in building, is or is not exhibitive.

The process of shaping, in order to be exhibitive, need not be methodical and purposive—it need not be a process of query.* An ordered constellation may function as such habitually rather than by design. And it may function as such not only without the intent of its producer but without his knowledge. The exhibitive emphasis is not something with which an agent has to endow a judgment. The judgment needs no official sanction; it must *be* exhibitive; it must exhibit a structure. A blacksmith who forges iron hinges without a sense of their character is yet pronouncing exhibitively in so far as the product, qualitatively considered, reflects his established make-up (the revelatory aspect of the judgment) and his tacit appraisal of the potentialities in iron (the substantive aspect). Even within methodical utterance, exhibitive judgment may lurk unawares. The author of a system of philosophy may be keenly conscious of the assertive content of his product and oblivious of its exhibitive function. For the combination of symbols, besides having conceptual value, may be entertained and possessed as a sheer edifice of ideas, and as such alone may compel or fail to compel.

It follows from these considerations that works of art—using the phrase, as we consistently shall, without honorific intent, and applying it to all instances whatever of methodical contrivance—are a subclass of exhibitive judgments. They are exhibitive judgments engendered by query. Making is more pervasive than methodical making. Philosophically, to detect the universal traits in all making and to emphasize the differentia of art are equally fundamental.

All judgment to some extent de-temporalizes nature, holds it in suspense. For what it selects from a large, various network of processes it

---

*Query is judgment that is inventive and deliberate. It is the interrogative spirit at work. This spirit is what animates the judgments of both science and art. Thus, science (inquiry) is only one kind of query; art is another.

also isolates and detaches. This capture of traits from process is itself a process, the most elemental means by which permanencies become available. It is most obvious in exhibitive judgment and least obvious in active judgment. To make something is to concretize in a manner readily discernible by the stubborn bluntness of common sense. The product is "there," mysterious and opaque, perhaps, but indubitably wrought. Nor can its possibilities of new meaning alter its established identity. The sock darned remains the same sock. From natural process the assertive judgment extracts no such tangible entity. Yet it is similarly arrestive. It is in itself fixed testimony; once completed, it says what it originally said, and forever more. Its constituent elements may be differently construed by the generations, or even a moment after its utterance, and its possible ambiguities may never be wholly resolved. In each of its uses or contexts, however, even if by the power and grace of human convention, it is irrevocably affirmative and constant.

An action is the most difficult mode of judgment to regard intelligibly. Not that actions are rarely isolated in common estimation—they are isolated too often, so far as interpretation is concerned, and arbitrarily disconnected from both their lineage and their effects. Nor is the temporal character of action its unique attribute. Each instance of asserting and of making likewise transpires. What accounts for the dubious unity of an action is its apparent evanescence. Once done, it ceases to be present, unlike the exhibitive judgment; and unlike the assertive judgment, it cannot be called back into being together with its original context. Whereas ordinarily assertions and contrivances are directly possessible and usable, actions are not. The paradox of all this is that in the case of assertions and contrivances society has small capacity for classification, while action it readily fits into preordained categories. Despite the fact that actions need to be recovered, and that they are recoverable only through memory and testimony; despite the fact that direct perception of them requires the keenest interpretative power, completable only in retrospect, existing garb will always be stretched to fit them and they will turn out to be proper or criminal, generous or reprehensible, noble or evil, white or black, with crushing inevitability. Judgment in any mode is susceptible of further or secondary "judgment," formal appraisal, commonly (with virgin simplicity) true or false (assertive), good or bad (exhibitive), right or wrong (active). An active judgment may be identified by the fact that it is subject to the application of moral predicates.

Strictly, an active judgment has the same type of unitary integrity as the other two modes. Once identified, located, and interpreted, whether reasonably or not, it can repeatedly be characterized, repeatedly be influential in human affairs, and as often as not be reenacted or duplicated in essential semblance of its original occurrence. An act, through a continuous progeny of acts, can persist in as powerful a form as the documents or monuments that are among its instruments of perpetuation. Documents and monuments are themselves never self-articulative and are equally dependent, in the last analysis, on the prevailing resources of men. The assertion and the contrivance, however tenacious their physical embodiment, persist only so long as communicative standards provide for them. A pertinent specimen of active judgment is a dent in a piece of wood. Whether it be trivial or important depends on the kind of dent it is, what object is dented and where, who prizes the object, and why he prizes it. The dent persists in its size and place, it remains a dent, despite the remote termination of the original act, as long as the wood exists, or until it is eradicated by the effect of another and different act.

The modes of judgment are the forms in which men render their experience tractable and expose their natural circumstances. We are addicted to the view of the human product as expressing "thought," "imagination," or "emotion." The experience of man, sprung, as we shall put it, from a union of manipulation and assimilation, and consisting in the permutations of this union, is too continuous and deep-rooted to sustain such a view. It is not the will that is free, said Locke, it is the man. In parallel manner we may say that it is not the mind that judges, it is the man. To think, as philosophers chronically do, of assertion alone as "judgment" is to miss the fact that even assertion cannot be understood adequately if understood merely as the product of mind. An assertion has a natural history, and its symbols reflect in their import varied natural situations, including the circumstances of human community. True, the substantive assertion is not to be identified with its circumstances; but the circumstances determine what the substance will be, and the activity of thought is only one of these circumstances. Ideas and meanings are by and large the outcome of living rather than of pure psychic invention. Assertion is not a name for a sudden unaccountable appearance, in the world, of propositions in the abstract. It is juster to say that assertion makes nature at large available to mind than that assertion about nature arises from mind. But even what assertion makes available to mind it makes available not to mind alone. For truth, though articulated, as we may say, by mind, is assimilated by life; mind being precisely, as Aristotle taught, the capacity of life to articulate truth.

Each judgment is the individual's situational recognition of his universe, a universe highly reduced in scale and present in the form of complexes that are to some extent uncontrollable. The judgment reflects both the impact of this universe and the momentum of the self. Now part of this reflected universe is the society of individuals in which the processes of communication obtain. The modes of judgment are also modes of communication. We communicate by acting and by making no less than by stating. The communicative power of products may far surpass the communicative intent of their producers. Becoming communal possessions, they affect conduct and understanding, or in general the content of individual judgment in every mode and the idiosyncrasies of future communication. The communicative power of a product is in no way dependent on the mode of its production, nor on the merit or moral quality of its utterance. One act by a Hitler or a St. Francis of Assisi may have a more pervasive communicative effect than the entire outpouring of assertion by most other men. And on the other hand, a single assertive product by an Aristotle or a Luther, in its communicative force, pales the totality of most human action.

The fact that all three modes of judgment may be efficacious in communication follows in part (though only in part, for there are other considerations) from a philosophic truth suggested in modern philosophy by Berkeley and generalized by Peirce and Royce, namely, that anything whatever may function as a sign. Anything is subject to interpretation and is therefore a possible vehicle of communication. The materials of communication are not a special ontological class. All matter, Alfred Lloyd said, is a "medium of exchange." Judgments in any mode may consequently function as signs, even as facts and objects not emanating from a producer may. But methodologically, the role of judgments, in contrast to the role merely of signs as such, is of especial importance. By their utterances men do more than feed material to one another. They compel and modify belief, assent, conduct, taste, feeling, and understanding. They affect the norms and the qualities of communication besides adding to the data of communication. At bottom, of course, products are events, events produced. Produced events can soften, intensify, illuminate, or darken unproduced events. Unproduced events, on the other hand, can influence the status of produced events by affecting the character of human production. Produced events are preceded, succeeded, and overwhelmed in number, though not necessarily in moral significance, by unproduced events. Production is a process within "proception," that is, within the natural process of individuated movement that we more loosely call "experience."

23

Epilogue

DESCARTES, BERKELEY, AND JAMES

DESCARTES. Delightful club you have here!

BERKELEY. Most kind of you to say that, my dear fellow, but I'm afraid it's nowhere as entertaining as those royal courts you're used to. I say, look out the window there, down the street—isn't that young James?

DESCARTES. It could be, but then again, it could be my eyes are deceiving me, and it's only a robot wearing clothes.

BERKELEY. It could be—it *could* be—but what *is* it, man, who *is* it?

DESCARTES. My senses tell me there are patches of color, but my mind judges the patches, and decides it's James and not a robot.

BERKELEY. Fiddlesticks! On what basis does the mind make its judgment?

DESCARTES. Why, on the basis of reason!

BERKELEY. Reason, my foot. It's nothing but sense experience, sir, nothing but sense experience. Look now, he's crossing the square. And what say you to his distance from us? Can your reason tell you how far away he is?

DESCARTES. Nothing would be easier than to measure it. I estimate it would turn out to be 100 yards.

BERKELEY. I say, come now—do you mean to tell me that our reason teaches us spatial distances? But we have no experience of space itself! The patch of brown that is his coat is not itself seen as distant. When we are infants, my dear Descartes, colors appear to us as patches floating at the surface of our eyes, just as sounds appear to be floating all about our ears. It is only when the child must crawl towards or away from the colors or sounds that he learns what distance is—by associating his muscular and tactile sensations with his visual ones.

DESCARTES. Ah, you're too much! You don't really imagine, do you, that the *extendedness* of the world rests merely upon our experience of it? Let me assure you that, on the contrary, extension is an independent substance, just as the mind is an independent substance. I am quite certain that extension exists in and of itself, regardless of the manner of sensory experience by which we become aware of it.

BERKELEY. What is it you mean when you proclaim that everything in the world is extended?

DESCARTES. Why, simply that they're measurable.

BERKELEY. Quite. And so qualities discriminated by measuring operations are called by you—

DESCARTES. Primary qualities.

BERKELEY. While the remainder, proper only to the mind and not in things themselves—

DESCARTES. I call secondary qualities, by which I refer to colors, sounds, tastes, odors, and the like.

BERKELEY. A most mischievous distinction, a most deplorable, a most absurd distinction, if you'll forgive my saying so.

DESCARTES. Think nothing of it.

BERKELEY. What we should think nothing of are things alleged to exist unperceived. In what way can we tell a shape exists unless we perceive it? How measure it without observing it? The criterion of existence is not reason (what can reason tell us about existence?), but perception! Hence, for something to exist unperceived is a logical self-contradiction.

DESCARTES. Do you deny, then, that there is a reality outside the mind?

BERKELEY. Is the mind in space, that it has an inside and an outside? I assert merely that the notion of anything existing "outside the mind" is quite unintelligible.

DESCARTES. Then the world is in our minds?

BERKELEY. Our perceptions are in our minds, for indeed, where else could they be? And the world, being the sum of all perceptions, must be likewise in some mind.

DESCARTES. Things are not what is perceived, but the sources of what is perceived. Stub your toe on a rock, and the pain is in your mind, but the rock is still on the ground. Surely you wouldn't say, would you, that you'd stubbed your toe on a *painful rock*, which then communicated its pain to you? Surely you don't think the rock had been lying there suffering, then on contact infected you with its pain? Surely if you were to consume yonder bottle of sherry at a sitting, the resulting intoxication would be in *you*, in your mind, but I'm certain you wouldn't want to say that the sherry had been standing there *dead drunk* in its bottle all the time prior to your drinking it! No, sir, there are real physical things outside the mind, and they cause certain impressions to appear within the mind. Some, the primary qualities, correspond to physical things; others, the secondary qualities, don't.

BERKELEY. I've no problem with what you say regarding the rock and the sherry. All I contend is that, if the sweetness of the sugar cube is in our minds, so is the rectangularity of the cube. If the colors of the flag are in our minds, so are its contours, for the criterion of existence is perception in every case, not just in some cases and not in others. But hold—here comes James.

JAMES. One needn't believe in mind-reading to be able to guess what you two have been discussing: whether things exist independently of the mind, right?

DESCARTES. True enough. I take it you believe in neither mind nor matter? That's even worse than Berkeley here maintaining that there's no matter, just mind.

JAMES. It amazes me that people should think that subjects and objects presuppose two separable types of entities or substances, rather than merely two different aspects of the same experience. Don't you see that what we begin with is experience; it's what we reflect upon, what we inquire into, what we analyze. Upon subsequent reflection we often decide to make distinctions that would apply to the experience just had; thus we distinguish subject from object, or matter from mind. But it is quite illegitimate to take these distinctions made *subsequent* to experience, and read them back as metaphysical characteristics of a world *prior to* experience. To do so would involve, as one of my colleagues has recently pointed out, what is probably the most fundamental of philosophical errors.

BERKELEY. I agree with you that the pain that resulted from the stubbed toe can't be read back into the rock that caused the stubbed toe. Likewise, the sweetness that resulted from tasting the sugar can't be read back into the sugar cube prior to its being tasted.

JAMES. Therefore I'm only generalizing on *your* principle when I deny that matter and mind can be read back as the causes of (or substances causing) the experiences in which we discover them.

BERKELEY. I wish you'd try, if you can, to keep three things separate in your mind: my psychology, my theory of knowledge, and my metaphysics.

JAMES. I'm not at all sure where each ends and the others begin. But I'll be very candid with you. You've neither Locke's profound respect for fact, nor Hume's profound concern for method, but your *Treatise* will always have its devastating impact, so long as there are people who constantly take for granted what they cannot possibly have experienced.

THE WORLD AT LARGE

24

Introduction

Every branch of philosophy has had its ups and downs—periods in which it has flourished, and periods in which it has languished. What is more, the very nature of each such branch of philosophy has undergone significant alterations as times have changed.

Take metaphysics. At one time, in Aristotle's day, it meant the study of all that is, in an effort to determine what it is for anything and everything to be—simply *to be*. In the eighteenth century, the great metaphysical systems of the previous century were treated with systematic scepticism by Hume, who sought to devastate them by showing that all knowledge comes from experience,which Hume believed is made up wholly of sensory observations. Since metaphysical categories such as causality are unperceived, and seem to have no warrant in our direct sense experience, Hume argued, they are wholly expendable and should be discarded.

Hume thereby opened to Kant the opportunity to redefine metaphysics in a radically different fashion. If metaphysics could not reveal the fundamental forms or categories of Being—or all that is, then metaphysics could at least be utilized to identify the forms of understanding—the categories that the mind stamps on the sensations flowing into it, and in terms of which categories it necessarily understands all that is. So Kant redirects metaphysical inquiry to the nature of the mind rather than to the world at large. But at the same time that Kant declares the actual world "off limits" to metaphysical speculation, he insists that metaphysics can deal logically and analytically with the world as a sheer possibility. To a very great extent, the practice of metaphysics in the twentieth century is either under the influence of the classical conception of Aristotle, Spinoza, and Leibniz—speculations about the ultimate nature of things—or under the influence of Kant—speculation about the nature of the mind and the character of possible worlds.

But seldom today is the position taken that the metaphysician seeks to vie with the scientist by devising metaphysical alternatives to scientific explanations. It is rather more common to conclude that metaphysics seeks to construct frames of reference *within* which scientific concepts can be located and explained or interpreted, along with all other human endeavors in their natural settings. The hope of the metaphysician, it has been said, is that no experience, whether of the future or of the present or past, should fail to fit consistently within such metaphysical frames of reference.

Metaphysics thus goes beyond the bounds of particular cultural activities such as religion, science, or art—though such disciplines may well provide the metaphysician with some of his methodological and conceptual underpinnings. But religion, science, and art lack in turn a unitary and comprehensive context—an overarching theoretical firmament, as it were—and it is this that the metaphysician seeks to provide. From the moment one steps out of the particular disciplines, one treads upon metaphysical ground and discovers the metaphysical bearings of each and every concept within such disciplines. Thus, a person may hesitate before deciding whether the choice he has to make is more properly subsumed under the discipline of moral theory or that of political theory, yet the decision as to the proper discipline will be neither ethical nor social, but metaphysical in character. To be metaphysical is thus to be lifted above the specific to the more comprehensive, with the result that, in the realm of ideas, the standpoint of metaphysics is the standpoint of our major intellectual freedom.

The forward thrust of metaphysics can in effect be construed as a kind of philosophical outreach. But this gives us no hint of its proper subject-matter: what is it *about*? Certainly there are the great metaphysical issues, such as, Is everything determined, or do some things happen by chance? Do all things change, or do they remain fundamentally the same? Are there appearances distinct from reality? Is nature constructed in levels, so that some things are intrinsically more basic than others? Is everything in nature made of some one stuff—like matter, or mind, or both of these, or neither? And speaking of mind, what is it? What is life? What is man? Indeed, a complete inventory of the subject-matters of metaphysics would include the most pervasive, perennial, and haunting questions that have arisen in the course of human history—such as of personal identity and death, of causality and immortality, of finitude versus infinitude, of human origins and human destiny.

If inference is a matter of going beyond what is given, then metaphysics would seem to be systematic inference that inquires into the most inclusive setting of what has been thus far encountered. Suppose it is asserted that what has been given, in a particular instance, is a particular sensation—an ache, a patch of green, a taste of coffee. But sensations do not occur in a void. The ache is to be located in bodily experience. The green is the green of a leaf, and a leaf comes from a particular tree. But the leaf is seen in the light of one's knowledge of other greens, other leaves, other trees—and perhaps even with a knowledge of botany and chemistry and agriculture. Hence, the green one observes is riddled through with inference and theory. Every perception must, moreover, be considered against a background of other experiences; experience is the ground or setting of every awareness. What then is the framework of things that makes experience itself possible? The universe, we are told. And suppose we ask the context of the universe? Some will say it has none. Others will give such answers as Nature or God, in terms of which our experience and the universe both would make some sense rather than be absurd. But always metaphysics would seem to be a going beyond—a search for some context or perspective in terms of which to understand what is given.

While some contemporary metaphysicians see metaphysics as a broadened form of description, and others see it as the analysis of the methods of such description, one could as well claim it to be existential interpretation. In this latter sense, metaphysical interpretations would be justified not by correspondence with facts, but by the effectiveness with which such interpretations help us make sense of our circumstances. Such concepts as *nature, existence, reality,* and *being*, since they are among the broadest and most comprehensive of our metaphysical notions, afford us some of our most far-reaching perspectives. In any case, wherever comprehensive and systematic interpretations of human experience and its various settings are to be found, there is metaphysics.

The conflict between science and religion can be overcome, Spinoza suggests, by recognizing that the terms by which God has traditionally been characterized (e.g., "one," "almighty," "infinite," "perfect," etc.) are precisely applicable to Nature itself, and to nothing else. Thus there is simply one being who happens to have the names "God" and "Nature," just as the same person may be variously known—by a last name, a first name, or even a nickname. To deny the existence of Nature or God would be to deny our own existence, which would be absurd, for we ourselves are parts of Nature. Since Nature is infinite in all respects, there cannot be another such Being, since this would limit Nature's infinitude. Nor can Nature change, since it is already infinite and perfect: any alteration would have to be for the worse. Thus, Nature is completely determined, in the sense that everything that happens in it, whether physical or mental, happens necessarily and inevitably. (The order in which things happen is both causal and logical.) While Nature or God may be incompletely understood by grasping its structure through the formulation of scientific laws, to know God fully requires a transcendent, panoramic insight that comprehends everything "under the aspect of eternity." Thus, Spinoza presents us with a vision of Nature as divine yet intelligible, as determined yet free of all outside coercion, and in its majestic infinitude a model of power and productivity that men can rightly endeavor to emulate.

Although Locke devised no metaphysical system in the sense that Spinoza and Leibniz did, his theory of knowledge touched upon many issues of a metaphysical character. His views provoked Leibniz to a lengthy reply, and the discussion contained in this volume includes selections from Locke's treatment of the notion of identity, together with certain of Leibniz's remarks upon Locke's presentation.

It may be noted that Locke is generally considered one of the major architects of empiricism. His *Essay* embodies the view that knowledge is restricted to ideas, which are themselves the products of experience. Experience is in turn of two forms—sensation and reflection. No ideas are to be found in the mind at birth. Knowledge then becomes the awareness of the structure of thought that is formed when our ideas are consistently connected with one another. With regard to identity, Locke holds that only one object can occupy a given space at a given time. Thus, different objects cannot take up the same space, nor can the same object be in different places at the same time. Each point of space is necessarily and irreducibly unique. The identity of the same man consists in a participation in the same organized living body by constantly changing particles of matter. But personal identity goes further: it involves a self. That is, it involves the consciousness of one's own perceptions, and is made possible by memory—by the consciousness that one's past actions or thoughts are those of the same rational being as one's present actions or thoughts.

Leibniz is concerned to distinguish himself both from Spinoza and from Locke. Unlike Spinoza, for whom Nature is devoid of purpose, Leibniz accepts the traditional notion of a supernatural creator of nature, a God whose purposes are those that the universe has been set in motion to realize. Nature is nevertheless a completely determinate mechanism, whose internal workings are of incredible complexity, for each of its basic units is to some degree alive, and is itself a microcosmic reproduction of the universe at large. Moreover, the relationships among the infinitely numerous entities that make up the world are not causal, since each is an independent version of the one universe at large, although synchronized by God to operate in an orchestrated fashion with all the others. But Leibniz rejects Locke's contention that personal identity must rest upon the individual's awareness of his own perceptions, since this would make individuality a subjective rather than objective matter. Nor can personal identity be simply a difference of spatial or temporal location. Instead, Leibniz argues that each unit of living force (monad) contains within itself a representation of the universe, but a representation slightly different from all others, for it represents the universe as perceived from the monad's unique and distinctive standpoint. Hence, although there is only one universe, no two individuals are alike, and individuality is both real and objective.

The introductory article by Glossop is a succinct account of some of the perennial themes and questions that metaphysics involves, as well as an able interpretation of the problem of cosmic purpose. On both counts it clears the ground for the essays that follow.

Bergson's case against determinism borrows from Hobbes' notion of freedom as "absence of restraint." For Bergson analogously defines possibility as "absence of hindrance," and proceeds to argue that possibilities cannot be ghostly copies, stored up in advance, of what may yet be. The future is not packed into the past and present, in the form of possibilities waiting to be unpacked and actualized. The future is rather,

Bergson argues, constantly novel and unprecedented, always to some degree unpredictable. Therefore, just as it would be meaningless to say of an as yet unpainted painting that it is possible (since it is the very painting of it that makes it possible), so what will happen in a constantly creative or innovative universe will involve the simultaneous invention of the possibility of that happening. Partially in answer to Bergson, Goodman argues that the foregoing argument assumes that our knowledge must be a picture of the world, and that our knowledge of particular possibilities must consist of advance images of those possibilities. But such assumptions are unwarranted, he maintains. The logical characteristics (such as simplicity and coherence) of our descriptions need in no way be copies of similar logical traits in the world itself. It is not that we cannot say what the world really is, but that every true way of characterizing the world captures *a* way the world is. Hence the world is all the ways it is truly formulated to be.

The Grünbaum essay is an assemblage of arguments in favor of determinism and refutations of attacks on determinism. While breaking little fresh ground, it usefully marshalls reasons to show why determinism should not be identified with either fatalism or compulsion. Thus Grünbaum contends that a person under duress may yet be said to be acting responsibly if he chooses his conduct so as to take into account the coercive conditions that surround him. To Melden, such a view can hardly be considered acceptable, insofar as it reduces human actions to physically caused events. Instead, Melden insists that a more careful analysis of the factual nature of a moral situation (typical of those cases in which determinists are said to deny human freedom) would show that it consists in part of intangibles that nevertheless essentially characterize what happens in that situation. A businessman's decision, for example, is made on the basis of economic considerations in the world of finance, amidst transactions that are essentially social and symbolic rather than physical. Only an enormously sensitive comprehension of such non-physical (and to Melden, non-deterministic) facts can lead us to an accurate understanding of human action, and to a recognition of its freedom.

The final essays in this section deal with various aspects of the mystery of things, and the perplexity it evokes in us. Nagel, recognizing the absurdity of countless life situations, nevertheless counsels us that the sense of absurdity puts us in touch with an authentic aspect of reality. Besides, he concludes, if it's a fact that nothing matters, then that fact doesn't matter either. The Lipman essay seeks to put in question some of the assumptions casually made about human experience, such as that human beings are naturally productive, originative, inquisitive, and so on. Instead, it is argued, such behavior is frequently a response to situations in which people find themselves—situations that extract conduct from them, that demand answers, that compel inferences, wrench works of art from them, and so on. Both Nagel and Lipman can therefore be seen as stressing the interplay between mystery and intelligibility that characterizes the relationship between the human creature and the world in which that creature lives.

25

Intelligibility in Nature

BENEDICT SPINOZA

(1632–1677)

Benedict Spinoza, a Jewish-Dutch philosopher, was a leading representative of seventeenth-century thought. In his early years, Spinoza mixed religious studies with an interest in optics, Descartes, and a rationalistic approach to religion, with the result that, at the age of twenty-four, he was excommunicated from the Amsterdam Synagogue. His essay, "On the Improvement of the Understanding," was written in 1660, and in 1670 he published his Tractatus Theologica politicus *anonymously. His* Ethic *(posthumously published in 1677) is a masterly metaphysical system that represents the major achievement of his lifetime. Four years before his death, he was offered a professorship of philosophy at Heidelberg, but refused it. He did not live to complete the popular exposition of his political views, which would evidently have represented one of the first modern philosophical defenses of democracy.*

NATURE DIVINE

DEFINITIONS

I. By cause of itself, I understand that, whose essence involves existence; or that, whose nature cannot be conceived unless existing.

II. That thing is called finite in its own kind (*in suo genere*) which can be limited by another thing of the same nature. For example, a body is called finite, because we always conceive another which is greater. So a thought is limited by another thought; but a body is not limited by a thought, nor a thought by a body.

III. By substance, I understand that which is in itself and is conceived through itself; in other words, that, the conception of which does not need the conception of another thing from which it must be formed.

IV. By attribute, I understand that which the intellect perceives of substance, as if constituting its essence.

V. By mode, I understand the affections of substance, or that which is in another thing through which also it is conceived.

VI. By God, I understand Being absolutely infinite, that is to say, substance consisting of infinite attributes, each one of which expresses eternal and infinite essence.

Explanation.—I say absolutely infinite but not infinite in its own kind; for of whatever is infinite only in its own kind, we can deny infinite attributes; but to the essence of that which is absolutely infinite pertains whatever expresses essence and involves no negation.

VII. That thing is called free which exists from the necessity of its own nature alone, and is determined to action by itself alone. That thing, on the other hand, is called necessary, or rather compelled, which by another is determined to existence and action in a fixed and prescribed manner.

VIII. By eternity, I understand existence itself, so far as it is conceived necessarily to follow from the definition alone of the eternal thing.

Explanation.—For such existence, like the essence of the thing, is conceived as an eternal truth. It cannot therefore be explained by duration or time, even if the duration be conceived without beginning or end.

Every substance is necessarily infinite.

Those who judge things confusedly erroneously ascribe to substances a beginning like that which they see belongs to natural things; for those who are ignorant of the true causes of things confound everything, and without any mental repugnance represent trees speaking like men, or imagine that men are made out of stones as well as begotten from seed, and that all forms can be changed the one into the other. So also those who confound human nature with the divine, readily attribute to God human affects, especially so long as they are ignorant of the manner in which affects are produced in the mind. But if men would attend to the nature of substance, . . . this proposition would be considered by all to be axiomatic, and reckoned amongst common notions. For by "substance" would be understood that which is in itself and is conceived through itself, or, in other words, that, the knowledge of which does not need the knowledge of another thing. But by "modifications" would be understood those things which are in another thing—those things, the conception of which is formed from the conception of the thing in which they are. Hence we can have true ideas of non-existent modifications, since although they may not actually exist outside the intellect, their essence nevertheless is so comprehended in something else, that they may be conceived through it. But the truth of substances is not outside the intellect unless in the substances themselves, because they are conceived through themselves. If any one, therefore, were to say that he possessed a clear and distinct, that is to say, a true idea of substance, and that he nevertheless doubted whether such a substance exists, he would forsooth be in the same position as if he were to say that he had a true idea and nevertheless doubted whether or not it was false.

God, or substance consisting of infinite attributes, each one of which expresses eternal and infinite essence, necessarily exists.

Inability to exist is impotence, and, on the other hand, ability to exist is power, as is self-evident. If, therefore, there is nothing which necessarily exists excepting things finite, it follows that things finite are more powerful than the absolutely infinite Being, and this (as is self-evident) is absurd; therefore either nothing exists or Being absolutely infinite also necessarily exists. But we ourselves exist, either in ourselves or in something else which necessarily exists. Therefore the Being absolutely infinite, that is to say, God necessarily exists.

Whatever is, is in God, and nothing can either be or be conceived without God.

There are those who imagine God to be like a man, composed of body and soul and subject to passions; but it is clear enough from what has already been demonstrated how far off men who believe this are from the true knowledge of God. But these I dismiss, for all men who have in any way looked into the divine nature deny that God is corporeal. That He cannot be so they conclusively prove by showing that by "body" we understand a certain quantity possessing length, breadth, and depth, limited by some fixed form; and that to attribute these to God, a being absolutely infinite, is the greatest absurdity. But yet at the same time, from other arguments by which they endeavour to confirm their proof, they clearly show that they remove altogether from the divine nature substance itself corporeal or extended, affirming that it was created by God. By what divine power, however, it could have been created they are altogether ignorant, so that it is clear they do not understand what they themselves say. But I have demonstrated, at least in my own opinion, with sufficient clearness, that no substance can be produced or created by another being. Moreover, we have shown that besides God no substance can be nor can be conceived; and hence we have concluded that extended substance is one of the infinite attributes of God. . . . All things, I say, are in God, and everything which takes place takes place by the laws alone of the infinite nature of God, and follows (as I shall presently show) from the necessity of His essence. Therefore in no way whatever can it be asserted that God suffers from anything, or that substance extended, even if it be supposed divisible, is unworthy of the divine nature, provided only it be allowed that it is eternal and infinite.

God acts from the laws of His own nature only, and is compelled by no one.

There are some who think that God is a free cause because He can, as they think, bring about that those things which we have said follow from His nature—that is to say, those things which are in His power—should not be, or should not be produced by Him. But this is simply saying that God could bring about that it should not follow from the nature of a triangle that its three angles should be equal to two right angles, or that from a given cause an effect should not follow, which is absurd. But I shall show farther on, without the help of this proposition, that neither intellect nor will pertain to the nature of God.

I know, indeed, that there are many who think themselves able to demonstrate that intellect of the highest order and freedom of will both pertain to the nature of God, for they say that they know nothing more perfect which they can attribute to Him than that which is the chief perfection in ourselves. But although they conceive God as actually possessing the highest intellect, they nevertheless do not believe that He can bring about that all those things should exist which are actually in His intellect, for they think that by such a supposition they would destroy His power. If He had created, they say, all things which are in His intellect, He could have created nothing more, and this, they believe, does not accord with God's omnipotence; so then they prefer to consider God as indifferent to all things, and creating nothing excepting that which He has decreed to create by a certain absolute will. But I think that I have shown with sufficient clearness that from the supreme power of God, or from His infinite nature, infinite things in infinite ways, that is to say, all things, have necessarily flowed, or continually follow by the same necessity, in the same way as it follows from the nature of a triangle, from eternity and to eternity, that its three angles are equal to two right angles. The omnipotence of God has therefore been actual from eternity, and in the same actuality will remain to eternity. In this way the omnipotence of God, in my opinion, is far more firmly established. Moreover—to say a word, too, here about the intellect and will which we commonly attribute to God—if intellect and will pertain to His eternal essence, these attributes cannot be understood in the sense in which men generally use them, for the intellect and will which could constitute His essence would have to differ entirely from our intellect and will, and could resemble ours in nothing except in name. There could be no further likeness than that between the celestial constellation of the Dog and the animal which barks. This I will demonstrate as follows. If intellect pertains to the divine nature, it cannot, like our intellect, follow the things which are its object (as many suppose), nor can it be simultaneous in its nature with them, since God is prior to all things in causality; but, on the contrary, the truth and formal essence of things is what it is, because as such it exists objectively in God's intellect. Therefore the intellect of God, in so far as it is conceived to constitute His essence, is in truth the cause of things, both of their essence and of their existence—a truth which seems to have been understood by those who have maintained that God's intellect, will, and power are one and the same thing. Since, therefore, God's intellect is the sole cause of things, both of their essence and of their existence (as we have already shown), it must necessarily differ from them with regard both to its essence and existence; for an effect differs from its cause precisely in that which it has from its cause. For example, one man is the cause of the existence but not of the essence of another, for the essence is an eternal truth; and therefore with regard to essence the two men may exactly resemble one another, but with regard to existence they must differ. Consequently if the existence of one should perish, that of the other will not therefore perish; but if the essence of one could be destroyed and become false, the essence of the other would be likewise destroyed. Therefore a thing which is the cause both of the essence and of the existence of any effect must differ from that effect both with regard to its essence and with regard to its existence. But the intellect of God is the cause both of the essence and existence of our intellect; therefore the intellect of God, so far as it is conceived to constitute the divine essence, differs from our intellect both with regard to its essence and its existence, nor can it coincide with our intellect in anything except the name.

In nature there is nothing contingent, but all things are determined from the necessity of the divine nature to exist and act in a certain manner.

Before I go any farther, I wish here to explain, or rather to recall to recollection, what we mean by *natura naturans* and what by *natura naturata*. For, from what has gone before, I think it is plain that by *natura naturans* we are to understand that which is in itself and is conceived through itself, or those attributes of substance which express eternal and infinite essence, that is to say, God in so far as He is considered as a free cause. But by *natura naturata* I understand everything which follows from the necessity of the nature of God, or of any one of God's attributes, that is to say, all the modes of God's attributes in so far as they are considered as things which are in God, and which without God can neither be nor can be conceived.

Things could have been produced by God in no other manner and in no other order than that in which they have been produced.

I wish now to explain in a few words what is to be understood by *contingent*, but firstly, what is to be understood by *necessary* and *impossible*. A thing is called necessary either in reference to its essence or its cause. For the existence of a thing necessarily follows either from the essence and definition of the thing itself, or from a given efficient cause. In the same way a thing is said to be impossible either because the essence of the thing itself or its definition involves a contradiction, or because no external cause exists determinate to the production of such a thing. But a thing cannot be called contingent unless with reference to a deficiency in our knowledge. For if we do not know that the essence of a thing involves a contradiction, or if we actually know that it involves no contradiction, and nevertheless we can affirm nothing with certainty about its existence because the order of causes is concealed from us, that thing can never appear to us either as necessary or impossible, and therefore we call it either contingent or possible.

From what has gone before it clearly follows that things have been produced by God in the highest degree of perfection, since they have necessarily followed from the existence of a most perfect nature. Nor does this doctrine accuse God of any imperfection, but, on the contrary, His perfection has compelled us to affirm it. Indeed, from its contrary would clearly follow, as I have shown above, that God is not absolutely perfect, since, if things had been produced in any other fashion, another nature would have had to be assigned to Him, different from that which the consideration of the most perfect Being compels us to assign to Him. . . . Since in eternity there is no *when* nor *before* nor *after*, it follows from the perfection of God alone that He neither can decree nor could ever have decreed anything else than that which He has decreed; that is to say, God has not existed before His decrees, and can never exist without them. . . .

4. Of Human Bondage, Preface

The impotence of man to govern or restrain the affects I call bondage, for a man who is under their control is not his own master, but is mastered by fortune, in whose power he is, so that he is often forced to follow the worse, although he sees the better before him. I propose in this part to demonstrate why this is, and also to show what of good and evil the affects possess. But before I begin I should like to say a few words about perfection and imperfection, and about good and evil. If a man has proposed to do a thing and has accomplished it, he calls it perfect, and not only he, but every one else who has really known or has believed that he has known the mind and intention of the author of that work will call it perfect too. For example, having seen some work (which

I suppose to be as yet not finished), if we know that the intention of the author of that work is to build a house, we shall call the house imperfect, while, on the other hand, we shall call it perfect as soon as we see the work has been brought to the end which the author had determined for it. But if we see any work such as we have never seen before, and if we do not know the mind of the workman, we shall then not be able to say whether the work is perfect or imperfect. This seems to have been the first signification of these words; but afterwards men began to form universal ideas, to think out for themselves types of houses, buildings, castles, and to prefer some types of things to others; and so it happened that each person called a thing perfect which seemed to agree with the universal idea which he had formed of that thing, and, on the other hand, he called a thing imperfect which seemed to agree less with his typal conception, although, according to the intention of the workman, it had been entirely completed. This appears to be the only reason why the words *perfect* and *imperfect* are commonly applied to the natural objects which are not made with human hands; for men are in the habit of forming, both of natural as well as of artificial objects, universal ideas which they regard as types of things, and which they think nature has in view, setting them before herself as types too; it being the common opinion that she does nothing except for the sake of some end. When, therefore, men see something done by nature which does not altogether answer that typal conception which they have of the thing, they think that nature herself has failed or committed an error, and that she has left the thing imperfect. Thus we see that the custom of applying the words *perfect* and *imperfect* to natural objects has arisen rather from prejudice than from true knowledge of them. For we have shown in the Appendix to the First Part of this work that nature does nothing for the sake of an end, for that eternal and infinite Being whom we call God or Nature acts by the same necessity by which He exists; for we have shown that He acts by the same necessity of nature as that by which He exists. The reason or cause, therefore, why God or nature acts and the reason why He exists are one and the same. Since, therefore, He exists for no end, He acts for no end; and since He has no principle or end of existence, He has no principle or end of action. A final cause, as it is called, is nothing, therefore, but human desire, in so far as this is considered as the principle or primary cause of anything. For example, when we say that the having a house to live in was the final cause of this or that house, we merely mean that a man, because he imagined the advantages of a domestic life, desired to build a house. Therefore, having a house to live in, in so far as it is considered as a final cause, is merely this particular desire, which is really an efficient cause, and is considered as primary, because men are usually ignorant of the causes of their desires; for, as I have often said, we are conscious of our actions and desires, but ignorant of the causes by which we are determined to desire anything. As for the vulgar opinion that nature sometimes fails or commits an error, or produces imperfect things, I class it amongst those fictions mentioned in the Appendix to the First Part.

JOHN LOCKE

(1632–1704)

One of the founders of political liberalism, as well as of English empiricism, Locke was educated at Oxford, and later became a physician. In the politically troubled 1670's and 1680's, he spent a number of years on the Continent, particularly in Amsterdam. His Treatises on Government *are variously interpreted as replies to the theory of divine right, and as defenses of the Glorious Revolution of 1688. In 1690 his* Essay Concerning Human Understanding *appeared and while largely indebted to Descartes, is nonetheless conspicuous for its denial of innate ideas, its insistence that all knowledge is ultimately derived from sense-perception, and its general tone of reasonableness, probity, and respect for the richness and variety of human experience. He is also known for his* Letters on Toleration *(1689, 1690, 1692) and his* Thoughts on Education *(1693).*

THE SENSE OF IDENTITY

1. *Wherein Identity consists.*—Another occasion the mind often takes of comparing, is the very being of things; when, considering anything as existing at any determined time and place, we compare it with itself existing at another time, and thereon form the ideas of identity and diversity. When we see anything to be in any place in any instant of time, we are sure (be it what it will) that it is that very thing, and not another, which at that same time exists in another place, how like and undistinguishable soever it may be in all other respects: and in this consists identity, when the ideas it is attributed to vary not at all from what they were that moment wherein we consider their former existence, and to which we compare the present. For we never finding, nor conceiving it possible, that two things of the same kind should exist in the same place at the same time, we rightly conclude, that, whatever exists anywhere at any time, excludes all of the same kind, and is there itself alone. When therefore we demand whether anything be the same or no, it refers always to something that existed such a time in such a place, which it was certain at that instant was the same with itself, and no other. From whence it follows, that one thing cannot have two beginnings of existence, nor two things one beginning; it being impossible for two things of the same kind to be or exist in the same instant, in the very same place, or one and the same thing in different places. That, therefore, that had one beginning, is the same thing; and that which had a different beginning in time and place from that, is not the same, but diverse. That which has made the difficulty about this relation has been the little care and attention used in having precise notions of the things to which it is attributed.

2. *Identity of Substances.*—We have the ideas but of three sorts of substances: 1. God. 2. Finite intelligences. 3. Bodies. First, God is without beginning, eternal, unalterable, and everywhere; and therefore concerning his identity there can be no doubt. Secondly, Finite spirits having had each its determinate time and place of beginning to exist, the relation to that time and place will always determine to each of them its identity, as long as it exists. Thirdly, The same will hold of every particle of matter, to which no addition or subtraction of matter being made, it is the same. For, though these three sorts of substances, as we term them, do not exclude one another out of the same place, yet we cannot conceive but that they must necessarily each of them exclude any of the same kind out of the same place; or else the notions and names of identity and diversity would be in vain, and there could be no such distinctions of substances, or anything else one from another. For example: could two bodies be in the same place at the same time, then those two parcels of matter must be

From Essay Concerning Human Understanding, *Ch. 27.*

one and the same, take them great or little; nay, all bodies must be one and the same. For, by the same reason that two particles of matter may be in one place, all bodies may be in one place; which, when it can be supposed, takes away the distinction of identity and diversity of one and more, and renders it ridiculous. But it being a contradiction that two or more should be one, identity and diversity are relations and ways of comparing well founded, and of use to the understanding.

Identity of Modes.—All other things being but modes or relations ultimately terminated in substances, the identity and diversity of each particular existence of them too will be by the same way determined: only as to things whose existence is in succession, such as are the actions of finite beings, v. g., motion and thought, both which consist in a continued train of succession: concerning their diversity there can be no question; because each perishing the moment it begins, they cannot exist in different times, or in different places, as permanent beings can at different times exist in distant places; and therefore no motion or thought, considered as at different times, can be the same, each part thereof having a different beginning of existence.

3. *Principium Individuationis.*—From what has been said, it is easy to discover what is so much inquired after, the principium individuationis; and that, it is plain, is existence itself, which determines a being of any sort to a particular time and place, incommunicable to two beings of the same kind. This, though it seems easier to conceive in simple substances or modes, yet, when reflected on, is not more difficult in compound ones, if care be taken to what it is applied: v. g., let us suppose an atom, i.e., a continued body under one immutable superfices, existing in a determined time and place; it is evident, that, considered in any instant of its existence, it is in that instant the same with itself. For, being at that instant what it is, and nothing else, it is the same, and so must continue as long as its existence is continued; for so long it will be the same, and no other. In like manner, if two or more atoms be joined together into the same mass, every one of those atoms will be the same, by the foregoing rule: and whilst they exist united together, the mass, consisting of the same atoms, must be the same mass, or the same body, let the parts be ever so differently jumbled. But if one of these atoms be taken away, or one new one added, it is no longer the same mass or the same body. In the state of living creatures, their identity depends not on a mass of the same particles, but on something else. For in them the variation of great parcels of matter alters not the identity: an oak growing from a plant to a great tree, and then lopped, is still the same oak; and a colt grown up to a horse, sometimes fat, sometimes lean, is all the while the same horse: though, in both these cases, there may be a manifest change of the parts; so that truly they are not either of them the same masses of matter, though they be truly one of them the same oak, and the other the same horse. The reason whereof is, that, in these two cases, a mass of matter, and a living body, identity is not applied to the same thing. . . .

6. *The Identity of Man.*—This also shows wherein the identity of the same man consists; viz., in nothing but a participation of the same continued life, by constantly fleeting particles of matter, in succession vitally united to the same organized body. He that shall place the identity of man in anything else, but like that of other animals, in one fitly organized body, taken in any one instant, and from thence continued, under one organization of life, in several successively fleeting particles of matter united to it, will find it hard to make an embryo, one of years, mad and sober, the same man, by any supposition, that will not make it possible for Seth, Ismael, Socrates, Pilate, St. Austin, and Cæsar Borgia, to be the same man. For, if the identity of soul alone makes the same man, and there be nothing in the nature of matter why the same individual spirit may not be united to different bodies, it will be possible that those men living in distant ages, and of different tempers, may have been the same man: which way of speaking must be, from a very strange use of the word man, applied to an idea, out of which body and shape are excluded. And that way of speaking would agree yet worse with the notions of those philosophers who allow of transmigration, and are of opinion that the souls of men may, for their miscarriages, be detruded into the bodies of beasts, as fit habitations, with organs suited to the satisfaction of their brutal inclinations. But yet I think nobody, could he be sure that the soul of Heliogabalus were in one of his hogs, would yet say that hog were a man or Heliogabalus.

7. *Identity suited to the Idea.*—It is not therefore unity of substance that comprehends all sorts of identity, or will determine it in every case; but to conceive and judge of it aright, we must consider what idea the word it is applied to stands for: it being one thing to be the same substance, another the same man, and a third the same person, if person, man, and substance, are three names standing for three different ideas; for such as is the idea belonging to that name, such must be the identity; which, if it had been a little more carefully attended to, would possibly have prevented a great deal of that confusion which often occurs about this matter, with no small seeming difficulties, especially concerning personal identity, which therefore we shall in the next place a little consider.

8. *Same Man.*—An animal is a living organized body; and consequently the same animal, as we have observed, is the same continued life communicated to different particles of matter, as they happen successively to be united to that organized living body. And whatever is talked of other definitions, ingenious observation puts it past doubt, that the idea in our minds, of which the sound man in our mouths is the sign, is nothing else but of an animal of such a certain form: since I think I may be confident, that, whoever should see a creature of his own shape or make, though it had no more reason all its life than a cat or a parrot, would call him still a man; or whoever should hear a cat or a parrot discourse, reason, and philosophize, would call or think it nothing but a cat or a parrot; and say, the one was a dull irrational man, and the other a

very intelligent rational parrot. . . For I presume it is not the idea of a thinking or rational being alone that makes the idea of a man in most people's sense, but of a body, so and so shaped, joined to it; and if that be the idea of a man, the same successive body not shifted all at once, must, as well as the same immaterial spirit, go to the making of the same man.

9. *Personal Identity*.—This being premised, to find wherein personal identity consists, we must consider what person stands for; which, I think, is a thinking intelligent being, that has reason and reflection, and can consider itself as itself, the same thinking thing, in different times and places; which it does only by that consciousness which is inseparable from thinking, and, as it seems to me, essential to it: it being impossible for any one to perceive without perceiving that he does perceive. When we see, hear, smell, taste, feel, meditate, or will anything, we know that we do so. Thus it is always as to our present sensations and perceptions: and by this every one is to himself that which he calls self; it not being considered, in this case, whether the same self be continued in the same or divers substances. For, since consciousness always accompanies thinking, and it is that which makes every one to be what he calls self, and thereby distinguishes himself from all other thinking things: in this alone consists personal identity, i. e., the sameness of a rational being; and as far as this consciousness can be extended backwards to any past action or thought, so far reaches the identity of that person; it is the same self now it was then; and it is by the same self with this present one that now reflects on it, that that action was done.

10. *Consciousness makes personal Identity*.—But it is further inquired, whether it be the same identical substance? This, few would think they had reason to doubt of, if these perceptions, with their consciousness, always remained present in the mind, whereby the same thinking thing would be always consciously present, and, as would be thought, evidently the same to itself. But that which seems to make the difficulty is this, that this consciousness being interrupted always by forgetfulness, there being no moment of our lives wherein we have the whole train of all our past actions before our eyes in one view, but even the best memories losing the sight of one part whilst they are viewing another; and we sometimes, and that the greatest part of our lives, not reflecting on our past selves, being intent on our present thoughts, and in sound sleep having no thoughts at all, or at least none with that consciousness which remarks our waking thoughts; I say, in all these cases, our consciousness being interrupted, and we losing the sight of our past selves, doubts are raised whether we are the same thinking thing, i. e., the same substance or no. Which, however reasonable or unreasonable, concerns not personal identity at all: the question being, what makes the same person, and not whether it be the same identical substance, which always thinks in the same person; which, in this case, matters not at all: different substances, by the same consciousness (where they do partake in it) being united into one person, as well as different bodies by the same life are united into one animal, whose identity is preserved in that change of substances by

the unity of one continued life. For it being the same consciousness that makes a man be himself to himself, personal identity depends on that only, whether it be annexed solely to one individual substance, or can be continued in a succession of several substances. For as far as any intelligent being can repeat the idea of any past action with the same consciousness it had of it at first, and with the same consciousness it has of any present action; so far it is the same personal self. For it is by the consciousness it has of its present thoughts and actions, that it is self to itself now, and so will be the same self, as far as the same consciousness can extend to actions past or to come; and would be by distance of time, or change of substance, no more two persons, than a man be two men by wearing other clothes to-day than he did yesterday, with a long or a short sleep between: the same consciousness uniting those distant actions into the same person, whatever substances contributed to their production.

11. *Personal Identity in Change of Substances.*—That this is so, we have some kind of evidence in our very bodies, all whose particles, whilst vitally united to this same thinking conscious self, so that we feel when they are touched, and are affected by, and conscious of good or harm that happens to them, are a part of ourselves; i. e., of our thinking conscious self. Thus, the limbs of his body are to every one a part of himself; he sympathizes and is concerned for them. Cut off a hand, and thereby separate it from that consciousness he had of its heat, cold, and other affections, and it is then no longer a part of that which is himself, any more than the remotest part of matter. Thus, we see the substance whereof personal self consisted at one time may be varied at another, without the change of personal identity; there being no question about the same person, though the limbs which but now were a part of it, be cut off.

GOTTFRIED WILHELM LEIBNIZ

(1646–1716)

The first of the great German philosophers, Leibniz appears to have been largely self-taught. His father, who had been a professor of philosophy, died in 1652. Young Leibniz ravenously absorbed the Greek and Latin classics in his father's library, then went on to enter the University of Leipzig, where he studied law mathematics. He continued his studies at Jena and Altdorff, obtaining his doctorate in 1666. Not yet twenty-one, he was already the author of some noteworthy essays, including "On the Principle of Individuation." Soon thereafter he entered into the diplomatic service of the Prince Bishop of Mainz, and visited Paris. Renewing his interest in mathematics, he discovered the differential and integral calculus, which Newton simultaneously but independently discovered. He returned to Germany in 1676, and for the next forty years was in the service of the Brunswick family, at Hanover. In 1700 he became the president of the Academy of Science, whose plans he had originated. His chief philosophic works were composed in the last twenty-six years of his life. Although he wrote prolifically, he never composed a systematic account of his ideas. The only complete work published in his lifetime was the Theodicy *(1710). The* Monadology *and* The Principles of Nature and of Grace *are sketches which appeared in 1714. The* New Essays *was published posthumously.*

UNIQUENESS AND UNIVERSALITY

1. *Ph.* A relative idea of the greatest importance is that of *identity* or *diversity*. We never find and we cannot conceive it possible that two things of the same kind exist in the same time in the same place. Therefore when we ask *whether a thing is the same or not*, the question always relates to a thing which at such a time exists in such a place; whence it follows that a thing cannot have two beginnings of existence, nor two things one beginning only in relation to the time and the place.

Th. [It is always necessary that besides the difference of time and place there be an internal *principle of distinction*, and, though there are many things of the same kind, it is nevertheless true that none of them are ever perfectly alike: thus although time and place (*i.e. external relation*) serve us in distinguishing things which we do not easily distinguish by themselves, the things do not cease to be distinguishable in themselves. The essence (*le precis*) of *identity* and *diversity* consists, then, not in time and place, although it is true that the diversity of things is accompanied by that of time or of place, because they bring with them different impressions of the thing; not to say that it is rather by the things that one place or one time must be distinguished from another, for in themselves they are perfectly alike, but they are not, therefore, substances or complete realities. The mode of distinguishing which you seem to propose here, as unique in things of the same kind, is based upon the supposition that penetration is not conformable to nature. This supposition is reasonable, but experience indeed makes it evident that it is not closely applied here, when the question concerns distinction. We see, for example, two shadows or rays of light which interpenetrate, and we might invent for ourselves an imaginary world wherein bodies would act in the same way. But we do not cease to distinguish one ray from another by the very rate of their passage even when they cross each other.]

3. *Ph.* What is called the *principle of individuation (principium individuationis)* in the schools, where they torment themselves so much to know what it is, consists in existence itself which determines each being to a particular time and place incommunicable to two beings of the same kind.

Th. [The *principle of individuation* reappears in individuals in the principle of distinction of which I just spoke. If two individuals were perfectly alike and equal and (in a word) *indistinguishable* in themselves, there would be no principle of individuation; and I even venture to assert that there would be no individual distinction or different individuals under this condition. This is why the notion of atoms is chimerical, and arises only from the incomplete conceptions of men. For if there were

From New Essays Concerning Human Understanding, *Section 26.*

atoms, *i. e.* bodies perfectly hard and perfectly unalterable or incapable of internal change and capable of differing among themselves only in size and shape, it is plain that in the possibility of their being of the same shape and size they would then be indistinguishable in themselves, and could be distinguished only by means of external denominations without an internal basis, which is contrary to the highest principles of reason. But the truth is that every body is alterable, and indeed actually changes so that it differs in itself from every other. I remember that a distinguished princess, who is of a pre-eminently excellent mind, said one day while walking in her garden that she did not believe there were two leaves perfectly alike. A gentleman of distinction, who was walking with her, thought he would easily find some. But although he searched long, he was convinced by his eyes that he could always note the difference. We see by these considerations, hitherto neglected, how far we have wandered in philosophy from the most natural notions, and how far we have departed from the great principles of true metaphysic.]

4. *Ph.* That which constitutes the *unity* (identity) of one and the same plant is the possession of such an organization of parts in a single body, as participates in a common life which endures while the plant subsists, although the parts change.

Th. [The organization or configuration without an existing principle of life, which I call a monad, would not suffice to cause the continuance of *idem numero* or the same individual; for the configuration can abide specifically without abiding individually. When a horseshoe is changed into copper in a mineral spring of Hungary, the *same* figure in kind remains, but not the same as *an individual;* for the iron is dissolved, and the copper, with which the water is impregnated, is precipitated and insensibly takes its place. Now figure is an accident which does not pass from one subject to another (*de subjecto in subjectum*). So we must say that bodies as well organized as others do not remain the same in appearance, and, speaking strictly, not at all. It is almost like a river which always changes its water, or like the ship of Theseús which the Athenians were always repairing. But as regards substances, which are in themselves a true and real substantial unity, to which may belong actions properly called *vital,* an as regards substantial beings, *quœ uno spiritu continentur,* in the words of an ancient jurisconsult, *i.e.* which a certain indivisible spirit animates, you are right in saying that they remain perfectly *the same individual* through this soul or this spirit which constitutes the ego in thinking beings.]

5. *Ph.* The case is not very different in animals and in plants.

Th. [If vegetables and animals have no soul, their identity is only apparent; but if they have, individual identity is in truth strictly speaking there, although their organized bodies do not preserve it.]

6. *Ph.* This also shows wherein the identity of the same man consists, viz. in the fact alone that he enjoys the same life, continued by particles of matter which are in a perpetual flux, but which in this succession are *vitally* united with the same organized body.

Th. [That may be understood in my sense. In fact, the organized body is not the same from one moment to another; it is only equivalent. And if it were not related to the soul, there would no longer be the same life or *vital* union. Thus this identity would be only apparent.] . . .

9. *Ph.* The word *person* carries with it a thinking and intelligent being, capable of reason and reflection, that can consider itself indeed as *the same*, as one and the same thing which thinks at different times and in different places; which it does only by that consciousness which it has of its own acts. And this knowledge always accompanies our sensations and our present perceptions [when they are sufficiently distinguished, as I have more than once before remarked] and it is by this that each one is to himself what he calls *himself*. It is not considered in his case whether the same self is continued in the same or in different substances. For since consciousness always accompanies thought, and is that which makes each one to be what he calls *himself* and by which he is distinguished from every other thinking being; it is also in this alone that personal identity consists, or that which makes a rational being always to be the same; and as far as this *consciousness* can be extended over actions or thoughts already past, so far the identity of this person extends, and the *self* is at present the same as it was then.

Th. [I am also of this opinion that consciousness or the perception of the ego proves a moral or personal identity. And it is by this that I distinguish the *incessability* of the soul of an animal from the *immortality* of the soul of man; both preserve *physical and real identity*, but as for man, he is conformed to the rules of divine providence so that the soul preserves also identity moral and apparent to ourselves, in order to constitute the same person, capable consequently of feeling chastisements and rewards. It seems that you, sir, hold that this apparent identity could be preserved, if there were no real identity. I should think that that might perhaps be by the absolute power of God, but according to the order of things, identity apparent to the person himself who perceives the same, supposes real identity to every *proximate transition*, accompanied by reflection or perception of the *ego*, a perception intimate and immediate naturally incapable of deception. If man could be merely a machine and with that have consciousness, it would be necessary to be of your opinion, sir; but I hold that this case is not possible at least naturally. Neither would I say that *personal identity* and even the *self* do not dwell in us and that I am not this *ego* which has been in the cradle, under pretext that I no more remember anything of all that I then did. It is sufficient in order to find moral identity by itself that there be a *middle bond of consciousness* between a state bordering upon or even a little removed from another, although a leap or forgotten interval might be mingled therein. Thus if a disease had caused an interruption of the continuity of the bond of consciousness so that I did not know how I came into the present state, although I remember things more remote, the testimony of others could fill the void in my memory. I could even be punished upon this testimony, if I had just done something bad of deliberate purpose in an interval that I had forgotten a little after on account of this disease. And if I had just forgotten all past things and would be obliged to let myself be taught anew even to my name and even to reading and writing, I could always learn from others in my past life in my previous state, as I have kept my rights without its being necessary for me to share them with two persons, and to make me the heir of myself. All this suffices to maintain moral identity, which makes the same person. It is true that if others should conspire to deceive me (as I might indeed be deceived by myself, by some vision, dream, or illness, believing that what I had dreamed had happened to me) the appearance would be false. But there are cases in which we can be morally certain of the truth upon the relation of another, and with God whose social connection with us constitutes the principal point of morality, the error cannot have place. As for *the self*, it will be well to distinguish it from *the phenomenon of self* and from consciousness. *The self* constitutes identity real and physical, and *the phenomenon of self*, accompanied by truth, joins thereto personal identity. Thus not wishing to say that personal identity extends no farther than memory, I would say still less that *the self* or physical identity depends upon it. Real and personal identity is proved with the utmost possible certainty by present and immediate reflection; it is proved sufficiently for ordinary purposes by our memory of the interval or by the conspiring testimony of others. But if God should change in an extraordinary manner real identity, personal identity would remain, provided man preserved the appearances of identity, as well the internal (that is to say, consciousness) as the external, like those which consist in that which appears to others. (Thus consciousness is not the sole means for constituting personal identity, and the testimony of another or even other proofs can supply it.) But there is some difficulty if contradiction occurs between those diverse appearances. Consciousness may be silent as in forgetfulness; but if it should alter very clearly things which were contrary to the other appearances, we should be embarrassed in the decision and as it were suspended sometimes between two possibilities, that of the error of our memory and that of some deception in external appearances.]

11. *Ph.* [You will say] that the members of the body of every man are a part of himself [and that thus, the body being in a perpetual flux, the man cannot remain the same].

Th. [I should rather prefer to say that *the I* and *the He* are without parts, because it is said, and with reason, that the same substance, or the same physical *ego*, is really preserved. But we cannot say, speaking according to the exact truth of things, that the same whole is preserved when a part is lost. Now whatever has corporeal parts cannot fail to lose some of them at every moment.] . . .

23. *Ph.* Could we suppose either *two* distinct and incommunicable *consciousnesses* acting by turns in the same body, the one constantly during the day, the other by night, or that *the same consciousness* acts at intervals in two different bodies; I ask if, in the first case, the day and night

man, if I may so express myself, would not be two as distinct persons as Socrates and Plato, and in the second case would he not be a single person in two distinct bodies? It matters not that this same consciousness which affects two different bodies, and these consciousnesses which affect the same body at different times, belong the one to the same immaterial substance, and the two others to two distinct immaterial substances, which introduce these different consciousnesses into these bodies, since personal identity would equally be determined by the consciousness, whether that consciousness were attached to some individual immaterial substance or not. Further, an immaterial thinking thing may sometimes lose sight of its past consciousness, and recall it anew. Now suppose these intervals of memory and forgetfulness return with every day and night, then you have two persons with the same immaterial spirit. Whence it follows that the *self* is not determined by the identity or diversity of substance, which it cannot be sure of, but only by the identity of consciousness.

Th. [I admit that if all the appearances were changed and transferred from our spirit to another, or if God made an exchange between two spirits, giving the visible body and the appearances and consciousnesses of the one to the other, personal identity, instead of being attached to that of substance, would follow the constant appearances which human morality must have in view; but these appearances would not consist in the consciousnesses alone; and it will be necessary for God to make the exchange not only of the apperceptions or consciousnesses of the individuals in question, but also of the appearances which present themselves to others regarding these persons, otherwise there would be a contradiction between the consciousnesses of the one and the testimony of the others, which would disturb the moral order of things. But you must also agree with me that the divorce between the insensible and sensible world, *i.e.* between the insensible perceptions which would remain in the same substances, and the apperceptions which would be changed, would be a miracle, as when you suppose that God makes the vacuum; for I have stated above why that is not in agreement with the natural order. Here is another supposition much more suitable: it may be that in another place in the universe or at another time a globe may be found which does not differ sensibly from this earthly globe, in which we live, and that each of the men who inhabit it does not differ sensibly from each of us who corresponds to him. Thus there are at once more than a hundred million pairs of similar persons, *i.e.* of two persons with the same appearances and consciousnesses; and God might transfer spirits alone or with their bodies from one globe to the other without their perceiving it; but be they transferred or let alone, what will you say of their person or *self* according to your authors? Are they two persons or the same? since the consciousness and the internal and external appearance of the men of these globes cannot make the distinction. It is true that God and the spirits capable of seeing the intervals and external relations of times and places, and even internal constitutions, insensible to the men of the two globes, could distinguish them; but according to your hypotheses consciousness alone discerning the persons without being obliged to trouble itself with the real identity or diversity of the substance, or even of that which would appear to others, how is it prevented from saying that these two persons who are at the same time in these two similar globes, but separated from each other by an inexpressible distance, are only one and the same person; which is, however, a manifest absurdity. For the rest, speaking of what may be in the course of nature, the two similar globes and the two similar souls of the two globes would remain so only for a time. For since there is an individual diversity, this difference must consist at least in the insensible constitutions which must be developed in the course of time.]

26

The Scope of Metaphysics

RONALD J. GLOSSOP

(b. 1933)

Since 1965, Glossop has been a member of the Department of Philosophy at Southern Illinois University. His published articles have tended to concentrate upon ethical issues, but metaphysics has been one of his major concerns.

QUESTIONS OF UTMOST GENERALITY

I

When confronted with the problem of putting a jigsaw puzzle together, most of us begin by trying to find the border pieces. After we get these pieces fit together to form the frame, it is easier to see where the other pieces belong. In a similar way, when confronted with the problem of organizing the information from all of our many experiences into a coherent view of the world, philosophers often begin by trying to find some very general truths that constitute the most basic principles concerning how the world is structured. Once these ultimate principles have been determined, it becomes easier to organize and evaluate the significance of other information acquired from our experience.

The ultimate questions philosophers ask about the nature of the world are of two kinds. On the one hand, we can seek to discover the ultimate principles that describe *the world as it exists at a given moment*. For example, we can try to formulate a true statement which has the pattern "Everything that presently exists depends on ___ for its existence." On the other hand, we can seek to discover the ultimate principles that describe *the changes the world undergoes from moment to moment*. For example, we can try to formulate a true statement that has the pattern "All events that take place in the world are the result of ___." These two examples are only examples. Philosophers ask other ultimate questions about the world as it exists at one moment and about the changes that take place in the world from moment to moment, but our present discussion will focus on the two examples given above.

II

Consider the first example: "Everything that presently exists depends on ___ for its existence. "What could go in the blank? One answer given by the ancient philosopher Democritus (460?–370? B.C.) is "physical atoms in empty space." According to Democritus objects such as stones and trees and lakes and animals all depend for their existence on the material particles of which they are made. If the particles were eliminated, the objects that are composed of them would cease to exist. This principle applies also to smaller objects. Regardless of how small an object may be, if it has any parts it depends on those parts for its existence. It would seem that ultimately there must be some very small particles that do not themselves have any parts. They cannot be broken down any further. Democritus called these ultimate physical particles that have no parts "atoms" (which in Greek means "that which cannot be divided"). He was mistaken about how small these indivisible particles were. He thought that the particles that today we call "molecules" were the ultimate particles. One-hundred-fifty years ago modern atoms were considered ultimate particles. Now even atoms are recognized to be composed of other smaller particles. But according to this way of thinking, there *must* be some ultimate physical particles, and whatever they are, everything that presently exists depends on them for its existence. Since this view claims that everything depends for its existence on material particles, it is called "*materialism.*"

For someone brought up in a science-oriented culture, materialism may seem quite plausible. The capacity of atomic bombs to vaporize living things as well as apparently solid physical objects makes the dependence of things on physical particles very evident. But is it true that *everything* depends on physical particles for its existence? What about our thoughts? Ideas seem to be non-physical things. Questions that are appropriate concerning physical objects ("How much space does it take up?" or "How much does it weigh?") seem not to be appropriate when dealing with ideas. "How much space is occupied by my idea of the solar system?" "How much does my idea of pink weigh?" Such questions seem ridiculous. Ideas just are not physical things. Do such non-physical ideas depend on physical particles for their existence?

The French philosopher René Descartes (1596–1650) thought not. He was ready to admit that our ideas depend on something else for their existence, but it had to be something non-physical. This non-physical thing upon which ideas depend for their existence is the mind. Being non-physical, minds cannot be seen or touched or weighed or detected by instruments that measure physical characteristics. Furthermore, although ideas depend on minds for their existence, minds do not depend on anything else for their existence. Especially they do not depend on physical particles or things made of physical particles such as brains. Descartes's view made it possible to believe in personal immortality, that is, that a person's mind could continue to exist after his physical body was destroyed. It also made it possible to believe that there could exist a superior mind (God) that has ideas but that has no physical aspects such as size or weight or location in space and time. If the materialists are correct, if ideas depend for their existence on brains that in turn depend on physical particles, then there could be no immortal mind or non-physical God. On the other hand, if Descartes is correct, there are some puzzling things to explain. Why does damage to one's physical brain affect his ideas? If destroying part of the brain destroys part of one's ideas, wouldn't it follow that destroying all of the physical brain would result in the destruction of all of one's ideas? Why do physical substances in the blood such as alcohol or LSD influence one's ideas? Don't these phenomena show that ideas and the state of the mind depend on physical things?

Descartes's argument that the existence of minds does not depend on anything physical was based on what he believed anyone could know on the basis of his own thinking. Anyone can know by introspection that he has a mind that thinks. Even if the various ideas one has are mistaken, even if one is being duped with regard to all his other ideas, still he knows that he must have a mind that thinks. His mind *must* exist in order to be duped. Indeed one can be more certain that his mind exists than that there is a physical world because his ideas about this world could possibly be mistaken; one could be merely dreaming that a physical world exists. George Berkeley (1685–1753) pursued this line of thought further. What is the physical world anyway? Isn't it simply a collection of ideas in some mind? What is an apple but ideas of shape, size, color, taste, texture, and so on? The apple is not some sort of non-perceptible thing that has various qualities. "The apple" is merely a short-hand way of speaking of all those qualities at once. The same is true of other physical objects. The materialist is wrong in thinking that the apple depends on some smaller physical particles that can themselves be only collections of other qualities. The apple depends for its existence on some mind having the ideas of the qualities that together constitute the apple. It might be objected that Berkeley has switched the question from "What depends on nothing else for its existence?" to "What can most readily be known to exist?" But to this objection Berkeley and other *idealists* would respond that it makes no sense to speculate about that which can't possibly be known. Our thinking must be about that which is knowable, and material objects as well as anything else that might exist are knowable only insofar as they are ideas in some mind. There are still problems for this view, however. How can I know what ideas are in other minds? How can I know that there are any other minds since I cannot have any perceptions of them? Don't I end up with the view that all which is knowable by me is that which I in fact know? But it seems implausible to say that everything that exists depends for its existence upon my knowing that it exists. That would imply that nothing existed before I existed and that nothing will exist after I cease to exist. The question of what depends on nothing else for its existence just seems to be a different question from what can be known to exist.

Another possible view of the relation between physical things on the one hand and ideas and minds on the other is the view that everything has both a physical and a mental aspect but is itself not wholly one or the other. The brain and the mind are not two different things as Descartes thought; they are merely two different ways of viewing something that is not wholly physical or wholly mental. Viewed from outside (perceptually) this thing is a brain that takes up space. Viewed from within (introspectively) this thing is a mind that has ideas. An analogy would be a cloud that from outside (when viewed from the ground) seems to be as substantial as a ball of cotton but that from within (when flying through it in a airplane) seems wispy and very unsolid. Benedict Spinoza (1632–1677) maintained that everything depends for its existence on something (call it "Nature" or "God") that is neither physical nor mental but that displays both these aspects. The main problem for this view is that as far as our experience is concerned mentality seems to exist only where there are physical brains while according to this view some kind of mentality would be just as pervasive as the physical dimension of reality.

So far we have been assuming that there is something that can fill the blank in the expression "Everything that presently exists depends on ____ for its existence." We have considered the *materialism* of Democritus, the *mind-matter dualism* of Descartes, the *idealism* of Berkeley, and the *neutral monism* of Spinoza as different views concerning how this blank should be filled. But it is also possible to deny that the blank can be filled. It is possible to say, as Heraclitus (fl. 500 B.C.) did, that there is no enduring sort of thing upon which all else depends for its existence. According to this *process philosophy* reality is like a flame. Particles pass through it, but there is no enduring thing upon which the flame depends for its existence. The world is a flowing thing. Thus, according to this view it is a mistake to assume that there is any answer to a question that suggests that there is some kind of enduring substance (physical or mental or both) on which all existence depends at any given moment. But this process view also runs into a difficulty. Even if there is no *enduring substance* on which other things depend for their existence, it seems that there still must be *something* that exists (even if only momentarily) that does not depend on something else for existence. Even a flame depends on the particles flowing through it. The process philosopher still needs to tell us the nature of that on which the existence of everything depends even if it is not an enduring sort of thing.

III

Let us now turn our attention to that other ultimate question we raised at the beginning, how ultimately to explain the changes that take place in the world. If possible, we want to form a true statement of the form "All events that take place in the world are the result of ____." Before considering how *all* events might be explained, however, let us consider two different ways in which a *single occurrence* might be explained. Then we can return to the larger question.

Suppose that we are in a room together. Among other things in this room there is a lamp with an electric filament-type light bulb that is not glowing. Then suddenly it begins to glow. Here is an event that needs to be explained. Why did the light come on? Let us suppose that someone has brought the ends of the wires attached to the socket for the bulb into contact with the terminals of a dry cell. But why should attaching these wires to the dry cell cause the filament of the bulb to glow? Because the filament glows whenever electrons are flowing through it, so when a flow of electrons was started the filament of the bulb began to glow. Our explanation has the following structure:

Whenever electrons flow through the filament, the filament glows.
Electrons began to flow through the filament.

Therefore, the filament began to glow.

The first statement is a general principle, a law of nature, which indicates how things just "naturally" or "automatically" happen with the passage of time. The second statement indicates that a particular event occurs. The statement below the line indicates what succeeding event *must* take place. The occurrence of this event is thus explained by referring to the two statements above the line that constitute the "causes" of the occurrence mentioned below the line.

The general pattern of this type of explanation can be schematized as follows:

Whenever events of type A occur, events of type B occur.
An event of type A occurs.

Therefore an event of type B occurs.

Because of the "natural" or "automatic" relationship expressed in the first statement, explanations of this type are called "*mechanistic*" (machine-like) explanations. There is no purpose or goal involved. Whenever an event of one type occurs, it is automatically followed by an event of another type. These mechanistic explanations are typical of the physical sciences.

The second type of explanation we want to consider is called a "*teleological*" (goal-connected) explanation because it explains events in terms of their being means to the accomplishment of some purpose or goal that is being pursued. Suppose someone asks you why you are taking college courses. You answer "Because I want to get a college degree and I must pass the courses in order to get it." Here the occurrence to be explained is your taking college courses, but the explanation is of a different type from the mechanistic explanations previously discussed. The structure of this teleological explanation looks like this:

I have the goal of getting a college degree.
Taking college courses is an appropriate means to achieving that goal.

Therefore I am taking college courses.

The first statement indicates that some goal is being pursued. The second statement indicates that a particular course of action is an appropriate means of reaching the goal. The statement below the line indicates what action is required. The doing of this action is justified by referring to the statements above the line that constitute the "reasons" for the action mentioned below the line.

The general pattern of this teleological type of explanation can be schematized as follows:

X aims for (wants, needs, desires) Y.
Z is an appropriate means to get Y.

X does Z

Note how this type of explanation suggests that X is a conscious agent aware of some goal. Just as mechanistic explanations seem well suited to explaining events in the physical sciences, so teleological explanations seem especially well suited to explaining actions of conscious beings in which some mentality or awareness is present.

A particular occurrence might be explained both mechanistically and teleologically. For example, if plants are grown in a dark place with light coming in only on one side, their stems bend toward the light. Why? We can explain this occurrence *teleologically* by saying that the plants need light and growing toward the light source is an appropriate means of their satisfying this need. The only trouble with this teleological explanation is that it suggests that the plants are aware of their need for light and consciously decide to grow toward the light source. We can also explain the bending of the plant stems by a complex *mechanistic* explanation: a growth-stimulating enzyme in the cells of the plant stems is partially destroyed by sunlight causing the cells on the side of the stem toward the light to grow less rapidly than the cells on the side away from the light where less of the enzyme has been destroyed; since the cells on the side of the stem away from the light thus grow to be larger and the number of cells on both sides of the stem is the same, the stem bends toward the light source. This explanation contains no suggestion of mentality because each event produces the succeeding event "naturally" or "automatically." Even though the growing of the plants toward the light source *can* be explained both teleologically and mechanistically, we might well say that only the mechanistic explanation is *proper* or *legitimate*. We might reject the teleological explanation on grounds that it suggests consciousness where there is none. On the other hand, we might reject the mechanistic explanation in favor of the teleological one on grounds that the mechanistic explanation suggests that plants are no different from non-living machines. In other words, it is important to determine not so much of what type of explanation *can* be given but rather what type of explanation is *appropriate* or *legitimate.*

Now we are ready to turn to the ultimate question of how changes in the world as a totality are to be explained. As we have just noted, the issue is not what types of explanations *can* be given but rather what types of explanations are *proper*. We have already noted that *mechanistic* explanations seem especially appropriate for explaining *physical* changes while *teleological* explanations seem especially appropriate where *consciousness* is present. We might expect therefore that various views on the issue of the proper way of explaining events will be related to the various views previously discussed on the issue of whether ultimate reality is physical or mental or some combination of the two.

Consider the materialistic view discussed earlier. The atomistic materialist believes that everything that exists depends ultimately for its existence on material particles that have no parts. Even ideas and minds are dependent ultimately on brains and the material particles of which they are composed. From the materialistic point of view all changes in the world would ultimately be physical changes. Since these changes are most appropriately explained mechanistically, it follows that for the materialist the proper way to explain any event is *mechanistically*. Teleological explanations suggest that there are minds that bring about changes by means of pursuing ends of which they are aware. They suggest that minds can really make a difference in what happens. But the materialist denies any ultimate reality to minds and thus must deny any ultimate legitimacy to teleological explanations. You may explain your taking college courses in terms of the goal of getting a college degree, but such an explanation does not get down to the foundations of things. It is superficial. Only mechanistic explanations that make reference to physical stimuli, nerve cells, and physical changes in the body are legitimate explanations for the materialist. Such a view treats humans as robots, but for the materialist ultimately that is just what they are. This view would also undermine all thinking about what is "good" and "bad" or "right" and "wrong" since these value expressions are all related ultimately to teleological explanations where some goal is being sought and there is a question about the value of a proposed means for reaching this goal. If all teleological explanations are to be abandoned as the mechanistic materialist proposes to do, so also must all issues related to making evaluations since they arise only in the course of goal-oriented thinking.

The mind-matter dualism of Descartes (somethings are ultimately mental while others are ultimately physical) generates a *dualistic view* concerning what kinds of explanations are legitimate. When we are dealing with physical objects, mechanistic explanations are appropriate to explain the changes that take place; but when minds enter in as ultimate causal factors, teleological explanations become appropriate. According to this view any single occurrence is either a physical event that should be explained mechanistically or an action of a mind that should be explained teleologically. The big problem for this dualistic view is to make clear how these two types of explanations mesh with each other when there is a series of events. How are the mechanistic explanations of neurological changes in the brain to be fitted together with the teleological explanations of the decisions made by the mind? The stimuli to which we react are ultimately physical changes. So also are the movements of the body that constitute our behavior. At what precise point in the process of explaining human behavior should mechanistic explanations give way to teleological ones, and then at what point should they give way again to mechanistic explanations? Are there any animals other than humans who have minds and whose behavior must consequently be explained in a teleological way at certain points? Many animals seem at times to act purposefully. If their apparently purposeful behavior is to be explained mechanistically, why not do the same with human behavior? On the other hand, if teleological explanations are sometimes legitimate when dealing with the behavior of some animals, precisely where as we descend in the animal kingdom will it become illegitimate to use these explanations that suggest mentality? Also, at what moment in the development of individual human beings does it become appropriate to use teleological explanations? At what moment does the human mind as an ultimate reality begin to exist? The dualist view seems to conform in some ways to our common-sense way of thinking but seems unable to handle the gradual appearance of mentality both in animals as a group and in the development of individual persons.

The idealist, who believes that everything ultimately depends on mind for its existence, can be expected to maintain that all occurrences should be explained teleologically rather than mechanistically. All events will be seen as means to some end. Even physical occurrences that the scientist explains mechanistically are not really understood unless one sees them as means to some end. This *teleological perspective* may not seem very closely related to what was said earlier about idealism. In order to better understand this approach we need to turn to religion and the notion that everything depends on God for its existence. God, the supreme mind, is the ultimate cause of every thing and every event. All that happens happens in accord with his will, that is, in accord with his purposes. Every event is thus a means used by God to reach some goal He has in mind. Acceptance of the teleological point of view is displayed by the believer who asks his priest or minister concerning some tragedy, "Why did it happen?" The believer is *not* looking for a mechanistic explanation. He wants a teleological one, one that gives a *reason* for the tragedy and not just a cause. His request for such an explanation indicates that he believes there is one, even though his religious leader may not know what it is. In accord with his faith he assumes that every occurrence has some reason, that is, that it can be explained *teleologically* with reference to the aims of the Deity. One of the great problems for such religious faith is that there are so many occurrences that seem on the surface not to have any purpose or even to be contrary to any desirable goal. If God is in control, why is there so much pain and undeserved suffering?

This discussion of the teleological view discloses how the issues being discussed here (mechanistic vs. teleological explanations) coincide with what many persons have seen as the conflict between science and religion. The program of science is to find mechanistic explanations for all occurrences including human behavior. On the other hand, the basic faith of religion is that ultimately all occurrences can be explained teleologically, that there is purpose not only in human behavior but in the world as a whole. The basic complaint of the believer against the view of the world presented by the scientist is that it is purposeless and has no place for values such as love and justice. There is no room in the scientist's world either for moral character based on devotion to doing one's duty or for a world in which ultimately justice prevails.

But must one choose between the mechanistic view of science and the teleological view of religion? Just as the neutral monist maintained that ultimately everything is both mental and physical (that these are but two aspects of the basic reality), so now one could maintain that ultimately *every occurrence can legitimately be explained both mechanistically and teleologically*. According to this view the scientist is right that ultimately every event can legitimately be explained as the natural or automatic consequence of the preceding state of affairs, but the religious believer is also right in believing that ultimately every event can legitimately be explained as a means of accomplishing the will of God. As attractive as this view may seem in the abstract, it still faces all those problems faced by the mechanist plus those faced by the teleologist. It suggests that men are merely robots while at the same time being confronted by occurrences that seem to be contrary to any purposes likely to be pursued by a benevolent Deity.

Until now we have been assuming that all occurrences can be explained. We have noted some different views concerning whether they should be explained mechanistically or teleologically or both ways, but we have not yet considered the possibility that some occurrences may be completely inexplicable. It seems at least conceivable that some events occur for which there is *absolutely no cause or reason*, but this possibility is not attractive to most persons. The human mind restlessly asks "Why?" It assumes that there is an order in the world that can be discovered. To say that an event has no cause or reason is to deny that with regard to this event the question "Why?" can be answered. Consider the fact that much money and effort has been spent, so far without much success, in trying to learn why people get cancer. What is its cause? Suppose that someone were to suggest that the search for the cause of cancer should be given up because there may be no cause. The suggestion seems ridiculous. There *must* be a cause. Perhaps we do not yet know what the cause is, but we are quite sure that this event of getting cancer cannot be something that just happens without any cause or reason. (How we can be so sure about this belief is itself a very interesting philosophical question.)

Yet some philosophers have maintained that some events occur without a cause or reason. They have usually maintained this view because they felt they needed to do so in order not to exclude "free will" for humans. For example, Epicurus (341?–270? B.C.), a mechanistic materialist with views similar to those of Democritus, maintained that there are chance (uncaused) occurrences partly on grounds that otherwise human beings would have no control over their own destiny. He was by no means the last philosopher to adopt this view.

On the other hand, there is some doubt whether the freedom (and responsibility) of humans can be saved by introducing the notion that some events have no cause or reason but just happen by chance. Suppose that such an uncaused event should occur in my arm resulting in its moving in a completely unpredictable and unintended way. It is *not* caused by my willing it to move, but moves without being caused in any way. Why should this random movement of my arm be viewed as in any way related to my "free will"? Suppose that this moving arm does some damage. Why should I be held responsible for an event that was in no way causally or intentionally related to my character? On the contrary, it seems that we should be held responsible for behavior only when it is voluntary, that is, only when it is intentional or consciously directed (teleologically determined). Despite the fact that Epicurus and other philosophers have maintained that human freedom and responsibility were incompatible with the view that all events are determined, a closer examination of the issue suggests that what is required for human freedom and responsibility is the *presence* of *teleological determination*. Once we have realized that freedom is linked with teleological determination, the next interesting question is whether the *presence* of *teleological* determination requires the *absence* of *mechanistic* determination.

27

Images of Nature

HENRI BERGSON

(1859–1941)

Bergson was born in Paris of Anglo-Polish parentage, and studied philosophy at the Ecole Normale Supérieure. After having taught at various schools, including the Ecole Normale, he became professor of philosophy at the Collège de France, a position he held until 1921. He was elected to the French Academy, and in 1927 received the Nobel prize for literature. Between the two world wars, Bergson sought actively to promote world peace, but he lived to see the collapse of these hopes with World War II and the occupation of France by the Nazis. One of his earliest works was Time and Free Will *(1889, translated 1910). Other works include* Matter and Memory *(1896, translated 1911),* Laughter, *(1900, translated 1910),* Creative Evolution *(1907, translated 1911),* The Two Sources of Morality and Religion *(1932, translated 1935), and* The Creative Mind *(1934, translated 1946).*

THE INVENTING OF POSSIBILITIES

I should like to come back to a subject on which I have already spoken, the continuous creation of unforeseeable novelty which seems to be going on in the universe. As far as I am concerned, I feel I am experiencing it constantly. No matter how I try to imagine in detail what is going to happen to me, still how inadequate, how abstract and stilted is the thing I have imagined in comparison to what actually happens! The realization brings along with it an unforeseeable nothing which changes everything. For example, I am to be present at a gathering; I know what people I shall find there, around what table, in what order, to discuss what problem. But let them come, be seated and chat as I expected, let them say what I was sure they would say: the whole gives me an impression at once novel and unique, as if it were but now designed at one original stroke by the hand of an artist. Gone is the image I had conceived of it, a mere prearrangeable juxtaposition of things already known! I agree that the picture has not the artistic value of a Rembrandt or a Velasquez: yet it is just as unexpected and, in this sense, quite as original. It will be alleged that I did not know the circumstances in detail, that I could not control the persons in question, their gestures, their attitudes, and that if the thing as a whole provided me with something new it was because they produced additional factors. But I have the same impression of novelty before the unrolling of my inner life. I feel it more vividly than ever, before the action I willed and of which I was sole master. If I deliberate before acting, the moments of deliberation present themselves to my consciousness like the successive sketches a painter makes of his picture, each one unique of its kind; and no matter whether the act itself in its accomplishment realizes something willed and consequently foreseen, it has none the less its own particular form in all its originality.—Granted, someone will say; there is perhaps something original and unique in a state of soul; but matter is repetition; the external world yields to mathematical laws; a superhuman intelligence which would know the position, the direction, and the speed of all the atoms and electrons of the material universe at a given moment could calculate any future state of this universe as we do in the case of an eclipse of the sun or the moon.—I admit all this for the sake of argument, if it concerns only the inert world and at least with regard to elementary phenomena, although this is beginning to be a much debated question. But this "inert" world is only an abstraction. Concrete reality comprises those living, conscious beings enframed in inorganic matter. I say living and conscious, for I believe that the living is conscious by right;

From The Creative Mind *(1934; trans. from the French, 1946), Philosophical Library, pp. 107–123.*

it becomes unconscious in fact where consciousness falls asleep, but even in the regions where consciousness is in a state of somnolence, in the vegetable kingdom for example, there is regulated evolution, definite progress, aging; in fact, all the external signs of the duration which characterizes consciousness. And why must we speak of an inert matter into which life and consciousness would be inserted as in a frame? By what right do we put the inert first? The ancients had imagined a World Soul supposed to assure the continuity of existence of the material universe. Stripping this conception of its mythical element, I should say that the inorganic world is a series of infinitely rapid repetitions or quasi-repetitions which, when totalled, constitute visible and previsible changes. I should compare them to the swinging of the pendulum of a clock: the swingings of the pendulum are coupled to the continuous unwinding of a spring linking them together and whose unwinding they mark; the repetitions of the inorganic world constitute rhythm in the life of conscious beings and measure their duration. Thus the living being essentially has duration; it has duration precisely because it is continuously elaborating what is new and because there is no elaboration without searching, no searching without groping. Time is this very hesitation, or it is nothing. Suppress the conscious and the living (and you can do this only through an artificial effort of abstraction, for the material world once again implies perhaps the necessary presence of consciousness and of life), you obtain in fact a universe whose successive states are in theory calculable in advance, like the images placed side by side along the cinematographic film, prior to its unrolling. Why, then, the unrolling? Why does reality unfurl? Why is it not spread out? What good is time? (I refer to real, concrete time, and not to that abstract time which is only a fourth dimension of space.) This, in days gone by, was the starting point of my reflections. Some fifty years ago I was very much attached to the philosophy of Spencer. I perceived one fine day that, in it, time served no purpose, did nothing. Nevertheless, I said to myself, time is something. Therefore it acts. What can it be doing? Plain common sense answered: time is what hinders everything from being given at once. It retards, or rather it is retardation. It must therefore, be elaboration. Would it not then be a vehicle of creation and of choice? Would not the existence of time prove that there is indetermination in things? Would not time be that indetermination itself?

If such is not the opinion of most philosophers, it is because human intelligence is made precisely to take things by the other end. I say intelligence, I do not say thought, I do not say mind. Along side of intelligence there is in effect the immediate perception by each of us of his own activity and of the conditions in which it is exercised. Call it what you will; it is the feeling we have of being creators of our intentions, of our decisions, of our acts, and by that, of our habits, our characters, ourselves. Artisans of our life, even artists when we so desire, we work continually, with the material furnished us by the past and present, by heredity and opportunity, to mould a figure unique, new, original, as unforeseeable as the form given by the sculptor of the clay. Of this work and what there is unique about it we are warned, no doubt, even while it is being done, but the essential thing is that we do it. It is up to us to go deeply into it; it is not even necessary that we be fully conscious of it, any more than the artist needs to analyze his creative ability; he leaves that to the philosopher to worry about, being content, himself, simply to create. On the other hand, the sculptor must be familiar with the technique of his art and know everything that can be learned about it: this technique deals especially with what his work has in common with other works; it is governed by the demands of the material upon which he operates and which is imposed upon him as upon all artists; it concerns in art what is repetition or fabrication, and has nothing to do with creation itself. On it is concentrated the attention of the artist, what I should call his intellectuality. In the same way, in the creation of our character we know very little about our creative ability: in order to learn about it we should have to turn back upon ourselves, to philosophize, and to climb back up the slope of nature; for nature desired action, it hardly thought about speculation. The moment it is no longer simply a question of feeling an impulse within oneself and of being assured that one can act, but of turning thought upon itself in order that it may seize this ability and catch this impulse, the difficulty becomes great, as if the whole normal direction of consciousness had to be reversed. On the contrary we have a supreme interest in familiarizing ourselves with the technique of our action, that is to say in extracting from the conditions in which it is exercised, all that can furnish us with recipes and general rules upon which to base our conduct. There will be novelty in our acts thanks only to the repetition we have found in things. Our normal faculty of knowing is then essentially a power of extracting what stability and regularity there is in the flow of reality. Is it a question of perceiving? Perception seizes upon the infinitely repeated shocks which are light or heat, for example, and contracts them into relatively invariable sensations: trillions of external vibrations are what the vision of a color condenses in our eyes in the fraction of a second. Is it a question of conceiving? To form a general idea is to abstract from varied and changing things a common aspect which does not change or at least offers an invariable hold to our action. The invariability of our attitude, the identity of our eventual or virtual reaction to the multiplicity and variability of the objects represented is what first marks and delineates the generality of the idea. Finally, is it a question of understanding? It is simply finding connections, establishing stable relations between transitory facts, evolving laws; an operation which is much more perfect as the relation becomes more definite and the law more mathematical. All these functions are constitutives of the intellect. And the intellect is in the line of truth so long as it attaches itself, in its penchant for regularity and stability, to what is stable and regular in the real, that is to say to materiality. In so doing it touches one of the sides of the absolute, as our consciousness touches another when it grasps within us a perpetual efflorescence of novelty or when, broadening out, it comes into sympathy with that effort of nature which is constantly renewing. Error begins when the intellect claims to think one of the aspects as it thought the other, directing its powers on something for which it was not intended.

I believe that the great metaphysical problems are in general badly stated, that they frequently resolve themselves of their own accord when correctly stated, or else are problems formulated in terms of illusion which disappear as soon as the terms of the formula are more closely examined. They arise in fact from our habit of transposing into fabrication what is creation. Reality is global and undivided growth, progressive invention, duration: it resembles a gradually expanding rubber balloon assuming at each moment unexpected forms. But our intelligence imagines its origin and evolution as an arrangement and rearrangement of parts which supposedly merely shift from one place to another; in theory therefore, it should be able to foresee any one state of the whole: by positing a definite number of stable elements one has, predetermined, all their possible combinations. That is not all. Reality, as immediately perceived, is fullness constantly swelling out, to which emptiness is unknown. It has extension just as it has duration; but this concrete extent is not the infinite and infinitely divisible space the intellect takes as a place in which to build. Concrete space has been extracted from things. They are not in it; it is space which is in them. Only, as soon as our thought reasons about reality, it makes space a receptacle. As it has the habit of assembling parts in a relative vacuum, it imagines that reality fills up some absolute kind of vacuum. Now, if the failure to recognize radical novelty is the original cause of those badly stated metaphysical questions, the habit of proceeding from emptiness to fullness is the source of problems which are non-existent. Moreover, it is easy to see that the second mistake is already implied in the first. But I should like first of all to define it more precisely.

I say that there are pseudo-problems, and that they are the agonizing problems of metaphysics. I reduce them to two. One gave rise to theories of being, the other to theories of knowledge. The first false problem consists in asking oneself why there is being, why something or someone exists. The nature of what is is of little importance; say that it is matter, or mind, or both, or that matter and mind are not self-sufficient and manifest a transcendent Cause: in any case, when existences and causes are brought into consideration and the causes of these causes, one feels as if pressed into a race—if one calls a halt, it is to avoid dizziness. But just the same one sees, or thinks one sees, that the difficulty still exists, that the problem is still there and will never be solved. It will never, in fact, be solved, but it should never have been raised. It arises only if one posits a nothingness which supposedly precedes being. One says: "There could be nothing," and then is astonished that there should be something—or someone. But analyze that sentence: "There could be nothing." You will see you are dealing with words, not at all with ideas, and that " nothing" here has no meaning. "Nothing" is a term in ordinary language which can only have meaning in the sphere, proper to man, of action and fabrication. "Nothing" designates the absence of what we are seeking, we desire, expect. Let us suppose that absolute emptiness was known to our experience: it would be limited, have contours, and would therefore be something. But in reality there is no vacuum. We perceive and can conceive only occupied space. One thing disappears only because another replaces it. Suppression thus means substitution. We say "suppression," however, when we envisage, in the case of substitution, only one of its two halves, or rather the one of its two sides which interests us; in this way we indicate a desire to turn our attention to the object which is gone, and away from the one replacing it.

We say then that there is nothing more, meaning by that, that what exists does not interest us, that we are interested in what is no longer there or in what might have been there. The idea of absence, or of nothingness, or of nothing, is therefore inseparably bound to that of suppression, real or eventual, and the idea of suppression is itself only an aspect of the idea of substitution. Those are the ways of thinking we use in practical life; it is particularly essential to our industry that our thought should be able to lag behind reality and remain attached, when need be, to what was or what might be, instead of being absorbed by what is. But when we go from the domain of fabrication to that of creation, when we ask ourselves why there is being, why something or someone, why the world or God, exists and why not nothingness, when, in short, we set ourselves the most agonising of metaphysical problems, we virtually accept an absurdity; for if all suppression is a substitution, if the idea of a suppression is only the truncated idea of a substitution, then to speak of a suppression of everything is to posit a substitution which would not be one, that is, to be self-contradictory. Either the idea of a suppression of everything has just about as much existence as that of a round square—the existence of a sound, *flatus vocis*,—or else, if it does represent something, it translates a movement of the intellect from one object to another, preferring the one it has just left to the object it finds before it, and designates by "absence of the first" the presence of the second. We have posited the whole, then made each of its parts disappear one by one, without consenting to see what replaced it; it is therefore the totality of presences, simply arranged in a new order, that one has in mind in attempting to total up the absences. In other words, this so-called representation of absolute emptiness is, in reality, that of universal fullness in a mind which leaps indefinitely from part to part, with the fixed resolution never to consider anything but the emptiness of its dissatisfaction instead of the fullness of things. All of which amounts to saying that the idea of Nothing, when it is not that of a simple word, implies as much matter as the idea of All, with, in addition, an operation of thought.

I should say as much of the idea of disorder. Why is the universe well-ordered? How is rule imposed upon what is without rule, and form upon matter? How is it that our thought recognizes itself in things? This problem, which among the moderns has become the problem of knowledge after having been, among the ancients, the problem of being, was born of an illusion of the same order. It disappears if one considers that the idea of disorder has a definite meaning in the domain of human industry, or, as we say, of fabrication, but not in that of creation. Disorder is simply the order we are not looking for. You cannot suppress one order even by thought, without causing another to spring up. If there is not finality or will, it is because there is mechanism; if the mechanism gives way, so much the gain for will, caprice, finality. But when you expect one of these two orders and you find the other, you say there is disorder, formulating what is in terms of what might or should be, and objectifying your regret. All disorder thus includes two things: outside us, one order; within us, the representation of a different order which alone interests us. Suppression therefore again signifies substitution. And the idea of a suppression of all order, that is to say, the idea of an absolute disorder, then contains a veritable contradiction, because it consists in leaving only a single aspect to the operation which, by hypothesis, embraced two. Either the idea of an absolute disorder represents no more than a combination of sounds, *flatus vocis*, or else, if it corresponds to something, it translates a movement of the mind which leaps from mechanism to finality, from finality to mechanism, and which, in order to mark the spot where it is, prefers each time to indicate the point where it is not. Therefore, in wishing to suppress order, you find yourself with two or more "orders." This is tantamount to saying that the conception of an order which is superadded to an "absence of order" implies an absurdity, and that the problem disappears.

The two illusions I have just mentioned are in reality only one. They consist in believing that there is *less* in the idea of the empty than in the idea of the full, *less* in the concept of disorder than in that of order. In reality, there is more intellectual content in the ideas of disorder and nothingness when they represent something than in those of order and existence, because they imply several orders, several existences and, in addition, a play of wit which unconsciously juggles with them.

Very well then, I find the same illusion in the case in point. Underlying the doctrines which disregard the radical novelty of each moment of evolution there are many misunderstandings, many errors. But there is especially the idea that the possible is *less* than the real, and that, for this reason, the possibility of things precedes their existence. They would thus be capable of representation beforehand; they could be thought of before being realized. But it is the reverse that is true. If we leave aside the closed systems, subjected to purely mathematical laws, isolable because duration does not act upon them, if we consider the totality of concrete reality or simply the world of life, and still more that of consciousness, we find there is more and not less in the possibility of each of the successive states than in their reality. For the possible is only the real with the addition of an act of mind which throws its image back into the past, once it has been enacted. But that is what our intellectual habits prevent us from seeing.

During the great war certain newspapers and periodicals sometimes turned aside from the terrible worries of the day to think of what would happen later once peace was restored. They were particularly preoccupied with the future of literature. Someone came one day to ask me my ideas on the subject. A little embarrassed, I declared I had none. "Do you not at least perceive, " I was asked, "certain possible directions? Let us grant that one cannot foresee things in detail; you as a philosopher have at least an idea of the whole. How do you conceive, for example, the great dramatic work of tomorrow?" I shall always remember my interlocutor's surprise when I answered, "If I knew what was to be the great dramatic work of the future, I should be writing it." I saw distinctly that he conceived the future work as being already stored up in some cupboard reserved for possibles; because of my longstanding relations with philosophy, I should have been able to obtain from it the key to the storehouse. "But," I said, "the work of which you speak is not yet possible."—"But it must be, since it is to take place."—"No, it is not. I grant you, at most, that it *will have been possible*." "What do you mean by that?"—"It's quite simple. Let a man of talent or genius come forth, let him create a work: it will then be real, and by that very fact it becomes retrospectively or retroactively possible. It would not be possible, it would not have been so, if this man had not come upon the scene. That is why I tell you that it will have been possible today, but that it is not yet so." "You're not serious! You are surely not going to maintain that the future has an effect upon the present, that the present brings something into the past, that action works back over the course of time and imprints its mark afterwards?"—"That depends. That one can put reality into the past and thus work backwards in time is something I have never claimed. But that one can put the possible there, or rather that the possible may put itself there at any moment, is not to be doubted. As reality is created as something unforeseeable and new, its image is reflected behind it into the indefinite past; thus it finds that it has from all time been possible, but it is at this precise moment that it begins to have been always possible, and that is why I said that its possibility, which does not precede its reality, will have preceded it once the reality has appeared. The possible is therefore the mirage of the present in the past; and as we know the future will finally constitute a present and the mirage effect is continually being produced, we are convinced that the image of tomorrow is already contained in our actual present, which will be the past of tomorrow, although we did not manage to grasp it. That is precisely the illusion. It is as though one were to fancy, in seeing his reflection in the mirror in front of him, that he could have touched it had he stayed behind it. Thus in judging that the possible does not presuppose the real, one admits that the realization adds something to the simple possibility: the possible would have been there from all time, a phantom awaiting its hour; it would therefore have become reality by the addition of something, by some transfusion of blood or life. One does not see the contrary is the case, that the possible implies the corresponding reality with, moreover, something added, since the possible is the combined effect of reality once it has appeared and of a condition which throws it back in time. The idea immanent in most philosophies and natural to the human mind, of possibles which would be realized by an acquisition of existence, is therefore pure illusion. One might as well claim that the man in flesh and blood comes from the materialization of his image seen in the mirror, because in that real man is everything found in this virtual image with, in addition, the solidity which makes it possible to touch it. But the truth is that more is needed here to obtain the virtual than is necessary for the real, more for the image of the man than for the man himself, for the image of the man will not be portrayed if the man is not first produced, and in addition one has to have the mirror."

That is what my interlocutor was forgetting as he questioned me on the theatre of tomorrow. Perhaps too he was unconsciously playing on the meaning of the word "possible". *Hamlet* was doubtless possible before being realized, if that means that there was no insurmountable obstacle to its realization. In this particular sense one calls possible what is not impossible; and it stands to reason that this non-impossibility of a thing is the condition of the realization. But the possible thus understood is in no degree virtual, something ideally pre-existent. If you close the gate you know no one will cross the road; it does not follow that you can predict who will cross when you open it. Nevertheless, from the quite negative sense of the term "impossible" you pass surreptitiously, unconsciously to the positive sense. Possibility signified "absence of hindrance" a few minutes ago: now you make of it a "pre-existence under the form of an idea," which is quite another thing. In the first meaning of the word it was a truism to say that the possibility of a thing precedes its reality: by that you meant simply that obstacles, having been surmounted, were surmountable. But in the second meaning it is an absurdity, for it is clear that a mind in which the *Hamlet* of Shakespeare had taken shape in the form of possible would by that fact have created its reality: it would thus have been, by definition, Shakespeare himself. In vain do you imagine at first that this mind could have appeared before Shakespeare; it is because you are not thinking then of all the details in the play. As you complete them the predecessor of Shakespeare finds himself thinking all that Shakespeare will think, feeling all he will feel, knowing all he will know, perceiving therefore all he will perceive, and consequently occupying the same point in space and time, having the same body and the same soul: it is Shakespeare himself.

But I am putting too much stress on what is self-evident. We are forced to these considerations in discussing a work of art. I believe in the end we shall consider it evident that the artist in executing his work is creating the possible as well as the real. Whence comes it then that one might hesitate to say the same thing for nature? Is not the world a work of art incomparably richer than that of the greatest artist? And is there not as much absurdity, if not more, in supposing, in the work of nature, that the future is outlined in advance, that possibility existed before reality? Once more let me say I am perfectly willing to admit that the future states of a closed system of material points are calculable and hence visible in its present state. But, and I repeat, this system is extracted, or abstracted, from a whole which, in addition to inert and unorganized matter, comprises organization. Take the concrete and complete world, with the life and consciousness it encloses; consider nature in its entirety, nature the generator of new species as novel and original in form as the design of any artist: in these species concentrate upon individuals, plants or animals, each of which has its own character—I was going to say its personality (for one blade of grass does not resemble another blade of grass any more than a Raphael resembles a Rembrandt); lift your attention above and beyond individual man to societies which disclose actions and situations comparable to those of any drama: how can one still speak of possibles which would precede their own realization? How can we fail to see that if the event can always be explained afterwards by an arbitrary choice of antecedent events, a completely different event could have been equally well explained in the same circumstances by another choice of antecedent—nay, by the same antecedents otherwise cut out, otherwise distributed, otherwise perceived,—in short, by our retrospective attention? Backwards over the course of time a constant remodelling of the past by the present, of the cause by the effect, is being carried out.

We do not see it, always for the same reason, always a prey to the same illusion, always because we treat as the more what is the less, as the less what is the more. If we put the possible back into its proper place, evolution becomes something quite different from the realization of a program: the gates of the future open wide; freedom is offered an unlimited field. The fault of those doctrines,—rare indeed in the history of philosophy,—which have succeeded in leaving room for indetermination and freedom in the world, is to have failed to see what their affirmation implied. When they spoke of indetermination, of freedom, they meant by indetermination a competition between possibles, by freedom a choice between possibles,—as if possibility was not created by freedom itself! As if any other hypothesis, by affirming an ideal preexistence of the possible to the real, did not reduce the new to a mere rearrangement of former elements! As if it were not thus to be led sooner or later to regard that rearrangement as calculable and foreseeable! By accepting the premiss of the contrary theory one was letting the enemy in. We must resign ourselves to the inevitable: it is the real which makes itself possible, and not the possible which becomes real.

NELSON GOODMAN

(b. 1906)

Goodman, a native of Massachusetts, received his bachelor's degree from Harvard in 1928, and his doctorate in philosophy from the same university in 1941. He has been a faculty member successively at Tufts College, University of Pennsylvania, and Brandeis University (where, from 1964 to 1967, he was Harry Austryn Wolfson Professor of Philosophy). He has also been a visiting lecturer at Harvard, Princeton, Oxford, and the University of London. In 1946, Goodman was awarded a Guggenheim fellowship, and he has been a research fellow with the Center for Cognitive Studies, as well as a fellow of the American Academy of Arts and Sciences. For thirteen years, until 1942, he operated an art gallery in Boston. His published works include The Structure of Appearance *(1951),* Fact, Fiction and Forecast *(1954), and* Languages of Art *(1968).*

THE WAY THE WORLD IS

1. INTRODUCTION

Philosophers sometimes mistake features of discourse for features of the subject of discourse. We seldom conclude that the world consists of words just because a true description of it does, but we sometimes suppose that the structure of the world is the same as the structure of the description. This tendency may even reach the point of linguomorphism when we conceive the world as comprised of atomic objects corresponding to certain proper names, and of atomic facts corresponding to atomic sentences. A *reductio ad absurdum* blossoms when an occasional philosopher maintains that a simple description can be appropriate only if the world is simple; or asserts (and I have heard this said in all seriousness) that a coherent description will be a distortion unless the world happens to be coherent. According to this line of thinking, I suppose that before describing the world in English we ought to determine whether it is written in English, and that we ought to examine very carefully how the world is spelled.

Obviously enough the tongue, the spelling, the typography, the verbosity of a description reflect no parallel features in the world.

Coherence is a characteristic of descriptions, not of the world: the significant question is not whether the world is coherent, but whether our account of it is. And what we call the simplicity of the world is merely the simplicity we are able to achieve in describing it.

But confusion of the sort I am speaking of is relatively transparent at the level of isolated sentences, and so relatively less dangerous than the error of supposing that the structure of a veridical systematic description mirrors forth the structure of the world. Since a system has basic or primitive terms or elements and a graded hierarchy built out of these, we easily come to suppose that the world must consist of corresponding atomic elements put together in similar fashion. No theory advocated in recent years by first-rate philosophers seems more obviously wrong than the picture theory of language. Yet we still find acute philosophers resorting under pressure to a notion of absolutely simple qualities or particles. And most of those who avoid thinking of the world as uniquely divisible into absolute elements still commonly suppose that *meanings* do resolve thus uniquely, and so accept the concealed absolutism involved in maintaining the distinction between analytic and synthetic propositions.

In this paper, however, I am not concerned with any of the more specific issues I have just touched upon, but with a more general question. I have been stressing the dangers of mistaking certain features of discourse for features of the world. This is a recurrent theme with me, but even this is not my main concern here. What I want to discuss is an uncomfortable feeling that comes upon me whenever I warn against the confusion in question. I can hear the anti-intellectualistic, the mystic—my arch enemy—saying something like this: "Yes, that's just what I've been telling you all along. All our descriptions are a sorry travesty. Science, language, perception, philosophy—none of these can ever be utterly faithful to the world as it is. All make abstractions or conventionalizations of one kind or another, all filter the world through the mind, through concepts, through the senses, through language; and all these filtering media in some way distort the world. It is not just that each gives only a partial truth, but that each introduces distortion of its own. We never achieve even in part a really faithful portrayal of the way the world is."

Here speaks the Bergsonian, the obscurantist, seemingly repeating my own words and asking, in effect, "What's the difference between us? Can't we be friends?" Before I am willing to admit that philosophy must make alliances that strange, I shall make a determined effort to formulate the difference between us. But I shall begin by discussing some preliminary, related questions.

2. *THE WAY THE WORLD IS GIVEN*

Perhaps we can gain some light on the way the world is by examining the way it is given to us in experience. The question of the given has a slightly musty sound these days. Even hardened philosophers have become a little self-conscious about the futility of their debates over the given, and have the grace to rephrase the issue in terms of "ground-elements" or "protocol-sentences." But in one way or another we hear a good deal about getting down to the original, basic, bare elements from which all knowledge is manufactured. Knowing is tacitly conceived as a processing of raw material into a finished product; and an understanding of knowledge is thus supposed to require that we discover just what the raw material is.

Offhand, this seems easy enough. Carnap wanted the ground-elements of his system in the *Aufbau* to be as nearly as possible epistemologically primary. In order to arrive at these, he says, we must leave out of ordinary experience all the results of any analysis to which we subject what we initially receive. This means leaving out all divisions along spatial or qualitative boundaries, so that our elements are big lumps, each containing everything in our experience at a given moment. But to say this is to make artificial temporal divisions; and the actual given, Carnap implies, consists not of these big lumps, but of one single stream.

But this way of arriving at the given assumes that the processes of knowing are all processes of analysis. Other philosophers have supposed rather that the processes are all processes of synthesis, and that the given therefore consists of minimal particles that have to be combined with one another in knowing. Still other thinkers hold that both these views are too extreme, and that the world is given in more familiar medium-size pieces, to which both analysis and synthesis are applied. Thus in views of the given we find duplicated the monism, atomism, and the intermediate pluralisms of metaphysics. But which view of the given is right?

Let's look at the question more closely. The several views do not differ about what is contained in the given, or what can be found there. A certain visual presentation, all agree, contains certain colors, places, designs, etc.; it contains the least perceptible particles and it is a whole. The question is not whether the given *is* a single undifferentiated lump or contains many tiny parts; it is a whole comprised of such parts. The issue is not *what* is given but *how* it is given. Is it *given* as a single whole or is it *given as* many small particles? This captures the precise issue—and at the same time discloses its emptiness. For I do not think any sense can be made of the phrase "*given as.*" That an experience is given as several parts surely does not mean that these parts are presented torn asunder; nor can it mean that these parts are partitioned off from one another by perceptible lines of demarcation. For if such lines of demarcation are there at all, they are there within the given, for any view of the given. The nearest we could come to finding any meaning to the question what the world is *given as* would be to say that this turns on whether the material in question is apprehended with a kind of feeling of wholeness or a feeling of broken-upness. To come that near to finding a meaning for *given as* is not to come near enough to count.

So I am afraid we can get no light on the way the world is by asking about the way it is given. For the question about the way it is given evaporates into thin air.

3. THE WAY THE WORLD IS TO BE SEEN

Perhaps we shall get further by asking how the world is best seen. If we can with some confidence grade ways of seeing or picturing the world according to their degrees of realism, of absence of distortion, of faithfulness in representing the way the world is, then surely by reading back from this we can learn a good deal about the way the world is.

We need consider our everyday ideas about pictures for only a moment to recognize this as an encouraging approach. For we rate pictures quite easily according to their approximate degree of realism. The most realistic picture is the one most like a color photograph; and pictures become progressively less realistic, and more conventionalized or abstract, as they depart from this standard. The way we see the world best, the nearest pictorial approach to the way the world is, is the way the camera sees it. This version of the whole matter is simple, straightforward, and quite generally held. But in philosophy as everywhere else, every silver lining has a big black cloud—and the view described has everything in its favor except that it is, I think, quite wrong.

If I take a photograph of a man with his feet towards me, the feet may come out as large as his torso. Is this the way I normally or properly see the man? If so, then why do we call such a photograph distorted? If not, then I can no longer claim to be taking the photographic view of the world as my standard of faithfulness.

The fact of the matter is that this "distorted" photograph calls our attention to something about seeing that we had ignored. Just in the way that it differs from an ordinary "realistic" picture, it reveals new facts and possibilities in visual experience. But the "distorted" photograph is a rather trivial example of something much more general and important. The "distortion" of the photograph is comparable to the distortion of new or unfamiliar styles of painting. Which is the more faithful portrait of a man—the one by Holbein or the one by Manet or the one by Sharaku or the one by Durer or the one by Cézanne or the one by Picasso? Each different way of painting represents a different way of seeing; each makes its selection, its emphasis; each uses its own vocabulary of conventionalization. And we need only look hard at the pictures by any such artist to come to see the world in somewhat the same way. For seeing is an activity and the way we perform it depends in large part upon our training. I remember J.B. Neumann saying that once when he happened to see the faces of a movie audience in the reflected glare of the screen he first realized how an African sculptor saw faces. What we regard as the most realistic pictures are merely pictures of the sort that most of us, unfortunately, are brought up on. An African or a Japanese would make a quite different choice when asked to select the pictures that most closely depict what he sees. Indeed our resistance to new or exotic ways of painting stems from our normal lethargic resistance to retraining; and on the other hand the excitement lies in the acquisition of new skill. Thus the discovery of African art thrilled French painters and they learned from it new ways to see and paint. What is less often realized is that the discovery of European art is exciting to the African sculptor for the same reason; it shows him a new way of seeing, and he, too, modifies his work accordingly. Unfortunately, while European absorption of African often results in an artistic advance, African adoption of European style almost always leads to artistic deterioration. But this is for incidental reasons. The first is that social deterioration of the African is usually simultaneous with the introduction of European art. The second reason is rather more intriguing: that while the French artist was influenced by the best of African art, the African was fed no doubt on calendar art and pin-up girls. Had he seen Greek and Mediaeval sculpture instead, the results might have been radically different. But I am digressing.

The upshot of all this is that we cannot find out much about the way the world is by asking about the best or most faithful or most realistic way of seeing or picturing it. For the ways of seeing and picturing are many and various; some are strong, effective, useful, intriguing, or sensitive; others are weak, foolish, dull, banal, or blurred. But even if all the latter are excluded, still none of the rest can lay any good claim to be the way of seeing or picturing the world the way it is.

4. THE WAY THE WORLD IS TO BE DESCRIBED

We come now to a more familiar version of the question of the way the world is. How is the world to be described? Does what we call a true description faithfully depict the world?

Most of us have ringing in our ears Tarski's statement that "it is raining" is true if and only if it is raining, as well as his remark (I think erroneous, but that is beside the point here) that acceptance of this formula constitutes acceptance of a correspondence theory of truth. This way of putting the matter encourages a natural tendency to think of truth in terms of mirroring or faithful reproduction; and we have a slight shock whenever we happen to notice the obvious fact that the sentence "it is raining" is about as different as possible from the rainstorm. This disparity is of the same sort for a true as for a false description. Luckily, therefore, we need not here concern ourselves with the difficult technical matter of the nature of truth; we can confine our attention to admittedly true descriptions. What we must face is the fact that even the truest description comes nowhere near faithfully reproducing the way the world is.

A systematic description of the world, as I noted earlier, is even more vulnerable to this charge; for it has explicit primitives, routes of construction, etc., none of them features of the world described. Some philosophers contend, therefore, that if systematic descriptions introduce an arbitrary artificial order, then we should make our descriptions unsystematic to bring them more into accord with the world. Now the tacit assumption here is that the respects in which a description is unsatisfactory are *just those respects in which it falls short of being a faithful picture*; and the tacit *goal* is to achieve a description that as nearly as possible gives a living likeness. But the goal is a delusive one. For we have seen that even the most realistic way of picturing amounts merely to one kind of conventionalization. In painting, the selection, the emphasis, the conventions are different from but no less peculiar to the vehicle, and no less variable, than those of language. The idea of making verbal descriptions approximate pictorial depiction loses its point when we understand that to turn a description into the most faithful possible picture would amount to nothing more than exchanging some conventions for others.

Thus neither the way the world is given nor any way of seeing or picturing or describing it conveys to us the way the world is.

5. THE WAY THE WORLD IS

We come now to the question: what, then, is the way the world is? Am I still threatened with the friendship of my enemies? It looks very much that way, for I have just reached the mystic's conclusion that there is no representation of the way the world is. But if our accord seems on the surface to have been reinforced, a second look will show how it has been undermined, by what we have been saying.

The complaint that a given true description distorts or is unfaithful to the world has significance in terms of some grading of descriptions according to faithfulness, or in terms of a difference in degree of faithfulness between true descriptions and good pictures. But if we say that all true descriptions and good pictures are equally unfaithful, then in terms of what sample or standard of relative faithfulness are we speaking? We have no longer before us any clear notion of what faithfulness would be. Thus I reject the idea that there is some test of realism or faithfulness in addition to the tests of pictorial goodness and descriptive truth. There are very many different equally true descriptions of the world, and their truth is the only standard of their faithfulness. And when we say of them that they all involve conventionalizations, we are saying that no one of these different descriptions is *exclusively* true, since the others are also true. None of them tells us *the* way the world is, but each of them tells us *a* way the world is.

If I were asked what is *the food* for men, I should have to answer "none." For there are many foods. And if I am asked what is the way the world is, I must likewise answer, "none". For the world is many ways. The mystic holds that there is some way the world is and that this way is not captured by any description. For me, there is no way which is the way the world is; and so of course no description can capture it. But there are many ways the world is, and every true description captures one of them. The difference between my friend and me is, in sum, the enormous difference between absolutism and relativism.

Since the mystic is concerned with the way the world is and finds that the way cannot be expressed, his ultimate response to the question of the way the world is must, as he recognizes, be silence. Since I am concerned rather with the ways the world is, my response must be to construct one or many descriptions. The answer to the question "What is the way the world is? What are the ways the world is?" is not a shush, but a chatter.

6. POSTSCRIPT

Near the beginning of this paper, I spoke of the obvious falsity of the picture theory of language. I declared rather smugly that a description does not picture what it describes, or even represent the structure of what it describes. The devastating charge against the picture theory of language was that a description cannot represent or mirror forth the world as it is. But we have since observed that a picture doesn't do this either. I began by dropping the picture theory of language and ended by adopting the language theory of pictures. I rejected the picture theory of language on the ground that the structure of a description does not conform to the structure of the world. But I then concluded that there is no such thing as the structure of the world for anything to conform or fail to conform to. You might say that the picture theory of language is as false and as true as the picture theory of pictures; or in other words, that what is false is not the picture theory of language but a certain absolutistic notion concerning both pictures and language. Perhaps eventually I shall learn that what seems most obviously false sometimes isn't.

28

Is Freedom a Form of Determinism?

ADOLF GRÜNBAUM

(b. 1923)

Born in Germany, Grünbaum studied at Wesleyan University and at Yale. He later taught philosophy at Lehigh University, and has been, since 1960, Mellon Professor of Philosophy at the University of Pittsburgh. He is the author of Philosophical Problems of Space and Time *(1963).*

HOW THINGS MUST BE

I. INTRODUCTION

Is man's possession of free will compatible with causal and/or statistical laws of human behavior? This problem has been one of the perennial issues of modern philosophy.[1] Its ramifications include the applicability of the scientific method to the study of our voluntary behavior, the logical consistency of *advocating* specific social changes while also predicting their occurrence, and the justice of making moral evaluations of human agents as a basis for meting out punishment or rewards to them. Thus, in his recent *Action and Purpose*, Richard Taylor has tried to show, by some new arguments, that if volitions are the causes of our actions, then we are not free but are compelled to act as we do. He therefore claims that our free actions must be exempt from the causal sphere.[2] And in a paper entitled "Some Limitations of Science," Thomas Murray of the United States Atomic Energy Commission wrote as follows:

> However useful science is to investigate the privacy of tiny chambers called atoms, it is all but useless to investigate the inner and higher life of man. You can't examine free-will in a test tube. Yet, much of what man does for weal or woe springs from this inner life of free choice.[3]

We are told that while causal and statistical laws characterize the physical world and thus make possible predictions and retrodictions of the careers of physical processes, the consciousness characteristic of man in some sense intrinsically defies any such characterization by laws. And since scientific mastery of a domain requires successful predictions, retrodictions, and/or explanations which only the existence of laws makes

From American Philosophical Quarterly, *Vol. 8, No. 4, Oct., 1971, pp. 299–304.*

[1]For a historical and critical treatment of some of the earlier literature on this problem, see Ernst Cassirer, *Determinism and Indeterminism in Modern Physics* (New Haven, 1956). A very useful recent anthology entitled *Free Will and Determinism*, ed. by B. Berofsky (New York, 1966) presents four fundamentally different approaches to the issue. Another valuable collection is the volume *Determinism and Freedom in the Age of Modern Science*, ed. by Sidney Hook (New York, 1961), and K. Lehrer (ed.), *Freedom and Determinism* (New York, 1966). See also H. Margenau, *Scientific Indeterminism & Human Freedom* (Latrobe, Pa., 1968), and Corliss Lamont, *Freedom of Choice Affirmed* (New York, 1967). For a contemporary account from the standpoint of dialectical materialism, see Tamas Földesi, *The Problem of Free Will* (Budapest, 1966).

[2]Richard Taylor, *Action and Purpose* (Englewood Cliffs, N.J. 1966)

[3]Thomas E. Murray, *Chemical Engineering Progress*, vol. 48 (1952), p. 22.

possible, it is claimed that consciously directed human behavior is beyond the scope of scientific comprehensibility.

It is ironic that this claim often finds adherents among executives like Murray, whose every step in the management of people is based on the unwitting assumption of *causal* connections between *influences* on men and their *responses*. But it is precisely this causal or *deterministic* conception of man which is repudiated by Murray. And in view of that conception's pivotal role in our inquiry, we shall need to make a careful assessment of its credentials. The deterministic conception of the *inorganic* sector of nature found its modern prototype in classical Newtonian mechanics, and in classical physics generally. These classical theories feature exceptionless functional dependencies relating the states of physical systems as follows: Given the state of a physical system at one or more times, its state at other times is uniquely determined. But, of course, these particular theories are not asserted by determinism as such and are only exemplifications of a deterministic kind of theory. Moreover, there is a notorious vagueness in determinism as a general thesis about the world and even as a regulative principle of scientific research. Yet the problems which we are about to discuss have significance, I believe, because they would confront any reasonably satisfactory explication of the notion of determinism which has evolved in modern science.

The deterministic conception of *human behavior* is inspired by the view that man is an integral part and product of nature and that his behavior can reasonably be held to exhibit scientifically ascertainable regularities just as any other *macroscopic* sector of nature. Determinism must be distinguished from predictability, since there are at least two kinds of situations in which there may be no predictability for special *epistemic* reasons even though determinism is true: (i) Though determinism may hold in virtue of the existence of one-to-one functional dependencies between specifiable attributes of events, some such attributes *may* be *"emergent"* in the sense of being unpredictable relatively to any and all laws that could possibly have been discovered by us humans in advance of the first occurrence of the attribute(s) in question, and (ii) there can be perverse persons who choose among alternative courses of action *not* in the light of the benefits that may accrue from the action but with a view to assuring that someone else's prediction of their choice behavior turns out to be false. And there may be conditions under which such perverse persons are bound to succeed in behaving *contra*-predictively.[4] For there may be conditions under which these perverse persons can make it *physically impossible* for the predictor to gain access to some of the information essential to the success of the prediction. Thus, there may be cases in

---

[4]Cf. M. Scriven, "An Essential Unpredictability in Human Behaviour," in *Scientific Psychology*, ed. by B. B. Wolman and E. Nagel (New York, 1965), pp. 411–425. For a criticism of Scriven's interpretation of the significance of contra-predictive behavior, see P. Suppes, "On an Example of Unpredictability in Human Behavior," *Philosophy of Science*, vol. 31 (1964), pp. 143–148.

which determinism is true even though prediction is not epistemically feasible even in principle. Indeed, it *may* be that for *external* predictors, either humans or computers, it is not physically possible to predict certain deterministic processes in the interior of the Schwarzschild radius of a Schwarzschild gravitational field of general relativity theory, and *perhaps* certain *deterministic* processes inside the so-called "black holes" of astrophysics are thus unpredictable for *outside* predictors.

Furthermore, as Popper has argued, no deterministically operating computing machine can calculate *its own future* in full detail, and hence the career of a deterministic system will *not* be completely predictable by a human or a computer if they themselves are constituents of that system.[5] Mindful of this result concerning self-referential or auto-predictability, Wilfrid Sellars has written as follows:

> . . . conceptual difficulties do arise about universal predictability if we fail to distinguish between what I shall call *epistemic* predictability and *logical* predictability. By epistemic predictability, I mean predictability by a predictor *in the system.* The concept of universal epistemic predictability does seem to be bound up with difficulties of the type explored by Gödel. By logical predictability, on the other hand, is meant that property of the process laws governing a physical system which involves the derivability of a description of the state of the system at a later time from a description of its state at an earlier time, without stipulating that the latter description be obtained by operations within the system. It can be argued, I believe, with considerable force, that the latter is a misuse of the term "predictability," but it does seem to me that this is what philosophers concerned with the free will and determinism issue have had in mind, and it simply muddies up the waters to harass these philosophers with Gödel problems about epistemic predictability.[6]

Thus, there are several weighty reasons for not identifying or equating determinism with universal predictability, i. e., with the physical possibility of universal prediction by predictors both inside and outside the system to which the prediction pertains.

The moral opponent of determinism, or "indeterminist libertarian," maintains that determinism is *logically incompatible* with the known fact that people respond meaningfully to moral imperatives. Specifically, this indeterminist says: If each one of us makes decisions which are determined by the sum total of all the relevant influences upon us (heredity, environmental background, the stimuli affecting us at the moment, etc.), then no man *can help* doing what he does. And then the conse-

---

[5]K. R. Popper, "Indeterminism in Quantum Physics and in Classical Physics," *The British Journal for the Philosophy of Science*, vol. I (1950), Pt. I, pp. 117–133; Pt. II pp. 173–195. In Sect. V below, I shall comment on the account of freedom of action which was proposed on the basis of Popper's result by D. M. MacKay in his 1967 Eddington Memorial Lecture *Freedom of Action in a Mechanistic Universe* (Cambridge, 1967).

[6]Wilfrid Sellars, "Fatalism and Determinism," in: K. Lehrer (ed.), *Freedom and Determinism* (New York, 1966), pp. 143–144.

quences are allegedly as follows: (*a*) It is impossible to allow for our feeling that we are able to act freely except by dismissing it as devoid of any factual foundation. (*b*) It is useless to try to choose between good and bad courses of action. (*c*) It is ill-conceived to hold people responsible for their acts. (*d*) It is unjust to punish people for wrong-doing, or reward and praise them for good deeds. (*e*) It is mere self-delusion to feel remorse or guilt for past misdeeds. (Hereafter the exponent of these views will be called "indeterminist" for brevity.)

Furthermore, the indeterminist sometimes makes the ominous declaration that if determinism became known to the masses of people and were accepted by them, moral chaos would result, because—so he claims—everyone would forthwith drop his inhibitions. The excuse would be that he cannot help acting uninhibitedly, and people would fatalistically sink into a state of futility, laziness, and indifference. Moreover, we are told that if determinism were believed, the great fighters against injustice in human history would give up raising their voices in protest, since the truth of determinism would allegedly make such efforts useless.

Thus, the indeterminist goes on to contend that there is a basic *inconsistency* in *any* deterministic *and* activistic socio-political theory. The alleged inconsistency is the following: to *advocate* a social activism with the aim of thereby bringing about a future state whose eventuation the given theory regards as assured by historical causation. This argument is applied to any kind of deterministic theory independently of whether the explanatory variables of the historical process are held by that theory to be economic, climatic, sexual, demographic, geopolitical, or the inscrutable will of God. Accordingly, the indeterminist objects to such diverse doctrines as (*a*) Justice Oliver Wendell Holmes's dictum that "the mode in which the inevitable comes to pass is through effort,"[7] and (*b*) St. Augustine's (and Calvin's) belief in divine foreordination, when coupled with the advocacy of Christian virtue. And correlatively, the indeterminist claims that if determinism is true, it is futile for men to discuss how to optimize the achievement of their ends by a change in personal or group behavior.

I do not regard the persistence of the polemics associated with these contentions as betokening the futility of the controversy. Instead, I believe that a good deal has already been clarified by the literature on it and that further progress is possible. Indeed, the present essay is an attempt to improve substantially upon my earlier defense of the thesis that man's "inner life of free choice" in principle no more eludes scientific intelligibility than does "the privacy of tiny chambers called atoms," to use Murray's parlance.[8]

---

[7] O. W. Holmes, "Ideas and Doubts," *Illinois Law Review*, vol. 10 (1915), p. 2.

[8] A. Grünbaum, "Science and Man," *Perspectives in Biology and Medicine*, Vol. V (1962), pp. 483–502; reprinted in *Value and Man*, ed. by Louis Z. Hammer (New York, 1966), pp. 55–66. There was also a shorter version of the present essay in *L'Age de la Science,* vol. 2 (1969), pp. 105–127.

II. THE ARGUMENT FROM MORALITY

To introduce the objections to the argument from morality given by *some* of the indeterminists, let us suppose, for argument's sake, that the truth of determinism would actually render moral imperatives ill-conceived by entailing that moral appraisals and exhortations rest on an illusion. This would indeed be tragic. But it could hardly be claimed that determinism is false on the mere grounds that its alleged consequences would be terrible. We would show concern for the sanity of anyone who would say that his house could not have burned down because this fact would make him unhappy. And it is a stubborn fact that no amount of Norman Vincent Peale's "positive thinking" can assure that the sun will warm the earth forever so that the human race will avoid the calamity of ultimate extinction.

But is it actually the case that there are data from the field of human responses to moral rules or from the phenomena of reflective action which refute the deterministic hypothesis? I shall argue that the answer is decidedly negative. For I shall maintain that in important respects the data are *not* what they are alleged to be. And in so far as they are, I shall argue that they are not evidence against determinism. Nay, I shall claim that in part, these data are first rendered intelligible by determinism. Furthermore, I shall show what precise meaning must be given to certain moral concepts like responsibility, remorse, and punishment within the context of a deterministic theory. Of course, determinism does exclude, as we shall see, *some* of the moral conceptions entertained by philosophical indeterminists like C. A. Campbell. But I shall maintain that this involves no actual loss for ethics. And we have already seen that even if it did, this would not constitute evidence against the causal character of human behavior, which is asserted by determinism. I wish to emphasize, however, that the categorical truth of that deterministic assertion can be established inductively *not* by logical analysis alone but requires the working psychologist's empirical discovery of specific causal laws.

To establish the invalidity of the moral argument of the indeterminist, I shall now try to show that there is no incompatibility between the existence of either causal or statistical laws of voluntary behavior, on the one hand, and the feelings of freedom which we actually do have, the meaningful assignment of responsibility, the rational infliction of punishment, and the existence of feelings of remorse or guilt on the other.

A. The Fallacious Identification of Determinism with Fatalism

In some cases, the charge that determinism rules out meaningful ethical injunctions springs from the indeterminist's confusion of determinism with one or both of two versions of fatalism. Let us now distinguish determinism from each of these versions in turn.

The first of these two forms of fatalism is the appallingly primitive prescientific doctrine that in every situation, regardless of what we do, the outcome will be unaffected by our efforts. We can grant at once that if we were to learn that the sun will become a supernova during the latter part of this century or that the earth will soon collide with a giant astronomical body, we would be helpless to avert total catastrophe. But if a diabetic is in glucose shock on a certain day, it is plainly empirically false to say that it is immaterial whether he is then administered insulin or sugar. The fatalist tells us that if the diabetic's time is up on that day, he will die then in either case, but that if he is destined to live beyond that day, he will survive it in either case. That a person dies at the time of his death is an utter triviality. And it is banal that for each of us, there is a time at which we die. But these truisms do *not* lend any credence to the fatalist, who tells us that a man dies when his time is up in the sense that human effort to postpone death is *always* futile.

The latter false thesis of fatalism does not follow at all from determinism. The determinist believes that specifiable causes determine our actions and that these, in turn, determine the effects that will ensue from them. But this doctrine allows that human effort be efficacious in *some* contexts while being futile in others. Thus, determinism allows the existence of situations which are correctly characterized by Justice Oliver Wendell Holmes's cited epigram that the inevitable comes to pass through effort. The mere fact that both fatalism and determinism affirm the fixity or determinedness of future outcomes has led some indeterminists to infer fallaciously that determinism is committed to the futility of *all* human effort. The determinist maintains that existing causes determine or fix whether certain efforts will in fact be made at certain times, while allowing that future outcomes are indeed dependent on our efforts in particular contexts. By contrast, the fatalist holds falsely that such outcomes are always independent of all human efforts. But the determinist's claim of the fixity of the outcome does not entail that the outcome is independent of our efforts. Hence determinism does not allow the deduction that human intervention or exertion is futile in every case. One might as well deduce the following absurdity: determinism guarantees that explosions are always independent of the presence of detonating substances, because determinism asserts that, in specified contexts, the effects of the presence of explosives are determined!

The misidentification of determinism with fatalism can now be seen to underlie two of the contentions by indeterminists which were stated in the Introduction.

The predictions that might be made by contemporary historical determinists concerning the social organization of industrial society, for example, pertain to a society of which these forecasters are themselves members. Hence such predictions are self-referential. But these predictions are made by social prophets who, *qua* deterministic forecasters, consider their own society externally, from *without* rather than as active contributors to its destiny. And the predictions made from that theoretically external perspective are *predicated* on the prior fulfillment of certain initial conditions. These conditions include the presence in that society of people—among whom they themselves may happen to be included—who are dissatisfied with the existing state of affairs and are therefore actively seeking the future realization of the externally predicted social state. To ignore that the determinist rests his social prediction in part on the existence of the latter initial conditions, just as much as a physicist makes a prediction of a thermal expansion conditional upon the presence of heat, is to commit the fallacy of equating determinism with fatalism. Thus, a person's role as *predictor* of social change from an "external" perspective, as it were, is quite compatible logically with his belief in the necessity of his being an *advocate* of social change internal to society. We see that the indeterminist has no valid grounds for the following objection of his: it is logically inconsistent for an historical determinist, *qua* participating citizen, to advocate that action be taken by his fellow-citizens to create the social system whose advent he is predicting on the basis of his theory. For it is now plain that the indeterminist's charge derives its semblance of plausibility from his confusion of determinism with fatalism in the context of self-referential predictions. This confusion is present, for example, in Arthur Koestler's claim, in his *Darkness at Noon*, that the espousal of historical determinism by Marxists is *logically inconsistent* with their reproaching the labor movement in capitalist countries for insufficient effort on behalf of socialism.

Equally fallacious is the indeterminist's claim that it is practically *futile* for a determinist to weigh alternative modes of social organization with a view to optimizing the organization of his own society. For the determinist does *not* maintain, in fatalist fashion, that the future state of society is independent of the decisions which men make in response to (*a*) facts (both physical and social), (*b*) their own *interpretation* of these facts (which, of course, is often false), and (*c*) their value-objectives. It is precisely because, on the deterministic theory, human decisions *are* causally dependent upon these factors that deliberation concerning optimal courses of action and social arrangements can be reasonably expected to issue in successful action rather than lose its significance by adventitiousness. In short, the causal determinedness of the outcome of a process of human deliberation does not at all render futile those deliberations which issue in true beliefs about the efficacy of specified actions.

There is another version of fatalism which Gilbert Ryle has articulated[9] and rightly criticized as a *non-sequitur*.[10] If Ryle went to bed at a particular time on a certain Sunday, then it was true a thousand years before then that he would go to bed a millennium later as stated. Indeed in the posited case, it was true forever beforehand that he would be going to bed on Sunday, January 25, 1953. But given this fact, it was impossible for Ryle not to have gone to bed at the specified time on that

[9] G. Ryle, *Dilemmas* (Cambridge, 1954), p. 28.

[10] *Op. Cit.*, ch. 11, "It Was To Be."

date. For it would be self-contradictory to assert that although it was true beforehand that Ryle would do something at a certain time *t*, he did not do it. Whatever is was to be. Thence the fatalist believes he can conclude the following: *irrespective of the antecedent circumstances,* "nothing that does occur could have been helped and nothing that has not actually been done could possibly have been done."[11]

My concern here is *not* with the fallaciousness of this argument, which Ryle has no difficulty demonstrating. Instead, I wish to point out that determinism as such is irrelevant to its truistic premisses and even denies its fatalist conclusion. Note that these premisses are compatible with indeterminism no less than with causal or merely statistical determinism.[12] And we already saw that far from asserting the independence of events from any and all circumstances prevailing at other times, the determinist explicitly affirms that kind of dependence.

The illicitness of saddling determinism with either version of fatalism is now apparent.

B. The Confusion of Causal Determination with Compulsion

Some of those indeterminists who do not equate determinism with fatalism fail to see, however, that psychological laws do *not* force us to do or desire anything against our will. These laws merely state what, as a matter of fact, we do or desire under certain conditions. Thus, if there were a psychological law enabling us to predict that under certain conditions a man will desire to commit a certain act, this law would not be making him act in a manner *contrary* to his own desires, for the desire would be his. It follows that neither the causes of our desires nor psychological laws, which state under what conditions our desires arise and issue in specified kinds of behavior, compel us in any way to act in a manner contrary to our own will. There is in the indeterminist's thinking a confusion of physical and psychological law, on the one hand, with statutory law, on the other. As Moritz Schlick emphasized decades ago, psychological laws do not coerce us against our will and do not *as such* make for the frustration or contravention of our desires. By contrast, statutory laws do frustrate the desires of some and are passed only because of the need to do so. Such laws are violated when they contravene powerful desires. But natural laws (as distinct from erroneous guesses as to what they are) cannot be broken. Anyone who steps off the top of the Empire State Building shouting defiance and insubordination to the law of gravitation will not break that law, but rather will give a pathetic illustration of its applicability.

We act under *compulsion*, in the literal sense relevant here, *when we are literally being physically restrained from without in implementing the desires*

---

[11] G. Ryle, *op. cit.*, p. 15.

[12] For details, see A. Grünbaum, *Modern Science and Zeno's Paradoxes* (Middletown, Conn., 1967; and London, 1968), ch. I, §5.

which we have upon reacting to the total stimulus situation in our environment and are physically made to perform a different act instead. In that case, our desires are essentially causally irrelevant to the act which we are being compelled to perform. For example, if I am locked up and therefore cannot make an appointment, then I would be compelled to miss my appointment. Of, if a stronger man literally forces my hand to press a button which I do not wish to press, then I would be compelled to blow up a bridge. The meaning of "compulsion" intended here should not, of course, be identified with the meaning of that term familiar to students of neuroses. In the case of neurotic compulsion, the compulsive person does *unreflectively* what he wishes, although his behavior is inspired by unwarranted anxiety, and hence is insensitive to normally deterring factors, as in the case of an obsession with germs issuing in handwashing every time a door knob is touched.

In using the locution "act under compulsion," I employ the term "act" in a somewhat Pickwickian sense. For I agree with Wilfrid Sellars' remark that "If an action is not voluntary . . . then it is not really an action, but rather behavior of a sort which *would* be an action if it *were* voluntary. An involuntary wink is not a wink at all, but rather a blink. . . . To go out the window propelled by a team of professional wrestlers is not to *do* but to *suffer*, to be a patient rather than an agent" (cf. 159–160 of the Sellars reference in footnote 6).

To emphasize the meaning of "compulsion" relevant to the issue before us, I wish to point out that when a bankteller hands over cash during a robbery upon feeling the revolver pressing against his ribs, he is *not* acting under compulsion in my literal sense, any more than you and I act under compulsion when deciding not to go out to play tennis during a heavy rain. When handing over the money in preference to being shot, the bankteller is doing what he genuinely wants to do *under the given conditions*. Of course, in the absence of the revolver, the teller would not have desired to surrender the cash in response to a mere request. By the same token, it was the heavy rain that induced the hopeful tennis player to wish to stay indoors. but both the bankteller and the frustrated tennis player are doing what they wish to do in the face of the existing conditions.

The relevant similarity of the bankteller case to a case of genuine compulsion in my literal sense lies only in the fact that our legal system does *not* decree punishment either in a case of genuine compulsion, like having one's hand literally forced to blow up a bridge by pressing a button, or in a case of *voluntary* action, like that of the bankteller. For, although the bankteller is actually physically free to hold on to the money and sound the alarm, he is not punished for surrendering the money because the alternative to such surrender would be to sound the alarm at the cost of his own life. The armed bank robber can therefore be said to have "compelled" the teller to surrender the money *not* in our literal sense, but only in the sense that the robber's threat was the decisive determinant of the *particular kind of voluntary action* that was taken by the teller. Similarly, when deference to their duties under the law "compels" a judge to sentence a dear friend to imprisonment or "compels" a policeman to arrest his own kin, the behavior of the judge and of the policeman are each voluntary. Their behavior is compelled only in the non-literal sense of springing from motives which had to overcome their affection for the culprits. Thus, what is common to genuine compulsion and voluntarily deciding to hand over money in preference to dying is that both of them are treated as *excusing conditions*.

But *causal determination of voluntary behavior is not identical with what we have called literal compulsion!* For voluntary behavior does not cease to be voluntary and become "compelled" in our literal sense just because there are causes for that behavior. The indeterminist needs to show that responsibility is rendered meaningless in every case of causation no less than in the case of literal compulsion. Unless he does, he is not entitled to assert that if determinism were true, the assignment of responsibility to people for their acts would be ill-conceived, just because such assignment is inappropriate in the case of literal compulsion. . . .

A. I. MELDEN

(b. 1910)

Born in Montreal, Melden was educated at U.C.L.A., Brown, and the University of California. He taught at the latter school briefly, and then served for many years in the Department of Philosophy at the University of Washington. More recently, he has been Department Chairman at the University of California at Irvine. Among his publications are Ethical Theories *(1955),* Rights and Right Conduct *(1959), and* Free Action *(1961).*

HUMAN ACTION AND NATURAL FACT

Any action is an event in nature and whether it be the action of a carburetor or that of a person at the controls of an automobile, in principle a complete causal explanation of it can be given. But if so, this seems to do violence to the sense we have that persons are sometimes responsible for what they do.

Consider a person driving his car home after having had too much to drink at a party. The drink has impaired his reflexes. His responses to the child that steps into the path of his car are slowed. He hits and kills her. Is he responsible? Surely a complete causal explanation of the event—the striking and the resulting killing of the child—is possible. Given the circumstances—the impairment of the driver's responses—the death of the child is as inevitable and as excusable as it would be if it had happened because of faulty brakes. But, you say, what determined the outcome was the excessive drink imbibed, or the decision, given the recognition of the intoxication induced, to chance it and to drive on the public road. But, each of *these* events is one for which a causal explanation is possible; and each therefore is as inextricably bound up in the web of necessity as the striking and killing of the child. A man's acceptance of a drink can be explained, if not by the same events, then at least generically in the same terms as the breaking of a windowpane, in the latter

From pp. 232–234, 237–245 of "Philosophy and the Understanding of Human Fact" by A. I. Melden in Epistemology: New Essays in the Theory of Knowledge *edited by Avrum Stroll.*

case by the dispositional property of glass—its fragility—and the activating force applied to its surface; in the former by the disposition of the driver to drink and the stimulus afforded by the sight of the proferred drink. To say that the man could have refused the drink, given the proferred drink and his disposition to accept it, is as absurd as the claim that he could have been someone else if only someone not the person, who was in fact his father, had met and married his mother, and in that way provided him with a different set of genes and dispositions. So too with the decision he made once he had accepted and imbibed the drink; he could no more have decided otherwise than he could have been someone else. And if to say that he could have done otherwise—whatever he did do—is only to say that if the conditions had been different he would have done otherwise, then each of us can do what in point of fact it is quite impossible for any of us to do. For in that sense of "could have," a fool could have been a man of genius, since if conditions had been otherwise, then he too could have been another Newton. And in that sense, too, our driver could have avoided killing the child, but in no sense that is material or relevant, since if he had been in Kalamazoo rather than in California, he would not have killed the child on the main street of San Diego. But he was in San Diego and he was just the sort of man he was, in just the sort of circumstances we have described, and he could no more have done otherwise than an exploding bomb once the fuse attached to it has been detonated.

The view that actions are causally determined—for the alternative would seem to imply some a priori restriction on the limits of scientific explanation—thus seems to rob persons of any responsibility for what they do. . . . It would be, in effect, to deny that the agent had anything to do with their occurrence, to rob the action of just that connection with the character of the agent which it does have in the deliberate *and* predictable actions of responsible men, and thus to reduce him to being a hapless spectator of the events of nature, in and beyond the limits of his own body, since all alike are events that are none of his doing.

Here, clearly, we need to reconsider the doctrine, not with a view to discovering a knock-down, drag-out argument that refutes it, but to determine what has given rise to it. And surely the trouble is not a mere matter of verbal ambiguity pertaining to some crucial terms like "cause." One could argue that, of course, in some sense of "cause" one can always cite a cause for any event in nature but that those human events that are called "actions" involve causes in some sense other than those relevant to the production of natural occurrences like the breaking of windowpanes and even the contraction of muscles and the reflex movements of the various parts of the body. And there are indeed interesting and peculiar linguistic features that mark our use of "cause" in connection with human actions. For we speak, not of the causes of actions but of what caused agents we cite as causes in the field of human actions—the things that cause persons to act in such-and-such ways—are reasons of peculiar sorts not encountered in the domain of physical events: reasons that are not the reasons an event took place but the reasons an agent has for doing, and which, as reasons that are relevant, good and sufficient, show the action to be right and reasonable, as distinct from the reasons we cite in physics or physiology which merely show how it is that events are brought to pass. For in the field of human actions we are concerned not merely, if at all, with the natural history of their production in the way in which this concerns us in the area of the natural sciences but with their rationale and even with their rationality; for here we are concerned, not with the causes *of* actions (this, surely, is a barbarism), but with what causes a *person* to act, and even with the causes an agent has *for* acting as he does which, if relevant, good and sufficient, show his action to be reasonable and right.

Observations of these sorts, sound indeed as they may be, do not however disclose the sources of our fatal determinism. A truly important and disturbing philosophical error, like the one with which we are here concerned and which gives those who commit it the sense that now they see things clearly enough to see through their surface look, never arises merely because of inattention to verbal ambiguities or grammatical constructions, but to troubles of a far more serious nature. For it is not that we make our philosophical mistakes because of inattention to these linguistic matters, but the other way around: we ignore and neglect the variety of linguistic idioms precisely because of the important philosophical mistake that already has been made. Once that has occurred, any commentary on the variety of linguistic forms, on the fact that in our present example "cause" is used in a wide variety of ways, must strike those who have succumbed to the mistake as a superficial consideration that does not touch upon the important insights they claim to possess. At best, therefore, attention to these linguistic forms can only prepare the ground for the further and far more important inquiry that needs to be undertaken. And this is shown by the manner in which our committed determinist will respond to the linguistic matters to which I have alluded: these, he will say, serve only to conceal from our view the truly causally effective determinants of human conduct. Of course, he will grant, we speak of causes relevant to actions in the sense in which these are the putative causes an agent has for doing what he does—causes that are the reasons *he* offers in his explanations and in his so-called self-justification—but all of these matters are mere rationalizations, matters of idle verbal show, by means of which we conceal from ourselves and each other the genuinely operative conditions of human conduct and which as operatives doom everything a so-called agent does to the senselessness of inevitable happening. The fact that a committed determinist of the thoroughgoing and extreme sort here imagined will dismiss these considerations (like the feelings all of us have that normally at least we could have done other than what in any given instance we have done) as matters of mere surface appearance, shows that the troubles lie elsewhere than in the failure to see that "cause" is a many-faceted item of our common discourse.

What has gone wrong is, rather, the insinuation of a conception of nature that is both plausible and pernicious. The conception to which I am referring is of course that of a realm of physical events associated, in the case of human beings at least, with mental occurrences—ideas, desires, emotions, sensations, etc.—which somehow are connected with each other and the physical events in the body in some sort of psychophysical mechanism.

The view is so much a part of our intellectual folklore that it seems rash to question it. And it is surely plausible. It is not only the legacy of the past, the intellectual construction of philosopher-scientists of the seventeenth century, it is also suggested almost irresistibly by every advance in the biological sciences. That what we think and feel and want and enjoy—and so with all of the various functions of intelligence—are most intimately connected with the relevant conditions within the body, is amply confirmed by every advance in the life sciences. And that an action executed through some bodily change—the movement of limbs, vocal chords, or whatever—is indeed a change in some relevant state of this bodily mechanism, seems to be too obvious for words. If we look closely at what happens when we observe some action being performed, e.g., the waving of one's arm in greeting a friend arriving at the airport, what surely occurs is that a certain part of the body, the arm, is in motion. This is the reality of the public performance, the thing that occurs *in rerum natura*, of which all of us are equally competent witnesses. And if we are to ascribe import to this public event, to be able to say not merely that it is an arm that is in motion but that it is an arm being moved in warm response to a friend, how else can one do this except by reference to the related or connected mental events—the sight of one's friend, the warm feeling this sight produces, and the response—the movement of the arm—that ensues? For these events are occurrences which take place at a given time and place. They have their properties and they stand in relations to each other and to the bodily events with which they are connected. When they occur we take note of them by means of an inner sense. And although they have characteristics which are peculiar to them as this or that kind of mental event, they are very broadly of the same very general sort of thing as physical events, differing from the latter in their shadowy and peculiarly private status within the theatre of the mind. In any case, they are events which function as causes or effects in some sort of mechanism of the mind, which at crucial points interacts with events in the body. When these mental events produce bodily movements in the way in which the sight of a friend and the warm feeling produces the motion of the arm, then we speak of the bodily movement in the way in which we do as the action of waving one's arm in friendly greeting. To perform the action is, strictly speaking, to make the relevant bodily movement happen in causal consequence of the interior mental event. And, strictly speaking, we do not observe the action, but only the bodily movement that takes place. "Seeing the action" is only a misleading, a somewhat inaccurate way of describing the facts: what we see is the bodily movement and we infer that it has occurred because of, i.e., as the effect of, the relevant mental events. We thus have a metaphysics in which nature is neatly divided into the mental and the physical, and where actions, which as public events are physical in their nature, are distinguished from other physical occurrences, not because of the features which they have as such observable occurrences, but only extrinsically because of their relations to the mental events that are their causes or their effects.

That such a metaphysics as I have here outlined has important revisionary consequences for our most deep-seated and widespread convictions is clear enough. Given these categories of the physical and the mental, it is not surprising that those who cheerfully embrace them as exhaustive and complete must deal as they do even with the simplest of human actions, e.g., that of raising one's arm. For this, being different from the bodily movement of the arm rising in the air, must now be viewed as a hybrid concoction, a bodily or physical movement to which a dash of mental bitters has been added.

But, secondly, the ingredients cannot possibly be mixed, since only one of these, the bodily movement, is observable, and the other, the mental event, is concealed. It follows that on this view no one ever saw anyone else ever do anything at all. All that one can see is some physical or bodily movement. Strictly speaking, no one has ever witnessed a signature, a theft, a robbery, or a killing; and the procedures adopted by the courts, in order to insure that witnesses confine their remarks to what they actually see, are necessarily wide of the mark when they address themselves to human actions. In respect of these, we must depart from what we actually see and engage in inferences or conjectures about the occurrence of mental events which, inescapably, are cut off from our view.

Third, an action, insofar as it is something observable, is physical or bodily in its nature, indistinguishable from the reflex movements of the body. As such, clearly, it cannot be right or wrong, any more than it can have the properties commonly ascribed to actions. For it is not the thing that we observe that is the morally right action of an agent: as something observed it is in its nature physical or bodily and hence neither an action nor anything that *could* be described as right or wrong. It is as if, looking at the moves of chess players, we suddenly saw them simply as movements of curiously shaped material objects on a checkered surface: where in such a scene do the adjectives that describe chess moves as clever, right, ingenious, etc. have any application? So what we mistakenly call the action, i.e., the thing we observe, namely the bodily movement, being physical, cannot be right or wrong. And moral philosophers on this ground have argued that what makes an action right is something having to do only with the character of its consequences; but of course this view is "derived" from a doctrine according to which the events that are normally termed "right" or "wrong" are not really actions at all. If there is anything that is strictly speaking an action, it must be relegated to some interior performance within the mind.

Fourth, there are those who are led by the kind of conceptual framework described to reject as intellectually indefensible the conception of responsibility inherent in the traditional criminal law. Instead, they offer us the panacea of the causal explanation and manipulation of the behavior of individuals, who have been "victimized" by the social conditions in which they have been reared, in order to achieve their socially desirable adjustment and reform. Now this may be testimony to their humanitarian purpose, but hardly to their logical acumen. It is nothing less than babel; it is speaking out of two sides of one's mouth at the same time, each side addressing the other in language it could not possibly understand. For if the conceptual model is taken seriously, there is no room for agency of any sort, since what happens, happens as it does, in accordance with discoverable causal laws relating to mental and bodily events but not in any way to persons as agents. And if so, there is not even the agency of the so-called behavioral scientist, not even the manipulation about which the would-be scientist speaks with such high-minded zeal for the good of those whose plight in courts touch his sentiments. Presumably *he* is to act with responsiblity in his manipulations on the basis of reasons which, if good and sound, deprive him of any agency in the matter and any moral responsibility.

Fifth, if the witnessable event is a bodily movement, what are its necessary and sufficient causal conditions? A desire, purpose, or anything else mental? Surely not. For the necessary and sufficient condition of the movement of one's arm is a contraction of the muscle. The causal explanation of the latter lies in the transmission of a nerve impulse to the muscle tissues. And so on it goes. There is no room for the causal agency of mental events in the explanation of the bodily movements. Or, if we are to speak of desires, hopes, expectations, etc. as causes, these must now be reinterpreted or redefined as events within the body. And if so, not only does this do violence to every ordinary view of the matter, it also entails a drastic revision of the very metaphysics with which we began: we no longer have the physical *and* the mental, but only the physical.

But supposing, finally, we do acknowledge that desires, for example, as mental events are causes that spark bodily movements into being, even this much involves a radical revision, this time in the concept of a desire. For what *is* the event that is the desire? Is it not essential to the very concept of a desire that a desire be a desire *for* something? But then how is that feature of intentionality to be secured? By supposing that the event that *is* the desire is somehow dissipated by the agent's obtaining the thing desired? Surely not. And is the connection between wanting and doing causal and hence contingent, not conceptual? Surely to think of a desire as an event whose features as the features of the desire can be read off by examining it all by itself, cut off as it were from all that connects it with the complexity of thoughts and actions of the agent—surely this is to construe a desire as a shadowy imitation of a physical event. It is, indeed, to think of it as something vaguely like an internal itch or twitch and, in so doing, to distort our view and to blind us to the complex texture of the life of the mind and of the person in which desires, *qua* desires, play their familiar roles. In the same way, any and all of the other incidents of our lives in which decisions, hopes, expectations, choices, emotions, etc., play their roles, must appear strangely distorted if, like desires, they are to be construed as events operating in some sort of mental mechanism.

In these comments, I have been doing much more than citing objections to the metaphysical preconception that prompts our radical determinism. Nor have I been merely exhibiting the ways in which this doctrine obliges us to revise or abandon this or that cherished belief. What I have wanted to emphasize is that this overly simplified conception of nature neatly divided into two bundles, one marked "physical," the other "mental"—each containing events that operate in some sort of causal mechanism—forces us to revise in one area after another the whole character of our thinking, our very sense of what happens in the area of human conduct. For the revisionary demands placed upon our thinking by our philosophical preconceptions are insatiable. It is as if suddenly we were to find ourselves in a situation even stranger than any imagined by Kafka, in which none of the concepts we employ in rendering intelligible and manageable the familiar incidents of our lives have any place at all.

How then are we to regain our sense of fact? And how are we to resist the conceptual model from which action, agency, responsibility, and all that is intelligible and familiar in our practical experience must be banished? Of course we need to take seriously the conception of a person and the conception of agency logically essential to it. Of course we must view the self not as a hidden or invisible chamber that provides a residence for Humean contents of consciousness or as a mysterious entity hovering in some transcendent region and connected in problematic ways to a body it inhabits in some sense altogether mysterious and unknown to us. But just how are these tasks to be accomplished? It is to these matters, albeit briefly, that I wish to address myself in my concluding remarks.

Our questions are not unrelated. Indeed, they invite the further query "Whence the fascination of the philosophical preconception?" It is not enough to note its pernicious consequences—it remains, despite the troubles to which it impels us, an inviting conceptual model. Part of the reason may lie in our desire to apply to matters of human fact the categories of explanation which, conspicuously in the natural sciences, have enjoyed signal success. This was Hume's motive in his famous *Treatise*, to do for the sciences of man what Newton had done for the physical sciences. Indeed, his association of ideas is clearly the mental analogue of the force of gravitation that explains both the fall of bodies and the motion of the planets. And modern-day psychologists, moved by this dream of how things must surely be, have been led to a metaphysics of human nature in which the a priori demand for causal explanations of the required sort has operated as a bed of Procrustes to which our human facts must forcibly be fitted even at their complete expense.

But this is not the whole truth of the matter. For, in a way, what operates to render plausible the conceptual model we wish to employ in matters of human fact and thus to becloud, distort and conceal what is all too familiar to any of us is the fact that we look at things from too close to. We concentrate our gaze upon the things at the very focus of our attention; and ignore the whole context of our lives in which these events enjoy their status as actions and passions, desires, decisions, and so on with the whole gamut of the incidents of the lives of intelligent beings like ourselves.

Thus we look closely at the action of a person raising an arm; and, ignoring this incident in the life of an agent, quite naturally see only a bodily movement. It is as if we could understand and see more clearly what a person was doing when he was writing a check if we ignored all of the circumstances surrounding this transaction between persons and confined our attention to the details of a cylindrical object (we call it "a pen") leaving a deposit of ink, of a curious design, upon a rectangular piece of paper we call "a check." As if, too, we could really know better and see more clearly what a person was doing if, watching someone play chess and move a king from this position to that, we concentrated our gaze upon the details of the movement of an object of a certain shape from one place to another on a checkered board. To do this is to lapse into the "seeing" of a child that is blind to the social transaction that is the writing of a bank check, and blind to what is going on in a game of chess. The truth is that we do not see if in our seeing we are oblivious to all that surrounds and imparts to what is seen the status it has in the lives and experience of those who only thereby are able to see well enough what is going on. . . . The concepts we employ are connected with the interests we have; and we are interested, not merely in offering causal explanations of bodily movements, but in these occurrences as the actions of agents in their dealings with one another. Just as it is one thing to consider the physics of the movements of chess pieces on the board—How much force needs to be employed to move this piece from here to there?—so it is another to consider the geometrical design traced by the movements, their aesthetic qualities, and the chess moves executed through such occurrences. Only a being trained and competent to play chess—this is the practical context within which the crucial terms we employ play their role—can *see* the movement of an object on the board as this or that move in the game, or recognize it as clever or foolish, right or wrong, as this or that tactical or strategic move. Only such a being can engage in the discourse in which moves are challenged for their propriety or wisdom, and reasons, excuses, and apologies are offered as indeed they are during and after the course of play. To insist that only the language of a causal explanation of what happens is relevant and pertinent to what takes place during the course of play, where the causes are the necessary and sufficient conditions of the physical movements of the material objects on the checkered surface, may strike some as hard-headed and tough-minded, but for those of us who are sensible of what is relevant and important, it may be learned and sophisticated, but it is nonetheless folly. Similarly, to insist that we employ only that language in which causal explanations can be given of the bodily movements that take place when a person does anything, is indeed to make a mystery of agency, responsibility, and rationality and all that is relevant and pertinent to our practical lives. And to conclude that no one, not even "the poor victim of his society" who brutally orders the execution of countless Jews, is really responsible for what he does, is intellectually incoherent and morally disastrous. For to see what happens as occurrences to be dealt with in these terms is not to see anything that anyone does at all and hence neither to invite nor justify any absolution of responsibility. Agency and responsibility simply have no place at all in events understood in such categorically impoverished terms. The application of these practical concepts lies elsewhere, in the lives of social beings of the sort that you and I are, beings who are morally concerned and accountable. To elucidate these concepts, in their complex connections with those other practical concepts involved in the whole body of the discourse we apply to ourselves and to others, is to exhibit the ways in which these concepts apply to events in the lives that are lived by such beings. And inescapably, this is to grasp, with increased perspicuity and a heightened sense of its complex and multivaried texture, the human facts that interest us, the way things really are with us in the daily living of our lives.

29

Enigmaticity in Nature

THOMAS NAGEL

(b. 1937)

Tomas Nagel sudied philosophy at Cornell, Oxford, and Harvard, and has taught at the University of California at Berkeley, and at Princeton, where he is now a member of the Department of Philosophy. He has published a number of significant articles in the areas of ethics and the philosophy of mind.

THE ABSURD

Most people feel on occasion that life is absurd, and some feel it vividly and continually. Yet the reasons usually offered in defense of this conviction are patently inadequate: they *could* not really explain why life is absurd. Why then do they provide a natural expression for the sense that it is?

I

Consider some examples. It is often remarked that nothing we do now will matter in a million years. But if that is true, then by the same token, nothing that will be the case in a million years matters now. In particular, it does not matter now that in a million years nothing we do now will matter. Moreover, even if what we did now *were* going to matter in a million years, how could that keep our present concerns from being absurd? If their mattering now is not enough to accomplish that, how would it help if they mattered a million years from now?

Whether what we do now will matter in a million years could make the crucial difference only if its mattering in a million years depended on its mattering, period. But then to deny that whatever happens now will matter in a million years is to beg the question against its mattering, period; for in that sense one cannot know that it will not matter in a million years whether (for example) someone now is happy or miserable, without knowing that it does not matter, period.

What we say to convey the absurdity of our lives often has to do with space or time: we are tiny specks in the infinite vastness of the universe; our lives are mere instants even on a geological time scale, let alone a cosmic one; we will all be dead any minute. But of course none of these evident facts can be what *makes* life absurd, if it is absurd. For suppose we lived forever; would not a life that is absurd if it lasts seventy years be infinitely absurd if it lasted through eternity? And if our lives are absurd given our present size, why would they be any less absurd if we filled the universe (either because we were larger or because the universe was smaller)? Reflection on our minuteness and brevity appears to be intimately connected with the sense that life is meaningless; but it is not clear what the connection is.

Another inadequate argument is that because we are going to die, all chains of justification must leave off in mid-air: one studies and works to earn money to pay for clothing, housing, entertainment, food, to sus-

From The Journal of Philosophy, *Vol. 68, No. 20 (October 21, 1971), pp. 716–727.*

tain oneself from year to year, perhaps to support a family and pursue a career—but to what final end? All of it is an elaborate journey leading nowhere. (One will also have some effect on other people's lives, but that simply reproduces the problem, for they will die too.)

There are several replies to this argument. First, life does not consist of a sequence of activities each of which has as its purpose some later member of the sequence. Chains of justification come repeatedly to an end within life, and whether the process as a whole can be justified has no bearing on the finality of these end-points. No further justification is needed to make it reasonable to take aspirin for a headache, attend an exhibit of the work of a painter one admires, or stop a child from putting his hand on a hot stove. No larger context or further purpose is needed to prevent these acts from being pointless.

Even if someone wished to supply a further justification for pursuing all the things in life that are commonly regarded as self-justifying, that justification would have to end somewhere too. If *nothing* can justify unless it is justified in terms of something outside itself, which is also justified, then an infinite regress results, and no chain of justification can be complete. Moreover, if a finite chain of reasons cannot justify anything, what could be accomplished by an infinite chain, each link of which must be justified by something outside itself?

Since justifications must come to an end somewhere, nothing is gained by denying that they end where they appear to, within life—or by trying to subsume the multiple, often trivial ordinary justifications of action under a single, controlling life scheme. We can be satisfied more easily than that. In fact, through its misrepresentation of the process of justification, the argument makes a vacuous demand. It insists that the reasons available within life are incomplete, but suggests thereby that all reasons that come to an end are incomplete. This makes it impossible to supply any reasons at all.

The standard arguments for absurdity appear therefore to fail as arguments. Yet I believe they attempt to express something that is difficult to state, but fundamentally correct.

II

In ordinary life a situation is absurd when it includes a conspicuous discrepancy between pretension or aspiration and reality: someone gives a complicated speech in support of a motion that has already been passed; a notorious criminal is made president of a major philanthropic foundation; you declare your love over the telephone to a recorded announcement; as you are being knighted, your pants fall down.

When a person finds himself in an absurd situation, he will usually attempt to change it, by modifying his aspirations, or by trying to bring reality into better accord with them, or by removing himself from the situation entirely. We are not always willing or able to extricate ourselves from a position whose absurdity has become clear to us. Nevertheless, it is usually possible to imagine some change that would remove the absurdity—whether or not we can or will implement it. The sense that life as a whole is absurd arises when we perceive, perhaps dimly, an inflated pretension or aspiration which is inseparable from the continuation of human life and which makes it absurdity inescapable, short of escape from life itself.

Many people's lives are absurd, temporarily or permanently, for conventional reasons have to do with their particular ambitions, circumstances, and personal relations. If there is a philosophical sense of absurdity, however, it must arise from the perception of something universal—some respect in which pretension and reality inevitably clash for us all. This condition is supplied, I shall argue, by the collision between the seriousness with which we take our lives and the perpetual possibility of regarding everything about which we are serious as arbitrary, or open to doubt.

We cannot live human lives without energy and attention, nor without making choices which show that we take some things more seriously than others. Yet we have always available a point of view outside the particular form of our lives, from which the seriousness appears gratuitous. These two inescapable viewpoints collide in us, and that is what makes life absurd. It is absurd because we ignore the doubts that we know cannot be settled, continuing to live with nearly undiminished seriousness in spite of them.

This analysis requires defense in two respects: first as regards the unavoidability of seriousness; second as regards the inescapability of doubt.

We take ourselves seriously whether we lead serious lives or not and whether we are concerned primarily with fame, pleasure, virtue, luxury, triumph, beauty, justice, knowledge, salvation, or mere survival. If we take other people seriously and devote ourselves to them, that only multiplies the problem. Human life is full of effort, plans, calculation, success and failure: we *pursue* our lives, with varying degrees of sloth and energy.

It would be different if we could not step back and reflect on the process, but were merely led from impulse to impulse without self-consciousness. But human beings do not act solely on impulse. They are prudent, they reflect, they weigh consequences, they ask whether what they are doing is worth while. Not only are their lives full of particular choices that hang together in larger activities with temporal structure: they also decide in the broadest terms what to pursue and what to avoid, what the priorities among their various aims should be, and what kind of people they want to be or become. Some men are faced with such choices by the large decisions they make from time to time; some merely by reflection on the course their lives are taking as the product of countless small decisions. They decide whom to marry, what profession to follow, whether to join the Country Club, or the Resistance; or they may just wonder why they go on being salesmen or academics or taxi drivers, and then stop thinking about it after a certain period of inconclusive reflection.

Although they may be motivated from act to act by those immediate needs with which life presents them, they allow the process to continue by adhering to the general system of habits and the form of life in which such motives have their place—or perhaps only by clinging to life itself. They spend enormous quantities of energy, risk, and calculation on the details. Think of how an ordinary individual sweats over his appearance, his health, his sex life, his emotional honesty, his social utility, his self-knowledge, the quality of his ties with family, colleagues, and friends, how well he does his job, whether he understands the world and what is going on in it. Leading a human life is a full-time occupation, to which everyone devotes decades of intense concern.

This fact is so obvious that it is hard to find it extraordinary and important. Each of us lives his own life—lives with himself twenty-four hours a day. What else is he supposed to do—live someone else's life? Yet humans have the special capacity to step back and survey themselves, and the lives to which they are committed, with that detached amazement which comes from watching an ant struggle up a heap of sand. Without developing the illusion that they are able to escape from their highly specific and idiosyncratic position, they can view it *sub specie aeternitatis*—and the view is at once sobering and comical.

The crucial backward step is not taken by asking for still another justification in the chain, and failing to get it. The objections to that line of attack have already been stated; justifications come to an end. But this is precisely what provides universal doubt with its object. We step back to find that the whole system of justification and criticism, which controls our choices and supports our claims to rationality, rests on responses and habits that we never question, that we should not know how to defend without circularity, and to which we shall continue to adhere even after they are called into question.

The things we do or want without reasons, and without requiring reasons—the things that define what is a reason for us and what is not—are the starting points of our skepticism. We see ourselves from outside, and all the contingency and specificity of our aims and pursuits become clear. Yet when we take this view and recognize what we do as arbitrary, it does not disengage us from life, and there lies our absurdity: not in the fact that such an external view can be taken of us, but in the fact that we ourselves can take it, without ceasing to be the persons whose ultimate concerns are so coolly regarded. . . .

VI

In viewing ourselves from a perspective broader than we can occupy in the flesh, we become spectators of our own lives. We cannot do very much as pure spectators of our own lives, so we continue to lead them, and devote ourselves to what we are able at the same time to view as no more than a curiosity, like the ritual of an alien religion.

This explains why the sense of absurdity finds its natural expression in those bad arguments with which the discussion began. Reference to our small size and short lifespan and to the fact that all of mankind will eventually vanish without a trace are metaphors for the backward step which permits us to regard ourselves from without and to find the particular form of our lives curious and slightly surprising. By feigning a nebula's-eye view, we illustrate the capacity to see ourselves without presuppositions, as arbitrary, idiosyncratic, highly specific occupants of the world, one of countless possible forms of life.

Before turning to the question whether the absurdity of our lives is something to be regretted and if possible escaped, let me consider what would have to be given up in order to avoid it.

Why is the life of a mouse not absurd? The orbit of the moon is not absurd either, but that involves no strivings or aims at all. A mouse, however, has to work to stay alive. Yet he is not absurd, because he lacks the capacities for self-consciousness and self-transcendence that would enable him to see that he is only a mouse. If that *did* happen, his life would become absurd, since self-awareness would not make him cease to be a mouse and would not enable him to rise above his mousely strivings. Bringing his new-found self-consciousness with him, he would have to return to his meagre yet frantic life, full of doubts that he was unable to answer, but also full of purposes that he was unable to abandon.

Given that the transcendental step is natural to us humans, can we avoid absurdity by refusing to take that step and remaining entirely within our sublunar lives? Well, we cannot refuse consciously, for to do that we would have to be aware of the viewpoint we were refusing to adopt. The only way to avoid the relevant self-consciousness would be either never to attain it or to forget it—neither of which can be achieved by the will.

On the other hand, it is possible to expend effort on an attempt to destroy the other component of the absurd—abandoning one's earthly, individual, human life in order to identify as completely as possible with that universal viewpoint from which human life seems arbitrary and trivial. (This appears to be the ideal of certain Oriental religions.) If one succeeds, then one will not have to drag the superior awareness through a strenuous mundane life, and absurdity will be diminished.

However, insofar as this self-etiolation is the result of effort, willpower, asceticism, and so forth, it requires that one take oneself seriously as an individual—that one be willing to take considerable trouble to avoid being creaturely and absurd. Thus one may undermine the aim of unworldliness by pursuing it too vigorously. Still, if someone simply allowed his individual, animal nature to drift and respond to impulse, without making the pursuit of its needs a central conscious aim, then he might, at considerable dissociative cost, achieve a life that was less absurd than most. It would not be a meaningful life either, of course; but it would not involve the engagement of a transcendent awareness in the assiduous pursuit of mundane goals. And that is the main condition of absurdity—the dragooning of an unconvinced transcendent consciousness into the service of an immanent, limited enterprise like a human life.

The final escape is suicide; but before adopting any hasty solutions, it would be wise to consider carefully whether the absurdity of our existence truly presents us with a *problem*, to which some solution must be found—a way of dealing with prima facie disaster. That is certainly the attitude with which Camus approaches the issue, and it gains support from the fact that we are all eager to escape from absurd situations on a smaller scale.

Camus—not on uniformly good grounds—rejects suicide and the other solutions he regards as escapist. What he recommends is defiance or scorn. We can salvage our dignity, he appears to believe, by shaking a fist at the world which is deaf to our pleas, and continuing to live in spite of it. This will not make our lives un-absurd, but it will lend them a certain nobility.[1]

This seems to me romantic and slightly self-pitying. Our absurdity warrants neither that much distress nor that much defiance. At the risk of falling into romanticism by a different route, I would argue that absurdity is one of the most human things about us: a manifestation of our most advanced and interesting characteristics. Like skepticism in epistemology, it is possible only because we possess a certain kind of insight—the capacity to transcend ourselves in thought.

If a sense of the absurd is a way of perceiving our true situation (even though the situation is not absurd until the perception arises), then what reason can we have to resent or escape it? Like the capacity for epistemological skepticism, it results from the ability to understand our human limitations. It need not be a matter for agony unless we make it so. Nor need it evoke a defiant contempt of fate that allows us to feel brave or proud. Such dramatics, even if carried on in private, betray a failure to appreciate the cosmic unimportance of the situation. If *sub specie aeternitatis* there is no reason to believe that anything matters, then that doesn't matter either, and we can approach our absurd lives with irony instead of heroism or despair.

---

[1]"Sisyphus, proletarian of the gods, powerless and rebellious, knows the whole extent of his wretched condition: it is what he thinks of during his descent. The lucidity that was to constitute his torture at the same time crowns his victory. There is no fate that cannot be surmounted by scorn" (*The Myth of Sisyphus*, Vintage edition, p. 90).

MATTHEW LIPMAN

(b. 1923)

Having studied at Stanford, Columbia, the Sorbonne, and the University of Vienna, Lipman taught for eighteen years at Columbia University. He is now Professor of Philosophy at Montclair State College, and Director of the Institute for the Advancement of Philosophy for Children. Among his publications are What Happens in Art *(1967) and* Contemporary Aesthetics *(1973).*

NATURAL OBLIGATION, NATURAL APPROPRIATION

"Man is born in a state of natural debt."—BUCHLER.

Our earliest discoveries of nature reveal to us our natural obligations, obligations which possess a primordial and foundational character, for they antedate our births and accompany and direct us to our deaths. Alive, we are committed to courses of behavior or to the achievement of satisfactions which we have no choice but to pursue. Insistent and urgent demands press upon us, the goals and deadlines of innovative as well as of routine existence. As these demands are inexorable and can never wholly be satisfied, incompleteness and unfulfillment come to be characteristic of man's natural condition. Far from being "unnatural," inadequacy, impotence, and failure are among the most natural things in the world.

When we say that nature obliges, we are being appropriately ambiguous. Nature is both compelling and compelled, subservient and coërcive. Insofar as it can compel us to discharge our obligations, nature is sovereign. Such sovereignty, of course, is not a contingent matter, nor is natural obligation a contractual affair. Being obligated is intimately involved in being human, and since nature is in a position to enforce its mandates, being human involves susceptibility to natural coërcion as well as to natural indebtedness and requiredness.

In different contexts, this requiredness takes on different forms. In one instance we see it as moral obligation; in a second, as esthetic obliga-

From *The Journal of Philosophy*, Vol. 56, No. 5 (Feb. 26, 1959), pp. 246-252.

tion; in a third, as logical obligation. There is no need to search for a natural basis for these obligations: they are already natural, for they are simply exemplifications of natural obligations in general.

A metaphysical pathology might concern itself with the various types of inadequate responses to natural obligations. Discussions of the "inability to develop one's constructive potentialities," or the "failure to realize one's ideal self," may suggest that the recognition of indebtedness brings on feelings of guilt. At any rate, this implication is apparent in the writings of Heidegger and Fromm. But it would also be possible to follow up the concept of natural obligation by examining its consequences in terms of the ways in which indebtedness is met or discharged. And if we pursue this line of inquiry, we find that in whatever manner a debt is discharged, it is fundamentally an instance of appropriation. Thus, the same necessity which imposes obligations on man may appropriate from him what is situationally required.

It should be noted that indebtedness is a natural, rather than a specifically human characteristic. We speak of man the debtor, but even if we referred to him as creditor, the fact of indebtedness would remain. For instance, a paucity of opportunities may manifest itself in terms of a surplus of human abilities or energy. Such a situation is nevertheless experienced as incompleteness, unfulfillment, or lack, just as is the situation in which the human being is impotent in the face of unavoidable challenges or invitations. The fact of incompleteness or precariousness remains, although at different times different factors may be held responsible. Whether we call the feeling of incompleteness "void" or "emptiness" or "nothingness," it is clear that its stimulus can be human or non-human, that its intensity can rise to anguish of tragic proportions, and that the behavior consequent upon it may diminish but can hardly eliminate the incompleteness and need, the imbalance and precariousness of the human situation itself.

Natural appropriation consists of those modes by which one's world compels the discharging of natural obligations. Where indebtedness takes the form of man exigent and his world deficient, we may speak of human appropriation. The modes of natural appropriation are production and extraction, while those of human appropriation are assimilation and irruption. Obviously the former modes are issues or emanations; the latter are absorptions or engrossments.

We can roughly distinguish production from extraction by noting that, in production, nature acts coërcively through man; while in extraction, it acts coërcively upon him. Extraction is peremptory, imperative, and undisguised. But in production man is manipulated, for it occurs in a manner which persuades him that the initiative is his own; it is subtle and indirect, often revealing nature as artful and designing.

The varieties of appropriation are phases of the ebb and flow of natural activity. (For example, a nursing mother is productive of milk, which the child assimilates after having extracted it or after having had it irrupt within him.) Analogous processes are involved when a confession is extracted by logic, persuasion, or torture, or when a painting is commissioned.

Extraction is coërciveness which, acting upon an individual, forces him to act, to assert, or to arrange. Production is coërciveness which, acting through an individual, likewise forces him to carry out active, assertive, or ordering forms of behavior. As it is customary to refer to the result of production as a product, we may similarly designate the outcome of extraction as an extract. Both terms may of course be employed to refer to the same object. A servile gesture can be produced, as by an actor in a play, or extracted, as by a master. A sigh may well up within us or be drawn out of us, and we may gasp because of overeating or because of a breathtaking sunset.

Once we recognize the significance of existential indebtedness, we can perhaps acknowledge that the concept of man as debtor is at least as fundamental as that of man as producer. Production and extraction stand on equal footing as dual modes of that natural appropriation by means of which our basic obligations are discharged. Modern philosophy has tended to exaggerate the role of production, by emphasizing such factors as "creativity," "originality," "initiative," and "expression." This tendency has been rightly criticized by Buchler:

> Activity which would ordinarily be ascribed to a positive impulse is often better interpreted as a response than as a drive, as a struggle to stand up rather than as a readiness to run. For the most part, 'activity' is best regarded as drawn from the individual rather than as contributed by him. [*Toward a General Theory of Human Judgment*, p. 61.]

This is not to imply that man, in the face of natural coërcion, is completely docile and acquiescent. Better to say that he is yielding. He yields to nature, giving in and giving up, bowing to it and yet bringing forth, as yield or crop, some appropriate issue. Only in the most rudimentary cases is the issue necessitated by a purely internal drive or need. The brute, far from being "more natural" than any other being, is less involved in nature (insofar as his behavior is determined by his individual organism alone) than one who is also susceptible to more remote and pervasive influences.

Consider the historical background of the conviction that what human beings make and say and do are products of drives and impulses, rather than the meeting of natural obligations or the response to natural imperatives. The purpose of envisaging man primarily as a producer was originally honorific and polemical. An earlier view had been contemptuous of man, and had portrayed him as basically inert or lazy, driven to act only by urgent needs or appetities, or forced to produce by external coërcion. Men did not naturally love to work or to invent: they did so only out of necessity. This apparent derogation of human dignity was subsequently subjected to bitter criticism. Men were now asserted to be productive by their very nature, instinctively workmanlike, although they could be corrupted by faulty social institutions. Laziness was not man's normal state but a consequence of the worker's alienation from participation in modern industrial life. The human organism was now described as a reservoir of energy, capable of being reduced to frustration or inertia by a stultifying environment, but fundamentally dynamic and active. Today we can see that productivity is dependent upon conditions which are highly complex and often obscure, and that it is usually more fitting to describe human behavior as responsive rather than initiative, as evoked by one's world rather than as expressed by one's self. We can also recognize more clearly now the significance of extraction as a process co-ordinate with production and frequently co-operative with it.

It is common to think of the productive individual as perhaps ill-adjusted to his society, but certainly well-adjusted in regard to nature itself. This belief is prevalent because it is related to the common belief that man is productive "by nature," or that he can have an efficient and balanced function in nature, characterized by spontaneity, fecundity, and absence of need. It is taken for granted that perpetual incompleteness does not have to be indigenous to the human situation. Yet incompleteness and precariousness may well be ineradicable factors of human existence (since civilization may multiply the obstacles to satisfaction at a faster rate than it diminishes them). Moreover, a man's natural obligation need not diminish proportionately to his productivity; on the contrary, it may well increase.

It would be incorrect to infer from what has been said that production and extraction, the two modes of natural appropriation, are to be categorized as evaluations rather than as descriptions. How these processes are appraised does not affect their status as natural issuances. At its worst, of course, extraction may disclose itself to be predatory and exploitative. In the face of such extortion or rapacity, man is victim, man is prey. But extraction similarly comprises processes which are subject to praise or condonation. Natural obligations arise in situations whose character may be esteemed or deplored, and our efforts to behave in a manner called for (i.e., appropriate to and appropriated by such situations) may be attended by consequences which we find harmful or beneficial. Thus acting, arranging, and asserting may be exacted from us by coöperative situations as well as competitive ones, and the need for retaliation can appear just as obliging as the need for justice.

Every extract, like every product, is a judgment. That is, it discloses an individual version of one's world, or of some aspect of it, and in so doing, discloses an aspect of oneself. It is a discovery of possibility and an invention of actuality. Every issue is a judgment by the individual and of the individual. By him, because through it he pronounces upon his significant involvements. Of him, because each issue throws open to the world a characteristic or symptom of the individual, so that it represents a judgment of oneself, and invites the judgment of others.

Extractive processes therefore fall into the same three classifications of judgment as those which, in Buchler's writings, are referred to as assertive, active and exhibitive. Consequently, we can take note of assertive, active, and exhibitive extraction.

Confessions, acknowledgments, admissions, all of these are assertive judgments in the form of verbal responses (either true or false) to demanding situations. It is clear that our utterances are solicited by countless environmental requisitions and invitations. If man is considered productive when, through inquiry, he puts questions to nature, then nature must be extractive when it demands responses of man. Assertive extraction is, in fact, a kind of natural interrogation. If many of our assertions seem to be made without duress, it is because circumstantial coërcion has been transformed into personal compulsion, and utterance perseverates of its own inertia. Or we may become so perceptive of the structure of natural interrogation that we develop an acute prolepsis, anticipating demands before they are imposed upon us, arriving at decisions and assertions in advance of the development of obligations that would require them and call them forth. In any case, when nature holds us answerable, we are obliged to reply. Hence our responsibility does not rest on our natural responsiveness, but conversely, it is because nature holds us responsible to our obligations that we respond as we do.

It is customary to use the term "conduct" to refer to behavior that is susceptible to moral evaluation. The term seems to suggest the productive aspect of moral behavior: initiative and self-control are strongly implied. One conducts oneself, deports oneself, behaves oneself. But action can also be conductive in the sense that it represents the active carrying out or discharging of natural obligations. Does this mean that conductive extraction is immune to moral appraisal? Certainly not, since ethical judgment relates to the fittingness or appropriateness of actions, as well as to the investigation into the degree of initiative exercised by the agents of those actions. Moreover, the assignment of natural responsibility does not logically necessitate the assignment of moral responsibility, for it is possible to be naturally responsible without being morally responsible.

Extraction has perhaps been most overlooked in the area of exhibitive judgment. Artistry and production are frequently taken as synonymous. The most honorific categories are those such as "creativity," "originality," and "expression," which are presumed to reflect the artist's innerness, uniqueness, and initiative. (However, extractive processes are customarily acknowledged to be at work in the case of "interpretive" artistry: it is readily enough granted that a conductor evokes music from his instrumentalists, or that an actor elicits fear, pity, or applause from his audience.) We have tended to misjudge the extent to which the discoveries and inventions of art are responsive rather than initiative. Perhaps it may be said that the freedom of art lies not in any ability to construct *ex nihilo*, nor in a supposed absence from coërcion, nor in the capacity to alter one's responses at will, but in the skill with which one recognizes the needs and requirements of a situation, organizes the sequence in which those obligations are to be faced and met, and controls the conditions under which artistic responses take place. Especially noteworthy is the degree to which artistic responses elicited by nature in turn demand responses to themselves, in a progressively evocative sequence which ultimately issues in a work of art at times utterly remote from and irrelevant to the natural complex whose coërciveness was first encountered. Moreover, artistic behavior involves the discharging of a multiple indebtedness, for if an artist is gripped by his subject-matter, he is controlled even more by the quality and requiredness of the developing work of art, and by his need to conform to the stringencies of the medium in which he operates.

It may be thought that our admissions, our conduct, or our orderings are extracted from us only on the occasional development of existential problems. But this would be incorrect. There is a continuity to requiredness which is the foundation of the needfulness of individually problematic situations. Nature is subtly and persistently evocative, manifesting a quizzical, enigmatic reserve which often functions as a powerful heuristic to inquiry and other forms of discovery. For just as the human need to investigate and pronounce upon the world is not sporadic, neither is it an innate disposition which would manifest itself under any circumstances. It is rather the pervasive enigmaticity of nature which elicits our inquisitiveness and stimulates our curiosity, as it is the precariousness of nature which commands our doubt and our constructive responsiveness.

If nature functions extractively then, if it is inquisitorial and demanding, surely it must be an oversimplification to identify experience merely with production or productivity. Too frequently we have interpreted experience as a matter of individual initiative and enterprise. It has even been assumed that one organizes experiences as an entrepreneur organizes corporations. Life should not merely be lived; it should be promoted. The error here, once again, is the assignment of initiative to man and man alone. Extractive processes are exemplifications not of human initiative, but of human initiation: the initiation of man by nature and into nature. If the productive interpretation of experience tends to identify it with experiment, with problem-solving, or, more grossly, with "trial-and-error" it is likely that for man seen as natural debtor, to exist is to be tried. To have an experience is to have, to some extent, a trying experience, for man is always, himself, on trial. This is equally true of experimentation, for just as judgment is always reflexive, doubling back on oneself, so trying out alternative modes of behavior places in jeopardy the experimenter, and makes him subject to appraisal.

Man has been described by Buchler as an animal that cannot help judging in more than one mode. For the judgments man makes in any one mode are usually not exhaustive: the plurality of modes of judgment is a reflection of the fact that nature is susceptible to various types of appraisal and pronouncement. In short: nature is not univocal but equivocal—hence a plurality of modes of judgment is possible. And nature is not passive but coërcive; hence judgment becomes necessary.

30

Epilogue

SPINOZA, LOCKE, AND LEIBNIZ

SPINOZA. Ah, you managed to get here together! Please come in; these Dutch winters can really chill a person's bones. Here, let me take your coats, and do stand over there by the fire. How about something to drink—some madeira, perhaps?

LOCKE. Most kind of you; yes, I am rather a bit chilled, and the fire is splendid, splendid.

LEIBNIZ. I'd not expected these creature comforts, Spinoza. You've a reputation for simple living, as indeed has our friend Locke as well. But don't you need—well, better accommodations?

SPINOZA. I'm afraid I don't limit my wants in order to find joy in living. Quite the opposite: it's when one finds joy in living that one finds one's wants naturally limited.

LOCKE. I'm beginning to thaw out now, a bit like Descartes' piece of wax.

SPINOZA. And are you the same person you were outside a little while ago, half-frozen then, but now ruddy-faced and hearty?

LOCKE. Naturally I am, since I remember my then being cold and miserable, while I am now aware of my being warm and comfortable, so I judge myself to be the same person.

LEIBNIZ. You think your identity is so feeble and precarious a matter as to rest on nothing more than your successive awarenesses of yourself? Ha, you rob it of its objectivity! You are the same John Locke as you were when you were conceived, when you were in your cradle, when you were a young student, just as the oak tree in my yard at home is the same as the acorn whose shape it took in an earlier state of its development. Its identity has nothing to do with my having first observed it as an acorn and later as a full-grown tree. Likewise, the caterpillar that turns into a butterfly is still the same creature it was; indeed its identity is imperishable, as is our own. Your making identity hang upon consciousness of self reminds me of the story of the poor ragged fellow who was found by the sultan lying in the street in a drunken stupor. The sultan had him brought to the royal palace, washed, robed and placed in the royal harem. After a time, during which the man was enjoying himself deliriously, the sultan saw to it that the man was returned to his state of intoxication, and replaced, in his rags, in the gutter. When the fellow finally awoke, he rubbed his eyes and exclaimed, 'What a wonderful dream I've just had!' Yet it was no dream at all, but a fact. So you too, when confronted with reality, think it no more than some passing fancies.

SPINOZA. Passing thoughts, if clear and distinct, can be no less real than anything else that happens. Reality is infinite, and infinitude is perfection, for anything less than infinite is finite and deprived.

LEIBNIZ. I follow you in more ways than I generally acknowledge, but I draw limits you fail to draw. I accept your determinism, but not your denial of universal purpose. I accept your salute to the reality of true ideas, but not your claim to the equal reality of matter. However, ideas and matter are both static notions, and reality is dynamic: it is substance, and substance is that which works.

LOCKE. My head is spinning. Is it the madeira, or these wild, metaphysical notions that you two keep tossing about?

SPINOZA. Leibniz, you have your own brand of determinism, perhaps, but you really shouldn't suggest that you accept mine. After all, when I contend that everything happens necessarily, I mean that effects flow from their causes with logical necessity as well as physical. But as I understand you, you make no allowance for causal interactions among the different individual entities in the world.

LEIBNIZ. When an orchestra plays, do the individual musicians move their horns and violins in response to one another, or rather does each follow, according to his own fashion, the same score as that followed by all? What are the characteristic features of a great orchestra, if not independence and concatenation? So the universe unfolds, in accordance with God's marvelous orchestration, with everything independent from everything else, yet concatenated with everything else.

LOCKE. I cannot concede that your universe is anything more than a fantastically complicated clockwork, in which each part is a clock made of infinite parts, each part being itself made of infinite parts, and so on infinitely—yet all the while, each miniscule part is a little world unto itself, a little replica of the one infinitely great universe at large. So I understand you.

LEIBNIZ. Not so far off, except that the parts are not exact replicas of the one great universe, for each, internal to itself, contains a representation of that universe from the unique point of view of the part. Thus, although medieval philosophers talked a great deal about particularity, it was I who first declared that every particle of Nature is utterly and necessarily unique. And in this I was absolutely modern. For to be unique and to have value have become the same for modern thinkers. Without such a notion, could Rousseau have announced, "I may not be better than other men, but at least I'm different"?

SPINOZA. Perhaps it's just a difference of emphasis between us. You stress the individuality of your monads, yet claim that each is a microcosmic version of the entire macrocosm. But I would prefer to say that each of us plays a unique role in the eternal order, so that the eternal order of things would not be what it is without each of us, just as we could not be what we are with it. When we see things under the aspect of eternity, in which all that has ever been possible has become actual, we see ourselves as parts of that one, seamless, timeless, deathless whole, unique and immortal parts of that sublime, endless panorama. To contemplate things under the aspect of eternity is to see Nature as one, all-powerful, perfect and divine, not from the partial perspectives permitted by time and space, but in its infinite and awesome majesty.

LOCKE. Ah, how you rationalists get carried away by your own eloquence!

LEIBNIZ. Our sense of fact is no less keen than yours, but our sense of order is more so. I agree with Spinoza about uniqueness—it is everywhere, and so is life. They permeate nature, and at no level are life and uniqueness ever totally absent. The world surges with life, and every particle in nature participates in it to some degree. The incredible error of atomists and sensationalists alike was to interpret the world as being made of *inert* elements which, in some unaccountable way, together produce life. I contend, however, that the elementary units that compose nature are packed with internal forces, and are directed towards their goals. We see this when the acorn bursts its shell, transforming itself inevitably into an oak; we see it in each human as he follows the necessary sequences of his development. Each makes the choices he must make in order to become—that is, to be—himself. Caesar chooses to cross the Rubicon. Had he not done so, he would not be Caesar. And had you not come here tonight with us, you'd not be Locke.

LOCKE. Possibly so, but whoever I'd have been, I'd not have been exposed to such extravagances as those to which you've been treating me.

SPINOZA. I'm a tedious host, and I apologize to you profoundly. But do reflect upon what we have said here tonight, strange and unpalatable though it now seems to you, for all things excellent are as difficult as they are rare.

LOCKE. Perhaps—but not all things difficult and rare are excellent.

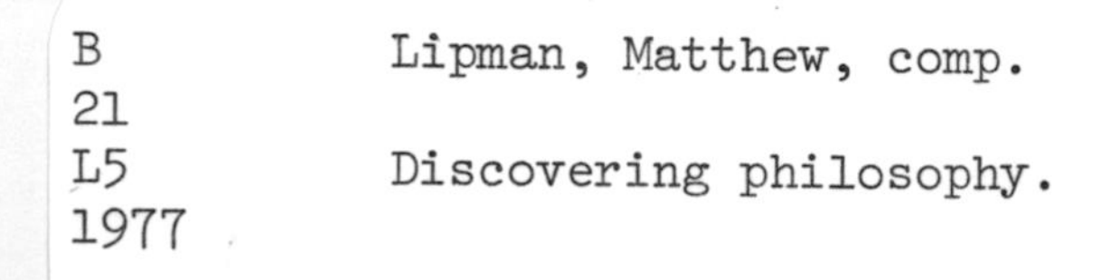
B
21
L5
1977
Lipman, Matthew, comp.
Discovering philosophy.

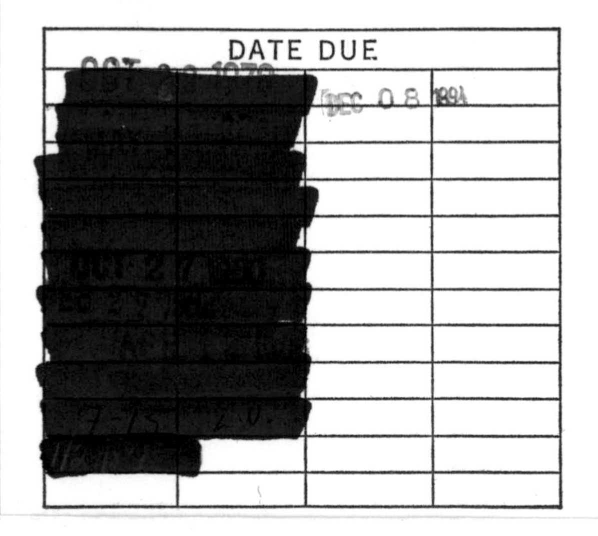
DATE DUE
DEC 0 8 1994